THE QUEST FOR PEACE

Dag Hammarskjöld 1905–1961

SECRETARY-GENERAL OF THE UNITED NATIONS

April 10, 1953–September 17, 1961

THE
QUEST FOR PEACE

THE DAG HAMMARSKJÖLD
MEMORIAL LECTURES

EDITED BY

Andrew W. Cordier and Wilder Foote

COLUMBIA UNIVERSITY PRESS
New York and London 1965

Andrew W. Cordier is Dean of the School of International Affairs, Columbia University. He is a member of the Board of Trustees and of the Executive Committee of the Dag Hammarskjöld Foundation and President of the United States Committee of the Dag Hammarskjöld Foundation.

Wilder Foote was formerly Director of the United Nations Press and Publications Bureau; he is currently a Research Associate in the School of International Affairs, Columbia University.

Acknowledgment is made to Little, Brown and Company for permission to quote four lines of "The Miraculous Countdown" by Odgen Nash, from *Everyone But Thee and Me*. Copyright © 1962 by Odgen Nash.

FOREWORD

Grayson Kirk

PRESIDENT, COLUMBIA UNIVERSITY

Once when a prominent French political leader had been felled by a stroke he was visited by a long-time and bitter opponent who later commented that, while the leader's speech and mobility had been impaired, "La méchanceté est intacte." Today, three years after Dag Hammarskjöld's tragic death, and despite the fact that he had been involved inescapably in serious international clashes of policy, few petty or partisan views have appeared about him. On the contrary, the world's appreciation of his greatness and its understanding of his remarkable qualities have continued to grow with each passing month.

Many tributes have been given to this man whose dedication to international peace was such that he gave his life for it. Many other memorials will be created to his memory in the future. But few, if any, have been, or could be, more relevant or more appropriate than the decision of the Dag Hammarskjöld Foundation and its United States Committee to sponsor a Memorial Lecture Series on the United Nations and world affairs, to be given by eminent men and women in various centers throughout the world.

It was the good fortune of Columbia University to serve as the host institution for many of these lectures. It is now Columbia's privilege through the publication of the present volume to make them available to that vast audience of men and women who recognize in the United Nations the world's best hope against the recurrence of another major war which could so devastate our restless planet.

All of us who had the privilege to Dag Hammarskjöld's friendship know that he would have preferred a memorial volume which dealt with the United Nations rather than with his own life and work. Since the two are so linked together, and since this volume is both a merited personal tribute and a trenchant analysis of the institution to which he was so devoted, the combination of the two purposes is appropriate and the results are significant.

THE
DAG HAMMARSKJÖLD
FOUNDATION

Alva Myrdal

PRESIDENT OF THE DAG HAMMARSKJÖLD FOUNDATION

The Dag Hammarskjöld Foundation has been glad to share in the sponsorship of the Dag Hammarskjöld Memorial Lecture Series with the United States Committee of the Dag Hammarskjöld Foundation and Columbia University. These lectures, without exception, covered United Nations and world problems which engaged the active concern of Dag Hammarskjöld during his service to the world community as Secretary-General. Reflecting the wide experience and deep engagement of the lecturers, these lectures, in a true sense, represent the continuation of his work and therefore constitute the type of living memorial which would have been in accord with his wishes.

Since the Dag Hammarskjöld Foundation was a principal sponsor of these lectures, it would seem appropriate to provide the readers of this volume with a brief sketch of the origins, purpose, and program of the Foundation, established in 1962 to provide a living memorial to the late Secretary-General of the United Nations.

Immediately after Hammarskjöld's death in September, 1961, at Ndola in Northern Rhodesia, on a flight undertaken as part of his endeavors to bring peace to the Congo, his Swedish compatriots were not only shocked but also stirred into action. A spontaneous collection of funds was begun to pursue the work for which he lived and died. Within a very short time fairly considerable funds had been collected. A similar interest to contribute funds to a purpose worthy of Hammarskjöld arose in other countries. To pool the resources and coordinate the ensuing activities, an international board was established in the spring of 1962 with representatives of several countries where national committees were, or were expected to become, active, for example, Norway, Tunisia, and the United States.

The main objective of the Dag Hammarskjöld Foundation was described in its statutes as "the promotion of social, political, economic and cultural progress within the nations whose development Dag Hammarskjöld had so closely at heart, by providing training for citizens of those countries to hold responsible positions." For its most immediate planning, the Board of Trustees interpreted its task within this mandate as that of providing specialized training facilities for people from less developed countries to hold responsible positions in public service, national and international. The Foundation can thus be instrumental in helping the newly independent countries to play their increasingly important role in world affairs, both through participation of their nationals in the work of international organizations and through their holding of posts within their national administrations where the tasks which call for international knowledge and international outlook are becoming ever more numerous and more important. Keeping in mind both the international character of the Foundation and the interests of Dag Hammarskjöld, it is natural that the Foundation should concentrate on such internationally-minded training activities as are particularly suitable for a nonofficial, nonnational body that can work with flexibility in response to shifting needs, with complete freedom from governmental pressure, and without being suspected of pursuing vested interests. Thus, the Dag Hammarskjöld Foundation embodies a new concept in the field of technical assistance. Although it is and will remain small in comparison with the programs of other international organizations and national foundations, it hopes to play a role of some strategic value to development.

The first two years of the Foundation's existence have been largely devoted to preparatory work: analysis of needs, contacts with institutions carrying on related programs, planning the training activities which might become specific to the Foundation, and experimenting with some practical projects. Such a period of preliminary work was foreseen; the Foundation was able only as of May, 1964, to utilize its capital assets. Realizing that the broader needs of public administration training are more and more generally being met at the national level, the Foundation has endeavored to find projects aiming at supplementing such programs. In particular, it focuses upon the teaching of the cross-national, comparative, and international aspects of national administrative problems. In this spirit the Foundation has offered gifts of select libraries to some schools of public administration in Africa. The main activity, involving really living currents of stimulation and contact, centers around a series of seminars intended mainly for young but high-level civil servants of new nations.

The first of these seminars was conducted at the Academy of International Law at The Hague in 1963. This six-week seminar was attended by fifteen senior officials from as many countries, most of them from Africa but also from the Middle East and the Caribbean. Among the participants were the secretaries-general of the ministries for foreign affairs of three African countries. At this seminar the participants discussed current problems of international law which affect the newly independent nations from a practical point of view.

A second six-week seminar, with a slightly different orientation, was held at The Hague Academy in the summer of 1964.

Another Hammarskjöld seminar was held in Addis Ababa, arranged by the United Nations Economic Commission for Africa. The discussions in the seminar centered upon the policies and activities of some international organizations in Africa, with particular emphasis upon the national administrative policies and procedures which would maximize the value of outside aid.

The above seminars have been bilingual. Officials attending them were recruited from both English- and French-speaking countries. This approach has value in a continent where there is need of a closer coordination of effort among nations having varied colonial backgrounds.

The seminar held in Lagos on the theme of international financing in its relation to development planning was conducted in English. It was attended by senior West African officials in planning commissions, ministries of finance, central and development banks, etc., and was planned as a high-level and confidential meeting of minds where the participants would have access to persons having done considerable research in the field under discussion.

A further seminar, conducted in French, which took place in Tunis, concentrated on methods of international cooperation, particularly in the economic field.

These seminars, through the select quality of their students, a carefully chosen faculty, and the use of educational techniques which throw new light on the problems under discussion, represent a valued educational contribution beyond the normal formalized educational programs.

While most senior officials can only absent themselves for seminars of fairly short duration, which is the reason for the Foundation's choice of this form of activity, programs will also be arranged for some participants to pursue their training through internships in international organizations and some national administrations.

The program planned provides, among other things, the possibility that the Foundation not only will increase its efforts to create a network of cooperation among trained national administration scholars, chiefly in Africa, but might also extend its function to certain lines of training for the international aspects of public administration work. If such training of a more regular academic type is justified, it will be in cooperation with various agencies and programs, particularly universities.

The United States Committee has been authorized by the Foundation to arrange a specially planned program at the Graduate School of Public and International Affairs at the University of Pittsburgh to train carefully selected graduate students in public administration, economic and social development, and international affairs. Most of these students have positions assured to them in their respective governments upon the completion of their work. A further program, held under the auspices of the United States Committee, was the Dag Hammarskjöld Conference on Leadership Training in Africa, held at the University of Denver, August 10 to 14, 1964. It was attended by some forty distinguished leaders—twelve of them Africans in the fields of politics and education, who assessed the current state of higher and specialized education and focused attention upon the needs of governments in the training area.

The Foundation, in conformity with the above objectives, is attempting at one and the same time to fill pressing practical needs in the new countries and to maintain the concepts and efforts of the late Dag Hammarskjöld.

INTRODUCTION

Andrew W. Cordier

DEAN OF THE SCHOOL OF
INTERNATIONAL AFFAIRS, COLUMBIA UNIVERSITY

The Dag Hammarskjöld Memorial Lectures on the "Quest for Peace" which are published in this book constitute a many-sided tribute to the man in whose honor they were given. The series was presented under the joint sponsorship of the Dag Hammarskjöld Foundation, the United States Committee of the Dag Hammarskjöld Foundation, and Columbia University. A generous grant by the Johnson Foundation of Racine, Wisconsin, made the series possible. The Johnson Foundation also took many effective measures, particularly through the press and radio, to present the lectures to a wider public.

Deep appreciation is due to the many universities and organizations which welcomed the privilege of acting as local sponsors of individual lectures. They were the University of Stockholm, the Swedish Bar Association, the University College of Dar es Salaam in Tanganyika, the Nigerian Institute of International Affairs at Lagos, the Johns Hopkins University Center at Bologna, Italy, the University of Strasbourg, the University of Leiden, Cambridge University, Carleton University, the University of Wisconsin, Princeton University, and Columbia University.

I owe a special debt of thanks to the distinguished personalities who gave the lectures and responded most readily to the invitation to share their thinking on the problems and prospects of peace and of nation building and thus give significance to this memorial to Dag Hammarskjöld. It is regretted only that others with equal claim and willingness to contribute to the series could not have been included in the current series, but future opportunities will be found to add the benefit of their analyses of United Nations and world problems to those given in these pages.

I express my appreciation for their cooperation to the executive heads of the other two sponsors of the lecture series—Dr. Grayson Kirk, President of Columbia University, and Ambassador Alva Myrdal, President of the Dag Hammarskjöld Foundation—who have also contributed prefatory notes. I wish also to add a word of personal thanks to Wilder Foote for his invaluable assistance in preparing the manuscripts for publication.

The contributors to this volume of lectures bring high qualifications to the discussion from their respective fields of government, diplomacy, the law, international administration, business, economics, and science. They speak from a platform solidly based on long practical experience and knowledge of international affairs. They hold or have held leadership positions of great responsibility in their governments or in international organizations.

All the contributors knew and admired Dag Hammarskjöld and many worked closely beside him or under his leadership during the eight pioneering and germinal years of his service as Secretary-General. In the opening lecture of this volume Mongi Slim, past President of the General Assembly and Foreign Minister of Tunisia, says that "by giving life and dynamism to the Secretary-General's office, Hammarskjöld gave by the same token life and impetus to the Organization itself" and that the Member States should be grateful to him for that reason alone. One of the concerns of these lectures is how to sustain and strengthen that impetus. Slim also recalls Dag Hammarskjöld's warning that the Member States must choose between two concepts of the United Nations—as static conference machinery or as a dynamic instrument of international action. The participants in this lecture series give the many reasons why world conditions require steadfast adherence to the second concept.

The lectures are not presented in the order in which they were given, but are arranged according to the themes with which they are concerned. There are two main groups: the lectures which deal primarily with the political problems of peace keeping and international organization and those which deal primarily with economic and human problems of the new and developing nations and their relationships with the industrialized nations. There is some overlapping between the two groups and, indeed, the problems are closely interrelated. Then there are five lectures concerned with human rights, international law, the peaceful uses of atomic energy, and the constitutional relationships within the United Nations family of intergovernmental agencies which do not fit these categories and have been placed in the concluding part of the book.

Following Mongi Slim's tribute to Dag Hammarskjöld, the first group of lectures opens with voices from Africa and Asia—President Nyerere of Tanganyika and Nehru's sister, Mrs. Pandit—speaking for reconciliation on all sides and for building bridges of understanding and cooperation, especially between the former colonial peoples and the West. Nyerere also engages in a long view of the evolutionary development of international order and puts his finger squarely upon the role of the United Nations in the present stage of that evolution, when the safety of the race calls for a world authority with sufficient sovereign powers to prevent general war, but the nations are not yet ready to carry cooperation that far. In the meantime, Nyerere points out, every United Nations peace-keeping intervention that can be agreed upon helps to build up an attitude of mind among the peoples of the world "which accepts—and will finally favor—international political action."

U Thant is an Asian, but he speaks as Dag Hammarskjöld's successor as Secretary-General in his conspectus of the problems facing the United Nations as it approaches its twentieth year, and of the prospects for solving them. He recalls that two world wars were fought to make the world safe for democracy and concludes that today we must engage on all fronts in a peacetime "war" that "has only one goal, and that is to make the world safe for diversity."

Ambassador Adlai Stevenson, Secretary of State Dean Rusk, and Ernest Gross, former Deputy United States Representative to the United Nations, reaffirm the strong support of the United States for a dynamic and developing role for the United Nations and spell out the reasons for this policy in terms of American national interest as well as of world peace. Stevenson and Rusk place special importance upon the peace-keeping functions of the Organization, both in its multilateral diplomatic aspects and in the use of United Nations Forces and other forms of a United Nations presence at points of conflict around the world. Rusk asks that fresh thought be given to such questions as adapting General Assembly procedures to the vast increase in membership, expanding the size of the Councils, the scales of payment for peace keeping and procedures for authorizing peace-keeping operations, as well as to the more general problem of equitable balance in the decision-making process as between the majority of smaller states and the larger states who must usually assume the primary responsibility and much of the cost for a given course of action. In his eloquent lecture Stevenson calls for strengthening the peace-keeping capacity of the United Nations by expanding its military and planning staff and by the establishment in Member countries of stand-by units, especially trained and equipped for United Nations service and ready to respond quickly to the Organization's call.

Gross examines the question as to how the United States can support the United Nations so as to promote effectively the United States national interest, rightly understood. In this regard, he describes the wide scope of national interest as reflected in the nature and purposes of the Organization, and in its continuing usefulness as a peace-keeping mechanism, an instrument of mediation, a forum of world opinion, an agency for the promotion of economic and social progress and of human rights.

Prime Minister Lester B. Pearson of Canada, who worked closely with Dag Hammarskjöld when the first United Nations Force was created, further develops Stevenson's theme. He suggests, among other things, that the "middle Powers" like Canada, the Scandinavian countries, and others cooperate directly with each other in creating, training, staffing, and maintaining stand-by forces until such time as it becomes politically feasible for the United Nations itself to organize and direct such an arrangement. These stand-by forces could be called into action, of course, only by the United Nations.

The limitations as well as the values of United Nations peace forces are clearly indicated in his review of the Congo operation by Under-Secretary Ralph Bunche, who has borne special responsibilities in this area from the beginning. Some of these limitations are imposed by the Charter itself, but others are caused by failures on the part of the Member States to give the necessary political and financial support. Bunche warns of "a vast and increasing discrepancy" between the responsibilities which the governments ask the United Nations to assume and the support which they give to the fulfillment of these responsibilities. Time and again, he points out, the governments turn in a crisis to the United Nations as indispensable to the chances of avoiding a war and then expect it to operate "not only largely by improvisation but on a shoestring."

The steadily worsening financial situation with which the Organization has been struggling for several years is caused partly by this dichotomy, but principally by a basic political and constitutional conflict. Agda Rössel gives an excellent factual summary of the status of the problem at the beginning of this year and U Thant, Rusk, Stevenson, and Pearson all discuss it. They were not able to offer in these lectures anything more than very tentative and preliminary thoughts as to how a way out of the deadlock might be found, while agreeing that somehow or other it must be found. The heart of the problem is that two of the great Powers, the Soviet Union and France, have, in effect, exercised a financial veto on United Nations peace-keeping operations. If they would pay up, there would be no financial crisis. The problem with the smaller developing countries is not *whether* they should pay a share of the costs but *how much* their share should be—and this is negotiable. Besides, the amounts involved in their delinquencies are comparatively small.

The positions of the Soviet Union and France are a different matter. To the extent that their stand may reflect a deliberate and sustained policy of cutting back the United Nations to the "static conference machinery" Dag Hammarskjöld warned against, and preventing its use as a peace-keeping instrument, it could produce a most serious crisis for the future of the Organization and for peace itself. To the extent that their stand may reflect only fears of erosion of the veto power and of hostile majorities, there is room for negotiation and persuasion. "Suppose it is agreed," says Dean Rusk, "that all Members, despite their deep differences, share a common interest in survival—and therefore a common interest in preventing resort to force anywhere in the world. . . . If this reality is grasped by the responsible leaders of all the large Powers, then the peace-keeping capacity of the United Nations will find some degree of support from all sides, _not as a rival system of order, but as contributor to, and sometimes guarantor of, the common interest in survival._" Let us hope for evidence that this reality has indeed been grasped by all.

U Thant, in his lecture, says that the nuclear arms race "has to be halted, and reversed, if humanity is to survive." All governments, in principle, endorse that statement but nineteen years of negotiation have led to no treaties except the nuclear test ban agreement, and the arms race goes on and on. Alva Myrdal, Sweden's delegate in the present Eighteen Nations Disarmament Conference discussions in Geneva, provides in her lecture an illuminating and realistic account of the issues as they stand now and of the flexible methods being used in pursuit of agreements on "collateral steps" that seem to be gradually building confidence and bringing hitherto insoluble problems within more manageable bounds.

In the course of his sound and descriptive discussion of the General Assembly's functions in the United Nations system, Zafrulla Khan points out the importance of its role as a school of political understanding not only for the representatives of the new countries but equally for the representatives of the older countries, who have often been saved from mistakes of policy by the knowledge gained from the sustained contacts and discussions with the new members that the Assembly makes possible. As a former Foreign Minister of the Asian country of Pakistan and as a past President of the General Assembly, Sir Zafrulla concludes that the Assembly, in addition to its many other functions, is making a very substantial and unique contribution toward establishing a pattern of sounder relationships between the new and developing nations and the older industrial countries.

That this is of high importance is made only too clear by the group of lectures which follows. They are concerned with economic development, with the present and prospective problems of nation building and the potentially explosive tensions between the small "class" of rich, white nations of the northern hemisphere and the two thirds who are desperately poor. The latter are for the most part also weak in the experience, skills, and institutions needed to sustain national independence. But they are the equals of the affluent in the capacity to learn and to aspire and they are a vast majority of the human race.

The lectures of Philippe de Seynes, Barbara Ward, and Paul Hoffman are commended especially to the attention of those who have become weary or discouraged about "foreign aid" and above all to those many in places high or low who have always misconceived "foreign aid" either as a form of bribery which should be abandoned when it fails to produce pliant and subservient allies or as a form of alms to be graciously bestowed without sacrifice by the rich upon the poor, who are expected to be deserving and grateful and to stay where they belong at the bottom of the ladder.

Dag Hammarskjöld rejected such concepts as morally wrong, economically unsound, and politically blind. Investment in economic development and other help to the new countries in building a viable national life and a self-sustaining economy should be provided in a spirit of solidarity and of partnership between rich nations and poor nations in a common war on poverty everywhere. These lectures—and others in the group take up that theme and examine in depth, with both realism and commitment, the very grave problems involved and the various means by which these may be surmounted or by-passed.

Philippe de Seynes points out that there is a built-in inequality of opportunity in the economic and trade relations of the developing nations with the industralized countries. This is causing the gap between rich and poor to grow wider despite all the present economic aid programs. New and special measures will have to be devised in the regulation of international trade if the trend is to be reversed and this inequality of opportunity at least reduced. Even then we shall have to think in terms of "trade *and* aid" rather than "trade not aid" for a long time to come.

Medicine, like the other sciences, is bringing changes faster than we can keep up with them. It is leading to a tremendous spurt in population. In the present decade half a billion people will be added, mostly in the developing countries. They tend to eat up the savings the poor countries need for investment faster than these can be accumulated. Yet the only hope of getting ahead of the growth in population, as Barbara Ward says, is "large investment in new productive technologies in farms and factories."

The target of the Decade of Development is a 5-percent growth rate for the developing countries by 1970. For this, in addition to other measures, it will be necessary for the industrially advanced countries to provide for financial investment and assistance the equivalent of at least 1 percent of their gross national product. These are probably minimum goals and 1 percent is a very modest share of affluence, but they are far above the current levels of growth and investment. Yet the productive capacity of the Atlantic Powers is surging ahead at a tremendous pace. Barbara Ward reminds us that "our abundance may overwhelm us unless we keep the expansion and maintenance of demand in pace with the fabulous expansion of supply." And where is this demand to come from unless we can repeat on a world level what we have largely accomplished at home by transforming the two billion poor into producers well paid enough to become consumers too?

Extensive, speedy, and reliable pre-investment surveys and training programs are required to prepare for capital investment on the necessary scale and Paul Hoffman describes encouraging progress in this area. How to transfer knowledge and skills both rapidly and effectively involves problems as difficult and as important as the provision of investment funds. Willard Thorp gives a stark description of the harsh realities faced by new nations in the absence of experienced leaders, trained administrators, technicians, and skilled workers, as well as in other respects. Douglas Ensminger and Ingvar Svennilson discuss what can be done to strengthen the process of transferring skills. The first speaks from long firsthand experience with successful community and economic development programs in India, the latter as a well-known expert in European economic planning.

The lecture of former President Galo Plaza of Ecuador also belongs with this group. He finds that Latin America's traditional educational systems constitute a serious obstacle to the success of the Alliance for Progress unless they can be reshaped to provide more vocational training for the skills required in economic development.

The significant lectures in the concluding part of the book begin with a scholarly and dispassionate examination of the subject of diversity and uniformity in the law of nations by Judge Philip C. Jessup of the International Court of Justice. Those opposite trends, he points out, are characteristic not only of the law of nations but also of national law. He stresses the legitimate claims of, and the values underlying, both diversity and uniformity and analyzes the creation of new law and the modification of existing law in response to great contemporary world and regional forces.

Jacob Blaustein and Judge Sture Petrén discuss the international promotion and protection of human rights on a universal basis through the United Nations and, in a region with common traditions, through the Council of Europe. Blaustein, citing the preamble of the Universal Declaration of Human Rights as "a common standard of achievement for all peoples and all nations," clearly sets forth the great scope of the political and moral authority that the Declaration has attained and outlines the further steps that should be taken to increase the effectiveness of its implementation, including among personal suggestions a proposal that "the General Assembly or the Secretary-General might appoint an independent person who would be a kind of international commissioner dealing with human rights, bearing perhaps the title of United Nations High Commissioner for Human Rights." Judge Petrén lucidly describes, against the background of widespread violations of human rights by dictatorships prior to and during World War II, the concern of European states in the protection of human rights against violation by states as expressed in the European Commission of Human Rights. He recites also the advances made in national constitutions, laws, and courts in the field of human rights through bringing them into conformity with the provisions of the European Convention for the Protection of Human Rights.

In his lecture on the peaceful uses of atomic energy Sir John Cockcroft surveys the past and potential role of the United Nations with the eyes of a Nobel prize-winning physicist. After describing the first United Nations conference on the peaceful uses of atomic energy and Dag Hammarskjöld's role in it, he traces the progress in nuclear power development and predicts that nuclear power costs will fall below conventional power costs in the 1970s.

Finally, Luther Evans, a former Director-General of UNESCO, gives a comprehensive historical account of the constitutional and practical working relationships within the United Nations family of agencies. Speaking from firsthand experience he gives a generally favorable picture of the dynamic growth and effective service of the specialized agencies and of their functional relationships with each other and with the United Nations, all engaged in vital tasks relating to human welfare, national growth, international cooperation, and peace.

CONTENTS

THE QUEST FOR PEACE

DAG HAMMARSKJÖLD'S
QUEST FOR PEACE

Mongi Slim

SECRETARY OF STATE FOR FOREIGN AFFAIRS OF TUNISIA

Given at Columbia University, November 27, 1963

By a strange and painful coincidence, my arrival in this country, where I was to speak in memory of Dag Hammarskjöld, coincided with the tragic death on that day of President John Fitzgerald Kennedy. Like people all over the world, the Tunisian people, who have always borne a great admiration for the late President, have been shocked and deeply pained by this great and sudden loss. We had watched with keen interest and close attention his unrelenting efforts for the promotion and maintenance of peace and justice in the world, his courageous dedication to the lofty principles of liberty, human rights, and dignity which lie at the root of our civilizations. May I say in all simplicity and sincerity that we of Tunisia deeply share the grief and consternation of the American people over this tragic loss.

I appreciate and welcome the opportunity to give this lecture on Dag Hammarskjöld's quest for peace. I feel doubly honored: honored to address a distinguished audience gathered in a most famous university of which the United States can be rightly proud; honored also and touched to speak about a great man whose name will ever remain identified with peace. For several years I was a personal witness at the United Nations of Dag Hammarskjöld's dedication and skill and on more than one occasion collaborated closely with him. I shall not attempt to assess all of his various achievements. It would take far more than one lecture to round them up. I shall, instead, speak mainly of the principles, conceptions, and methods he brought to his quest for peace, as I observed and understood them in several of the crises that confronted him. These are contributions that did not die with him. They remain relevant now—and for the future.

When to his great surprise Hammarskjöld was assigned ten years ago to succeed Trygve Lie as Secretary-General of the United Nations, he made a brief inaugural speech in the General Assembly which he ended with a line of Swedish poetry: "The greatest prayer of man is not for victory but for peace." This gives a clue to the philosophy of the man, and to the approach to human and international problems which it inspired. The goal of an enduring peace was not to be found along the road of conflicts of power in which victory is won and defeat imposed. Such an outcome nourishes the desire for revenge and leads to renewal of the struggle. Instead a result should be sought which both parties would feel able to accept as honorable. This does not mean compromise at the expense of principle. Hammarskjöld affirmed again and again the importance of strict "adherence to the principles of law, justice, and human rights" in settling disputes. But he was not one to believe that good was the exclusive possession of one side and evil of the other. Soon after his inaugural he paid tribute to Count Folke Bernadotte in these words: "We bow before an ideal of life, and an example of profound faith, faith in the dignity and also the good sense and fundamental decency of men. Without this ideal and this faith, who would seek to follow the course of patient negotiation, of ceaseless effort to conciliate, to mediate, to compose differences, to appeal to men's reason in order to build agreement?" The words were prophetically true of Hammarskjöld's own career as Secretary-General.

Hammarskjöld was one of a line of many great men stretching far back in history who have been dedicated to peace. His dedication was admirable but it was not original. His originality, his genius lay in the ways and means he used to work for peace. These won him such popular descriptions as "watchdog for peace," "custodian of the brushfire peace," "trouble shooter."

Hammarskjöld was as rational as he was dedicated. He was also a prodigious worker with a lightning-fast and penetrating mind. Whenever a conflict arose he would immediately gather all the relevant data, all the elements necessary for a thorough understanding of the situation. With his acute sense of timing, he would then act, whenever his responsibilities called upon him to do so, either to prevent violence or to secure a cease-fire in case a fight had started. He would use every conceivable means, explore all possible avenues that might lead to a settlement. Hammarskjöld believed in and promoted personal diplomacy. No effort would be spared, no minute lost. Telephone calls would be put through in rapid succession to the top people on the spot and to those either directly or indirectly concerned with a solution as well as to others remote enough from the conflict to remove any suspicion of partiality in efforts at mediation. In the choice of the people who would be approached lay one of the keys to the solutions he secured and the successes he won.

Hammarskjöld was a highly cultivated person, an accomplished diplomat who had a deep comprehension and understanding of man. His wide culture gave him a sense of modesty, of humility; he was self-effacing, unobtrusive, discreet, dedicated to his duty and bent on performing it efficiently. He inherited a sense of duty from his father, who had served his country, Sweden, with great zeal and patriotism. Though Sweden had remained neutral in World Wars I and II, Hammarskjöld shared in the sorrow and anxieties of the whole world and was confirmed in his desire for peace.

One of his major traits was the courage to uphold and to abide by his principles. When he was first elected Secretary-General, very few suspected the great determination, the courage, the soundness of the convictions of the man. Hammarskjöld said: "No life was more satisfactory than one of selfless service to your country—or humanity. This service required a sacrifice of all personal interests, but likewise the courage to stand up unflinchingly for your convictions." And stand up for his convictions he did. Against France, Great Britain, and Israel during the Suez crisis; against the USSR and Belgium during the Congo crisis; against France again during the Bizerte crisis. By so doing, he earned even more respect from the countries he stood up against, because he was impartial. And being impartial he saw the solution more clearly than others. In return for his peace-keeping endeavors he had virtually universal respect, if not always gratitude.

Hammarskjöld gave another dimension to the role of the Secretary-General. The United Nations Charter contained, fortunately, provisions conferring upon the Secretary-General the right to take the initiative in matters threatening peace and security in the world. It was on this ground that he based his resourceful, imaginative actions. This dynamic, active interpretation enriched and strengthened the role of the Secretary-General, who otherwise might have been confined to a mainly administrative role of limited political importance. Hammarskjöld explored to the fullest extent the powers and responsibilities vested in the Secretary-General. He said it was "his duty to use his office and, indeed, the machinery of the organization to its utmost capacity and to the full extent permitted at each stage by circumstances."

The first major demonstration of the uses to which his office could be put came in December, 1954. The United States government called upon the United Nations to help release fifteen Air Force men who had been captured by Communist China during the Korean War and sentenced to prison terms on spying charges. The General Assembly passed a resolution condemning Communist China for holding the men and calling on Hammarskjöld to take whatever action he deemed fit to secure their release. This was a very delicate matter, for Communist China was not represented in the United Nations Organization which condemned her. She could very well disregard the mandate entrusted to Hammarskjöld and dismiss it altogether as a maneuver used by the United States against her. At the same time many members of the American Congress were pressing for the intervention of the United States Seventh Fleet to try to compel the Chinese government to release the airmen through force.

The picture was rather bleak and it took all the sagacity, diplomacy, and skill of a Hammarskjöld to avoid a dangerous worsening of the situation.

Hammarskjöld decided to rely on personal diplomacy—this was his first but by no means his last use of this method in the major crises in which he participated—and he took off for Peking after making sure that Chou En-lai was prepared to receive him—in his personal capacity as Secretary-General rather than on the basis of the General Assembly resolution of condemnation.

In Peking, Hammarskjöld had long private discussions with Chou En-lai, under the seal of secrecy. The talks ranged over a wide political field. Hammarskjöld argued the case for release of the fliers on grounds of both law and humanity. He also established his role as a world citizen whose only aim was to uphold the principles of the United Nations Charter and who was in the service of all the nations and the instrument of none. The talks ended without a firm commitment from Chou En-lai to release the fliers but Hammarskjöld left for home convinced that the ground had been prepared for their release in a few months on "humanitarian" grounds. Contact was also maintained in an exchange of messages. Six months later, just as some began to believe that his mission was a failure, Hammarskjöld received for his birthday an unexpected gift: a cable from the Foreign Minister of Communist China announcing that the United States airmen were being released. That was a rewarding, gratifying victory for Hammarskjöld. He was to declare later: "Many things have happened during my time as Secretary-General for which I have reason to be grateful. But no event ranks higher on that list than my trip to Peking."

Consistent with his doctrine concerning the dynamic role of the Secretary-General, Hammarskjöld construed the role of the United Nations to be to serve as an "instrument for the negotiation of settlements, as distinct from the mere debate of issues." Nothing would be gained if each representative of a country were to come to the United Nations merely to expound his government's viewpoint on an issue, indulge in a sometimes arid debate, refute the other party's arguments, and then return to his country without making any progress on the problem at issue. If this course were followed the United Nations Organization would progressively lose in efficacy, would fall into decay and undergo the same fate as that of the League of Nations. Hammarskjöld warned that Members had to choose between these two concepts of the United Nations: as a "static conference machinery" or as a "dynamic instrument" in which executive action is brought to bear upon preventing conflicts or resolving them. From the

Charter and United Nations decisions Hammarskjöld sought guidance for his own role. He believed also "that it is in keeping with the philosophy of the Charter that the Secretary-General should be expected to act also without such guidance, should this appear to him necessary in order to help in filling any vacuum that may appear in the system which the Charter and traditional diplomacy provide for the safeguarding of peace and security."

Both in the Suez and in the Congo crisis Hammarskjöld acted strictly on the basis of the Charter and of decisions of the Assembly and Security Council, but the responsibilities delegated to him were very wide and much of the initiative was his also. Hammarskjöld stood up to his responsibilities and acted in the most expeditious and efficacious manner to bring to the points of conflict a peace-restoring United Nations presence in forms that were new to the world. In this sense he did, indeed, help to fill a vacuum in the traditional systems for safeguarding peace.

In the Suez crisis the aggression perpetrated by Britain, France, and Israel was halted by a cease-fire, and a United Nations Emergency Force contributed by smaller nations neutral in the conflict was created and flown to Egypt within days. It supervised the withdrawal of the invaders and has remained ever since in Gaza and along the armistice demarcation line between Egypt and Israel on guard against a renewal of conflict from either side. UNEF, with its soldiers from such countries as Canada, Sweden, Brazil, and India, is an admirable example of the power of a nonfighting force to secure the observance of United Nations decisions by its presence.

In the Congo, the task of the United Nations had to be carried even further. The United Nations was called upon to send troops to help restore and maintain order in a collapsing country. This Hammarskjöld did at once by addressing himself mainly to the African countries themselves in order to prevent the Congo from falling a prey to the Cold War. He called on such African countries as Ghana, Ethiopia, Tunisia, the United Arab Republic, and Morocco. I am happy to say that, answering his appeal, the Tunisian forces were the first to disembark in the Congo. Shortly thereafter more forces arrived and constituted what was called later the ONUC (from the French: Operations des Nations Unies au Congo, or United Nations

Operation in the Congo). The situation was unfortunately deteriorating rapidly in the Congo and the United Nations was faced not only with the task of restoring peace but also with granting a badly needed technical assistance on a large scale to enable the administrative, social, health, telecommunication, and other services, to operate.

The political situation, jeopardized by the threat of secession of Katanga under the incitement of Tshombe, the Union Minière, and the Belgians, deteriorated to such an extent that the normal civilian operations of the United Nations became an almost impossible task. Yet Hammarskjöld never despaired. He gave strict instructions that United Nations troops were not to meddle in the domestic affairs of the Congo and that they were not to shoot at anyone except in self-defense.

In spite of his usual strict neutrality, Hammarskjöld came under severe attack on account of the United Nations operations in the Congo, mostly on the part of the USSR. Much controversy arose on the merits of such operations, with many pros and cons. But what can be asserted beyond any doubt is that the United Nations presence prevented the Cold War from settling in the Congo, that the unity of the Congo was reestablished thanks in large measure to the United Nations efforts, and that the United Nations helped avoid an impending chaos that threatened peace and security not only in the Congo but in the whole African continent.

It took a strong, outstanding personality like that of Hammarskjöld to give to the Secretary-General's office such an impetus. All who are Member States of the United Nations should be grateful to Dag Hammarskjöld for this reason alone. For by giving life and dynamism to the Secretary-General's office, Hammarskjöld gave by the same token life and impetus to the Organization itself.

To achieve this, Hammarskjöld used his intellectual and moral gifts: tact, talent, imagination, efficiency; he always took into consideration the feelings of the parties concerned and avoided hurting them in any way. Underlying all his actions were the same qualities of strict objectivity, fairness, absence of prejudices, and, I should add, a strong urge to help the small countries. It is not for the big Powers that the United Nations is most useful, he used to say, but for the small countries. This was also in line with his strong sense of justice.

Hammarskjöld believed that, in order to eliminate one of the major factors of trouble, the wide gap between the highly developed big Powers and the less economically developed countries must be gradually bridged until a reasonable balance is created between nations. The number of small nations emerging into independence was increasing the needs for foreign assistance to ensure their development. Hammarskjöld felt the necessity of channeling such assistance as much as possible through the United Nations in order to avoid any race of the two power blocs to grant assistance with ulterior motives and designs to expand their zones of influence. Hammarskjöld was one of the principal initiators of a number of United Nations special operations designed to give technical and operational assistance to the new nations. A double service was thus rendered: (1) to the welfare of the new nations and (2) to the maintenance of peace and security in the world.

He used to say that, "to the diplomat of the twentieth century, war must be averted at almost any cost." His contribution to peace, as these examples show, was one of the greatest made in our times. He fully deserved the Nobel Peace Prize which was bestowed upon him posthumously.

All those who knew him will treasure in their memories, and history will record, the achievements of this relentless peacemaker, adamant in his determination to use every conceivable effort to serve peace and humanity at large, convinced that in the most entangled situations there always glimmers a ray of hope—hope for relaxation of tensions, hope for peace and prosperity. We shall keep in our minds also, and history will record, the everlasting lesson of the invaluable service rendered to humanity by a man who perished in his quest for peace among men but whose example is and shall always remain imperishable.

THE COURAGE OF RECONCILIATION

Julius K. Nyerere

PRESIDENT OF THE UNITED REPUBLIC OF
TANGANYIKA AND ZANZIBAR

Given at the University College, Dar es Salaam, January 23, 1964

From the world point of view, the important thing about the late Secretary-General of the United Nations was the work he was trying to do. It is this which made Dag Hammarskjöld great, which made him loved and hated—and which made his death in Africa a tragedy for all mankind.

Hammarskjöld's name will be associated with many incidents, many details of history. But they all add up to one thing—the search for peace in the world. He recognized that peace can only be obtained on certain conditions; that inherent in it is compromise, tolerance, and a devotion to the principles of human equality and brotherhood. As Secretary-General he tried both to promote these conditions, and —just as important—to gain time for them to become effective. He saw his task as that of reconciling those who were quarreling before their dispute had developed into violent conflict, and his main purpose in doing this was so that a world society based on fundamental human rights could be built. He believed that only when this had been achieved would the constant threat of war recede from the lives of men.

I

The need for this work of reconciliation and construction arises out of the basic conflict which is inherent in society. Living in a community gives man an enlarged opportunity to improve his well-being and develop himself to the full; only by cooperation with his fellows can man really live in maximum freedom. Yet, at the same time, it is life with his fellows which restricts his freedom. He can no longer do exactly what he wishes, when he wishes to do it.

By working together, two men can cut and transport a log of wood which is too heavy for either of them alone. With it they can jointly make a canoe large enough to go farther away from land than one made by either of the men alone. Through their cooperation each of the men will have increased his power to travel—will have enlarged his effective freedom on earth.

But, at the same time, each of the men has lost his individual freedom in relation to that log. Neither, for example, can decide alone that it would after all be better to use it for building a house, or for firewood. And once the canoe has been made as a result of their joint effort, neither of them can use it for fishing on his own, or exchange it for something entirely different—however much he might need the proposed exchange object. Their joint effort has enlarged the freedom of them both; but it has also introduced new possibilities of conflict which did not exist when each of them built a small canoe on his own.

Cooperation and conflict are two sides of the same coin; both arise out of man's relationship with his fellows. The larger the group, the greater the possibility of development through cooperation, and the greater the possibility of conflict. The peace which is essential between two men if they are to work together in making and using one large canoe is also most endangered by their joint activity.

It is law and authority which transform this situation of cooperation, constantly endangered by conflict, into a situation of expanding human development. Only a system of rules governing interpersonal behavior, plus the enforcement of these rules, makes cooperation between men possible and fruitful.

Law, that is the rules governing human behavior, can of course be imposed by force; people can be made to abide by certain regulations through fear of what will happen to them if they do anything else. This does—for a time—bring peace in the sense that men work within a particular framework of rules without fighting each other. The history of man is filled with examples of this kind of law in societies large and small, poor and rich. But the peace resulting from imposed law is short-lived. The moment a man feels himself strong enough he tries to throw off this law and substitute another more to his liking. Or he may even break out in sheer destructive desperation if the law appears to him to be threatening his life or that of his family, or even just demanding too high a price in terms of liberty and manhood.

The only system of law which brings stable peace is a system based on the fundamental human equality of all the people under its suzerainty, and aimed at reconciling to the greatest possible degree man's conflicting desires for individual freedom and the benefits of communal life. Such law will not be a static thing, for changes in the physical or technological environment, and even changes in the balance of men's desire for contact with or isolation from their fellows, will require changes in the laws and ultimately perhaps in the system of law. But for peace in a society to be ensured these three things are essential: a system of law which respects the equal human rights of every member of the society; a system of law which treats every member equally in both its guarantees of protection and its restrictions on individual license; and a system of law which can be changed by peaceful agreement of the citizens governed by it.

Nothing else will suffice. The fact that each of its members is of different physical, mental, or moral strength does not allow any society to assume with impunity that its citizens can be separated one from another as regards the law which applies to them. For however small the number of men who are discriminated against, their existence remains a threat. It does not matter on what grounds these differences are excused; anyone who is deliberately excluded from the benefits of certain laws will have less interest than others in the maintenance of the society and of peace within it. He will therefore be a constant threat to the other members; their attempts to make him less than a man will rebound on them. For if such a person is to keep his self-respect he will have no alternative but to retaliate on the society and its other members the moment an opportunity presents itself. It is in fact men's inequality in every visible respect which makes peace between them possible only on the basis of their fundamental equality.

Yet although peace is not possible without law, it is equally true that no law is possible without authority. Within a small community law may not be written down, and there may be no formal arrangements for its enforcement; but the peace of that community is maintained only because the law is known and transmitted orally, and because the law is capable of being enforced by pressure of public opinion or by threat of punishment. If there is no means of enforcing the law, the temptation to secure immediate personal advantage is often too great for the knowledge of the law's reasonableness to prevail. Every individual under some circumstances or other requires assistance to fulfill his basic desire to live in peace with his fellows. There must therefore always be an enforcement authority; law which cannot be enforced is liable to deteriorate into an expression of pious hopes. Thus there is, and must be, in every society a balance between that voluntary agreement which is necessary to give stability and that decision to pay the price of social living.

And just as law must be impartial between men if it is to bring lasting peace, so the enforcement of it must be impartial between them. It is essential that both the law and its enforcement depend on something other than the brute force of the men involved in a relationship—who in times of conflict become the contestants. There must be an outside authority in which men acquiesce, which is both willing and able to act fairly between them.

Once families or groups of people have worked out a satisfying internal relationship on the basis of law and authority their contact with others changes its form. Their society itself becomes a unit in relation to the outside, and all the complications of human contact are renewed in contacts between societies—with the additional problem of the multiple membership of the unit. But the same principles apply. The tribal wars, that is the wars between different societies, which scarred Africa in the past have now been replaced by systems of law and by authorities which cover the members of many tribal groups. The conflicts resulting from contact between members of different tribes have not completely stopped, but the sovereign authority which had previously been transferred from the individual to the tribal unit has now been transferred to the larger group—the nation. It is this which has enabled peace to be developed over the wider area.

All modern nation-states have grown out of such small and possibly conflicting groups of people. All of them have developed their different combinations of force and agreement; but each of them is now the repository of the sovereignty which an individual surrenders when he enters society.

The nation-states have thus become the basic unit in relation to the world community which the individual was to the village, the village to the tribe, and the tribe to the nation. And the same dichotomy—of desiring closer relations with other units but not wanting to lose the freedom to act individually—therefore automatically reappears on the international scene in the guise of conflict between cooperating nation-states.

II

These nation-states are themselves composite units, and contain within themselves great possibilities for human cooperation. But nation-states are inevitably and inescapably members of the world society. With the irresistible force of a glacier inching down to the sea, the movement toward greater human contact and unity has continued since the world began. The citizens of one nation trade with noncitizens, visit other parts of the earth, dispute with neighbors who happen to live across the line on a map which marks the "national boundary." And even if the state desires to prevent its citizens from making individual outside contacts, its duty to protect itself and its people from the repercussions of outside events forces it to take an interest in the rest of the world. In the modern world all nations border on each other; no sea, no range of mountains, constitutes a barrier to events outside.

The same necessity for law and authority which exists in a small village society, and is the only basis for a national society, is also therefore the unavoidable concomitant of contact on a world scale.

Citizens from different nations trading together, for example, will end by quarreling unless they are operating on a common basis, unless they both accept the same rules. It does not matter in the short run what those rules are, whether the goods are weighed in kilos or in tons, or the price set in terms of dollars or pounds or rubles. But chaos and conflict will result if one partner has agreed to supply 100 tons at a price of £1,000 and the other has agreed to purchase 100 tons at a price of $1,000. The "rule" for that transaction may be dollars or pounds or rubles, but it must exist.

Similarly in all other aspects of contact; there must be one common rule which regulates both parties even when these parties are sovereign states. The system of rules—the law—can be the result of voluntary agreement among all those involved, or it can be imposed by one party on all the others as a result of that party's overwhelming strength. In the short run this would be of less importance than the existence of the law, and the existence of a power willing and able to enforce it. When Napoleon and Hitler claimed that the result of their ambition for world domination would be world peace, they were, I presume, really saying that if they were successful there would be one world system of law, and an authority able to maintain it.

It is certainly true that many of our present-day nation-states exist as a result of force; their unity is the direct result of one law being imposed over a wide area and being maintained by force until it had become accepted by the people. Tanganyika is an example of this; until we were colonized this "nation" did not exist, different laws operated among the constituent tribes, and there was conflict between them. It was the colonial Power which imposed a common law and maintained it by force, until the growth of the independence movement put the flesh of an emotional unity on the skeleton of legal unity.

But the unification which was a by-product of settling disputes through force in earlier centuries is no longer a practical proposition. Two major power blocs now exist, neither of which can destroy the other without itself being destroyed, and both of which are for the present powerful enough to prevent other nations expanding to challenge them in importance. We have indeed achieved a "balance of terror" in the world which effectively prevents the establishment of a system of world law by force. The only way in which this can now be achieved is therefore by agreement between the contending Powers. Impossible as this may sometimes seem, there is no alternative except mutual extermination. The nations are interdependent. Contact between them cannot be avoided; it must therefore be regulated by a mutually acceptable system of law and enforced by an impartial authority which is universally accepted.

At any level, however, there is only one way in which law can be made by agreement. And there is only one way in which disputes can be settled peacefully when there is no law. That is by talking until agreement is reached. There is no short cut, and no alternative. Unless one can agree to this system, with a full recognition of the time which will be taken, and the money which will be spent, and the compromises which will be necessary before a conclusion is reached —unless one can agree to this, one is not giving up the idea of violence as a part of life. Further, unanimity in the final conclusion will be necessary, except to the extent that it can be imposed on those who remain in disagreement, without the cost of enforcement being too great to be countenanced on either physical or moral grounds.

The purpose of any system of international law thus established must be the same as that of village or national law—to enable men to live and work together in harmony. This international law, however, can only be established by agreement among nations, each of which speaks for its citizens. It is true that in a sense the institutions of nationalism are now an interjection between men and the total community of which they are members—which is a world community. But we have to deal with two facts: firstly, that almost all the men of the world think now in national terms; and secondly, that it is conflict between nations which at present destroys the peace of the world. The first task of a world system of law must therefore be to harmonize relations between the different nation-states, to get each of them to agree on certain common practices which will be followed by their own citizens.

III

These are the things which give the United Nations its current importance, and which constitute its current limitations. It is a meeting place for governments, a place where they can talk about their disputes and about problems which might give rise to dispute. It has no other powers except power to talk, unless those powers are specifically given to it, and maintained for it, as a result of agreement in that talking. But its existence as a talking place is a recognition that there is an alternative to war. While people are talking they are not fighting and they may find a compromise which saves them from this disaster. Further, the United Nations is a multinational talking place. It constitutes a recognition that a dispute between two countries— and any solution they arrive at—may affect many others besides themselves.

All these things mean that the very existence of the United Nations is an advance along the path to peace.

At the same time the existence of the United Nations is not itself a solution to the problems of the world, and expecting too much from it can lead to disenchantment with the Organization and with the method of settling disputes by discussion. This is a very real danger, and one which is intensified by the terminology we use. When there is trouble in the world we criticize the United Nations; we criticize its procedures or the existence of veto powers of the permanent members of the Security Council, or we shrug our shoulders when resolutions passed by the General Assembly are not implemented and suggest that the whole discussion is a waste of time.

What we ought to be doing in such cases is to express criticism of the governments for failing to agree on a matter in dispute; the fault lies not with the Organization but with the fact that talking has not resulted in agreed action. It is the several governments which ought to be disparaged—but often it is the United Nations itself which is! Similarly, the application of the veto is not a criticism of the Organization, it is an indication that the permanent members of the Security Council have not talked until they agree. Its reservation to them can be defended as a practical recognition of the fact that these are the states against whom action by the rest would be most destructive in terms of world peace.

To reiterate: the first purpose of the United Nations is to facilitate and encourage talking. Its other powers stem from the results of that talking. The extent to which the nations of the world agree to talk, and agree to disagree until the next time they discuss a particular matter, is the extent to which there is an overwhelming desire for peace among the national governments and their citizens. The danger to peace comes when failure to agree at a particular time leads to action other than more talking—for example, when, having disagreed, the contestants send troops into an area about which there is a boundary dispute. And the real problem is that there are many situations in which action cannot wait for the period necessary if agreement is to be reached. Further, it is possible to use talk to obstruct, as well as to seek, a settlement.

It is in this respect that certain regional and ideological associations have an advantage over the United Nations. As a means of preventing or settling disputes, talking is more productive, and certainly easier, the greater the general feeling of sympathy and friendship among the participants. Progress can be made when each representative is willing and able to understand the internal difficulties which face the other members of the conference. Agreement on any dispute always involves compromise and the adjustment of plans. The existence of mutual trust and a common objective makes this politically possible, while lack of trust makes each compromise appear like a defeat.

In an argument over the boundary of my farm I will more easily give way to my brother than I will to a man whom I dislike because he beats his wife—even though his marital problems have nothing to do with the point at issue. Similarly, I will find it easier to agree with other men who share my desire to build a dam than with those who wish to cultivate the area instead; our common objective will make other questions appear of subsidiary importance.

It is for this sort of reason that the Addis Ababa Conference of African Independent States held in May, 1963, was such a success. Having different languages, size, and resources, we could yet agree that the objective of African unity is in the interests of us all; that our boundaries are so absurd that they must be regarded as sacrosanct; that there shall be united action against colonialism in Africa; and that other steps should be taken to harmonize our development in different social and economic fields. For a conference lasting one week this was quite an achievement. It was made possible because each of us recognized that the others also have problems of their own, and that the only legitimate concern of all of us was that these internal difficulties should not be dealt with in such a manner as to have adverse repercussions on the rest of Africa.

Of course the Addis Ababa Conference did not solve all the problems of inter-African relationships. This requires the achievement of the unity to which we are now only aspiring. Until then there is always the danger that local disagreements will lead to disputes, and disputes to bad feeling and war, and this to an end of the common objective of unity. But this is only to say again that until there is a common law governing contact between different nations there will be a danger of conflict developing between them. It remains true that the easiest time to establish these common laws and institutions of justice is when there is such a feeling of unity and sympathy that it seems inconceivable that they will ever be required.

At any particular moment the real danger of conflict exists between those who do not trust each other, and who have a deep-seated dislike of each other's philosophy. We do not feel very much afraid of the arguments between Britain and America, but we feel very apprehensive about disputes between either of these two and the USSR. No ideological association is going to be able to deal with that problem, any more than it can deal with disputes between smaller antipathetic countries. Only within the framework of a world organization is there any hope of this really dangerous type of dispute being dealt with by discussion. Let regional and ideological conferences agree on what unity they may—all of them can contribute to the growth of world unity. But no partial gathering can do the job which must be tackled now if a holocaust is to be avoided.

IV

The United Nations is the only meeting place we have which claims the wider ambition. Yet there are states which are not Members of it—Switzerland, Germany, the People's Republic of China, to mention a few. Some of these states are not Members because the United Nations was conceived and brought to birth by the allied Powers in World War II. Their failure to agree on the reorganization of Europe after the end of hostilities has meant that, for example, the seventy million people of Germany are not represented. Other states are kept out because they are regarded—by one Member State or another—as not being "peace-loving," or as being in some other way suspect.

As it stands now, therefore, the United Nations is neither an association of friends nor a really universal meeting place, and there is at present a widespread attitude that it is a privilege to belong to the United Nations. I find myself having a degree of sympathy with this idea. It implies that there is a minimum level of behavior expected of every member of the world community, and those who sink below it should be ostracized and excluded from communion with the rest.

There is, however, a certain lack of logic in our attitude. If this is the conception of how the United Nations should work, then there should be no contact at all with nonmembers; all trade should cease, all diplomatic contact, and all international telecommunications; and every United Nations Member should stand solidly with those who share a border with the country which the United Nations has declared to be nonexistent. This does not happen, and the only case in which it is seriously advocated is in relation to South Africa—which is still a Member of the United Nations!

The fact is that we all have to live together; a country does not cease to exist as an international entity because other states have disputes with it. On the contrary, that is when it becomes most important that a state should be a member of the conference which is supposed to settle disputes. Who is a "peace-lover" is one of the points we should be arguing about inside the Organization.

Once you accept the principle that a state of whom some Members disapprove should be excluded from the peace-keeping Organization, then the whole character of the United Nations changes. It becomes an association of states which don't have too much objection to each other even if they are not actively friendly. Yet for conflicting countries to lose the one place where they sit down together would be to say that their particular dispute cannot be settled by argument and must be settled by extermination.

The maintenance of peace requires that the United Nations should, in principle, be universal. If any state is then excluded from the United Nations it can only be because the other Members have unanimously decided that they do not wish to keep the peace with that state; they have outlawed it from world society. In that case they have no alternative but to act as a group against the excluded state and—by whatever means are necessary—cause such changes in its administration or practices as would make it fit to become again a member of the world society. The question of universality should override all other considerations unless this final action can be and is to be taken, because these are the alternatives: either war, or talking until there is agreement. If, therefore, we expect, or hope, that problems are going to be solved peacefully, then we cannot deny, to any state, membership in the Organization which aims to provide the place and the institutional machinery for discussion.

This means that we should accept into the United Nations all states which themselves claim to be qualified for membership. Further, qualification should be simple and formal; it should consist only of *de facto* existence as a state with sovereign powers, and a willingness to affirm three things. These are: that it desires peace; that it is willing to talk about disputes which others have with it, and it with others, with a view to settlement by negotiation; and that it accepts the principle of human equality and, for practical purposes, the equality of nations.

Once this threefold statement has been made, any nation should be admitted to membership, regardless of whether others doubt the genuineness of these claims to accept the principles of peace between nations. Allegations that particular actions are not in accordance with these principles are then matters for discussion.

In making this statement I am fully aware that in her desire to force the Union of South Africa to cease its racial persecution, Tanganyika has joined with others in calling for the expulsion of South Africa from the United Nations. I believe there is no inconsistency in this, for what we are really demanding is that South Africa be ostracized by the world community. We are in fact not nearly as interested in pushing that government away from the conference table as we are in forcing it to adhere to the resolutions which the United Nations has passed. No one will be more pleased than we if this can be effectively achieved by the progressive success of an international trade boycott while South Africa remains a member of the United

Nations. But the use of the United Nations meeting place to bolster up the immoral and dangerous philosophy of racialism is intolerable. While this continues we have no alternative but to advocate South Africa's expulsion.

Expulsion, or exclusion, should always be the ultimate step, however, and must presuppose further action by the Members as a united group, because the first purpose of the United Nations must be to establish peace, and the conditions for peace. I believe that, with all its imperfections, it can serve these purposes.

V

The United Nations is a center for conference diplomacy, a place where the nations of the world submit their point of view for public examination. It is also the place, beyond anywhere else, for private diplomacy, for those quiet discussions where compromises can be brought to life and viewpoints exchanged. In the corridors and lobbies of the United Nations building almost all the nations of the world meet, disagree, and meet again. The man who has nothing to gain on either side in a dispute—but everything to lose if there is war—can talk to the contending representatives and put his—and our—point of view. Thus, through its unique combination of public and private discussion the United Nations Headquarters provides a basis for the work of building peace through talking.

The United Nations is also the one organ through which international action can be taken. Once agreement has been reached by the different governments, a "fire brigade" can be sent to the places where trouble is likely to break out, or where a breakdown of authority has created the kind of power vacuum which is an invitation to outside intervention and conflict. The present world situation makes this ability to get "impartial" intervention of the greatest possible importance. Whenever a single state intervenes in a local conflict, it inevitably spreads that conflict; when the United Nations intervenes effectively the conflict is isolated.

There is another aspect of United Nations intervention, the importance of which has not so far been fully appreciated. When the Member States of the United Nations agree to the dispatch of a United Nations force, or to a "good offices mission," they have voluntarily surrendered their own power to intervene in that dispute. Their reason may be simply fear that the intervention of their enemies would be more effective than their own, but the effect is a *de facto* surrender of power by a sovereign state to an international organization.

Certainly this is only a beginning, and on each occasion this right has to be surrendered all over again. But it is a beginning, and we may hope that, as the sufficiency of the present *ad hoc* arrangements becomes more obvious through increasing use, some more permanent arrangement for an "international police force" will be agreed to.

Sufficiency alone, however, will not enable the present arrangements to be replaced; any permanent United Nations police force implies a United Nations authority to govern it. And this is where we really do come up against the present insufficiency of the United Nations. At present we have a General Assembly made up of government delegates whose judgment must be exercised in the interests of their own nation and not necessarily in the long-term interests of the world as a whole. Also there is no executive authority at all; the Security Council is not really much more than a committee of the General Assembly which has special powers, and although these powers enable it to give a lead to the major body, it is not representative of it, and cannot be certain that it will get support for any proposals it makes.

Under these conditions, the work of the United Nations civil service is extremely difficult but extremely important. The international civil servant is the only person whose primary responsibility is to the world, and to peace on the basis of the Charter principles. The instructions he receives from his governing "political" body are often vague in the extreme, and it is his responsibility to interpret these in highly dangerous situations. Yet he is responsible to a collection of national governments, each of which is concerned first and foremost with the interests of its own country. This means that, whatever decision the civil servant makes in this exposed position, he is bound to be criticized, and not bound to be either praised or supported.

Yet just because his masters are divided, and because he is serving an ideal, the international civil servant can do a great deal for world peace. He can take the initiative in situations where any one else's proposals are suspect, and can thus get discussions going again, or get a compromise agreed upon. He can put himself as a buffer between contending groups, and interpret his instructions in such a manner that the concept of world unity is served rather than the interests of any one nation or ideology. But all this presupposes that he is a man of great courage and sagacity. He has to take decisions knowing that he is probably offending many of his masters, and he has to do this with no certainty of support from anywhere except his own conscience.

The real problem for the international civil servant is that he is expected to be a nonpolitical politician. He is required to be "neutral" in highly political situations, and to do this in the absence of a political authority able to do anything more than give the most general—and often conflicting—guidelines. The United Nations servant is, in fact, filling a power vacuum created by the inability of individual nations to govern the world and the absence of a real political governing authority. He remains subject to correction, but he takes the initiative, and he acts as a catalyst to secure international accommodation simply because there is no one else in a position to do so.

This situation can only be safely changed when some elements of sovereignty are surrendered by the individual nation-states to a world body.

Recent efforts to achieve unity in Europe and East Africa, however, have shown how difficult it is to achieve a surrender of sovereignty even among friendly nations. A universal surrender by nations suspicious of one another is certainly not a practicable proposition in the near future. We have to accept the fact that there is not going to be a "world government" in time to deal with the present problems of peace, just as we have to accept the fact that in every other respect the nations are moving ever closer to each other and thus increasing the possibility of conflict. This is the situation we have to deal with now.

Nonetheless, I do not believe there is reason for despondency. We are making progress—even despite ourselves. When there is a dangerous flare-up in the world, or a fear of a local power vacuum, many of the nation-states now think in terms of calling for international action. Every United Nations intervention which is agreed upon is making stronger the concept that individual states should keep out of power conflicts, but that the United Nations should go in to maintain law and order, or separate opposing armies. In other words, an attitude of mind is being built up among the peoples of the world which accepts—and will finally favor international political action. Certainly this acceptance is at present confined to fairly restricted fields, and a major failure by the United Nations officials to live up to their hard calling could still destroy it. But we have begun to form a habit, and habitual interpersonal behavior gradually becomes common law, and eventually statutory law.

In other ways too we have inched forward toward international law. Every institution develops its "accepted practices," its customary code of behavior, and I do not think the United Nations will be any exception to this. I think there can already be discerned the growth of an accepted standard of international practice. True, it is only just beginning—but the various national United Nations representatives do advise their governments about how a particular action is likely to be received, and the effect it is likely to have on the prestige of their countries in the United Nations.

The growth of the position of the Secretary-General is also a starting point for real internationalism, because it has evolved out of need and not out of personal ambition. Each Secretary-General has been elected because he was regarded as "safe," "neutral," and "modest." But each in his turn has contributed to the development of an international consciousness by virtue of his own world responsibility.

From these and a myriad of other small things will develop that law of nations which is our only real protection against international war. But we have first to accept the implications of this.

Our protection against others must inevitably imply their protection against us, for the law which protects also restricts. Unfortunately, it is often the restriction which is most noticeable. Nations, like people, tend not to think about absent dangers, and the more effective a protection the less it is noticed. Thus the keystone of peace—law—is never popular, and to ask that all the laws which are there to protect should be kept voluntarily is to ask more than one can expect to obtain.

In this respect the world has only just started. The International

Court has a long history, but the number of states which have accepted the jurisdiction of the Court in all legal disputes is severely limited—I have discovered that Tanganyika is not one of them! The usual reason given is that most quarrels are more political than legal. This is rather like a thief claiming that he stole from the rich to help the poor; it might be true, but it is quite irrelevant to the existence of law! The main difficulty, however, about using the International Court to enforce international law is that it is very slow and has no way of implementing its decisions. When finally issued, a judgment becomes one of a number of factors considered if the matter is submitted to the Security Council. Yet it is worth considering just how many of the present danger spots in the world could have their temperature reduced if the International Court were made into a more speedy and effective body—and if all the nations agreed to implement its decisions.

There is, however, one further factor to be considered.

VI

Whether there is an enforcement authority or not, whether law is statutory or not, peace will still only be secured if the international law is based on certain fundamental principles. Law which offends against basic human rights, or which fails to secure those rights, does not fulfill the purpose of law, because it does not secure man's life in society.

There is nothing new in this; the American Declaration of Independence is the most famous assertion of man's right to revolt if "certain inalienable rights" are not secured by his government, and a refusal to obey laws is nothing less than a revolt. Neither is it necessary to think in these large and national terms; within a nation-state there are occasions on which, if the law does not act against an individual, other men will do so—and receive the support of their fellows. The world-wide sympathy for those who plotted to kill Hitler did not arise simply because he was the leader of a nation at war. It resulted from the fact that he was the dominant figure in a conspiracy against the humanity of men, and the law was not only powerless against him but had even been twisted to his service.

Similarly, if international law is powerless against those who transgress against basic human morality, there will be nation-states which will take matters into their own hands, and themselves act as judges and executioners. What is more, they will demand—as of right—that others support them, and they will claim a moral basis for their actions—regardless of any law which might or might not exist in international affairs.

This means that a concern with international peace must be a concern for justice as well as a concern for "law and order." The debates on human rights at the United Nations are not a pleasant diversion from the quest for peace; they are an integral part of it. Yet we have to acknowledge that every new state has as its first priority the creation of peace, the establishment of conditions where a man can walk down the street without fearing for his life. Questions of justice for and between the citizens always come second, and too often never arrive. But just as the absence of justice leads ultimately to revolution within a state, so its absence in international relations will ultimately destroy peace, whatever system of law and authority is evolved. Law and human justice have to develop side by side, the one supporting the other. Only under these conditions are we moving toward the position where human development is a story of constructive endeavor and not of bloodshed.

Yet to say all this is merely to outline the objectives which have to be aimed at and the path which has to be followed. Peace in the future, as well as peace now, depends upon men. Ultimately, it depends upon all men, all the citizens of all the countries. But it is those who hold positions of responsibility, particularly in the political field, who must carry the real burden. Every national leader can make a contribution to our progress, or he can give way to the pressure of old-fashioned loyalties and lead the way to another era of mass destruction. For there is nothing more obvious in the modern world than the fact that it is easier—from a political point of view—to fight than to talk.

The world's past is the era of nationalism, and because it is our past it is also the present. Our educational systems have led to the development of exclusive national loyalties and to concepts of national pride and superiority. They are still doing so. These are the values of the vast mass of the world's citizens. They mean that to discuss differences and difficulties with the representative of another state is often to be accused of being "unpatriotic," of favoring "appeasement." They mean that great personal popularity can be won by bellicose statements and aggressive attitudes. They mean that national leaders have almost to apologize if they sit down and talk over actual or potential disputes with another state.

Few things are more difficult for a national political leader than getting an opportunity to talk to his opposite number in a country with which there is a history of disputes. If he wants to do this he has to make excuses, use threatening language to the person with whom he is trying to negotiate, perhaps make a "show of strength," or do other things which make the actual discussions infinitely more difficult. Further, once a compromise has been arranged, it is often necessary for both sides to demonstrate that the discussions have really resulted in a "victory" for their own nation; claiming victory for common sense and sanity is not enough.

This is not a problem confined to the leaders of any one continent, or to leaders of countries which have a multiparty system of government—though these do have some special difficulties at election times! It is a problem facing all leaders in nation-states throughout the world. It is not necessary for me to quote examples; we all know that to stand on a public platform and announce that you favor discussions with the "national enemy" is not always popular!

Yet how else are these problems to be solved, if not by talking? The only alternative is violence and war. It is understandable that nations in dispute should refuse to cooperate in constructive tasks, for these require a basic common trust and understanding. But a refusal to talk about the dispute which has undermined that mutual trust is a refusal to face up to the basic dilemma of man—that for his own freedom he needs unity with his fellows, and this requires from him compromise, toleration, and a concept of justice. The real enemy in the modern world is, in fact, the man who refuses to talk about the disputes in which he is involved.

The challenge of the twentieth century is the conversion of nationalism into internationalism. Our success depends on whether we have the courage to place our trust in world institutions of which we each are such a small part, and whether the leaders of nation-states will lead in the direction of unity on the basis of equality.

The search for peace is a long and wearisome job. It has been going on for a long time; Dag Hammarskjöld once quoted the story of the Chinese philosophers in the year 350 B.C. who "went round from state to state helping people to settle their differences." But it is now more urgent than ever before. Wars of old affected the soldiers and the people over whose land the wars were fought; now they affect every individual in the world, and all those yet unborn. The solution to the problem is easy to describe, but it has perhaps never been so difficult to carry out. Working for it requires more courage than war does; it requires patience and the firm adherence to principles under all sorts of countervailing pressures. The big question is whether we can move fast enough—in education, in attitudes, and in institutions —to avoid a third World War.

I believe that if two conditions are fulfilled we can yet succeed. The nations must have the courage to talk about their differences, and must hold fast to the principles of our common humanity while recognizing that the path to their implementation is likely to be long and unlikely to be straight. In addition, there must exist a focus of loyalty beyond the nation-state, and men who are willing, if necessary, to sacrifice their reputation and even their lives for that greater loyalty.

Dag Hammarskjöld was such a man. He was willing to be unpopular with everyone in support of the United Nations Charter and, beyond that, in support of what the United Nations ought to be. He was a great servant of humanity. And not the least of his services was the example he provided: a man of principle who accepted the equality of those most unequal to him; a man of patience and tolerance with the impatient and intolerant; and a man of such courage that it was one of his least courageous acts to go voluntarily on the dangerous mission of peace which led to his death.

BUILDING BRIDGES
IN SUPPORT OF PEACE

Vijaya Lakshmi Pandit

FORMER PRESIDENT OF THE UNITED NATIONS GENERAL
ASSEMBLY AND CHAIRMAN OF THE DELEGATION OF INDIA

Given at Columbia University, December 9, 1963

I am conscious of my privilege in being asked to deliver one of the Dag Hammarskjöld Memorial Lectures. My association with Dag Hammarskjöld was brief but its impact is still with me. It was during the year 1953, soon after his appointment as Secretary-General of the United Nations, that I was elected President of the General Assembly; during the months that followed I saw him constantly, worked with him closely, benefited in many ways by his wisdom, and learned to call him friend.

It is not necessary for me to speak about Dag Hammarskjöld's contribution to the cause of peace. His life and the manner of his death are testimony of his dedication to the great causes for which men live. He was sensitive and a rather remote person but sometimes one had a glimpse of the real man, and during the period we worked together I had several such glimpses. Dag Hammarskjöld's scholarship was impressive and he was undoubtedly a statesman. He always seemed to me a man in a hurry—anxious to set things moving. This quality appealed to me, for I, too, am always driven by a sense of urgency. Delays in any work that has once been undertaken seem to me not only bad but frustrating. Life is never long enough for the implementation of all our dreams but if life is cut short at a moment when its earlier promise is about to be fulfilled, then it is a sad day for the world. In Dag Hammarskjöld's death we witnessed such a tragedy. Recently another great tragedy has moved the world. In both cases, the men killed were dedicated to the cause of building a better world, pledged to the service of humanity, unswerving in their pursuit of peace, and devoting their time, energy, and rare gifts toward this goal. That such men should die before the allotted human span leaves all mankind the poorer for their going.

The present Memorial Lecture is about "Building Bridges in Support of Peace." Both Dag Hammarskjöld and John Fitzgerald Kennedy were trying to build such bridges, and we who wish to honor their memory must labor at the task. It is not easy.

War is older than history but the quest for peace has also been pursued for centuries. Men have tried to devise institutions to provide for the settlement of international disputes, efforts have been made to reduce the scope of war and lessen its horrors. In 1919, a great document of international law, the Covenant of the League of Nations, came into being but it was unable to prevent the worst war history has so far known. Now we have the United Nations with its Charter which "reaffirms faith in fundamental human rights, in the dignity and worth of the human person, in the equal rights of men and women and of nations large and small" and which promises "to promote social progress and better standards of life in larger freedom." Through its various agencies, assistance of many kinds has reached the far corners of the earth and created new hope in people's minds, but the shadow of war continues to darken our lives. During the relatively short period of its existence, the United Nations has been the instrument by which, on several occasions, conflicts have been localized and ended, but no formula for peace has yet been devised.

We now accept the fact that peace is not the reverse of conflict. Peace has been described as "subtle and varied in its manifestation—more intricate in the problems it lays bare." In my childhood the picture of peace depicted an anemic young woman in a nightgown clasping a frightened dove to her breast. This has no message for the present. Our need now is for a peace in which the qualities of dynamism and radiance can be found—a peace which is a continuing process, bringing with it the guarantee of freedom, justice, and security, until it embraces all the nations of the earth. Science has forced the recognition of one world upon us but only peace can provide the cement which will bind these nations to each other. There is no short cut to this end.

Man's growing knowledge has opened new doors into a land of promise. Part of that promise is already being translated into our lives, which have become richer in many ways, but unless knowledge walks hand in hand with wisdom, peril looms ahead. Like the Indian fable, science has given us the power of death as well as the enrichment of life. The Indian fable tells us that once, long years ago, the Gods and the demons decided to churn the ocean, for they knew that within the ocean were great treasures. And so the churning began on the distinct understanding—a sort of gentleman's agreement that whatever came out of the ocean would be shared equally between them. All was well until the elixir of everlasting life—Amrita—came from the ocean and immediately a quarrel started; neither side would give up this priceless gift. While they argued and fought for possession of the Amrita the ocean yielded up another less appealing gift— poison, or Vish. Now the problem was again one of sharing but this time no one was willing to take the poison. Though this is a fable, it has a message for us today, for we have in our hands the power of enriching and making life abundant, more abundant than man has ever known before. We also have it in our power to destroy life and civilization itself. Because of the inability to share and the inability to control ourselves, we are poised on the precipice.

The problem facing us is whether man will readjust his mind to the new situation in which he lives or, drunk with his power, reduce its value, by wrong actions, to nothingness. Man's conquest of space, his ability to orbit the globe, are indeed dramatic landmarks of our century, but the need to conquer prejudice, to change outworn methods of thinking, and to follow this by decisive action has still to be answered. The threats to peace stem largely from our own limitations. As the distinguished Prime Minister of Canada stated in the General Assembly a few weeks ago, it has become possible for man to communicate with a missile or a planet millions of miles away but it is still not possible for us to communicate with each other on this small planet of ours. However, it is good that this realization is being borne in upon us and the fact that solid work directed toward change is being done by the United Nations is encouraging. While we work for the removal of the causes of conflict we must remember it is necessary to build bridges by which the members of the human race may cross over to each other. This, of course, is a universal responsibility since no bridge can be built from one side only. We have a saying in India which is very descriptive. We say that you cannot clap unless you use two hands. And we cannot have peace unless all parties to the peace are in agreement.

During the last quarter of a century, several of the causes of war have been attacked and partially uprooted. The colonial system was among the major factors which involved the world in misery and indignity. One of the miracles of the age has been the elimination of this system. The way in which established imperialist systems have, within the past two decades, given place to a new relationship based on mutual understanding and cooperation is surely a thing of great value. Since India was the country where this process first began, a word about the way in which our freedom was achieved may be appropriate. Events move so swiftly these days that memories have become short and there are some things it is good to remember.

The technique followed by Gandhi in the national struggle in India was unique. He spoke all the words of which the world seems to be suspicious—love, truth, purity, fearlessness, nonviolence. These he combined into a national creed which became the instrument of our freedom. He did more. He taught us that one does not fight against men but against systems; one opposes evil in all its forms, whether at home or outside. Further, he identified our struggle with all those who like ourselves were pawns of colonialism, thus releasing the movement from narrow national boundaries and placing it on the highest plane. The Indian people under his guidance grew to great stature and the movement itself, in spite of occasional lapses from his teachings, became a crusade. The transfer of power from Great Britain to India was one of the most outstanding events of this century. The fact that after this the relationship between the two countries became one of partnership in a common endeavor is something of which both the people of Great Britain and the people of India are justly proud. It was a civilized ending—the turning over of an ugly page in history and the beginning of a new chapter.

India's freedom was the first step in the process of the liquidation of colonialism. Rapidly new nations emerged in Asia and took their place in the United Nations. Even more significant has been the emergence of Africa, many of whose countries' representatives are now valued members of the United Nations Assembly, adding dignity and strength to that august body. These things are good, but it is a matter of regret, and of considerable concern, that there are still areas under colonial domination. Even a single thorn in the finger of one's hand can lead to suppuration. So long as any area remains under foreign domination we cannot regard the future with equanimity, for we have arrived at the stage when the indivisibility of freedom is not merely a slogan but hard practical realism.

Racialism is another threat that hangs over us and comes in the way of crossing the bridge of peace. Discrimination on grounds of color, religion, or sex is abhorrent to most people and yet this pernicious practice still continues to divide human beings and degrade them. We believe that such discrimination is bad for those who practice and preach it as well as for its victims. No group of human beings—no government—can act unjustly and inhumanly toward their fellows without disastrous consequences to themselves. The human spirit is destroyed in the process. There is a moral law which must be recognized and obeyed if mankind is to continue its onward march to a brave new world. Because of this belief democratic governments—mine among them—seek to implement the promise of justice and equality enshrined in their constitutions in the lives of every citizen. The pace may sometimes be slower than we wish, but nevertheless we move on and strive to break down all artificial barriers which separate men from each other. There are, unfortunately, some governments who make a virtue of brutal and senseless policies and even in this day and age seek to justify them. It is obvious these policies will have to end, for enlightened world opinion is against them, but meanwhile the values on which our civilization is built stand in jeopardy. A strong bridge is needed so that those who have suffered the indignities of separation from their fellows for no fault of their own may cross over and make their special contribution to the prosperity and progress of the world.

Two resolutions recently passed in the General Assembly will be helpful in this connection. The first requests the Economic and Social Council to invite the Commission on Human Rights to give absolute priority to the preparation of a draft international convention on the elimination of all forms of racial discrimination, to be submitted to the Assembly for consideration at its next session. The other provides that the United Nations, the specialized agencies, states, and nongovernmental organizations should do all in their power to ensure the abolition of all forms of discrimination based on race, color, or ethnic origin, and requests the Secretary-General and the specialized agencies to ensure the immediate and large-scale circulation of the Declaration on the Elimination of All Forms of Racial Discrimination already adopted.

The recent United Nations vote in the Security Council on the question of apartheid in South Africa is most significant and shows the new realistic trend of thinking in the United Nations. These and others are moves in the right direction, small steps on the road to peace.

When one speaks about peace, it is inevitable that one's thoughts should turn toward the existing economic imbalance. I speak as one of the millions who are concerned about the underprivileged parts of the world, who, as citizens of a developing country, desire a richer and fuller life for the people of India and all the vast areas of Asia and Africa where the struggle for the basic things of life takes precedence over all else. This is another explosive situation and the efforts made by the United States and the United Nations to assist developing countries show complete awareness of the threat that faces the world because of this present economic imbalance. Two thirds of the world's population has only 17 percent of the world's annual income. Half the world's population, living in Asia, possesses only one fourth of the world's food supplies. The appalling misery and poverty in these areas is a continuous reminder that it is such conditions that breed revolution. It would be equally correct, I think, to say that an Asia with a better, fuller life, with higher standards, with hope for the future, would provide guarantees of democracy and peace on which the world could rely.

The richer countries might, in their own enlightened self-interest, step up help to improve the lot of the people in the developing countries. It is not my suggestion that the development of the underdeveloped countries should be made at the cost of the further development of the industrialized countries. What I plead, however, is that while maintaining their own growth, they should set apart a small portion of their own resources for the development of the poorer countries. Until there has been a reasonable amount of economic development it will not be possible for these countries to achieve complete social justice. People must first be fed, housed, given education, health, and equality of opportunity. Each one of these objectives is linked to the other—how does one allot priorities? The needs are desperate and all require to be tackled together. Speaking recently in the United Nations, the Vice-Chairman of India's Planning Commission said:

While many millions in the poor countries labor to forge a new future for themselves, to deny them essential aid while unused capacity of production remains in some of the highly industrialized countries is a reversal of reason and humanity. In the war against hunger and want, we in the poorer countries are now fully engaged. Here, as on an earlier famous occasion, we ask for tools, and we promise to do the job. The rich nations, whether from the West or the East, are invited to join the peaceful competition to become the great arsenals of development. It is not aid, or even trade, that encompasses our vision, it is the quickening of mutual aid and cooperation. Poor as my country is, our contribution to the United Nations Special Fund is the seventh largest. Not India alone, but every developing country is anxious to contribute to the common pool, as they are to benefit from it. But this requires the blasting of the inhibiting influences in the rich countries that prompt them to view political boundaries as of equal significance in economic life too. Here at least the truth is that we grow only by sharing.

The world's economic resources, as well as its political energies, have for years past been diverted toward the arms race. Nearly $200 billion are spent the world over on armaments. If a tenth of this amount could be diverted to peaceful purposes, dramatic and far-reaching changes could be achieved in the world. It would become possible to erect an edifice to peace which would be a testimony to man's wisdom and his abiding faith in his fellow man instead of the lofty memorials we build to those he has slaughtered in senseless wars of hate and revenge.

It is, therefore, with a sense of relief and hope that one welcomes a small first step in the lessening of fear and tension and mutual suspicion which has come to us as a result of the Moscow Treaty. The problem of most concern and of the utmost urgency is total disarmament. The atomic and outer space revolutions of our time have brought forcefully to the attention of the international community the basic choice between the destruction of humanity and human civilization and international cooperation for peace, progress, and justice and the settlement of differences by peaceful negotiations. The development of weapons of mass destruction makes it absolutely necessary that the foremost principle of the United Nations Charter, which is to outlaw war, should be fully implemented and preparations of war and threats of war should be completely banned.

Paradoxically the hydrogen bomb is helping to usher in a world without nuclear war. Nurclear war is outmoded. There would be no victor, nor vanquished, in such a war. The belligerents themselves— and perhaps all life on this planet—would be destroyed. Nuclear arsenals may still be able to hold the peace, through the balance of terror, but they cannot be used any longer. The struggle between rival ideologies will continue but this will be through peaceful competition or example, described recently by Mr. Gromyko as "peaceful coexistence," and by President Kennedy as a "contest of peace." That this may, in fact, become the international way of life is the prayer of each one of us.

Recognizing the need to divert people's attention to the vast fields in which nations are cooperating with each other, the Prime Minister of India suggested two years ago that the United Nations might consider declaring one year as a year of international cooperation. This would focus attention on the positive and meaningful aspects of the United Nations which we so often lose sight of. It would confirm that we are trying to build the defenses of peace in the minds of men, as the Charter of UNESCO asks us to do. It would be an encouragement to thousands of people, especially the people of the prosperous countries, to realize that work at the grass roots level is being done quietly and effectively by United Nations agencies in the far-flung corners of the globe. It is important for the largest possible number of people in the United States to know that when an endemic disease is conquered in some far-off corner of the world, when a starving child is fed and given education, when schoolhouses and hospitals, roads and industries spring up in rural areas, there the seeds of democracy are being sown. It is here that the people, if permitted, will give an answer to the challenge of our time. Let us examine what Prime Minister Nehru said about the international cooperation year which he advocated. I feel sure many of us share the thoughts he has expressed.

In his statement he referred to the numerous areas of conflict which afflicted the world. He said frankly that he could not suggest any rapid or magic ways of dealing with the problems, but he found that the worst difficulty we had to face was to fight something one could not grip: an atmosphere, the imponderables of life, people filled with fear, passion, and hatred. These were the problems to be dealt with. One of the facts of life is that, surrounded by conflicts of all kinds, the world still manages to go on. This points to the existence of considerable cooperation between nations and individuals in spite of disagreements and disputes in political and other fields.

The tendency to play down such cooperation and to highlight the smallest points of disagreement has led to the prevalent idea that the world is full of conflict and that we live poised on the verge of disaster. Surely, the realities of the world could be more faithfully reflected if the existing cooperation on all levels was presented in its true perspective to the people.

Recalling that some years ago it had been resolved to have an International Geophysical Year, Prime Minister Nehru said that the Assembly might call upon all countries of the world to devote a year, not to speeches about peace, but to the furtherance of cooperative activities in any field—political, social, cultural, and others— through which nations have come closer together. This would direct our energies and our thinking to cooperation, thereby creating a better atmosphere for the solution of big issues of the day.

This idea is not a new one, he said. Indeed, there is little that is new in the world; truth is as old as time itself and yet we must remind ourselves of it from time to time. Violence and hatred are bad for countries, as they are bad for individuals. The great men of the world have been those who have fought hatred and violence and not those who have encouraged them. The crisis that we now face is forcing men and women to a new way of thinking. We are at a moment in history when new thoughts must be followed rapidly by new action. This is the challenge of the present and we must meet it, for what shall it profit the world if it conquers its material problems and then commits suicide because it cannot control its own mind.

Such a year of international cooperation might play a considerable role in lifting, somewhat, the burden of fear that lies heavy on the human heart and bring the reassurance that ways and means can be found and will be found to remove the fear entirely. I am again reminded of a little Eastern fable.

Once upon a time, there lived a king. He was a good king, he was a just man, and his people loved and honored him. One morning he was going out to hunt, and at the gates of the city he saw Death coming in. He stopped Death and asked, "Why do you go into my city?" Death answered: "It is ordained that 200 people must die today, but since you are a good and wise man and a just king, I promise you I will not take more than 200 lives." With this assurance the king had to be content and he went on his way with a heavy heart. Returning late at night he heard sounds of weeping and wailing coming to him from the city. On arrival, he discovered that the population of the city was almost all dead. He was appalled, and looking around he saw that Death was still sneering in one corner. He said, "Why have you broken your promise to me? You said you would take 200 people and you have taken many thousands." And Death replied, "Sire, I took but 200, the rest died because my brother Fear lived among them."

And so let us build these bridges of peace before we fall further in the grip of fear. Let us work for the elimination of things which cause conflict and wars and for the consolidation of things which bring men together in comradeship and love.

Let us not die of our fear, let us not die at all; rather let us *live* by our hopes, by our faith in ourselves, in our fellow man, and in God.

LOOKING AHEAD

U Thant

SECRETARY-GENERAL OF THE UNITED NATIONS

Given at Columbia University, January 7, 1964

I deem it a privilege to be able to participate in the Dag Hammar-skjöld Memorial Lecture Series. When my distinguished predecessor was killed on September 17, 1961, there was a genuine feeling of sad-ness and a keen sense of tragedy, which we experienced again when President Kennedy was snatched away from our midst. The contribu-tion that Dag Hammarskjöld made to the development of the United Nations and to the whole concept of international cooperative action to solve major problems will surely go down in history as something unique, since it came at a time when the Organization itself was in its formative stage.

I remember participating as the representative of Burma in the 1,010th plenary meeting of the General Assembly on the afternoon of Wednesday, September 20, 1961, along with so many of my distin-guished colleagues. Tributes were paid to the great personal qualities of the man, his wide culture, his penetrating intelligence, his amazing grasp of the most complicated international issues, his intellectual integrity, his courage of conviction, his tenacity of purpose, his inde-fatigable industry, and his tireless stamina. Surely, this was a unique combination of qualities in one human being, who dedicated the best years of his life to the cause of the United Nations and the pursuit of peace!

I admired his principles even more than his remarkable personal qualities. To him, the provisions of the Charter were so important—

almost sacred—that he was willing to forego any temporary advantage that could be gained by following the easier path of expediency. To him, too, the institution, the United Nations Organization and its collective interest, was far more important than the separate interests of the individual Member States. With his great gift for innovation and improvisation, he discovered new ways to help keep the peace—witness the practical application of the principle of an emergency force in one situation, of an observer group in another, and of a United Nations presence in a third context.

Dag Hammarskjöld had a dynamic concept of the Organization. To him the United Nations was not merely a forum for debate, although he realized that this was a very important function of the Organization. It was more important, in his view, that it should be a center for harmonizing the actions of nations in the attainment of common ends. While realizing that many important decisions, whether they related to the halting of the nuclear arms race or the implementation of general and complete disarmament, could be settled only by agreement among the major Powers, he emphasized at the same time the stake of the nonmilitary Powers, in fact of all mankind, in the survival of the human race. He viewed the United Nations, therefore, as providing the occasion and the opportunity for the nonmajor Powers to affirm their interest in peace and survival. He also regarded the Organization, not as a substitute for normal diplomacy, but rather as an additional and perhaps novel instrument which was available to Member governments and which could be used by them in situations where conventional methods of diplomacy might be precluded for a variety of reasons.

I believe that I was the first on the occasion of that 1,010th meeting of the General Assembly to give expression to a thought which, no doubt, had crossed the minds of many of my friends. I said: "Who could be more deserving of a Nobel Peace Prize than Mr. Dag Hammarskjöld, who fell in the unrelenting fight for peace, even though the award would be posthumous?" Not long afterward, we all had the satisfaction of learning that the Nobel Prize Committee had in fact decided to award the Peace Prize for 1961 to the late Secretary-General.

I shall now turn to the theme I have chosen. I should perhaps begin by explaining the title of my address. I would like to take advantage of this occasion, which comes at the beginning of a new year, to look ahead in the light of the past and to see what the major problems are which we face and what the prospects are for solving them. I would thus hope to have an opportunity to give a conspectus of the situation facing the World Organization in the nineteenth year of its existence.

Twenty-five years ago, when the League of Nations was also nineteen years old, it was already tottering and on its last legs. On the other hand, I believe I will not be accused of partiality if I say that, despite its shortcomings, the United Nations has a substantial record of solid achievement during its nineteen years of existence, and I hope I will not be charged with overoptimism if I predict that its most fruitful years are still ahead of it. The great advantages that the United Nations has over the League are its greater universality of membership and the fact that it gives as much importance to economic and social development, the protection and promotion of human rights, and the equal rights of nations, large and small, as to its over-all objective of saving succeeding generations from war. If we are to justify the faith of humanity in our international Organization and to live up to the promises of the Charter, we can do so only by living up to the principles of the Charter.

I believe therefore that 1964 is a crucial year in the history of the United Nations. This is the time when the Organization has to face up to its responsibilities and solve the problems which hinder its effectiveness. Among the most important of these is the financial problem. The Organization is in debt to the tune of some $134 million. True, its creditors are for the most part Member governments, but I believe it is imperative for the Organization to be financially solvent. I also believe that a bankrupt Organization is bound to be an ineffective one. I am advised that the outlook for 1964 is discouraging, not only because of the serious financial position, but also because of the implications of Article 19 of the Charter. On the other side of the ledger it is noteworthy that a terminal date has been set by the General Assembly for the military operations in the Congo, which are due to be wound up by the middle of the year. In regard to the United Nations Emergency Force in the Middle East we have undertaken a recent review as a result of which we have been able to reduce the expenditure a little. Most of the other peace-keeping operations we have undertaken are on the basis that the Member governments mainly concerned reimburse the Organization for the expenses involved.

But the basic problem remains, and that is the question of solvency of the Organization. I believe that it is time for all countries, whatever their stand on the merits of particular peace-keeping operations may have been in the past, to make a special effort in 1964 to put the Organization back on its financial feet. If this can be done perhaps we may be able to ensure, with respect to future peace-keeping operations—large or small—that the Organization might be called upon to undertake, that a situation does not arise in which, in the pursuit of peace, the Organization bankrupts itself. I realize that the difference of views among Member governments stems not only from their varying evaluation of specific peace-keeping operations but also from their interpretation of the provisions of the Charter. Even so, I believe that if there is a will to solve this problem a way out may be found without prejudice to the questions of principle involved.

Unless the financial picture improves I am afraid that the effectiveness of the Organization in its various fields of activity, whether they be political or economic, social or humanitarian, or whether they relate to development or decolonization, to disarmament or *détente,* will be impaired. The present world outlook is, I believe, propitious for settling some of the problems which have plagued international relations in the years following World War II. I cannot help thinking that this congenial atmosphere is also favorable for settling this basic issue of the solvency of the Organization.

I propose to refer later, and in somewhat greater detail, to the efforts being made by the major Powers to reduce defense expenditures. At this point I would simply like to mention that, including the regular budget of the United Nations, the peace-keeping operations, and the contributions to all the voluntary programs, the total cost of the United Nations to the international community in 1964 will be around $330 million. With these funds the United Nations undertakes a variety of tasks in the field of diplomacy, in the peaceful settlement of controversial and potentially dangerous issues, in furthering the progress of dependent territories to political independence and sovereignty, in promoting economic and social development of the developing countries, in advancing international trade, and in safeguarding human rights. If we think in terms of the defense expenditures of the major military Powers alone, all the costs involved in discharging these manifold responsibilities of the United Nations, including its voluntary programs and peace-keeping operations, are approximately one quarter of one percent. If Member governments could be persuaded to see the problem in this perspective and with this sense of proportion, I am sure that they would not feel it a strain to make a special effort to solve the problem of the financial solvency of the Organization.

I would now like to undertake a conspectus of the work of the Organization, as I promised earlier. In its political work the United Nations deals with certain global problems such as nuclear and conventional disarmament as well as certain regional and local problems. I may perhaps begin by dealing with some of the regional and local problems with which the United Nations is directly concerned at the present time.

I mentioned earlier that the military phase of the Congo is to come to an end in the middle of 1964, but that the United Nations Emergency Force is to continue with a little reduction in expenditure. Through the good offices of the United Nations Truce Supervision Organization we were recently able to arrange for the exchange of some prisoners between Syria and Israel. But the over-all outlook in the Middle East today is threatening, and I am very much afraid that there will be more than one occasion in 1964 when Middle Eastern problems will engage the attention of the United Nations. In Yemen we have reduced the military contingent to a handful of observers assisted by a small air arm. The character of the United Nations representation in Yemen has also changed, with the emphasis on the political rather than the military aspects. I hope that, by the time the extended term of the United Nations Mission in Yemen is due to come to an end, the situation may have stabilized sufficiently for us to be able to leave with the assurance that stability may continue.

Another important part of the political work of the United Nations is in the field of decolonization. Both the General Assembly and the Security Council have recently adopted resolutions on the subject of territories under Portuguese administration. I sincerely hope that a just and lasting solution may be found for this problem in 1964. Elsewhere in Africa, especially in Central Africa, it appears that the process of decolonization will continue and that we may have the opportunity to welcome at least two more countries from this part of Africa in the United Nations at the nineteenth session of the General Assembly.

On December 10, 1963, we celebrated the fifteenth anniversary of the Universal Declaration of Human Rights. One of the achievements of the eighteenth session of the General Assembly was the adoption of the Declaration on the Elimination of All Forms of Racial Discrimination. I am encouraged to find that everywhere there is increasing preoccupation with the abolition of discrimination, so that one of the main purposes of the Charter, namely, to promote and encourage respect for human rights and for fundamental freedoms for all without distinction as to race, sex, language, or religion, may become a reality.

History has recorded many examples at different times of man's inhumanity to man, but today we see an awakening of the human conscience to the evils of discrimination. I realize that, even so, traditions die hard, and that the process of elimination of discrimination may take time. There is, however, one country where discrimination is one of the principles of state policy. This policy has been unequivocally condemned by both the General Assembly and the Security Council. I hope that the day is not far off when the impact of public opinion in the rest of the world begins to be felt in that country so that here too there may be an awakening of conscience and a change of direction.

The Charter also emphasizes the importance of employing international machinery for the promotion of economic and social advancement. In recognition of this responsibility of the world community, the sixteenth session of the General Assembly decided to designate the current decade as the United Nations Development Decade. Unfortunately, the resources available to the United Nations have never been wholly adequate to discharge its responsibilities in this field, and as a result it has concentrated on pre-investment and technical assistance. While the World Bank and its affiliates have been able to give some capital assistance for economic development, the bulk of such assistance has been on a bilateral basis between the donor and the recipient countries.

Recently there has been a growing recognition of the many advantages of multilateral assistance for promoting economic development. I believe that this is a welcome trend and I hope that this will have the effect of augmenting and raising to more adequate levels the resources available to the United Nations. At the same time I feel that even if the United Nations is not able, in the immediate future, to offer capital aid to the developing countries it can, and should, make its assistance in the pre-investment field more effective. During the last two years and more I have had the opportunity of observing at first-hand the multiplicity of sources from which technical assistance is provided. To some extent I realize that this proliferation is inevitable; however, I believe that the time has come when we should streamline our own Organization and make it easier for the developing countries to receive aid from us. I also believe that this streamlining could be coupled with better coordination, not only at United Nations Headquarters, but also in relation to the specialized agencies, which have such a distinguished record of achievement in this field. I consider that this need not affect present interagency relationships and that we should be able to preserve the best elements of existing programs in a new setup. Most important of all, I believe that it would enable us to be better prepared for the day when, whether as a result of progress toward disarmament or otherwise, really substantial resources become available to the United Nations, enabling it to offer capital aid to the developing countries.

Before leaving the field of economic development I would like to make one more observation. In the first half of 1964 the United Nations will be convening a major conference in the economic field, namely the United Nations Conference on Trade and Development. While it is true that aid is an important element in promoting the economic development of the developing countries, trade is an even more important factor. The problems of the developing countries in regard to their terms of trade are well known and I do not wish to expatiate on these problems on this occasion. I hope that following the trade conference we will be able to set up some machinery which might be able effectively to harmonize the interests of the advanced and developing countries in regard to international trade. Here is a field where generosity, imagination, and mutual understanding will surely lead to increased prosperity for all.

I said at the beginning that the times are propitious for a settlement of some of the major issues which the world has been facing from the very end of World War II. Surveying the international scene a couple of years after the end of the war, a wit observed that peace had broken out everywhere. The outlook is even more spotty today. For one thing, there is an atmosphere of *détente* following the conclusion of the test ban treaty in Moscow in August last, an occasion in which I was privileged to participate. I then made a statement in which I detailed some of the measures which had been recommended by the United Nations and which had as their object the relaxation of tensions. In some quarters this statement was misinterpreted as being partial to one or another point of view. This, of course, was not and could not have been my intention and I was only going by the fact that the Assembly had recommended certain measures. I referred then to the question of wider dissemination of nuclear weapons and the dangers of proliferation. I pointed out that the Assembly had called upon all governments to make every effort to achieve a permanent international agreement, subject to inspection and control, on the prevention of the wider dissemination of these weapons of mass destruction. I referred to the problem of the means of delivering nuclear weapons and the proposals for limiting the production of delivery systems and for the destruction of all but an agreed limited number in the early stage of an agreed program of general disarmament. I also mentioned the problem of surprise attack, the proposals for convening a general conference for signing a convention on the prohibition of the use of nuclear and thermonuclear weapons for military purposes, and, finally, a proposal to establish denuclearized zones in different geographical areas of the world. I believe that all these proposals deserve serious consideration and that any progress made in reaching general agreement in regard to any of these proposals will lead to an improvement of the international climate.

The eighteenth session of the General Asembly met in a mood of hope, and the conciliatory statements made by President Kennedy and Foreign Minister Gromyko in the very early stages of the session raised our hopes. In actual fact, however, the only concrete accomplishment of the eighteenth session in the field of disarmament was the agreement of the major nuclear Powers, as embodied in a resolution of the General Assembly, not to use space vehicles for purposes of nuclear warfare. Thus there is no sign that a golden age of better understanding has dawned.

However, there are some silver linings among the clouds. Before the close of 1963 two very significant and encouraging developments took place without much fanfare and therefore without generating strong public comments. President Johnson announced, within three weeks of his assumption of office, that military operations at thirty-three military bases—twenty-six of them in the United States—would be halted or curtailed and that more cuts were coming. In a speech made on November 18, 1963, Defense Secretary Mr. McNamara made the important announcement that he believed the Soviet Union had cut its armed forces by 2,250,000 men between 1955 and 1962, thus indicating Washington's desire to reduce arms expenditure. President Johnson's dramatic decision was made about the same time as Chairman Khrushchev announced his government's decision to cut Soviet military spending by $600 million in 1964. More recently a reduction of $1 billion in the over-all defense expenditure of the United States for 1964 has been announced.

These decisions were not the result of negotiations at the conference table, but unilateral decisions. They were obviously reached by the two super Powers with the realization that their previous assumptions regarding the other's military might and intentions were not based on full information. I have no doubt that their actions were also motivated by a sincere response to humanity's yearning for peace and greater understanding. Although the United States and the Soviet Union have not subscribed to the policy of unilateralism, they seem to have come to the conclusion that no progress toward ending the arms race will be made unless and until they slow down themselves. I want to take this opportunity of congratulating the two governments for their courage and vision in arriving at these decisions. It is worth recalling the basic fact that an overassessment of the other's military power is as dangerous as an underestimate. The former risks economic ruin and generates an atmosphere of fear and even panic. The latter invites military adventurism.

The year 1964 starts with the auspicious prospects of arms reduction and cutback of armed forces. The real challenge faced by the developed countries is how to promote economic growth and public welfare without the stimulus of arms production, and then to ensure the proper use of that growth and expansion to ease the contrast between their abundance and the poverty of the rest of mankind.

It is the experience of history that, if we do not press forward when there is a favorable atmosphere, there is a relapse and we are apt to drift helplessly from crisis to crisis, until eventually we find that we are pretty close to open war. This is certainly true of the First and Second World Wars. In this context may I recall the words of the late President Kennedy. In an address that he delivered at the University of Maine on October 19, 1963, he said:

> Historians report that in 1914, with most of the world already plunged in war, Prince von Bulow, the former German Chancellor, said to the then Chancellor Bethmann-Hollweg: "How did it all happen?" and Bethmann-Hollweg replied: "Ah, if only one knew."
>
> If this planet is ever ravaged by nuclear war—if 300 million Americans, Russians, and Europeans are wiped out by a 60 minute nuclear exchange—if the survivors of that devastation can then endure the fire, poison, chaos, and catastrophe—I do not want one of those survivors to ask another "How did it all happen?" and to receive the incredible reply: "Ah, if only one knew."

If today we are not able to make more rapid progress toward lasting peace it is not for lack of diagnosis of the causes of war. The greatest danger facing the world today is the nuclear arms race. This race has to be halted, and reversed, if humanity is to survive. Two world wars were fought to make the world safe for democracy. Today we have to wage a third war on all fronts. This war has to be waged in peacetime, but it has to be waged as energetically and with as much concentration of total national effort as in times of war. The war we have to wage today has only one goal, and that is to make the world safe for diversity.

The concept of peaceful coexistence has been criticized by many who do not see the need to make the world safe for diversity. I wonder if they have ever paused to ask themselves the question: What is the alternative to coexistence? The world is inhabited by over three billion human beings, and yet the fingerprint experts tell us that no two human beings have identical fingerprints. Human beings come in all sizes and shapes and in a variety of colors. This rich diversity is matched by an equal diversity in regard to religious beliefs and political ideologies. We are thrown together on this planet and we have to live together. That is why the Charter imposes the imperative on all human beings to practice tolerance and to live together in peace with one another as good neighbors. To my mind this is the simplest definition of peaceful coexistence.

Looking ahead, I hope that in the coming years we may all be inbued with this spirit of tolerance. If all human beings and all nations large and small were to be moved by this spirit we could indeed make the world safe for diversity, and for posterity.

FROM CONTAINMENT TO CEASE-FIRE AND PEACEFUL CHANGE

Adlai E. Stevenson

UNITED STATES REPRESENTATIVE TO THE UNITED NATIONS

Given at Princeton University, March 23, 1964

The United Nations—and therefore the world—has been fortunate to have had three strong Secretaries-General—Trygve Lie of Norway, Dag Hammarskjöld of Sweden, and U Thant of Burma. While serving on the American delegation in London in the first days of the United Nations and latterly in New York, I had something to do with the selection of Trygve Lie and U Thant. And it was my good fortune to know Dag Hammarskjöld well, and my sad lot to attend his funeral in the lovely old cathedral at Uppsala. Like the others who came from all over the world, I walked behind him to the cemetery through the streets of the ancient town, lined with thousands of silent, reverent people. Uppsala was the world that day when he was laid to rest in the northern autumn twilight, for he was a hero of the community of man.

Norman Cousins tells a story that says a lot about Dag Hammarskjöld as a peacemaker.

Hammarskjöld had scheduled an interview with a magazine writer one evening. The writer suggested that they have dinner at a restaurant, which the Secretary-General accepted. He further suggested that they take his car, which the Secretary-General also accepted.

Upon leaving the building, the writer recalled to his embarrassment that he had driven into town in a battered old jeep. The Secretary-General was delighted. "Sometimes I think I was born in one," he said. But the writer's embarrassment had only begun. Four blocks away, a taxicab darted in front of the jeep and there was a harmless collision.

I don't have to suggest the reaction of the cab driver or the quality of his prose. But the writer was not without a temper himself, or the prose to match the cab driver. It looked as though the disagreement was about to escalate into active hostilities. At this point, Hammarskjöld climbed out of the jeep and stepped around to the cab driver.

"You know," he said, "I don't think anyone quite realizes how tough it is to drive a cab in New York City. I don't know how you fellows do it—ten, twelve, fourteen hours a day, day after day, with all the things you've got to contend with, people weaving in and out of traffic and that sort of thing. Believe me, I really have to take my hat off to you fellows."

The cab driver defused immediately. "Mister," he said, "you really said a mouthful." And that was the end of the incident. But it wasn't the end of the story. A few blocks later the unfortunate writer ran out of gas. And who should drive by? The same cab driver pulled up and said, "What's the matter, chum, any trouble?"

"Out of gas," said the disgruntled writer.

Well, the end of the story should be obvious: The cabbie offered to get some gas, invited the driver's "nice friend" to come along with him, and drove off with the Secretary-General of the United Nations in the front seat—leaving the writer to ponder the role of the peacemaker in today's tense society.

I

No one ever doubted Dag Hammarskjöld's selfless dedication to peaceful settlement of any and all disputes among men and nations. None questioned his deep personal commitment to the principles of the Charter of the United Nations, whose first business is the peaceful settlement of disputes.

But this can be said of other men. Hammarskjöld was unsurpassed, but he was not alone in his devotion to peace. What distinguished his service to the United Nations is that he came to see it for what it is, a specific piece of international machinery whose implicit capabilities can only be realized by the action of the Members and the Secretariat working within its constitutional framework.

There was no doubt in Dag Hammarskjöld—nor is there in many others that the United Nations is the most remarkable and significant international institution ever conceived. But Hammarskjöld also understood that the machinery not only needs lofty goals and high principles but it has to work in practice—that it has limited, not unlimited, functions; that it has finite, not infinite, capabilities under given circumstances at a given time. He saw that the effectiveness of the Organization is measured by the best consensus that can be reached by the relevant majority of the relevant organ and that reaching that consensus is a highly pragmatic exercise.

Understanding all this, Dag Hammarskjöld—himself a key part of the machinery—helped make the machinery more workable, more adaptable, more relevant to the immediate political needs. By doing so, he helped expand the capacity of the machinery to act effectively. This, I think, was his greatest contribution to the United Nations, and thus to world peace. His was dedicated service, backed by diplomatic skill, by administrative talent, and by a sharp sense of political reality.

The overwhelming political reality of Hammarskjöld's day was the division of the world into opposing and rigid military alliances, led by two incomparable centers of power and influence—with the two halves of this bipolar world engaged in a Cold War paced by an uncontrolled and seemingly uncontrollable nuclear arms race—while everyone else held his breath lest the "balance of terror" get too far out of balance.

Many came to accept this as a continuing—almost natural—state of affairs which would continue until one side collapsed or the two sides collided in World War III. We now know that it was a transitory and unhealthy condition of the world body politic.

The Cold War has not sunk out of sight, but the field of contest may be shifting radically—and for the better. The nuclear arms race has not passed into history, but at least it has, for the first time, been brought within a first stage of control.

For these and a large variety of other reasons, the world is a very different world from that which existed when Dag Hammarskjöld went down to his death in that cruel crash in Africa. We therefore will be wise to tailor our thinking about the role of the United Nations he served so well not to his world of 1961 but to our world of 1964—which is to say:

—a world which is no longer bipolar but in which multiple centers of power and influence have come into being;

—a world which at long last is approaching the end of the historic struggle for military superiority—by acquiring absolute military power;

—a world in which the myth of monolithic blocs is giving way to a bewildering diversity among nations;

—a world in which realities are eroding the once rigid political dogmas;

—a world in which not only imperialism but paternalism is dying;

—a world in which old trading systems, monetary systems, market systems, and other elements of the conventional wisdom are being challenged and changed;

—a world which at once makes breath-taking new discoveries and is crippled by ancient feuds—which is both fabulously rich and desperately poor—which is making more progress than ever before and seeing much of it wiped out by an explosive population growth;

—and, finally, a world in which fundamental issues of human rights—which have been hidden in closets down the long corridor of history—are out in the open and high on the agenda of human affairs.

For the first time in history the world is being changed radically within the span of an average lifetime. We enter one world and leave quite a different one. As E. B. White once said of New York, "The miracle is that it works at all."

Not even the sloganeers have caught the full essence of these times; we do not yet know what to call this particular passage of history. Since the end of World War II we have spoken of the "atomic age" and the "jet age"—of the "era of rising expectations" and the "epoch of the common man"—of the "first age of space" and the "first age of mass politics." Each of these labels identifies at least one of the swirling phenomena of our times, but none of them will do as an over-all title.

II

We should try to come to grips with the central theme of our times—with that aspect of current affairs which gives them their characteristic stamp and flavor—with that label which may not tell all but puts its finger on the most important thing that is going on.

Back in 1947 a certain "Mr. X"—who turned out to be my friend George Kennan—wrote an article for *Foreign Affairs* in which he introduced the famous label, the "Policy of Containment." He invented the phrase but he did not invent the doctrine; the United States already was busily, heavily, expensively, and dangerously involved in containing the ruthless, heavy-handed outer thrust of Stalin's Russia—wherever it might strike or lean.

This was the main pattern of world events for a number of years and "containment" was a meaningful description of the main purpose of United States policy. It was therefore a great public service, for in the free world effective foreign policy is difficult without the understanding and appreciation of the public. How can one rally support for a policy if one cannot even describe it? In the absence of a suitable description, each individual action of government is dangerously exposed to attack and suspicion, but if it is known to be part of a larger and well-understood design, it becomes less difficult to act quickly and coherently. However, this is not a lecture on the glorious virtues and crippling vices of sovereign public opinion in a genuine democracy.

When we look back with pride on the great decisions that President Truman made, we see now that he had the inestimable advantage of public understanding. He could react to Korea quickly because he did not have to stop to explain, to pull public opinion up alongside. It was quite clear to all that this was but another phase of containment, just like the Berlin airlift, and the guerrilla war in Greece, and NATO.

Up until the postwar years, Americans had been brought up on the idea of fighting every conflict to a decisive finish—to total victory, to unconditional surrender. But when the nuclear age revealed the hazards of this course, it was neither easy nor popular to introduce the concept of limited action, primarily to preserve the status quo. This nuclear necessity went against the American grain; it was (and to some still is) both confusing and frustrating. It took patient explaining, and all of us can be grateful that "Mr. X." gave identification and illumination to a policy that was already being practiced. He showed us why the Greeks thought it so important to have "a word for it."

We can, as I say, be proud of our performance under the containment policy. Above all we can be proud that the tendency once noted by Lord Acton did not operate in our case: the possession of great power—unprecedented and overwhelming power—did not corrupt the American government or the American people.

But as unquestioned leader of an alliance constantly threatened by external military pressure, we had to stand up and be counted for more; we had to stand firm; we had to confront force with force until the tanks faced each other gun barrel to gun barrel along Friedrichstrasse in Berlin—until the Korean invaders had been thrown back across the 38th Parallel—until the Navy drew an armored noose around Soviet missile sites in Cuba—and until, at long last, Soviet leaders became convinced that free men will answer steel with steel.

During this whole period the positions and actions taken by the United States government to contain aggression had broad public understanding and support. In a sense the policy of containment was too easy to understand. It tended to reinforce a simplistic view of a black-and-white world peopled by "good guys" and "bad guys"; it tended to induce a fixation on military borders to the exclusion of other things; and it tended to hide deep trends and radical changes which even then were restructuring the world.

And, of course, the policy of containment—being a reaction to Soviet communist aggressiveness—necessarily had a negative and static ring to it. This had the unfortunate effect of partially obscuring the positive and progressive purposes of United States policies in support of the United Nations, in support of regional unity in Europe and elsewhere, and in support of economic and social growth through-

out most of the world where poverty was a centuries-old way of life.
Nevertheless, the doctrine of containment was relevant to power
realities of the times—to the struggle to protect the independent
world from Stalinism—and to the defense of peace—which is quite
a lot! Indeed, the doctrine may not yet have outlived its usefulness. If
the present Soviet leaders have come to see that expansion by armed
force is an irrational policy, it is by no means clear that the Chinese
Communists—pretending to read out of the same book—have yet
come to the same conclusion.

No doubt we shall have to stand firm again—and face danger
again—and run risks again in the defense of freedom. We cannot and
will not resign from whatever degree of leadership is forced upon us
by the level of threat used against us, our allies, and our friends. But
as anyone willing to see clearly already knows, the current course of
world affairs calls for something more than a "policy of containment."

III

What, then, *is* the dominant theme that marks the character of
contemporary world affairs? I would suggest that we have begun to
move beyond the policy of containment; that the central trend of our
times is the emergence of what, for lack of a better label, might be
called a policy of cease-fire and peaceful change. I would suggest,
further, that we may be approaching something close to a world
consensus on such a policy.

No analogy is ever perfect, but if the policy of containment stands
for "limited war," then the policy of cease-fire perhaps stands for
"limited peace." I believe this mutation is occurring simply because
the H-bomb has made even "limited war" too dangerous.

Cease-fire and peaceful change may strike some as a curious way
to describe a period so jammed by violence, by disorder, by quarrels
among the nations—an era so lacking in law and order. But I do not
speak wistfully; I speak from the record. It is precisely the fact that
so much violence and so many quarrels *have not led to war* that puts
a special mark on our times.

Only a few decades ago, if a street mob organized by a government
sacked and burned the embassy of another government, if rioters tore

down another nation's flag and spit upon it, if hoodlums hanged or burned in effigy the head of another state, if ships or planes on lawful missions were attacked, one would expect a war to break out forthwith. Lesser excuses than these have started more than one war before.

And only a few decades ago, once hostilities broke out between the armed forces of two nations, it was assumed with good reason that, since the war was started, the war would proceed until one nation or one side had "won" and the other had "lost"—however foolish or futile the whole thing might be. It also was assumed that the only way fighting could be stopped was by surrender—unconditional or negotiated—confirmed by signatures on a document and ritualized by the presentation of swords by the vanquished to the victors. That was in the nature of the institution called war. This is how it was.

But this is *not* the way it has been for well over a decade now and I think we should begin to notice that fact. Scores and scores of what used to be called "incidents"—far too many of them—have occurred around the world without leading to hostilities or even ultimatums. The fact is that in the last decade nearly every war, partial war, incipient war, and threat of war has either been halted or averted by a cease-fire. It is still a very foolish and dangerous thing to insult another nation or desecrate its property or take pot shots at its citizens or equipment. But there are other forms of penalty than mass slaughter and, happily, the world is beginning to avail itself of them. Firing has started and then stopped—organized hostilities have been turned on and then called off—without victory or defeat, without surrender or peace treaty, without signatures or swords.

This is what seems to be happening. If so, it is perhaps the most important and certainly the most hopeful news for many a moon. As Al Smith kept saying, let's look at the record.

Just after the last war, the Soviet Union sent two armored divisions through northern Iran toward the Turkish and Iraqi frontiers while Bulgaria massed troops on its southern frontier to form the other prong of a huge pincers movement against Turkey. Then the Security Council of the United Nations met in London for the first time, and presently the Soviet troops went back into the Soviet Union. Not a shot had been fired.

Since that time there have been some twenty occasions on which the armed forces of two or more nations engaged in more or less organized, formal hostilities, which in another day would have been accompanied by declarations of war—wars to be fought until "victory" was attained by one side or the other. Eight of these could be classified as outright invasions, in which the armed forces of one nation marched or parachuted into the territory of another. Only one of them—the mismatched affair between India and Goa—was settled in the traditional way in which wars have been settled in the past. On at least another twenty occasions there has been minor fighting on disputed frontiers, or armed revolts which usually involved the national interests of an outside state. Any of them would have qualified as a *casus belli* in another day.

At this very moment the agenda of the Security Council of the United Nations lists fifty-seven international disputes. Some of them have been settled, some are quiescent, and others could flare again at any moment. The point here is that more than half a hundred international quarrels have been considered by somebody to be enough of a threat to the peace to take the case to the court of last resort.

This is not exactly peace—at least not the kind of peace that people have dreamed and hoped and prayed for. But the record suggests that, if fighting breaks out somewhere tomorrow, the chances are good that the next step will not be the sound of trumpets but the call to cease-fire. And the chances are good that the step after that will not be an exchange of swords but an exchange of words at a conference table. This is no guarantee that a way will be found to remove the root of the trouble: in the Middle East, Southeast Asia, and the Far East there are temporary armistice lines that have been temporary now for more than a decade. But in these affairs there are no victors and no vanquished—and in this sense we are all winners.

This record of violence-without-war suggests, then, that we may have slipped almost imperceptibly into an era of peaceful settlement of disputes—or at least an era of cease-fires while disputes are pursued by other than military means. Without making light of life-and-death matters, one can conclude that it has become distinctly unfashionable to march armies into somebody else's territory. I can think of no better evidence than the fact that the Organization of African

Unity—an institution hardly out of its swaddling clothes—quickly arranged cease-fires when fighting broke out on the borders between Morocco and Algeria and again between Somalia and Ethiopia.

How has all this come about? I shall not attempt anything like a definite answer. I would only suggest in passing that *perhaps* Korea was the end of the road for classical armed aggression against one's next-door neighbor; that *perhaps* Suez was the end of the road for colonial-type military solutions; and that *perhaps* Cuba was the end of the road for nuclear confrontation.

Perhaps man is adjusting once again to his environment—this time the atomic environment. *Perhaps* the leaders of nations around the world—small as well as large nations—have absorbed the notion that little wars will lead to big wars and big wars to annihilation. *Perhaps* we are edging toward a consensus on the proposition that nobody can afford an uncontrolled skirmish any more—that the only safe antidote to escalation is cease-fire.

I emphasize *"perhaps"*—for we must work and pray for that historical judgment on these times.

Yet skirmishes will occur—and will have to be controlled. Countless borders are still in dispute. Nationalism and rivalry are rampant. Ethnic and tribal and religious animosities abound. Passions and hatreds—ignorance and ambition—bigotry and discrimination—are all still with us.

IV

The question is what can be done to make sure that this is in fact an era of peaceful settlement of disputes among nations.

For one thing, we can pursue this consensus on recourse to nonviolent solutions. Most of the world is in agreement on this right now—though there are a few who would make a small exception for his own dispute with his neighbor. Yet there is reason to hope that the aggressors are extending their doctrine of "no nuclear war" to a broader doctrine of "no conventional war"—on the grounds that one cannot be sure there will be no nuclear war unless one is sure there will be no conventional war either.

For another thing, we can get on with the urgent business of expanding and improving the peace-keeping machinery of the United

Nations. Most of the cease-fires I have been speaking about have been arranged by the United Nations and the regional organizations. Most of the truces and negotiations and solutions have come about with the help of the United Nations. Even if the will had existed, the way would not have been found without the machinery of the United Nations.

Violence—which there will be without war—which there must not be—is unthinkable without an effective and reliable system of peace keeping.

How should we and how can we improve the peace-keeping machinery of the United Nations?

Cyprus has vividly exposed the frailties of the existing machinery. The Security Council, by an impressive unanimous vote, first saved the situation with a cease-fire resolution providing for a United Nations peace-keeping force, but shortly afterward war nearly broke out again before the United Nations could put the resolution into effect.

There were no troops immediately available, and the Secretary-General could not marshal the United Nations force with the speed so urgently required. Then there was no assurance of adequate funds to pay for the operation. While these handicaps were overcome, the Secretary-General had not yet found a mediator of the conflict. It took over two weeks, instead of two days or two hours, to get the peace-keeping operation going, and then only because armed intervention appeared imminent.

In short, when time is of the essence, there is a dangerous vacuum during the interval while military forces are being assembled on a hit-or-miss basis. And we further risk an erosion in the political and moral authority of the United Nations if troops trained only for national forces are thrust without special training into situations unique to the purpose and methods of the United Nations. For a United Nations soldier in his blue beret is like no other soldier in the world —he has no mission but peace and no enemy but war.

Time and again, we of the United States have urged the creation of a United Nations International Police Force, trained specifically for the keeping of the peace. Perhaps it is too early to contemplate a fixed United Nations international force which would be permanently maintained for use for any and all purposes, for the world's emergencies differ one from another, and there can hardly be one treatment for all of them. But surely it would make sense for Member countries of the United Nations to indicate what forces, equipment, and logistic support they would be willing to train for peace-keeping service and to supply on a moment's notice. And surely it would make sense for the United Nations itself to add to its military and planning staff so that peace-keeping operations can be set in motion with the utmost speed and effectiveness.

There are some encouraging signs of progress. Recently it was announced that Scandinavia would create a permanent force for use on United Nations peace-keeping missions. This would include Denmark, Sweden, Norway, and Finland, although it is not yet clear if Finland would join in an integrated command or form an independent unit. Other nations, such as Canada and the Netherlands, have also shown interest in creating a United Nations stand-by force. So things are moving. There is also movement on the fiscal front. Last year it seemed hopeless that the United Nations General Assembly would be able to agree on a financing formula which would permit its vital Congo operations to continue. But it did, and in the process paved the way for further developments in this all-important area.

This next month a United Nations working group will be meeting in an endeavor to formulate agreed methods for financing future peace-keeping operations, so that there will be less need for controversy each time such an operation is to be financed. It is true that every United Nations peace-keeping effort is and probably always will be different from any other, and that no simple financing formula can fit them all, but agreement on certain principles and improvements in mechanisms should be possible and useful for the future. The United States will join wholeheartedly in the search for such agreements.

There will, however, be a shadow over that working group—the shadow of unpaid assessments for past United Nations peace-keeping operations. No less than $92 million of such arrears are owed by the Soviet bloc and a few other countries that have refused to pay their share of the cost of such operations—principally those in the Middle East and in the Congo. The Soviet claim that the assessments for these operations were not legally imposed and are not legally binding was rejected by the advisory opinion of the International

Court of Justice in 1962, and that opinion was accepted by a decisive vote of the General Assembly that fall. Yet the Soviets are still refusing to pay.

What can be done about it?

Article 19 of the United Nations Charter provides that a Member whose arrears amount to as much as its last two years' assessments "shall have no vote" in the General Assembly. This article has caught up with the Soviet Union and certain other countries, which means that, if at the time the next General Assembly meets the Soviet Union has not paid at least some $9 million of its arrears, it will have no vote in the Assembly. The United States and, I believe, all the Members want to avoid such a situation in the only way it can be avoided, namely, by a Soviet payment—in whatever form.

We think the best way to avoid the penalty and preserve the financial integrity of the United Nations is for the Members to make it abundantly clear that they support peace-keeping operations, that they want all Members to pay their fair share of the cost, and that the Charter must be applied in accordance with its terms, and without fear or favor. It is our earnest hope that the overwhelming sentiment of the Members will prevail, and that the Soviet Union and others will find the means, in one way or another, to provide funds that will make unnecessary any Article 19 confrontation.

At the same time, the United States and others are exploring the possibility of adjustments to avoid the recurrence of this unhappy situation. Not many Members would agree with the Soviet Union's contention that the General Assembly has no right to recommend a peace-keeping operation and that the Security Council should have the exclusive right to initiate such operations. Nor would many agree to abolish the General Assembly's exclusive right, under the Charter, to apportion and assess expenses.

But it should be possible to give new emphasis to the position of the Security Council by providing that all proposals for initiating a peace-keeping operation should first be presented to the Council, and that the General Assembly should not have the right to initiate such an operation unless the Council had shown that it was unable to act. Also, when it comes to the apportionment of the costs among the Members by the General Assembly, we are exploring possible arrangements whereby the viewpoints of the major Powers and contributors to the cost could be assured of more adequate consideration, and also the possibility of more flexible methods of distributing the cost.

I mention the fact that these possibilities are being discussed to make clear that the United States is using every effort to reach agreement as to future peace-keeping arrangements, in the hope that agreement as to the future will facilitate solution as to the past and provide a more firm foundation for a peace-keeping structure that has already proved itself so valuable.

Let me make it quite clear that it is the Charter that imposes the penalty of loss of voting privileges for nonpayment of assessments. The United States has never presumed to think it could negotiate this requirement of the Charter with the Soviet Union and it has not entered into these exploratory talks for this purpose. But we are eager to discuss a sound system for financing future peace-keeping operations, a system which involves no change in the terms of Article 19 of the Charter and, indeed, presupposes settlement of the arrears problem. We hope and believe that these efforts to preserve the peace-keeping function will have the support of all Members, and certainly of all Members who believe in the efficacy, indeed the indispensability, of the United Nations as a force for peace in the world.

V

Finally, if we are going to get the nuclear genie back in the bottle and keep it there, we shall have to improve our techniques for arriving at basic solutions to problems which remain even when a cease-fire has gone into effect.

I referred earlier to the point that the doctrine of containment was essentially a negative and static concept—as it had to be for its purpose. But a simple cease-fire is static, too; it is a return to the *status quo ante*. And that is not good enough for a world in which the only question is whether change will be violent or peaceful. The world has known periods of relative peace and order before. Always the order was assured by a system designed to preserve the status quo. And this is precisely why the system of order broke down—because the status quo is indefensible in the long run.

What the world needs is a dynamic system of order—a system capable of bringing about not just a precarious halt to hostilities but a curative resolution of the roots of hostility. This is to say that a dynamic system of order must be one which helps parties to a dispute to break out of rigid stalemates—to adapt to new times—to manage and absorb needed change. It is easier to write this prescription than to fill it. But if conflicts are to be resolved and not just frozen, it is manifest that only through the United Nations, the community of nations, can the workable system of peaceful change evolve. The United Nations is a shared enterprise; it speaks for no nation, but for the common interest of the world community. And most important, the United Nations has no interest in the status quo.

VI

To conclude: I believe there is evidence of new beginnings, of evolution from containment to cease-fire, and from cease-fire to peaceful change. We have witnessed the first concerted and successful effort to avoid the confrontation of naked force. The Cuban crisis has been followed by the nuclear test ban treaty and a pause in the arms race. We see growing up in the interstices of the old power systems a new readiness to replace national violence with international peace keeping. The sheer arbitrament of force is no longer possible and less lethal methods of policing, controlling, and resolving disputes are emerging. Do we perceive, perhaps dimly, the world groping for, reaching out to, the fuller vision of a society based upon human brotherhood, an order in which men's burdens are lifted, a peace which is secure in justice and ruled by law?

As I have said, I believe that now, as in the days of the Founding Fathers, even the faintest possibility of achieving such an order depends upon our steadfast faith. In their day, too, democracy in an age of monarchs and freedom in an age of empire seemed the most remote of pipe-dreams. Today, too, the dream of a world which repeats at the international level the solid achievements—of law and welfare —of our domestic society must seem audacious to the point of insanity, save for the grim fact that survival itself is inconceivable on any other terms.

Once again we in America are challenged to hold fast to our audacious dream. If we revert to crude nationalism and separatism, every present organ of international collaboration will collapse. If we turn in upon ourselves, allow our self-styled patriots to entice us into the supposed security of an impossible isolation, we shall be back in the jungle of rampant nationalisms and baleful ambitions and irreconcilable conflicts which—one cannot repeat it too often—have already twice in this century sent millions to their death, and next time would send everybody.

I believe, therefore, that at this time the only sane policy for America—in its own interests and in the wider interests of humanity —lies in the patient, unspectacular, and, if need be, lonely search for the interests which unite the nations, for the policies which draw them together, for institutions which transcend rival national interests, for the international instruments of law and security, for the strengthening of what we have already built inside and outside the United Nations, for the elaboration of the further needs and institutions of a changing world for a stable, working society.

If we in the United States do not carry these burdens, no one else will. If we withdraw, retreat, hesitate, the hope of today, I believe without rhetoric or exaggeration, will be lost tomorrow.

We have called this land the "last best hope" of man—but "last" now has overtones of disaster which we would do well to heed. With Churchill, I can say that "I do not believe that God has despaired of His children." But I would say also, in the words of the Scriptures: "Let us work while it is yet day."

THE FIRST TWENTY-FIVE YEARS OF THE UNITED NATIONS: SAN FRANCISCO TO THE 1970s

Dean Rusk

SECRETARY OF STATE OF THE UNITED STATES

Given at Columbia University, January 10, 1964

I regard this lecture as a welcome opportunity—and a command performance. Any invitation bearing the name of Dag Hammarskjöld is compelling for me.

In my job, I often think of Hammarskjöld's reply to a newsman who asked about his interest in mountain climbing:

What I know about this sport is that the qualities it requires are just those which I feel we all need today: perseverance and patience, a firm grip on realities, careful but imaginative planning, a clear awareness of the dangers but also of the fact that fate is what we make it and . . . the safest climber is he who never questions his ability to overcome all difficulties.

Dag Hammarskjöld was an intensely practical idealist; and I think this is why his name will live. He never wore his devotion to world peace as a personal adornment. Instead, he worked for peace through action. It was selfless and tireless action—and for this we honor the man. But it also was rational, considered, calculated action—and for this we respect his method.

During the regime of Dag Hammarskjöld the United Nations found its capacity to act and to grow. As the institution grew in stature, so did he. But he never subscribed to the idea that any man was indispensable to the United Nations; he knew that what counts is the creation and use of the machinery and procedures for peaceful settlement and peaceful change. He helped build that machinery and passed it on to the world when death met him on a mission of peace.

My assignment—to talk about the first twenty-five years of the United Nations—is unusual punishment for a Secretary of State. It is difficult enough to be a reasonably accurate historian of world affairs years later, after all the evidence is in. It is nothing short of foolhardy to foretell the future, especially when you are trying to tinker with the future to make it come out the way you think it should.

However, the punishment is self-inflicted. For the hazards of my situation I have only myself to blame. Andrew Cordier gave me a free choice of topic. And I decided to try to look ahead as well as to look back. For, if we are to act wisely in world affairs, we must have some sense of direction, some conviction about the way human events are moving, some expectations about the forces and counterforces just over the horizon. I do have some expectations for the United Nations over the next five or ten years, and I might as well state them straightaway.

I believe that the influence of the United Nations will be even greater in the 1970s than it is today.

I believe also that the executive capacity of the United Nations to act in support of the purposes of the Charter will be greater in the 1970s than it is today.

I hold these convictions despite valid cause for concern and some necessary reservations. I shall try to explain why.

I

Let me begin by observing that it means little to study the performances of an institution against abstract standards without reference to the realities, and even the illusions, of the total environment in which it must operate. In that context, the first thing that strikes one about the United Nations is that international organization is a plain necessity of our times. This is so for both technical and political reasons.

The technical reasons stem, of course, from the headlong rush of scientific discovery and technological advance. That process has overrun the hypothetical question as to whether there is to be an international community that requires organization. It has left us with the practical question of *what kind* of international community we have the wit to organize around the scientific and technical imperatives of our time. In the words of Ogden Nash:

> When geniuses all in every nation
> Hasten us towards obliteration,
> Perhaps it will take the dolts and geese
> To drag us backward into peace.

World community is a fact because instantaneous international communication is a fact; because fast international transport is a fact; because matters ranging from the control of communicable disease to weather reporting and forecasting demand international organization; because the transfer of technology essential to the spread of industrialization and the modernization of agriculture can be assisted by international organizations; because modern economics engages nations in a web of commercial, financial, and technical arrangements at the international level.

The advance of science, and the technology that follows, create an insistent demand to build international technical and regulatory institutions which lend substance to world community. Few people seem to realize just how far this movement has gone. The United States is now a member of 53 international organizations. We contribute to 22 international operating programs, mostly sponsored by these same organizations. And last year we attended 547 international intergovernmental conferences, mostly on technical subjects. We do these things because they are always helpful and often downright essential to the conduct of our national and international affairs.

It is obvious that in the 1970s we shall require more effective international organization, making for a more substantial world community, than we have today. We already know that in the next decade we shall become accustomed to international communication, including television, via satellites in outer space. We shall travel in aircraft that fly at speeds above a thousand and perhaps above two thousand miles per hour. Industrialization will pursue its relentless course. Cities and their suburbs will keep on growing. The world economy will become increasingly interdependent. And science will rush ahead, leaving to us the task of fashioning institutions—increasingly on the international level—to administer its benefits and circumscribe its dangers.

So, while nations may cling to national values and ideas and ambitions and prerogatives, science has created a functional international society, whether we like it or not. And that society, like any other, must be organized.

Anyone who questions the *need* for international technical organizations like the United Nations agencies dealing with maritime matters, civil aviation, telecommunications, atomic energy, and meteorology simply does not recognize the times in which we live.

In a world caught up in an urgent drive to modernize areas containing two thirds of the human race, there is need also for the United Nations specialized agencies dealing with health, agriculture, labor standards, education, and other subjects related to national development and human welfare. A massive effort to transfer and adapt modern technology from the more to the less advanced areas is a part of the great drama of our age. This sometimes can be done best through, or with the help of, the institutions of the international community.

And the international organizations concerned with trade and monetary and financial affairs are important to the expanding prosperity of the world economy.

II

The need for political organs at the international level is just as plain as the need for technical agencies.

The decision to try to form a new international organization to preserve peace grew out of the agonies of World War II. The United States took the lead in this enterprise. President Franklin D. Roosevelt and Secretary of State Cordell Hull sought to avoid repeating what many believed to have been mistakes in political tactics which kept the United States from joining the League of Nations. They consulted at every stage the leaders of both political parties in both houses of Congress. They insisted that the formation of this new organization should be accomplished, if possible, *before* the end of the war. Most of our allies readily endorsed this objective and cooperated in achieving it. The Charter conference at San Francisco convened before the end of the war against Hitler and the United States Senate consented to ratification of the Charter in July, 1945, before the end of the war in the Pacific. The vote in the Senate was 89 to 2, reflecting a national consensus bordering on unanimity. The significance of that solemn action was especially appreciated by those of us who were in uniform.

The commitment of the United States to the United Nations was wholehearted. We threw our best efforts and some of our best men into getting it organized and moving. We set about binding the wounds of war. We demobilized our armed forces and drastically reduced our military budget. We proposed—not only proposed but worked hard to obtain agreement—that atomic energy should be put under control of an agency of the United Nations, that it should be devoted solely to peaceful purposes, that nuclear weapons should be abolished and forever forbidden.

What happened? Stalin refused to cooperate. Even before the guns were silent, he set in motion a program of imperialistic expansion, in violation of his pledges to the Western allies and in contravention of the principles of the United Nations.

The United Nations was designed on the assumption that the great Powers in the alliance destined to be victors in World War II would remain united to maintain the future peace of the world. The United Nations would be the instrument through which these Powers, in cooperation with others, of course, would give effect to their mutual determination to keep the peace against any threats that might arise from some future Mussolini or Hitler. World peace was to be enforced by international forces carrying the flag of the United Nations, but called into action and directed by agreement among the major Powers. Action without big Power agreement was not ruled out by the Charter, but such agreement was assumed to be the prior condition of an effective peace organization. Indeed, it was stated repeatedly by early supporters of the United Nations that the Organization could not possibly work unless the wartime allies joined in collective action within the United Nations to exert their combined power to make it work.

That view of the postwar world rapidly turned out to be an illusory hope. One might well have expected, as many good people did, that, when the conceptual basis for the United Nations fell to the ground, the Organization would fall down beside it.

But all great institutions are flexible. The United Nations adjusted gradually to the political and power realities of the quite different world that came into being. In the absence of major Power agreement in the Security Council, it drew on the Charter's authority to balance the weakness with a greater reliance upon the General Assembly.

By adapting to political reality, the United Nations lived and grew in effectiveness, in prestige, and in relevance. It could not act in some of the ways the founding fathers intended it to act, but it went on to do many things that the founding fathers never envisaged as being necessary. The most dramatic reversal of its intended role is seen in the fact that, while the United Nations could not bring the great Powers together, it could on occasion keep them apart by getting between them—by becoming the "man in the middle"—as it did in differing ways in the Middle East and in the Congo.

In short, the political organs of the United Nations survived and did effective work under the shadow of a nuclear arms race of awesome proportions, despite the so-called Cold War between the major Powers whose unity was once presumed to be its foundation.

This was not bound to happen. It is evident that in the political environment of the second half of the twentieth century both technical and political reasons dictate the need for large-scale and diversified international organizations. But it does not necessarily follow that the United Nations was destined to work in practice—or even to survive. Indeed, its very survival may be more of an achievement than it seems at first blush. That it has steadily grown in its capacity to act is even more remarkable.

It has survived and grown in effectiveness because a great majority of the nations of the world have been determined to make it work. They have repulsed those who sought to wreck or paralyze it. They have remained determined not only to keep it alive but to improve and strengthen it. To this we owe in part the peace of the world.

III

Indeed, it is difficult to avoid the conclusion that the existence of the General Assembly and the Security Council these past eighteen years was a plain necessity for the preservation and repair of world peace. The failures would still have been failures, but without the United Nations some of the successes might not have been possible.

In the world of today any breach of the peace could lead to the destruction of civilization. In the thermonuclear age, any instrumentality with a potential for deterring war can hardly be described as less than indispensable to mankind. In eighteen brief years, the United Nations has helped to deter or to terminate warfare in Iran and Greece, in Kashmir and Korea, in the Congo and the Caribbean, and twice in the Middle East and in the western Pacific. It is not fanciful to speculate that any or all of us may owe our lives to the fact that these dangers were contained, with the active and persistent help of the processes of the United Nations.

With half a dozen international disputes chronically or repeatedly at the flash point, with forces of change bordering on violence loose in the world, our very instinct to survival informs us that we must keep building the peace-keeping machinery of the United Nations— and keep it lubricated with funds and logistical support.

If we are to entertain rational hopes for general disarmament, we know that the United Nations must develop a reliable system for reconciling international conflict without resort to force. Peace in the world community—like peace in smaller communities—means not an end of conflict but an accepted system of dealing with conflict and with change through nonviolent means.

Traditional bilateral diplomacy, of the quiet kind, has a heavier task today than at any time in history. But with the annual agenda of urgent international business growing apace, with the birth of more than half a hundred new nations in less than two decades, an institution that can serve as an annual diplomatic conference becomes almost a necessity. As a general manager of our own nation's diplomatic establishment, I cannot imagine how we could conduct or coordinate our foreign affairs if we were limited to dealing directly through bilateral channels with the 114 nations with which we have diplomatic relations today.

At the last General Assembly representatives of 111 countries met for more than three months to discuss, negotiate, and debate. Two more countries became United Nations Members, to make the total 113. When the tumult and the shouting had died, the General Assembly had adopted, curiously enough, 113 resolutions. This is what we have come to call parliamentary diplomacy.

But outside the formal agenda the General Assembly also has become the world's greatest switchboard for bilateral diplomacy. For many of the young and small nations, lacking a fully developed diplomatic service, the United Nations is the main, sometimes the only general, mechanism available for the conduct of their diplomacy.

Without formal decision, the opening of each new Assembly has turned into something like an informal conference of the foreign ministers of the world community. In New York last fall, in a period of 11 days, I conferred with the foreign ministers or heads of government of 54 nations.

I believe that too many items are placed on the agenda of the General Assembly. Too many issues are debated and not enough are negotiated. I feel strongly that members should take more seriously Article 33 of the Charter which pledges them to seek solutions to their disputes "first of all . . . by negotiation, enquiry, mediation, conciliation, arbitration, judicial settlement, resort to regional agencies or arrangements, or other peaceful means of their own choice" before bringing disputes to the United Nations at all.

But the point here is that it is hard to imagine the conduct of diplomacy throughout the year without a meeting of the General Assembly to deal in one forum, and in a more or less systematic manner, with subjects which demand widespread diplomatic attention among the members of the world community.

The need for an annual diplomatic conference, the need for a peace-keeping deterrent to wars large and small, and the need for an international monitor of peaceful change are plain enough. They seem to me to warrant the conclusion that the political organs as well as the technical organs of the United Nations have been very useful to the world at large for the past decade and a half. Common sense informs us that they can be even more useful in the years ahead.

I suspect that the near future will witness another period of adjustment for the United Nations. Some adjustments are, indeed, required because the political environment is changing and so is the structure of the United Nations itself.

For one thing, the cobweb syndrome, the illusion that one nation or bloc of nations could, by coercion, weave the world into a single pattern directed from a single center of power, is fading into limbo. That other illusion, the bipolar theory, of a world divided permanently between two overwhelming centers of power with most other nations clustered about them, is fading too. The reality of a world of great diversity with many centers of power and influence is coming into better focus.

Meanwhile, a first brake has been placed on the nuclear arms race and the major Powers are searching for other agreements in areas of common interest. One is entitled to hope that the major Power conflicts which so often have characterized United Nations proceedings in the past will yield more and more to great Power cooperation; indeed, there was some evidence to sustain such a hope in the actions of the Eighteenth General Assembly.

As long as a Member possessing great power is intent on promoting conflict and upheaval—the better to coerce the world into its own image—that Member might well regard the United Nations as a threat to its own ambitions.

But suppose it is agreed that all Members, despite their deep differences, share a common interest in survival—and therefore a common interest in preventing resort to force anywhere in the world. Then the peace-keeping capacity of the United Nations can be seen realistically for what it is: an indispensable service potentially in the national interest of all Members—in the common interest of even rival states.

If this reality is grasped by the responsible leaders of all the large Powers, then the peace-keeping capacity of the United Nations will find some degree of support from all sides, not as a rival system of order, but as contributor to, and sometimes guarantor of, the common interest in survival.

It would be a great service to peace if there could develop common recognition of a common interest in the peace-keeping capacity of the United Nations. That recognition is far from common now. My belief that it will dawn is based on the fact that it would serve the national interests of all nations, large and small—and because sooner or later nations can be expected to act in line with their national interests.

Peace will not be achieved by repeating worn-out propaganda themes or resetting rusty old traps. But if our Soviet friends are prepared to act on what Chairman Khrushchev says in part of his New Year's message—that war over territorial questions is unacceptable, that nations should not be the targets of direct or indirect aggression, that we should use the United Nations and every other means of peaceful settlement—then let us together build up the peace-keeping machinery of the United Nations to prevent even small wars in our flammable world. For small wars could too easily, too quickly, lead to nuclear war, and nuclear war can too easily, too quickly, prove fatal to friend and foe alike.

IV

Meanwhile, the internal structure of the United Nations has been changing radically over the past several years. The United Nations began life with 51 Members. When its headquarters building was designed, United Nations officials believed they were foresighted in planning for an eventual membership of 75. This year major alterations will be undertaken to make room for the present 113 Members and more. It is a fair guess that membership of the United Nations will level off during the next decade at 125 to 130 Members.

This more than doubling of the membership of the United Nations is proud testament to the tidal sweep through the old colonial areas of the doctrine of self-determination of peoples. It is a triumph of largely peaceful change. It is a tribute to those advanced countries which have helped bring dependent areas to self-government and independence and made possible their free choice of their own destiny. It is a striking and welcome result of the greatest wave of national liberation in our time. It also has important implications for all United Nations Members—the new Members and the older Members too—and for the United Nations itself.

The most prosaic—but nonetheless important—implication is for methods of work in the General Assembly. With more than twice as many voices to be heard, views to be reconciled, and votes to be cast and counted, on a swelling agenda of business, there is obvious danger that the General Assembly will be swamped.

I already have suggested that the agenda may be unnecessarily bloated, that in many cases private discourse and real progress are preferable to public debate and symbolic resolution, and that the United Nations might well be used more as a court of last resort and less as a forum of original jurisdiction.

But I think still more needs to be done. If the expanded Assembly is to work with reasonable proficiency, it must find ways of delegating some of its work to units less cumbersome than committees of one hundred and thirteen members. The General Assembly is the only parliamentary body in the world that tries to do most of its business in committees-of-the-whole. The Assembly has, in fact, moved to establish several subcommittees, including one to consider financing peace-keeping operations; and perhaps more thought should now be given to the future role of such committees in the work of the Organization.

The radical expansion of the membership raises problems for the newer and smaller nations. They rightly feel that they are underrepresented on some organs—notably the Security Council and the Economic and Social Council—whose membership was based on the original size and composition of the United Nations. The growth of membership also raises problems for the middle-range Powers, who were early Members and have reason to feel that they are next in line for a larger voice. And it raises problems—or potential problems—for the larger Powers too.

The rapid and radical expansion of the General Assembly may require some adaptation of procedures if the United Nations is to remain relevant to the real world and therefore effective in that world. Theoretically, a two-thirds majority of the General Assembly could now be formed by nations with only 10 percent of the world's population, or who contribute, altogether, 5 percent of the assessed budget. In practice, of course, this does not happen; and I do not share the dread expressed by some that the General Assembly will be taken over by its "swirling majorities." But even the theoretical possibility that a two-thirds majority, made up primarily of smaller states, could recommend a course of action for which other nations would bear the primary responsibility and burden is one that requires thoughtful attention.

There are two extreme views of how national influence should be expressed in the work of the United Nations. At one extreme is the contention that no action at all should be taken by the United Nations without the unanimous approval of the permanent members of the Security Council. This is a prescription for chronic paralysis. The United Nations was never intended to be kept in such a box. The rights and duties of the General Assembly are inherent in the Charter. The United Nations has been able to develop its capacity to act precisely because those rights were not blocked by the requirement of big Power unanimity.

At the other extreme are those few who feel that nothing should matter except the number of votes that can be mustered—that what a majority wants done must be done regardless of what states make up the majority. This notion flies in the face of common sense. The plain fact of the matter is that the United Nations simply cannot take significant action without the support of the Members who supply it with resources and have the capacity to act.

Some have suggested that all General Assembly votes should be weighted to reflect population, or wealth, or level of contributions, or some combination of these or other factors. I do not believe that so far-reaching an answer would be realistic or practical. The equal vote in the General Assembly for each Member—however unequal in size, wealth, experience, technology, or other criterion—is rooted in the idea of "sovereign equality." And that idea is not one which any nation, large or small, is eager to abandon.

I do not pretend to have the final answer, nor is it timely or appropriate for any Member to formulate the answer without wide and careful consultations with others in the world community.

However, extended discussions lie ahead on such questions as ex-

panding the Councils, scales of payment for peace keeping, and procedures for authorizing peace-keeping operations.

I shall not discuss United Nations finances in detail. But let me say
that the first principle of a healthy organization is that all its members
take part in its work and contribute their proper shares to its financial
support. Two years ago more than half the United Nations Members
were behind in their dues—some because of political objections but
many simply because they were not paying. I am glad to see that most
Members are now beginning to act on the principle of collective financial responsibility. But there remains a serious problem of large
nations that have not been willing to pay for peace-keeping operations.

I would hope that the discussions which lie ahead will not only
strengthen the financial underpinnings of the United Nations but,
among other things, develop an acceptable way for the General Assembly to take account of capacity to act, of responsibility for the
consequences, and of actual contributions to the work of the United
Nations. Such a way must be found if the United Nations machinery
is to be relevant to the tasks that lie ahead—in peace keeping, in
nation building, and in the expansion of human rights.

All adjustment is difficult. Adaptation of the United Nations to
recent changes in the environment may take time. It will require a
shift away from some hardened ideas and some rigid patterns of
action and reaction—perhaps on all sides. It will require—to come
back to Hammarskjöld's words—"perseverance and patience, a firm
grip on realities, careful but imaginative planning, a clear awareness
of the dangers."

To ask all this may seem to be asking a great deal. But I am
inclined toward confidence because the United Nations already has
demonstrated a capacity to adapt under the flexible provisions of the
Charter to the realities of international politics.

I am further persuaded that all, or most, of the smaller Members
are realistic enough to know that their own national interests lie with,
not against, an effective United Nations; that the United Nations can
be effective only if it has the backing of those who have the means to
make it effective; that the United Nations is made less, not more,
effective by ritualistic passage of symbolic resolutions with no practi-

cal influence on the real world; that only responsible use of voting power is effective use of voting power; that true progress on behalf of the world community lies along the path on which the weak and the strong find ways to walk together.

V

These are some of the reasons, derived from analysis of the current state of world affairs, why I expect the United Nations to evolve and to grow in executive capacity to act in support of its goals. And apart from the issue of human survival, the greatest of these goals is, of course, the steady extension of human rights.

Dedication to the principle of the universality of fundamental human rights collides in practice with dedication to the principle of national sovereignty. Most violations of human rights are committed within the confines of national societies, often by the very governments that have ratified the Charter's prescription for "fundamental freedoms for all." Yet securing equal rights for all individual members of the human race is the ultimate goal of world community—and the ultimate challenge to the United Nations as the elementary but principal expression of that community. Somehow, the United Nations must learn how to increase respect for the rights of the human person throughout the world.

It is here that we sense the permanent value and the final force of the basic principles of a Charter which dares to speak for "We, the peoples of the United Nations." Sometimes I feel that we talk too much about the universality and brotherhood of man and too little about the valuable and interesting differences that distinguish all brothers. But the lessons of recorded history, and the teachings of the world's great teachers, make clear the basic wants of mankind.

Men and women everywhere want a decent standard of material welfare for themselves and their children. They want to live in conditions of personal security. They want social justice. They want to experience a sense of achievement, for themselves and for the groups with which they identify themselves.

But men and women everywhere want more. They want personal freedom and human dignity. Individuals and societies place differing values on these aspirations. But surely these are universal desires, shared by all races in all lands, interpreted by all religions, and given concrete form—or lip service—by leaders and spokesmen for every kind of political, economic, and social system.

Peace and security, achievement and welfare, freedom and dignity —these are the goals of the United Nations for all peoples. And any nation which questions for long whether we should seek these aims is destined to become a pariah of the world community.

Because the kind of world projected in the Charter is the kind of world we want, the United Nations—despite its quarrels and its shortcomings—commands our continuing support.

As President Johnson said to the General Assembly on December 17, 1963: "More than ever we support the United Nations as the best instrument yet devised to promote the peace of the world and to promote the well-being of mankind."

Because the kind of world projected in the Charter is the kind most people everywhere want, I believe that others will join with us in improving and strengthening the United Nations. That is why I am confident that the executive capacity of the United Nations—its machinery for keeping peace, building nations, and promoting human rights—will be greater on its twenty-fifth birthday than on its eighteenth.

THE UNITED STATES NATIONAL INTEREST AND THE UNITED NATIONS

Ernest A. Gross

FORMER DEPUTY UNITED STATES
REPRESENTATIVE TO THE UNITED NATIONS

Given at Columbia University, December 16, 1963

The late President of the United States, John F. Kennedy, and the late Secretary-General of the United Nations, Dag Hammarskjöld, both typified the strength of mind and character by which society generates, as well as responds to, leadership. Each bequeathed a legacy of true leadership: the capacity of institutions to surmount grievous and sudden loss with orderly processes of continuity. This is a test of maturity of any system, whether it is—like the United States —an indivisible and permanent union under law, or—like the United Nations—a voluntary association of sovereign states linked by a treaty without a term.

The two fallen leaders also shared a conviction concerning the dynamic values of the United Nations and an understanding of its spiritual foundations. Appropriate to their respective responsibilities, one viewed the Organization from the perspective of the international civil servant, the other as servant of his own nation. But it would be wrong to suppose that moral or political principles vary with national perspective or individual interest. The contrary assumption, implicit in the Soviet troika proposal, is not intelligible to the religious faiths of mankind and is rejected by all free nations, large and small.

Indeed, as Dag Hammarskjöld proved by his life and work, a great international civil servant must be a great citizen of his own nation, loyal to the deepest values of its heritage and traditions. Wide appreciation of this fact in our country would help further our national interest in encouraging devoted Americans to share in the duties of a strong and honorable international civil service.

At the height of World War II, the great Powers agreed upon "the necessity of establishing, at the earliest practicable date, a general international organization for the maintenance of international peace and security" (Moscow Declaration; October, 1943).

In the intervening twenty years, five United States Presidents successively have accepted the validity of that premise, without question or rhetoric.

One of the last official acts of President Kennedy was his Report to the Congress on United States Participation in the United Nations in 1962, which he signed two days prior to his assassination. Like his predecessors—and his successor—he pledged support to the United Nations, with characteristic realism:

Like most institutions devised by man, the United Nations exhibited both accomplishments and shortcomings. But despite non-cooperation from certain Members and wavering support from others, the Organization moved significantly toward the goal of a peace system worldwide in scope. The United States will continue to lend vigorous support to the building of that system.

From this point of departure, consideration must be given to ways by which the late President's successors, with the help of an informed public, can effectively carry out his pledge. The question for discussion may be phrased thus: "How can the United States support the United Nations so as to promote effectively the United States national interest, rightly understood?"

An attempt to answer this question must take into account, first the nature and purposes of the Organization, and then at least three major premises, or imperatives, which condition its use. These are: the limitation of power; the needs of nations; the claims of the individual.

I

It is necessary first to note that, true to the law of continuity in life and in change, the United Nations was built largely with parts taken from the League of Nations. What makes an institution "new" is not novelty of design so much as the use to which it is put. History suggests that, if the United Nations were to suffer the same fate as the League, the survivors would again anxiously search the rubble for salvage.

The builders of the United Nations, for divergent reasons, agreed on one major premise, which proved wrong: that the great Powers would jointly underwrite international peace. The fact that peace never became a joint venture has bred an illusion that, because the premise turned out to be false, the necessity for a "general international organization" to maintain peace has somehow disappeared. The contrary is so obviously true that any such illusion must be accounted for by motives of frustration or fear.

There is, indeed, a certain inconsistency between the United States emphasis upon the special role of the great Powers, on the one hand, and the central position of the General Assembly in the scheme of the Organization, which the United States has likewise stressed from the beginning.

At San Francisco, the United States government—contrary to the British and Soviet views—strongly favored the creation of a popular body with broad deliberative, administrative, elective, and budgetary functions. In his 1945 Report to the President, Secretary of State Edward R. Stettinius urged that "an effective international organization must be constructed on the most broadly democratic basis." He noted that the Assembly would be "concerned with the promotion of constructive solutions of international problems in the widest range of human relationships, economic, social, cultural and humanitarian." And he predicted, almost twenty years ago, that the General Assembly "will come to be regarded by all nations as the forum in which their interests can be effectively represented and promoted."

It would be a mistake to regard this as prophetic vision; it was a practical projection of the obvious teachings of our own traditions.

One of the fundamental issues in appraising United States national interest and the United Nations is confronted right here: What is the role of opinion as an element of strength—both national and international?

The 1945 Report on the San Francisco Conference takes a flat stand: "In the contemporary world, public opinion plays a greater part internationally than it has ever played before . . . modern instruments of communication, with the continuing interchange of expression among nations and peoples which they make possible, create a situation in which a true world opinion can form."

Many in our country, accounted as realists, question such views, often with a vehemence surprising on the part of any bred in a tradition summarized in Jefferson's phrase: "Opinion is Power."

American ambivalence on this matter is shared, although in a quite different ideological context, by the Soviets.

On the one hand, Mr. Khrushchev derides what he terms "majoritarian democracy." On the other hand, the Communists expend large sums and scarce materials to disseminate, through all modern media, their views and versions of fact, to countless millions, whose opinions they regard as prime targets of the Cold War.

The reciprocal U.S.–USSR ambivalence, like almost everything else of international significance, is likewise reflected in the United Nations.

The Soviets, rebuffed by lack of support for untenable positions, complain of an "automatic majority." Americans, fearful of the implications of a large, new membership, sometimes warn of an "irresponsible majority."

Both of these mutually conflicting viewpoints are false, and both proceed from a common error concerning the true nature of the Organization. The United Nations is not a corporate entity, control of which can be won by an international proxy fight. It is a center of diplomatic activity, complementary to, and in many respects indistinguishable from, other forms of diplomacy—bilateral and regional. When 75 foreign ministers and 11 heads of state gathered in New York during the opening weeks of the 1963 General Assembly, their discussions with each other and with our Secretary of State fell into no neat category. Good old-fashioned bilateral diplomacy has lost none of its importance in furthering national interest, although one of its functions has become that of shaping and advancing the other two forms.

It is readily observable from the record of the United Nations that divisions take place on different issues and at different seasons, depending upon considerations of national interest, interplay of power, and the effects of prestige and persuasion. With respect to matters in which large majorities consistently form, such as colonial questions or economic development, the majorities are not to be regarded as either "automatic" or "irresponsible," but as an expression of keenly felt needs or aspirations. These could, no doubt, be more effectively submerged if there were no forum in which they found expression. But history teaches that pressures thus submerged often erupt with volcanic force. Inasmuch as United States national interest and tradition more usually than not are ranged alongside these aspirations and claims, we would not be the first to benefit by their submersion, nor the last to suffer from their explosion.

The American pledge to support the United Nations is impeded also by ambivalence concerning the role which the Organization is expected to play in the world of nations.

The United Nations is called upon—and justly so—to perform the most diverse and mutually inconsistent functions. It must serve as a forum for both recrimination and conciliation. By the same resolution, for example, the United Nations roundly denounced Red China for imprisoning eleven American fliers and simultaneously called upon the Secretary-General to exert influence with the Communists to obtain their release. Mr. Hammarskjöld privately questioned the practical statesmanship of so inconsistent a diplomatic strategy.

The United Nations likewise is used to derive advantage in ideological conflicts, and as a shield to avoid commitment or confrontation in the same conflicts.

It is an agency for alleviating endless need; yet it may not exact undue sacrifice.

The United Nations must be prepared to cope with crisis, or be reviled as a mere debating society. It must, nevertheless, avoid all appearance of a superstate, any pretension to which it would in any event lack means to enforce.

No one is to be criticized for demanding that the United Nations serve such utterly inconsistent purposes. What may be questioned is unwillingness of Members to face up to the inevitable consequences of demands which, in the case of more familiar domestic enterprises, would be expected inevitably to produce erratic performance.

These are some of the considerations relevant to the question of how the United States can effectively advance its national interests through the United Nations, taking into account the origin and nature of the Organization.

The question must also be considered in the light of the three international imperatives already referred to: the limitation of power; the needs of nations; the claims of the individual.

II

One of the major premises of foreign policy was stressed by President Johnson in his first address to the Congress of the United States, on November 27, 1963:

In this age, when there can be no losers in peace and no victors in war, we must recognize the obligation to match national strength with national restraint. We must be prepared at one and the same time for both the confrontation of power and the limitation of power.

Not long before, the Secretary of Defense of the United States had expressed the same point in more guarded strategic terms:

We are approaching an era when it will become increasingly improbable that either side could destroy a sufficiently large portion of the other's strategic nuclear force, either by surprise or otherwise, to preclude a devastating retaliatory blow.

Formal repudiation of the doctrine of massive retaliation is, of course, not a bid for weakness but a call to greatness. Danger of war is not eliminated by the missile. The risks of miscalculation or escalation through the use of force become so great that traditional forms of coercion become untenable. They are replaced by subversion, insurgency, harassment, and other forms of indirect aggression. Our diplomatic armory must, therefore, command resources adequate to respond to any level of covert aggression, just as our military strength must be able to oppose any level of overt provocation with an appropriate reaction.

Keeping in mind the mutually supporting role of bilateral, regional, and multilateral diplomacy, what are the implications of the nuclear deadlock—that is to say, the "limitation of power"—with respect to the uses of the United Nations, from the standpoint of United States national interest?

Replacement of overt coercion by indirect aggression places a high premium upon the attitudes and opinions of peoples. Those who ask where so-called world opinion is to be found need only be reminded of Jefferson's dictum, of the insight of the American architects of the United Nations, and of those undefinable forces which are reflected in polls and watched by anxious politicians. The General Assembly is a parliamentary forum in which truth can be revealed and falsehood exposed. No man on horseback has ever yet devised a better system for informing and persuading free men.

The limitation of power generates diffusion of power which, in turn, imposes even greater limits upon the uses of power. One effect upon our national interests of the working of this cycle is the loosening of ties of alliance.

It is commonplace to observe that as the Cold War loses its bipolar character, and as the nuclear deadlock holds force in leash, smaller nations express their claims, needs, and aspirations with greater insistence. Evidence that the process is taking place even behind the Iron Curtain is summed up in Mr. Khrushchev's rueful comment that quite a few of the captive nations of eastern Europe are "getting too big to spank." One of the objectives sought by the Kremlin in a nonaggression pact undoubtedly is to cut the captive nations down to size, by diminishing their hopes of liberation and their will to resist.

The United Nations offers small nations a useful forum for concerting, as well as pressing, their demands. It is logical for them to seek the benefits of ever-widening circles of common interest and action.

The movements of this tide erode the solidarity of even the most important regional arrangements to which the United States is party, including the OAS and NATO.

The Secretary of Defense has remarked that the primary strategic contribution of the Organization of American States to the common defense is assistance in antisubmarine warfare. This is another way of saying that the OAS has become essentially an ingredient of the United States military capability. On the economic and social aspects of the hemisphere organization, the Alliance for Progress is basically a cooperative enterprise for administering United States assistance. With regard to peace-keeping functions, the OAS continues to play its accustomed role of mutually reenforcing bilateral and universal processes of pacific settlement.

The importance of NATO to the defense of the United States remains undiminished. At the same time, the diffusion of power has unstabilized and loosened the alliance. The Foreign Relations Committee of the United States Senate emphasized in 1949 that the North Atlantic Treaty was "conceived within the framework of the United Nations Charter," that its major objective was to "strengthen the system of law based upon the purposes and principles of the United Nations," and that the Treaty itself "makes clear the overriding character of the Charter with respect to the obligations of the signatories."

The limitation and diffusion of power since 1949 have brought to the Senate's high-sounding phrases a literal and prescriptive significance which may cause surprise even to the authors.

In 1949, stress was given to the role of NATO in helping Europe defend *itself* against speedy and overwhelming aggression on the ground. Today, the focus has shifted to NATO's role in helping Europe defend *us* against the same kind of aggression from the skies.

The United States emphasizes the role of NATO as ensuring a means of response to intermediate levels of aggression, thus providing the alliance with an option against nuclear war. The history of an earlier age suggests to some Europeans a resemblance between the United States concept and the temptation of princes to offer the marches to a marauder, in the hope of saving the castle. General de Gaulle's insistence upon independent European nuclear capability is in an ancient, if obsolete, tradition.

If ties of alliance become loosened through conflict as to strategic concepts and coordination of defense—the very heart of the North Atlantic Treaty system—it seems overoptimistic at the same time to expect a tightening of political bonds in the same community. NATO has not in fact evolved processes for giving effect on a NATO-wide basis to the commitment in Article 2 of the Treaty, "to encourage economic collaboration" among the parties. Economic undertakings involving NATO members collectively have developed within the United Nations and its framework of economic, technical, and financial agencies, of which all NATO members except Germany are active members.

Nor have NATO-wide political mechanisms or institutions matured, with the important exception of consultations pursuant to Article 4 of the Treaty. Even with respect to the latter, issues of vital concern to parties to the Treaty, such as Algeria, Cyprus, and Suez, have wound their painful way through the United Nations rather than NATO, thus sparing the latter from ordeals which might have torn it apart.

The history of such cases demonstrates the limitations of NATO as a forum for political action. It reveals also the lightning-rod function of the United Nations in shielding the United States from the total destruction of alliance which might result if we had to take decisions in lonely and conspicuous isolation, on the many matters in which the United States has conflicting interests or mutually inconsistent commitments.

It is, indeed, difficult to imagine any major threat to the peace or an act of violence in which some Member would not seek recourse to the United Nations. Although this does not mean that the Organization is always the appropriate forum, the interests of the United States benefit from the availability of the United Nations as part of a mutually reinforcing diplomatic process.

The Cuban missile crisis of October, 1962, illustrates the workings of this process in a situation in which the limitation of power, the diffusion of power, and the specter of the actual use of power were inextricably combined.

President Kennedy's final Report to Congress on United States Participation in the United Nations, already referred to, appraises the uses of the United Nations in this confrontation. In the late President's words: "From the start it was clear that the United Nations would have a crucial role." The role, in fact, consisted of several parts.

Firstly, as the Report states, the United Nations provided a "forum in which the evidence of Soviet guilt could be most convincingly exposed to a world-wide audience and where world opinion could be mobilized, and the world verdict pronounced."

There is a moving quality in this echo of Jefferson's precept that "opinion is power" and of the prediction of the American architects of the United Nations that a world in which "war would be fought with weapons capable of reaching every part of the earth" was one "in which a true world opinion can form," and that the United Nations would provide a powerful means of forming it.

Secondly, the United Nations proved to be a "ready and efficient mechanism for diplomatic communication . . . and served as a site where United States and Soviet negotiators could easily meet."

This had, of course, been true also in earlier crises, notably in the Jessup-Malik conversations, leading to the lifting of the Berlin blockade in 1949.

Thirdly, "the Secretary-General himself supplied an important link between the parties, particularly during the first days when tension was highest."

That a parliamentary system, however rudimentary, must be supported by executive action was a lesson constantly taught by Dag Hammarskjöld. Whether or not an extension of the "hot line" is installed in the Secretary-General's office, it is certain that, in the event of its use, his own telephone will not long remain silent.

Fourthly, the United Nations "proved itself able and willing to devise acceptable mechanisms for inspection and verification," although Cuba prevented their employment. The implications with regard to armaments are obvious, particularly considering that, by acquiescing in such processes on Cuban soil, the Soviets weakened their own moral and political case for rejecting similar measures as a part of a general plan for disarmament.

In appraising the undoubted significance of the role played by the United Nations in the Cuban crisis, it is appropriate to underline that it was only one part of a total diplomatic process.

The Organ of Consultation of the OAS was convoked without delay, and recommended that member states "take all measures, individually and collectively, including the use of armed force," to meet the threat to the security of the hemisphere.

Recourse to the United Nations and the OAS thus supplemented and supported our own strategic and political actions, which included quarantine of Cuba, reinforcement of Guantanamo, marshaling of military force, and diplomatic approaches to all world capitals, of course including the stern and direct warning to the Soviet government "to eliminate this clandestine, reckless and provocative threat to world peace."

The significant words of the sentence are the last two; and it was, indeed, the whole world which responded to the threat.

III

Effective use of the United Nations in furtherance of United States national interest requires appraisal of another international imperative: the needs of nations.

A member of the United Nations Committee on Colonialism recently warned of a disturbing contradiction between nationalist aspirations and national needs. He remarked:

In a world marching toward greater integration of sovereignties, of economies and peoples in the search for unity, it seems to be a backward step to put the emphasis on division, dismemberment and disintegration, whether of a political, economic, social or cultural nature.

When the Colonialism Committee was created in 1961, sixty-four colonial territories were listed, some with a population of less than 1,000 living on an island of five or six square miles. At least a dozen are not economically or politically viable.

The Anticolonial Declaration of the United Nations sweepingly proclaims that "all peoples" have the right freely "to determine their political status."

The principle remains an abstraction—often an illusion—until it is given practical dimensions in time and space. Independence may come too suddenly as well as too soon. Transitional arrangements, supervised by the United Nations, should be welcomed, not resisted, by the governing Power.

Questions concerning the proper size or composition of the group likewise involve the application of rational standards unique to each case. It is in the national interest of the United States, which bears so large a portion of the cost of errors, that decisions concerning the unit appropriate for self-determination be made collectively and objectively, with the full weight of United States influence brought to bear. This becomes progressively important as the remaining "hard core" problems come to the fore with ever greater insistence.

Future historians will have to evaluate the role played by the United Nations in the birth rate of new states. Although the existence of the forum facilitates and encourages the exchange of ideas, the actual sources of change are, of course, in the ideas themselves rather than in the place they find expression.

It is reasonable to assume, though impossible to prove, that the massive liquidation of colonialism could not have occurred without major wars, in the absence of an institution to channel and moderate tensions by means of restraints imposed under the leadership of the United States and like-minded nations. The Congo is only one example.

Marx would, no doubt, be astonished to learn that the great Powers are not locked in bloody conflict to capture the resources of new colonies, as he predicted, but in a determined contest to capture the allegiance of new states.

Pressing internal problems of the new states, conflicting interests among them, and competitive exploitation of their difficulties by the Chinese-Soviet rivalry foreshadow increasingly insistent demands for assistance from the United States in modernizing their economies.

As the principal, though not by any means the only, target of such pressures, we must be concerned by whatever hinders the United Nations from effectively aiding the United States to discharge its international responsibilities in this area.

United Nations programs for economic and social development in 1962 cost more than $200 million, of which the United States paid almost 40 percent. Our own bilateral technical assistance programs came to an additional $400 million. Large as these figures are, they cover only 7 percent of the total costs of world-wide economic aid. The overwhelming demand and need is for capital and goods of which at least 90 percent is furnished by governments on a bilateral basis.

Although the role of the United Nations in economic development and technical assistance thus may be called marginal in absolute terms, it is nevertheless expensive in itself. Moreover, it may be highly important in particular cases, as the Congo demonstrates.

A State Department Advisory Committee on International Organizations has recommended specific methods for improving (1) the financial management of the United Nations system, (2) the administration and coordination of the United Nations Technical Cooperation Programs, and (3) the staffing of international organizations. Reports reflecting these recommendations were published by the Department of State in 1963.

In addition to the matters covered by the Advisory Committee, several other considerations seem pertinent:

(1) Channeling of aid through the United Nations, rather than through bilateral or regional processes, is not entitled to a presumptive right of way or first priority. Choice of methods, singly or in combination, depends not upon moral but upon pragmatic judgments, including maximum effectiveness in the recipient country, greatest sharing of the burden, and the like.

(2) The United Nations is not necessarily the best antiseptic for every international wound. Deployment of United Nations personnel does not in itself ensure impartial or competent administration. The Cold War exists in the United Nations, as it does everywhere else in international life, and the United Nations "presence" does not automatically insulate areas or operations from ideological conflict. Care must be exercised, as indeed it is, by the devoted international civil servants directing the technical assistance programs to ensure equally devoted personnel, serving under clearly defined instructions.

(3) Decisions concerning budgets for United Nations technical cooperation should give greater weight to the views of the principal contributors. This does not necessitate the creation of a "donors' club" or intricate systems of weighted voting. If recipients do not exercise greater self-restraint than has often been the case, however, tax-paying pressures will be exerted either for weighted voting or, failing that, for decrease in appropriations for allocation through multilateral channels.

(4) Finally, the United Nations Development Decade goal of a 50 percent rise in the per capita income in the developing nations as a whole cannot possibly be approached without vigorously self-disci-

plined effort on their part to meet the demands in their own countries for social and economic reform. United States national interest in conditions of world stability and progress is too great to shrink away from noisy charges of "intervention" when we impose sensible restrictions upon United States assistance. Warnings of turning to the Communists for help are threadbare. Moreover, those who bind their own people with ropes have no standing to complain of "strings" tied to our aid, designed to ensure its fair and effective use.

IV

The uses of power and the satisfaction of the needs of nations are dedicated to only one end, the promotion of the peace, dignity, and well-being of the individual.

In an age of mass consumption, mass distribution—and mass destruction—we tend to forget that "mass" is merely an impersonal term for describing the family of man.

Secretary of State Dean Rusk has recently observed that "history could come to know the 20th Century as the Age of the Rights of Man."

In fact, the twentieth century opened upon a world unaware of the emergent claims of individual and national freedoms. The Covenant of the League of Nations made no reference whatever to human rights, reflecting the traditional view that the fate of the individual rests solely in the hands of his state.

The validity of Secretary Rusk's prediction, therefore, is likely to depend upon the course of events in the second half of the twentieth century.

The decisive role of the United Nations in the history of our times may well be played in the vaguely discerned, though fiercely debated, context of human rights and fundamental freedoms.

Soviet-Chinese rivalry assumes increasingly ominous aspects of racial conflict. Chinese leaders are probing sensitive areas of Africa in order to test their response to anti-white appeals, accusing the Soviet leadership of conspiring with the West to abandon the Leninist policy of support for "wars of national liberation."

In the southern third of Africa, it is difficult to predict whether Angola and Mozambique, representing colonial vestiges, or South and Southwest Africa, representing obsolete internal racial policies, will be the first to slide to disaster.

The United Nations Charter calls for "promoting and encouraging respect for human rights and for fundamental freedoms for all without distinction as to race, sex, language or religion." Even-handed enforcement of this provision requires machinery for implementation which was not provided in the Charter and which has not yet been created.

Efforts to give to the Human Rights Commission of the United Nations an operational, rather than a merely declaratory, function have been obstructed by political and social elements within the United States which fear that international promotion of civil rights may bring surveillance or other pressures to bear upon the evolution of civil rights programs within our own country. Such fears have long since ceased to serve the national interest of the United States.

No debates or resolutions in the United Nations General Assembly could approximate the effectiveness with which our own media of communication disseminate news concerning domestic trials, challenges, and crises in the field of civil rights, accompanied by searching self-criticism. In this situation, crouching behind the domestic jurisdiction clause of the United Nations Charter does not advance our own cause. It plays the game of the repressive systems, Communist and otherwise, which do not hesitate to use the United Nations forum to attack the open societies, even while disclaiming all obligation to respond to the very Charter provisions they invoke.

It is, therefore, past time to establish a United Nations agency to receive and air grievances, whether by individuals, groups, or nations, alleging violations of human rights and fundamental freedoms. A United Nations executive agency should likewise be created, charged with the duty to investigate complaints, to screen out the many which will (as in any domestic society) be frivolous, malicious, or unfounded, and to present to the Human Rights Commission any which merit hearing. The United States should support the creation of an international penal tribunal to try individuals guilty of defined international crimes, such as piracy, slavery, or genocide. We should, without delay, ratify the Genocide Convention, which the United States signed in 1948, but which has lain dormant since.

The opening words of the Charter, echoing those of the United States Constitution, proclaim the United Nations as an alliance not of rulers or states but of peoples. They remind us that no nation, however powerful, can dominate the universal field of action in the nuclear age.

In the endless struggle for a just peace, victory over the ancient enemies of men can be won only by mastery over the self. It is a truth as old as Paul's admonition that "every man prove his own work," which is to say that each must measure his own achievement by searching himself. No better formula for building self-discipline, either in men or in nations, has ever been devised.

It may be said, indeed, that the United Nations Charter embodies a code which demands no less.

KEEPING THE PEACE

Lester B. Pearson

PRIME MINISTER OF CANADA

Given at Carleton University, Ottawa, May 7, 1964

I

When I received the invitation to speak in this Dag Hammarskjöld Memorial Lecture Series, I considered it a privilege to be included among those close collaborators and friends of the late Secretary-General who would be paying tribute to his memory, and to his work, in this way. It is most fitting that in Canada this lecture should be given at Carleton University, from which Dag Hammarskjöld received the first honorary degree given by this university and the first offered to him by any Canadian university.

I have chosen the subject "Keeping the Peace" because Mr. Hammarskjöld gave so much of himself to the task of developing the peace-keeping work of the United Nations. Indeed, he was on active service for peace when his life so tragically and so prematurely ended.

Dag Hammarskjöld died, as he would have wished, in the service both of peace and of the United Nations. I had the privilege of knowing him well and of working with him at the United Nations during some difficult years. I admired and respected the high character of the man and the great qualities of the statesman. He was tireless and selfless and wise. He was as sure and as resolute in carrying out instructions from the United Nations for international action in the cause of peace as he was skillful and objective in seeking to establish a basis for that action in the Charter.

His life was a triumph of service and achievement and his passing at the very height of his career was a tragic loss. His death must continue to inspire us all to do what we can to secure the triumph of the cause for which he died, peace and security in the world, through the United Nations.

At a press conference early in 1959, Dag Hammarskjöld said this:

The policy line, as I see it, is that the United Nations simply must respond to those demands which may be put to it. If we feel that those demands go beyond the present capacity, from my point of view, that in itself is not a reason why I, for my part, would say no, because I do not know the exact capacity of this machine. It did take the very steep hill of Suez; it may take other and even steeper hills. I would not object beforehand unless I could say, and had to say in all sincerity, that I know it cannot be done. Then I would say it. So far, I do not know of any question that has been put to which I would have to give that very discouraging reply. For that reason, my policy attitude remains . . . that the United Nations should respond and should have confidence in its strength.

In this lecture I am concerned with ways and means of increasing that strength and capacity to respond.

To this end I wish to review developments in the field of United Nations peace keeping in order to illustrate the various demands which have been made of the Organization and its response to them. I hope, as well, to suggest ways in which the capacity to respond can be strengthened, as it must be strengthened, if the United Nations is to fulfill its primary purpose of maintaining peace and security in future.

II

As the nineteenth century came to an end, governments were be-ginning to think about international organization to prevent war. But in the main they continued to rely for security on their own power, supplemented by military alliances which had replaced Metternich's earlier "Concert of Europe." Like the little old lady in *Punch* of 1914, they consoled themselves with the thought that, if threats to the peace occurred, such as the assassination of an archduke in a Serbian town, "the Powers are sure to intervene." After the shot at Sarajevo they did so—against each other and for national ends. The war to end war was on.

After World War I, experts on international affairs debated

whether it could happen again. They hoped that war could be avoided by strengthening collective security. They looked to the new League of Nations for this. But most governments still showed a preference for arms and military pacts. When collective security and sanctions under the Covenant *were* advocated, it was primarily with a view to possible use against Germany. Later, in Italy's attacks on Ethiopia, the League rejected effective international action for peace. In consequence, we lost the race with rearmament, while Hitler and Mussolini scorned the treaties intended to maintain the balance of power. "Intervention," a dirty word in the case of Ethiopia, Spain, and Czechoslovakia, became a necessity in Poland. Peace in our time dissolved in the global devastation of World War II.

Again there was a kind of peace, this time soon followed by the Cold War, which had become so intense by the fifties that great Power deadlock was in danger of destroying or rendering impotent the improved League which we now called the United Nations. Yet the World Organization, in spite of limitations and with varying success, tried to keep the peace on the periphery of potential war—in Greece and Kashmir, in Palestine and Indonesia. Its method was one of persuasion and "watchdog" presence. It seemed a frail basis for collective security in the face of Soviet aggressiveness—and in the shadow of the Bomb.

Since the main communist challenge at that time was in Europe, the North Atlantic states responded to the weakness of the United Nations by exercising their right of collective self-defense under the Charter. They formed NATO to ward off the threat of military attack in the Treaty area and, in essence, to safeguard peace by deterring aggression. NATO was not an alternative to the United Nations but a practical and regional means of cementing cracks which had appeared in the Charter security system.

In some ways, the situation in 1950 was unpleasantly like that of 1935. The international peace-keeping machinery was virtually stalled; the Powers were once more turning to defense pacts. Tension in Europe remained explosive. A single incident from this tension could, and more than once almost did, result in general disaster.

But the flash of fighting actually occurred on a distant horizon—in Korea. This was no mere incident with possible alarming repercussions. This was an armed aggression, carefully calculated and prepared, and bolstered by the conventional military weapons of the communist arsenal. It was a direct challenge which had to be met squarely by the western Powers if there was to be any hope of containing communist military expansion. They were able to use the United Nations for this purpose because, luckily, the Russians stayed away from the Security Council when the Korean resolution was passed. It was an absence not likely to be repeated.

If the great Powers had intervened in the manner of earlier times, Korea could have been the spark which ignited nuclear world war. Instead, the conflict was localized by improvising a collective response from the United Nations, by carefully defining the objectives of the United Nations military action, and by making effective but limited use of United States military strength. In his thoughtful lecture in this series, Mr. Adlai Stevenson suggested that *"perhaps* Korea was the end of the road for classical armed aggression against one's next-door neighbor."* It may also have signified the end of communist gambling on *direct* aggression in areas of great Power interest.

III

In any event, Korea was the beginning of a new development in international affairs—the deployment of armed military force under the control and the flag of the United Nations. At San Francisco, this possibility had been provided for in Chapter VII of the Charter. But the international security force of that chapter—intended to be the strong arm of an effectively functioning Security Council and to include all its permanent members—withered in the angry Cold War debates of the late forties.

With the Security Council "frozen in futility," the General Assembly, under the stimulus of the Korean emergency, took its own action to give sinew to the United Nations peace-keeping arm.

It adopted certain recommendations under the heading "Uniting for Peace," including one to the effect that each Member should maintain within its national armed forces elements so trained, organized, and equipped that they could promptly be made available for service as a United Nations unit or units upon recommendation by the Security Council or General Assembly. The same resolution provided for the General Assembly to act on short notice when there was a threat to the peace and the Security Council had failed to act because of the exercise of the veto.

Neither the procedure nor the collective measures proposed were pursued with any vigor in the next few years. The fighting in Korea died down. The wave of that crisis receded and with it the urge to be ready next time. The Soviet bloc was naturally opposed to the "Uniting for Peace" resolution and violently denounced it as a violation of the Charter. In any event, East-West tension had eased after the summit meeting at Geneva and the West lost interest in the matter. In short, great Power deadlock destroyed the hope of establishing the United Nations Security Council force envisaged in the Charter. Inertia and wishful thinking, among Members generally, postponed any significant action on the 1950 resolution calling for the alternative of stand-by units. The world community was to wait for another crisis.

It came in 1956, mounting with increasing menace in the Middle East. In late October, Israeli armed forces raced to the Suez Canal. Britain and France delivered their ultimatum and moved in. The Soviet Union and later Communist China issued threats. War seemed imminent and the United Nations was called upon to intervene for peace.

The main demand was to end the fighting and bring about the withdrawal of the British, French, and Israeli forces. What was needed to accomplish this was an impartial military force to secure a cease-fire and withdrawal and to supervise a buffer zone, first near the Canal and later along the line dividing Israel and Egypt. Some security had to be restored after the shock of fighting, the humiliation of defeat, and the frustrations of withdrawal. But the United Nations force to be organized for this purpose would do no fighting except in self-defense and would rely mainly on its presence as representing the United Nations to accomplish its aims. "Intervention" by the United Nations was to acquire new meaning.

IV

The "Uniting for Peace" procedure had made it possible for the Assembly to meet in emergency special session to deal with the Suez crisis. It was able quickly to adopt broad directives governing the establishment and functioning of the United Nations Emergency Force. But the Secretariat found little in their files concerning collective measures which might give a lead on how to proceed. It was a new course on new ground. Some experience could be drawn from the earlier activities of the military observer groups but no real precedent existed for a major, genuinely United Nations military operation which had to be carried out with speed, efficiency, and even daring, if it were to succeed.

The Secretary-General and the participating governments had to start virtually from zero. There was no time for detailed planning, either in New York or in national capitals. An international command staff had to be gathered in the Canal zone, and an *ad hoc* team of military advisers assembled overnight in United Nations Headquarters. Contingents, selected from the offers made, had to be moved to Egypt within a few days after the adoption of the Assembly resolution.

That UNEF did succeed in its initial tasks can largely be attributed to the ingenuity, skill, and energy of Dag Hammarskjöld; to the solid core of support which existed in the Assembly; to the prompt response of the ten governments which provided the original contingents; finally, to the fact that the parties directly concerned with the Suez conflict consented to the stationing and functioning of the force in the area.

There were many anxious days in the long weeks from November, 1956, to March, 1957, when the withdrawal from Egyptian territory was completed and the United Nations force was fully deployed. There was noisy and acrimonious debate. There was also quiet and earnest consultation. At times it looked as though the UNEF experiment might fail, mainly because of political objections but also because of practical difficulties of establishing, organizing, and directing an international force which was the first of its kind in history.

A major question for Canada was the nature of its own participation. Our experience was revealing. To support our political initiative in the Assembly, the government offered to provide a self-contained infantry battalion group. But after these troops had begun to move to the port of embarkation, it emerged that, of some two dozen offers of military assistance to the United Nations, most of the contingents were infantry units and practically none included the supporting and technical services which the force would need—including an air component. Since the great Powers were not participating in the force, Canada was one of a very few countries which was able, because of its military know-how and experience, to provide administrative and logistic specialists. In the end, the Canadian contingent included reconnaissance, transport, maintenance and supply units of the Canadian Army, and an observation and transport squadron of the RCAF. They were sneered at by some in the heat of partisan debate as a typewriter army, but they were indispensable to the success of UNEF. They played, and are still playing, a courageous and essential role.

This last-minute need to reorganize the Canadian contingent was not only a source of political embarrassment but a cause of delay in getting Canadian troops to Palestine. Both could have been avoided if there had been advance United Nations planning for such peace-keeping operations and coordinated preparations in the military establishments of the contributing countries.

Similar problems—the political problem of achieving balanced composition and the practical problem of finding qualified units and personnel for maintaining a mixed force—arose when the Congo crisis broke in 1960 and the United Nations was again asked to provide a peace-keeping force. There was no lack of infantry contingents and it was very desirable that the countries of Africa should provide most of them. Technical units and specialists were also needed, however, and national establishments had to be combed for suitable personnel.

The UNEF experience was available because the Secretary-General had produced a very useful study in 1958. But the United Nations faced a very different situation in the Congo and the demands on its military force were much more complicated. Quite apart from the political difficulties, which multiplied as the operation progressed, once again, as in the case of UNEF, there were technical delays and administrative and other difficulties.

Again our own experience can be cited. For both UNEF and ONUC (United Nations Operation in the Congo), mainly because of the nature of our participation, it was necessary to organize new

Canadian units to form the contingent. This caused some disruption in our armed services, for specialists had to be drawn from units and formations already committed to other tasks. While the personnel were well trained in their technical duties, they had been taught, as part of their regular training, to think and act as fighting soldiers. In a peace-keeping role—largely passive and supervisory in nature—the troops were called upon to perform unaccustomed and difficult duties, often without clear directions.

I do not wish to leave the impression that the Canadian Armed Services in both the Suez and the Congo did not respond to United Nations needs with speed, efficiency, tact, and inventiveness. The opposite is true. They were magnificent. What I do suggest is that the launching of these two vital peace-keeping operations—from the point of view both of the United Nations and of participating countries—would have been accomplished more easily and effectively if steps had been taken in advance to ensure technical and other forms of preparation for this kind of peace keeping.

Now I am aware that earlier conditions are not likely to be duplicated when the United Nations embarks on a peace-keeping mission. The political circumstances vary; the composition of the force usually has to be adjusted to suit them; the climate and terrain in the area of operations may be quite different.

We also have to recognize that the kind of United Nations presence required may vary greatly from situation to situation. Mr. Hammarskjöld spoke about the "uniqueness of the UNEF setting." He maintained that such a force could not have been deployed in Lebanon or in Jordan in 1958, although there was a need for other forms of United Nations presence on these occasions in which unarmed military observers in Lebanon were able to play a significant part in restoring stability. Similar operations—but with local variations—were carried out more recently in West New Guinea and in Yemen.

The method of operation has to be adapted to each situation. The truce supervision teams in Kashmir and Palestine investigate complaints about incidents; the observers in Lebanon, moving about in jeeps and helicopters, sought to check the illegal entry of arms and infiltrations. In Gaza, UNEF had been stationed at fixed posts. In the buffer zone and in Sinai it has engaged in mobile reconnaissance on the ground and in the air. In the Congo, the force has occupied key points in the main centers of the country. In some areas, the task has been one of patrolling demilitarized zones; in others, of calming and controlling local populations; and in still others, of persuading opposing factions to refrain from hostile acts.

The very fact that forces are composed of national contingents with their own military traditions and methods and disciplines adds to the complexity of the operation. Language can be a barrier and problems of supply a difficulty. The many variations which occur require careful organization, thorough training, and standardization of procedure.

But, in spite of all the difficulties and differences, the shocks and surprises, the United Nations has shown itself capable of brilliant improvisation and has succeeded in making its peace-keeping presence effective. Its record of achievement has been good; all the more so because it was never permitted to be prepared.

V

How can we be complacent about this chronic state of unpreparedness, this necessity of improvising during a crisis when failure could mean war? Today, in Cyprus, the United Nations is facing another severe test of its capacity to respond, without preparation, to a challenge to peace. On tomorrow's horizon there may be other sudden and equally exacting demands. The halting response which the Organization made, after the Cyprus issue had been raised in the Security Council, reflected the deep-seated political dilemma which handicaps the United Nations peace-keeping role. It also served to remind us again that the protection of international peace should not be left to preparations made on the brink, to *ad hoc* arrangements and hasty organization.

Hesitations and difficulties over Cyprus were increased by division among the great Powers. But this was a normal situation in the United Nations and outside it. More disturbing was the widespread disinterest or suspicion on the part of many middle and small Powers. Some were too preoccupied with national and regional interests, which dulled their sense of danger at tensions smoldering in other parts of the world. Others had grown weary of the burden of international crises and of financing them, which, in recent years, has fallen heavily on the shoulders of a few states. All-pervading also was the suspicion that the Cyprus conflict was just too difficult and too domestic for United Nations treatment. It was too small a local tail to wag such a big international dog.

But, as in the Suez and the Congo, the United Nations, while hesitant and unprepared, did not abandon its peace-keeping responsibilities, thanks to the initiative taken by certain of its Members.

So we can take comfort from the fact that in the Cyprus crisis, occurring even before the liquidation of the Congo problem, the Security Council decided to establish a force in that troubled island; that five Member governments agreed to provide contingents and ten to make contributions to the voluntary fund for financing the operation; that the force became quickly operational and that a mediator was chosen who took up his difficult assignment without delay.

While this result gives cause for satisfaction, it should not blind us to the need, demonstrated once more, to organize, plan, and prepare in advance for prompt United Nations engagement in peace-keeping operations. It has become glaringly apparent that the Organization and its individual Members must improve their capability to act quickly. I believe that there is a growing resolve to do this, reflecting a conviction that United Nations preparedness in the field of peace keeping falls far short of the urgent demands being made on the Organization with increasing frequency.

The requirements of peace preservation in the future may not always be satisfied by skillful improvisation and by the willingness of a few to do their duty. The growing interest in improving peace-keeping methods must be broadly stimulated into encompassing advance planning and preparation. Canada, I know, is resolved to draw on its own experience in a way which will give leadership and encouragement in this effort.

VI

What can be done, then, to prepare the United Nations for the kind of peace-keeping operations which we have seen in the past and others which we can expect in future? Ideally the Organization should have its own permanent international force in being, under its orders, for peace-keeping duties. But this is not now feasible for political reasons.

As a next best solution, all Member governments should have elements in their armed services earmarked, trained, and equipped for United Nations service, ready for call to such service. There should be a military planning staff in United Nations Headquarters to coordinate the national preparations and to improve the operating procedures of the Organization.

It has become apparent in the past ten years, however, that formal action by and in the United Nations to achieve even these limited ends is not immediately feasible because of political and practical difficulties. The most recent occasion when the United Nations showed some disposition to deal with the question of stand-by arrangements was in 1958. Dag Hammarskjöld had made his report on the experience derived from the establishment and functioning of UNEF. A number of countries, including the United States, wished to take action in the General Assembly, based on that report. Political circumstances, however, were not favorable. United States support roused all the worst Soviet suspicions. So the matter was dropped. The report was not even discussed by the Assembly.

The Soviet bloc remained firmly opposed to any international security or peace-keeping force or any plan for such a force. The West was not willing to force the issue. The Arab world had been rocked by disturbances in Lebanon, Jordan, and Iraq. Some nonaligned countries, suspicious of Western motives and not wishing to become involved in East-West argument, were unwilling to authorize the United Nations to put force behind international decisions and organize for the purpose. They failed to appreciate that by strengthening the United Nations capacity to meet threats to the peace they would be strengthening as well their own security and creating conditions favorable to the economic and social development which they so badly needed.

Since that time, 1958, there has been some shift in the attitude of Member States but not sufficient to ensure the kind of support needed if formal United Nations stand-by arrangements are to succeed. Nevertheless, the need continues and increases.

A few Members have recognized this. Like Canada, they have earmarked units for United Nations service. Following an announcement last year, the Nordic countries—Denmark, Finland, Norway, and Sweden have introduced legislation setting up contingents which are designed for United Nations service and each of which may be used in conjunction with those established in the other Nordic countries. This is an encouraging development. The Netherlands has followed suit by earmarking troops. There have been indications that other states, representing other geographical areas, have begun to think along those lines.

This is why I proposed recently that, if the United Nations itself remains unable to agree on permanent arrangements for a stand-by peace force, Members who believe that stand-by arrangements should be made could discharge their own responsibility, individually and collectively, by organizing such a force for use by the United Nations. I do not wish to be misunderstood on this point. The stand-by arrangements made by the interested countries, because of existing circumstances in the United Nations, would have to be made outside its constitutional framework. But those arrangements would be squarely within the context of United Nations purposes, within the Charter.

The stand-by contingents which resulted from such an arrangement would not be used unless and until they had been requested by the United Nations to engage in one of its duly authorized peace-keeping operations. In some situations this stand-by force might not necessarily serve as an entity; only some of its national contingents might be selected to serve. Parts might be used alone or be combined with contingents from other United Nations Members not included in the stand-by arrangements. Political requirements would determine its role.

I emphasize this because there has been some disposition to interpret my proposal as an intention to turn away from the United Nations. The whole point of it was to strengthen the capability of the Members concerned to serve and support the United Nations. When I suggested that at first the stand-by arrangements might be confined to half a dozen or so middle Powers, I had in mind, of course, the countries which have already earmarked contingents for United Nations service. They would be ready—and willing. Soon, I hoped, others would be added until all the continents would be represented.

Coordination would be a first requirement. This could be achieved in several ways. The governments concerned could consult closely about the kind of units and personnel which might be needed in future operations. They could perhaps agree to some allocation of responsibility for organizing and training their earmarked contingents. Exchanges of ideas, experience, and key personnel could be arranged on a regular basis.

An international staff would be needed to coordinate the training and other activities of the earmarked contingents; to analyze and correlate with future needs the experience of past operations; to prepare contingency plans and operating procedures for a variety of situations. No stand-by arrangements would be complete without making provision for such a staff—at least in embryo.

It would be even better if a compact military planning staff could be set up in the office of the Secretary-General, one which could cooperate with the Member States who have decided to work together in the United Nations peace-keeping field. It is a matter of some satisfaction that the Secretariat now includes a Military Adviser. He should have a supporting staff to assist him in advising the Secretary-General on the establishment and conduct of military operations. The same staff could be planning ahead for possible peace-keeping missions.

I believe that, if a group of middle and small Powers could be persuaded to work together along the lines indicated above, an effective stand-by arrangement could be brought into being. I do not expect that even the most modest of such arrangements could be accomplished quickly. Nevertheless, the Canadian government is determined to push ahead toward this goal. We have been considering plans for confidential discussions with certain other governments, primarily of military problems arising out of the past and current peace-keeping operations. As a first stage, such discussions would be confined to countries which have taken steps to establish stand-by units for United Nations service. Later they might be extended.

Out of these discussions may come suggestions for improving the United Nations ability to conduct peace-keeping operations and for strengthening and coordinating arrangements for national participation in these operations. That is what I intended when I suggested at the eighteenth General Assembly that there should be a "pooling of available resources and the development in a coordinated way of trained and equipped collective forces for United Nations Service." We shall be following up these exploratory talks with a more formal approach to the other governments concerned. We have reason to hope that they share Canadian views on the need to improve on the present improvised and haphazard approach to peace keeping.

VII

My concentration so far on the organization and employment of military force reflects my deep concern about the present operation in Cyprus, as well as a conviction which I have held for many years.

However, just as the United Nations is not the only instrument for keeping the peace in today's world, international military force is not the only peace-keeping United Nations machinery which should be readily available. There remains a growing need for unarmed supervisory teams, for experienced mediators and conciliators. This need should also be planned for.

As a result of past operations, the United Nations has been able to compile an impressive list of individual soldiers and civilians who have demonstrated their qualification for serving as impartial international servants. Some Member governments are aware of the need to keep this list up-to-date and up to strength. They have been proposing additional names to it. They know that there will be more situations requiring the prompt dispatch of observers and mediators ready and able to serve the Organization.

In many cases, the functions performed by an international force more closely resemble those of the police than the military. This is especially true in a country experiencing the breakdown of internal order or torn by civil disturbance.

Police training is not usually a part of military training but it should be, under any stand-by arrangement, for an international peace force. I would go further. If the United Nations, as such, cannot now organize its own peace-keeping force, it should at least recruit a small professional international police force specifically trained for such duties as traffic and crowd control, property protection, escort duty, and crime investigation. Cyprus is showing the importance of having such a police force to supplement the soldiers.

Mr. Trygve Lie, the first Secretary-General, had this kind of force in mind when he put forth his proposal for a United Nations Guard in 1948. His proposal, like many others at that time, was a casualty of the Cold War. But it had great merit then, as it has even greater merit today in the light of recent experience of the United Nations in the field of peace keeping.

Whatever may be the role of United Nations representatives in the field, it will always call for special qualities, in civilians and soldiers alike. They must make a quick transition from being a loyal citizen of one nationality to being a member of an international team with loyalty to the Organization and the Charter.

This means that training for United Nations service is of particular importance. Such training—military or paramilitary or civilian—should have a certain uniformity in all countries likely to participate in peace-keeping operations. It should take into account the training requirements of individual units. It should include a substantial content of United Nations philosophy. Personnel of all categories should be educated in the aims and purposes of the United Nations, in its political methods and administrative procedures, in the significance of the peace-keeping role.

This is particularly true for the soldiers of all ranks, who have been trained to be nonpolitical and to owe one allegiance. It is a tribute to the character and discipline of United Nations troops that there have been very few instances in which they have broken the code of international service.

In the tasks of separating armies, supervising truce lines, or calming hostile factions, the United Nations soldier will be frequently called upon to exert a mediatory rather than a military influence. He will be required to display unusual self-restraint, often under severe provocation. In many cases, an explosive situation can be brought under control through coolness, good humor, and common sense. And this applies not only to high-ranking officers but to NCO's and other ranks.

Behind this self-restraint and common sense there must, however, be force. The problem of the use of such force in United Nations peace-keeping operations can be a complicated and difficult business, especially for the commander on the spot. But the basic principles are clear enough and follow logically from the initial premise: that a United Nations force is a peace force and there is no enemy to be defeated. Therefore, the United Nations does not mount offensive actions and may never take the initiative in the use of armed force.

This means the use of arms by a United Nations force is permissible only in self-defense and when all peaceful means of persuasion have failed. It is important to appreciate, however, what is involved in this right of self-defense. Thus, when forcible attempts are made to compel United Nations soldiers to withdraw from positions which they occupy under orders from their commanders, or to disarm them, or to prevent them from carrying out their responsibilities, United Nations troops should be and have been authorized to use force.

What can be done in any situation depends on the mandate given the Force. It is always open to the Security Council or the General Assembly, as the case may be, to enlarge this mandate and authorize the use of the necessary amount of force to achieve specified objectives. This was done during the Congo operation as the developing situation required, and with the aim of preventing civil war clashes and apprehending mercenaries. The mandate thus determines the extent to which any United Nations peace-keeping force can employ arms for the discharge of responsibilities which have been clearly assigned to it.

VIII

In this lecture I have put forward some modest proposals whereby the United Nations could be better prepared for keeping the peace. There are, however, two large and related issues which make such proposals difficult to carry out. The first is financial. The second, and more important, is political.

We know that for the past few years the United Nations has been teetering on the edge of bankruptcy. There have been heavy burdens assumed in the Middle East and the Congo. A number of Member States—including two great Powers—with full capacity to pay have failed to assume their share of these burdens and pay their share of the costs. Others have been slow in paying, even when reductions were granted to take into account their relative incapacity to pay.

This is a deplorable, indeed an intolerable, situation for a World Organization established to maintain peace and security. It is especially urgent in view of the growing demands for peace-keeping operations, which have demonstrated not only their worth but their cost. The situation is moving toward a climax this year because a number of states, including the Soviet bloc, now have accumulated arrears of payment which make them subject to Article 19 of the Charter, which provides for the loss of vote in the General Assembly. When it next meets, the Assembly will have to deal with this critical situation, which has far-reaching political and financial implications, unless steps have been taken in the meantime by those in default to liquidate their arrears.

Canada is convinced that the principle of collective responsibility is the only sensible basis for financing peace-keeping operations. We believe that Article 19 was intended to provide, and should provide, the sanction for that principle. We do not seek to force this issue but we are ready to face it if the delinquent states are not prepared to join in a search for a constructive solution. The financial dilemma must be solved.

Even more important is the political conflict which underlies finance and everything else. This conflict has made it all the more necessary to redefine the political basis for United Nations action in the field of peace preservation. It has also made such redefinition more difficult to bring about. The powers and functions of the Security Council, the General Assembly, and the Secretary-General have to be clarified in an agreed manner. In particular, the Security Council needs to reassert its authority in a way which will be effective when the peace is threatened.

To exert its proper influence, the Council should be enlarged to permit a balanced composition in its membership, with equitable representation for all geographical areas. It must be made more capable of preserving the peace. For this, its functions may have to be modified to meet the changing situation in the world.

The United Nations must put its house in order so that it can exercise to the full its responsibility for maintaining peace and security. Stand-by arrangements for peace forces and for the other forms of United Nations presence are part of that process. But this does not embrace the whole responsibility for keeping the peace in our nuclear age.

The World Organization, as such, plays its part but the individual Members cannot escape their own responsibility for maintaining peace; for refraining from the use of force in the pursuit of national policy; for leaving aside shortsighted and debilitating maneuvering, designed for national, regional, or ideological purposes.

The great Powers have a special responsibility in this regard. The Charter gives them a position of privilege but it also imposes a corresponding obligation to cooperate and show the way in preventing war and securing peace; to strive to avoid major clashes among themselves and to keep clear of minor ones.

The middle Powers also have their own position of responsibility. They are and will remain the backbone of the collective effort to keep the peace as long as there is fear and suspicion between the great Power blocs. They have a special capacity in this regard which they should be proud to exercise.

Finally, there is the particular responsibility of the parties themselves to a dispute. U Thant, the courageous and worthy successor to the Secretary-Generalship, underlined this in his recent report to the Security Council on Cyprus: "It is the parties themselves who alone can remedy the critical situation of Cyprus. The authorities . . . must, with a high sense of responsibility, act urgently to bring completely to an end the fighting in Cyprus, if that island is to avoid utter disaster." This meant, he added, a voluntary and immediate renunciation of force as the first essential to finding a peaceful solution of the problems of Cyprus.

The United Nations can and will assist the process of peace making whenever it is given the chance. Its peace forces can restore and have restored the conditions necessary to a peaceful solution of a dispute when they are permitted to operate effectively.

I know that for this purpose and in the long run the political conflicts and above all the East-West conflict inside the United Nations must be resolved or at least reduced.

But there is also a growing necessity for planning and preparation so that the machinery for peace making can operate swiftly and effectively even under present conditions and when required.

To this end, we must do what we can now and hope that we will soon be able to do more.

In this effort Canada has played and I know will continue to play a good and worthy role.

THE UNITED NATIONS OPERATION IN THE CONGO

Ralph J. Bunche

UNITED NATIONS UNDER-SECRETARY

FOR SPECIAL POLITICAL AFFAIRS

Given at Columbia University, March 16, 1964

I have chosen as my topic in the Dag Hammarskjöld Memorial Lecture Series "The United Nations Operation in the Congo" (called ONUC for short), primarily because that operation meant so very much to Dag Hammarskjöld, and he far more to it, and also because I have been directly associated with the operation from its inception. Dag Hammarskjöld initiated the Congo operation in midsummer of 1960, encouraged it to become the biggest of all United Nations operations to date, and gave his major attention to it through many tense and unpleasant months until, in September, 1961, he gave his life while serving it.

It is especially appropriate, I think, to introduce this particular lecture with a few remarks about Dag Hammarskjöld himself. It is, of course, never easy to talk about one's chief or former chief, and Dag Hammarskjöld was my hard-working and demanding "boss" for eight years. It is even less easy to present a balanced judgment about a man as remarkable and as remarkably complex as Dag Hammarskjöld.

One need not elaborate here on the widely accepted fact that he was one of the truly great men of our times; on his widely known and deserved reputation for being uniquely gifted in intelligence, wisdom, statesmanship, and courage; or on his literally total dedication to the causes of peace and human advancement and the United Nations efforts to promote them. We who worked with him came to know Dag Hammarskjöld also as bold, sometimes daring in his moves and approaches to problems, but not reckless. He was not given to acting without cool and thorough calculation, and was never one to act impulsively, although when an idea firmly commended itself to him he would pursue it doggedly. It is not suggested, however, that he was above anger, even fury, or other emotions. He could and at times did erupt. He had an uncanny and almost intuitive sense of political timing and this may have been one of his greatest assets throughout his years of devoted service to the United Nations.

The course taken by Dag Hammarskjöld's career in the United Nations was something of a surprising revelation to many. At the time of his first election as Secretary-General his strength was considered to be very largely on the side of administration and conservatism in action. He was expected to be safe and sound. In the early period of his regime at the United Nations, in fact, he did give a good bit of attention to administration, bringing about some administrative improvements in the internal workings of that United Nations structure which he liked to refer to as "this house." These improvements made a very helpful impact on the morale and the *esprit de corps* of the Secretariat, at a time when Senator Joseph McCarthy's attacks had seriously impaired the spirit and hopes of much of the staff, particularly its American members. But his interest and immersion in political problems soon began to leave him less and less time for the administrative aspects of his responsibilities and both his attention to and interest in them steadily diminished. It also soon became clear that he would not be lacking in political initiative backed by courage, as demonstrated by his audacious mission to Peking in the interest of the release of the American prisoners. It cannot be said that Dag Hammarskjöld displayed any reluctance about being carried in this direction, and he never seemed to be sorry about becoming more and more exclusively a "political man." Quite the contrary.

The former Secretary-General was a man of great reserve in his personal relations, to the extent even of shyness; he was not easy to know, even for those who worked closely with him. It sometimes seemed as though he was reluctant to let anyone see his relaxed side, as though out of fear that it might be regarded as a weakness, just as he stubbornly sought to avoid ever admitting an illness or an ache. But there was a warm and attractive human side of him which in time was gradually revealed to those closely associated with him and who came to know him well, or rather whom he came to know well. This congenial side of the austere man would be revealed in many ways: in the form of personal gifts, usually carefully selected by himself, either through shopping expeditions in town or brought back from a trip; through an arresting narration of some personal reminiscence which unfailingly would be a gem from life; some startling hops of elation on receiving unexpectedly good news, perhaps from one of his field operations or an effort in quiet diplomacy; his poignant affection for "Greenback," the little monkey he was given during his trip to Somaliland in the winter of 1960—the lively little pet who was a monkey in every sense, wildly playful, an irrepressible show-off, a born "ham" whenever visitors were present; or in an animated discussion of some lately published novel or essay in almost any language.

Although Dag Hammarskjöld became increasingly consumed by his dedication to the United Nations—even to the extent of giving up his mountain climbing, his walks, his occasional exercise at squash rackets, and his browsing in bookstores and antique shops—he did maintain to the end some of his other interests, such as his devotion to literature, by late night and early morning reading at the expense of his sleep. His interest in the arts, music, poetry, and painting gave him continuing pleasure and relaxation.

Dag Hammarskjöld was himself a dynamic person and he strove with, I believe, no little success to make the United Nations a dynamic force for peace and human advancement. Wherever in the world there was a conflict situation, actual or threatening, he believed the United Nations should actively seek to contain or avert it: by quiet diplomacy, when the circumstances permitted, in the form of good offices if the parties themselves demonstrated an inability to deal with the situation; and, if necessary, by overt United Nations action. He saw more clearly than any man I have known that the United Nations must do more than hold meetings and talk and adopt resolutions. It was good for the General Assembly to be the forum of the world, and to afford a unique opportunity for a meeting of statesmen from all over, and for those statesmen to exchange views. But this in itself, he knew, could never be enough to save the world. In his conception, the United Nations must play an ever more active role, must project itself into the very area of conflict.

It was in pursuance of this line of thought that under Dag Hammarskjöld came the numerous acts of quiet diplomacy and the establishment, for peace-making and peace-keeping purposes, of the United Nations "presence" in a number of places, whether by a representative of the Secretary-General, by the stationing of United Nations military observers, or by a United Nations peace force. It was his firm conviction that it was not only possible to conceive of but that there actually had been built up at the United Nations—at the very heart of world events—a body of thoroughly objective, if not "neutral," international officers who, under his leadership, when given opportunity and resources and the confidence of enough governments, could play a vital and at times even decisive role in averting conflict.

Thus Dag Hammarskjöld strengthened the United Nations truce and cease-fire operations in the Near East and Kashmir, which had begun under Trygve Lie, his predecessor, giving increasing attention particularly to the United Nations Truce Supervision Operation (UNTSO) in Jerusalem. At the time of the Suez crisis in 1956, even though it was an untried idea, without precedent and without any prior provision for its financing, Mr. Hammarskjöld helped to initiate and proceeded speedily to establish the United Nations Emergency Force (UNEF) in Gaza and Sinai, in pursuance of a resolution of the General Assembly. He made an enormous miscalculation in this instance, for he had anticipated that UNEF would be needed in the Near East for only a few months, and he could not have imagined how indispensable it would become. After almost six and a half years at an annual cost to the United Nations of approximately $19,000,000, that peace force is still deployed along the Gaza-strip armistice line and the international frontier between Israel and the United Arab Republic, and there is little prospect that it can be withdrawn in the foreseeable future without risking a new war.

The United Nations Operation in the Congo was mainly Hammarskjöld's in conception and reflected Hammarskjöld's boldness. From the beginning, it was apparent that this would be by far the largest and most costly operation ever undertaken by the United Nations, and it also soon became distressingly clear that it would be the most difficult and trying of all United Nations efforts. It began in mid-July, 1960, and still goes on, although, in accordance with General Assembly action, the United Nations Force is definitely scheduled to be withdrawn from the Congo at the end of June, 1964, which will be just short of four years after its arrival in the Congo.

In the three and a half years to date of the Congo operation, the United Nations has expended some $400,000,000 in its military and civilian assistance activities.

The Congo task posed the sort of stern challenge that brought out the imaginative and courageous best in Dag Hammarskjöld. He loved to rise to a challenge. He was never so stirred and inspired—or inspiring—as when entering the lists with a tough new issue.

Dag Hammarskjöld anticipated the possibility of trouble in the Congo after its independence, even before that independence was achieved on June 30, 1960. It was well known even then, of course, that the Congolese had had very little preparation for independence. How totally unprepared they were was to become fully and tragically revealed soon after independence day. In late May of that year, Mr. Hammarskjöld called me into his office to inform me that he wished me to go to the then Belgian Congo toward the end of June to represent the United Nations at the Congo's independence ceremony. He also informed me I was to stay on in the Congo for some time after independence to be of such assistance as might be required of me by the new government, bearing in mind, he added, that there might well be trouble in that new country.

His anxiety was justified. There was to be trouble in the Congo, profound and shattering trouble, and it came only a week after independence, when the ANC (the Armee Nationale Congolaise, which had been the Force Publique under Belgian rule) mutinied in early July and arrested or chased away all of its Belgian officers, which at that time meant quite literally *all* of its officers.

Soon after the mutiny of his troops, Patrice Lumumba, the Congo's first Prime Minister, who only a few months later was to come to such a tragic end, called me into a meeting of his Cabinet members to make the government's first request for assistance from the United Nations. At that time the government was thinking only of military technical assistance and not a military force. When, however, only a few days later, the Belgian troops, to protect Belgian nationals, moved outside of their bases in the Congo without the consent of the Congolese government, Mr. Lumumba, on July 12, 1960, urgently called on the United Nations for military assistance in getting the Belgian troops to withdraw and in helping to protect the country's territorial integrity.

There was not at this time very much understanding on the part of any Congolese official about the nature of the United Nations, or about what it could or could not do, its functioning and structure, and particularly about the meaning and status of the United Nations Secretariat. Indeed, even today, one could wish for much more understanding along these lines. The feeling in Leopoldville in July, 1960, seemed to be that the United Nations would quickly respond with everything that was wanted and needed and that the United Nations personnel, military and civilian alike, would be constantly at the bidding of Congolese government officials, even at times to serve most petty personal aims. Mr. Lumumba bluntly stated in his bitter letter of August 14, 1960, to Mr. Hammarskjöld, that the Security Council, by its resolution of August 9, 1960, "is to place all its resources at the disposal of my government." Congolese officials holding such views have naturally suffered profound disillusionment.

The United Nations experience in the Congo has demonstrated, sometimes painfully, the serious difficulties that will inevitably be encountered by a United Nations peace force stationed in a country under a specific mandate to provide the government with military assistance in preserving its integrity and in maintaining internal law and order, without clear, precise, and full directives about its function and authority in relation to the government of the country in which it is to be deployed, and prior agreement about these with the government concerned.

In July and August of 1960 I was seeing Patrice Lumumba almost daily. He was an electric figure; his passionate oratory could entrance an audience and, as it sometimes appeared, even himself; he was indefatigable; he was quickly perceptive and shrewd; also he was deeply suspicious of almost everyone and everything. He may have been subject to leftist influence but I did not regard him as anyone's stooge and felt that he was not greatly concerned with ideology. Mr. Lumumba, it must be said, was one of the few Congolese who seemed to grasp the vital necessity of national unity in a new nation and he strove against all the divisive forces of tribalism and special interest to promote this unity. Unfortunately, however, he and most of his colleagues in his Cabinet had little knowledge of and apparently no deep interest in government and administration as distinct from crude politics and political maneuver. It was this, combined with the mutiny of the ANC, the inability, which was all too clear from the beginning, of Kasavubu and Lumumba to reconcile their differences, the extraordinary atmosphere of rumor, fear, suspicion, and violence which pervaded the Congo at that time, that soon brought the Congo to near chaos.

It must be said that the Belgian decision to move their troops out of their Congo bases against the will of the Congo government, or, at least, the manner in which it was done, was a disastrous step. Some in Leopoldville at that time, including myself, had advised Belgian authorities that it would likely be so, before the fateful move was undertaken. I had suggested that a wiser tactic than unilateral military action would have been an appeal to the Security Council for assistance in protecting the thousands of Belgian nationals remaining in the Congo. The move of the Belgian troops left Mr. Lumumba furious and desperate, and led him to broadside appeals for outright military aid to the United States (President Eisenhower advised him to turn to the United Nations), to the USSR, and, only as a last resort, to the United Nations. In response to this second appeal, I assured Mr. Lumumba that the United Nations would most likely respond sympathetically, but even with my deep faith in the United Nations I could not have imagined at that time that the United Nations response to Mr. Lumumba's call would be as rapid and as immense as it turned out to be.

It developed that virtually the entire international community was sympathetic to the cries from this newly emerged country in the very heart of Africa, and wished to help. As mentioned earlier, the second appeal was received at the United Nations on July 12, 1960, and the first Security Council resolution in response to it, promising assistance, was adopted in the before-dawn hours of July 14, 1960. The follow-up action by the United Nations was unbelievably rapid, for the first United Nations troops—the Tunisians, quickly followed by Moroccans, Ethiopians, and Ghanaians—landed at Ndjili airport in Leopoldville on July 15, 1960. For this swift and effective response, my friend and former colleague in the Secretariat, Dean Andrew Cordier, deserves major credit.

The United Nations had no reasonable alternative to its favorable response to the Congo's appeal—the appeal of a weak government in a new state. In so doing, the United Nations strengthened itself morally and won new prestige. And it also gave to itself, no doubt unknowingly at the time, a far wider role and meaning in world affairs than it had ever had, and made indispensable a much stronger position for the Secretary-General as the executive arm. An unfettered executive with authority to act is imperative to the effective conduct of a peace-keeping field operation.

The Congo issue, when it came before the United Nations, was not in the context of the East-West conflict or of the Cold War. This accounted for the unanimity and spontaneity of the early support for the Congo's appeal, the Security Council resolutions, and ONUC. But it was not long before this changed and the United Nations Operation in the Congo came to be an issue between East and West, with Dag Hammarskjöld caught squarely in the cross-fire because of his responsibility, as Secretary-General, for the conduct of the operation. In any case, the United Nations, by having ONUC on the spot without delay, was able to fill what otherwise, because of the collapse of government in the Congo, would have been an inviting and most dangerous vacuum of authority in the heart of Africa, with obvious implications for rival East-West interests.

As soon as the July 12th appeal was received from the Congolese government, Dag Hammarskjöld began intensive consultations, particularly with the representatives of a number of African governments. He had seen immediately, with his usual keen perception, that the solid support of the Africans would be a decisive factor in getting the Congo operation launched. It was from these discussions that the idea—and the necessity—of a United Nations force which should be basically although not exclusively African in composition emerged.

The African Members, although they later became much less of one view on questions relating to the Congo operation than at first, have continued to exercise a decisive influence on matters affecting the operation. It was their unified voice, for instance, that led the General Assembly last fall to respond favorably to the appeal of Prime Minister Adoula to extend the stay of the United Nations Force in the Congo from the end of December, 1963, when it was originally scheduled to be withdrawn, to the end of June, 1964.

The near anarchy and chaos which occurred in the Congo so soon after independence and continued for so long led to a most unfortunate if unavoidable diversion to military assistance of the major part of the United Nations resources for the Congo from the hoped-for program of massive *technical* assistance, designed to help the country get on its feet after the departure of the Belgians who had been doing just about everything in the government, in administration, and in the economy. This military assistance was provided to help induce, as it did, Belgian troops to return to their bases and ultimately to leave the country, and to assist the government in maintaining law and order and preserving its territorial integrity. For the United Nations, this really meant undertaking for some time virtually the entire responsibility of holding things together in the Congo, while not trespassing on the authority of the government, at a time when governmental machinery was just about nonexistent owing to lack of experienced officials and the incessant quarrels of the politicians, and when the ANC was not only weak but dangerous, owing to lack of officers and discipline.

In a United Nations operation which, in both its military and its civilian aspects, must be in such close and daily contact with a government which has to lean so heavily on United Nations assistance, the problem of relations with that government is a most serious one. The operation, obviously, must meticulously avoid any interference in the internal political affairs of the country or any appearance of such interference, although many persons unconnected with the operation seem to take it for granted that there is such interference. The government, on its part, requests and is dependent upon the assistance the operation can afford, but many of its officials actually resent the need for it, or at least having to seek and ask for it. The government also, of course, would resent any United Nations political intervention unless it could be directed against the opposition, when it would, naturally, be entirely welcome.

Considering all the delicate circumstances, the relations between the Congolese government and the United Nations by and large have been tolerable, although they have seldom been really happy. They are, in truth, none too good at this very moment, although there has been no change in the policy of the United Nations or Secretary-General U Thant toward the Congo, which is to afford that country the maximum assistance possible with the resources available. The difficulties leading to strained relations usually arise when the United Nations, most likely for reasons of sound principle, finds it impossible to grant one or another request of the government. In this regard, I cannot help but recall my own experience with Mr. Lumumba, Mr. Gizenga, and other members of the Lumumba Cabinet back in August, 1960, when I was rejecting almost daily demands from them that elements of the United Nations Force be put instantly at the disposal and under the command of the Congolese government, which would then dispatch them to Katanga to fight Mr. Tshombe, or to Kasai or to Kivu to fight someone else—the ANC itself being unable to do so for lack of officers, retraining, and discipline.

I suppose one cannot speak of the United Nations Operation in the Congo without some reference to the attempted secession of Katanga, which has, perhaps more than any other single factor, the ANC mutiny excepted, complicated and bedeviled the post-independence history of the Congo. I say "attempted" advisedly because Katanga's secession never actually took place, and, indeed, Moise Tshombe, from his retreat in Spain, was recently avowing without a smile that, after all, the secession of Katanga was never his intention.

Although Mr. Tshombe had attended the Brussels Conference before independence and had agreed with the other Congolese leaders on the arrangements for independence, including the provisional constitution, it seems certain that the idea of secession was actively on his mind, possibly for a combination of personal political and financial reasons. I first met Mr. Tshombe in my suite at the Stanley Hotel in Leopoldville a few days after Congo independence. He was peeved, rather justifiably I think, at having been ignored by Messrs. Lumumba and Kasavubu. Mr. Tshombe at that time also expressed great dissatisfaction that the concept of a centralized government had been adopted, and informed me, with a surprising knowledge of the United States Articles of Confederation, that he favored a loose (and weak) federation in the Congo along those lines. He seemed only to be encouraged when I protested strongly that the United States Articles of Confederation had failed woefully to work.

A few days later, Mr. Tshombe returned to Katanga and proclaimed secession. This declaration of July 11, 1960, was about the only basis Katangese secession ever had, and it would have had little or no meaning if Mr. Tshombe had not acquired disputed access to very large financial resources as well as the support of the European community in Katanga and of mining interests in and outside of that province. He was thus able to raise a Katangese army and employ non-African mercenary officers to lead it. Even so, Mr. Tshombe and Katanga and the mercenaries would not have been able to cause nearly as much trouble as they did had it not been for the utter incapacity of the Central Government and its army.

It deserves passing mention that Mr. Tshombe had at his bidding throughout the secession effort a quite formidable propaganda apparatus which was very active in the Western world and had especially strong impact in the United States. In this country, strangely, it succeeded in blinding a surprisingly large number of people, including some in public position, to the verities of the Katanga situation particularly and the Congo situation generally, and led them to oppose the policy of the United States government on the Congo.

The specter of Katanga and Mr. Tshombe always had highest priority in the thoughts of Congolese government officials, sometimes to an obsessive and paralyzing degree. Although this may be less the case today than it was three years ago, it could become so again very quickly should Mr. Tshombe emerge onto the active scene, as he may well do, once the United Nations troops are withdrawn from the Congo at the end of June. In fact, at this very time we are receiving a number of increasingly disturbing reports from reliable sources of a renewed concentration of the relics of Tshombe's army and of the mercenary officers' corps along the Angolan-Congolese border.

I recall an evening in Leopoldville in August, 1960, at Patrice Lumumba's home when he was vigorously lodging a series of complaints against ONUC until, in sheer self-defense, I took out of my case a cable that I had just received from Dag Hammarskjöld, giving the text of the long message he had recently sent to Mr. Tshombe firmly rejecting the latter's claim for Katanga's membership in the United Nations. Mr. Lumumba's face lighted up with near ecstasy when he read the message. He immediately dropped the subject of his complaints and asked only that he be permitted to make a copy of that message.

It is a most difficult situation for any government, and particularly for a new and proudly sensitive one, to have a right to a certain line of action, and a desperate need to take it, as in the case of the Congo's opposition to the attempted secession of Katanga, but to lack completely the means to launch the action, while at the same time there is in their country an international agency which they think has the right, as well as the means, to undertake the action for them, but which refuses to do it except in its own way and time. The resulting emotions and frustrations lead to many unrealistic attitudes. For example, on one of his visits to the Congo, Mr. Hammarskjöld informed Mr. Gizenga, who was Acting Prime Minister in the absence of Mr. Lumumba, and his colleagues, of his intention to send me to Katanga to prepare the way for the entry of the United Nations Force into Katanga. This was in early August, 1960. Mr. Gizenga was insistent that several members of the Congolese government should accompany me on the flight, although he knew very well that the only possible result of this would be that all of us would be promptly arrested on landing at Elisabethville, if not shot down before landing there. Mr. Gizenga was furious when Mr. Hammarskjöld decided that only United Nations personnel would take this trip. We went alone and got into trouble anyway.

While it was apparent that Katanga had no military force of consequence at that time, Mr. Tshombe was appealing by every means to the people of Katanga to resist United Nations entry. It would clearly put the United Nations Force in an untenable position if it had to fight the people of Katanga to enter that province and to remain there, for this would give it the posture of an army of occupation. Therefore I advised Mr. Hammarskjöld not to send the force to Katanga for the time being. I greatly doubt that a United Nations peace force could be stationed for very long in any country if, even in self-defense, it would have to turn its guns on civilians rather than military forces. The political realities of the United Nations, I imagine, would not long permit a peace force to be in the posture of an army of occupation.

Subsequently, the Secretary-General, with characteristic decisiveness and courage, decided to go himself to Katanga to talk with Mr. Tshombe, following a quick visit to New York to report to the Security Council. He went and succeeded in convincing Mr. Tshombe that the United Nations troops should be permitted to come into Katanga without resistance, and this they promptly did. Far from pleasing Mr. Lumumba, however, this accomplishment infuriated him, and on Mr. Hammarskjöld's return to Leopoldville from Katanga he received some incredibly angry and insulting letters from Mr. Lumumba about his trip to Katanga and his interpretation of Security Council resolutions. In fact, from that time on, Mr. Lumumba rejected all normal relations with the United Nations.

Before concluding this lecture I feel in duty bound to take advantage of the opportunity to try to clear up or dissipate certain misconceptions and myths about the Congo operation.

The United Nations Operation in the Congo at no time has had any executive authority there, or any share in executive authority. Its role has been exclusively that of assistance and advice. We do not participate in governing the country and have no responsibility for the actions of government. There are those, for example, who still say that the United Nations made a fatal mistake in the early days of the operation in that it did not disarm the mutinous ANC. It is quite possible that if the United Nations could have done this at that time —although to do it would almost certainly have involved considerable fighting—the course of events in the Congo might have been considerably different. But the United Nations had no authority to do this except at the request of the Congolese government, and that request never came, although it had been made clear to the government that the United Nations would also undertake this type of assistance upon request of the government.

There has been much talk also, and some still persists, about United Nations "offensives" in the Congo, about the United Nations thwarting secession, conquering Katanga and returning it to the Congo, and otherwise using force to achieve its ends. The United Nations Force in the Congo has always adhered strictly to the principle that it is a peace force and that its arms are for defensive purposes only, although they may be used for its protection when it is discharging responsibilities assigned to it by Security Council resolutions, such as the prevention of civil war or the removal of mercenaries. In its three and a half years in the Congo the United Nations Force has had to use its arms on remarkably few occasions. It has *not* undertaken any offensive actions in Katanga. If it had, it could very easily have dealt with the problem of Katanga secession in 1960, or at any other time in the last three and a half years. It did, in pursuance of directives from United Nations Headquarters based upon Security Council action, undertake to round up Tshombe's mercenaries in Katanga. In September, 1961, this led to fighting in Elisabethville, with the United Nations troops being on the defensive. The attempt of the mercenaries, now admitted in various memoirs, to liquidate the United Nations Force in Elisabethville in December, 1961, led to heavier fighting, which stopped the moment the security and freedom of movement of the United Nations Force had been restored.

In the classic manner of propaganda, naturally, the Katangese Information Service asserted on both these occasions that Tshombe's troops were the victims of "an offensive," and this distortion received credence in quite a wide circle.

The decisive fighting in Katanga occurred in December–January, 1962–63. Then, it may be said quite frankly, the Katangese troops, led by mercenaries, played into the hands of the United Nations Force by launching an attack on United Nations positions in Elisabethville and continuing that attack for several days with no reaction from the United Nations troops. Finally, however, when Mr. Tshombe's own cease-fire orders to his troops were disregarded by them, the United Nations Force was commanded to react firmly and it then proceeded to clean out all threatening pockets once and for all, and also to assert and realize fully for the first time its undoubted right, under an agreement with the Congolese government, to freedom of movement throughout the Congo, including Katanga. Tshombe, however, remained as President of Katanga Province and was even at times given physical protection by the United Nations when it seemed that his personal security might be in danger.

We speak of the Congo, but the unhappy fact is that at the time of its independence, and to a considerable degree still, there was not, and there is not, a true national spirit or wide sense of national statehood and government in the Congo. The divisive factors of tribalism and sectional, or even personal, interests are still very strong, and there are too few leaders who stanchly believe in and well understand the concepts of centralization, central government, and national loyalty.

While there are some who charge that the United Nations Operation in the Congo has not taken a strong enough line and has failed to exercise the necessary authority, there are others who have from the early days of the operation used the unkind expression of "neo-colonialism" to describe United Nations action in the Congo. In truth, the United Nations operation has bent over backwards to avoid most scrupulously the least basis for any such charge and has carefully refrained from any interference in Congolese internal affairs except upon the specific request of Congolese authorities. Thus, for example, the United Nations in 1961 at the request of such authorities as there were, in a situation in which there was no constitutional government, undertook to find, transport, and protect the members of Parliament throughout the country, many of whom were in fear of their lives and in hiding, in order that the Congolese Parliament might convene in Leopoldville and establish a new government. The successful search for its members and the protection of the reconvened Parliament prevented the country from falling into anarchy. In brief, the United Nations operation has been criticized most unjustly by groups who, in theory at least, are at the opposite poles of political thought, the one crying "Communist agent" and the other crying "neo-colonialist." This testifies to the genuine objectivity and impartiality of the United Nations in the Congo.

One still hears it said occasionally that Dag Hammarskjöld took an unnecessary risk in going to the Congo in 1961, on a trip that tragically proved to be his last. There was always a risk, of course, when he went to the Congo, as there was when he went to a number of other places, but to say that there was an unnecessary risk is to say that it was not necessary, or at least not important, for him to go to the Congo when he did, and even to imply that he was acting recklessly in doing so. In view of the situation and of what Dag Hammarskjöld had in mind, his trip to the Congo in September, 1961, was of major importance. He went on the eve of the sixteenth session of the General Assembly, knowing that the issue of the Congo was likely to arouse a bitter and divisive debate in the Assembly.

Dag Hammarskjöld did not go to the Congo in gracious response to a polite and not at all pressing invitation received from Prime Minister Adoula, but for more compelling reasons. He had it definitely in mind to try to induce Mr. Tshombe to enter into talks with Mr. Adoula, preferably in Leopoldville. He knew that if this could be achieved it might well relieve the Assembly of the necessity of extensive and poisonous debate on the subject of the Congo, which would do neither the Congo nor the United Nations any good. In this regard, I wish to present a passage never before published from a message which Mr. Hammarksjöld addressed to me from Leopoldville on September 15, 1961, two days before his death. I had informed him of certain criticisms of the operation, and he replied:

However, the key question is this one: What have our critics done in order to bring Mr. Tshombe to his senses? . . . It is better for the United Nations to lose . . . support . . . because it is faithful to law and principles than to survive as an agent whose activities are geared to political purposes never avowed or laid down by the major organs of the United Nations. It is nice to hear . . . parties urge . . . that we do everything in our power to bring Adoula and Tshombe together after having gone, on our side, to the extreme point in that direction without any noticeable support at the crucial stages from those who now complain.

It was Mr. Hammarskjöld's misfortune that a totally unanticipated fighting situation should have developed in Elisabethville at the very time of his arrival in the Congo. While there were standing instructions to the United Nations people in Katanga to seek to round up and evacuate all mercenaries, Dag Hammarskjöld had not authorized any specific action involving fighting and was indeed surprised and shocked to learn about it. This is established beyond a doubt by another passage from the message just mentioned, one of the last he sent from Leopoldville before his fatal trip. He said the following with reference to the fighting that had broken out in Elisabethville on September 13, 1961: "It belongs to the history . . . that the first I knew about this development, I learnt by a tendentious Reuters report in Accra on my way to Leopoldville."

The "tendentious Reuters report," by the way, was a press story to the effect that Conor Cruise O'Brien, the United Nations representative in Elisabethville, had announced the end of Katangese secession, a statement which O'Brien subsequently denied to the United Nations that he had ever made. One can readily imagine Mr. Hammarskjöld's feelings at such a report in the light of his intention to try to bring Tshombe and Adoula together.

Because of the success that has attended the deployment of the United Nations peace forces in Gaza-Sinai and in the Congo, there has been a recent tendency to regard a United Nations peace force as a panacea for conflicts. It has happened increasingly, lately, that whenever a conflict situation is brought to the United Nations there will be some automatic suggestions that a United Nations force should be organized and dispatched. This is a misconception which overrates the true possibilities in the employment of a peace force, which are, in fact, limited.

First of all, a peace force is a very expensive device. The Congo force, for example, at its peak strength of 20,000 was costing over $10,000,000 a month; and the small UNEF force—just over 5,000 officers and men—has been costing approximately $19,000,000 per year.

The locus of responsibility for the cost is a controlling factor in determining ability to obtain contingents for a force. If the United Nations is able to defray all extra expenses, the force can be recruited rather easily and quickly; otherwise not.

The composition of such a force has to be most carefully selected in the light of the particular conflict situation and the political considerations that apply to it. A basic determinant is the definition of acceptable contingents by the government of the country on whose territory the force is to be stationed. This is a serious and built-in limitation which has also vital implications for the extent to which the troops of a standing force could be used in a particular situation, as, for example, in Cyprus.

The nature of the conflict situation with which the force is to be involved also affects the ability to obtain contingents, for naturally the countries providing the contingents never fail to examine carefully the situation in which their troops will be placed before they agree to make them available to the United Nations. The states providing contingents also wish to know in advance the extent of danger for their troops, the likelihood that they would have to fight, and particularly the prospect that they might become embroiled in fighting with the civilian population or segments of it, or be charged with intervening in the internal affairs of a country.

Such considerations have all come very much to the fore in establishing the United Nations Peace-keeping Force in Cyprus in response to the decision of the Security Council in its resolution of March 4, 1964, not the least the financial restriction and the limitation on acceptable contingents. Here was to be found the reason for the delay in constituting the Cyprus force. All necessary preparations—transport, logistics, etc.—had been made; only the contingents were lacking.

The United Nations Operation in the Congo, in the light of its mandates, has certainly had great success; it may even be considered the most successful operation the United Nations has undertaken when measured in terms of what it was called upon to do and has in fact done. Striking evidence of the success of the operation is found in the almost complete cessation of organized attacks on it from whatever source, West or East. It is especially noteworthy that some governments that had been most critical of the military aspect of the operation became the strongest voices in urging the retention in the Congo of the United Nations Force.

There is very, very much still to be done in the Congo, of course, particularly in the realm of civilian assistance. The anxious question now is what will happen when the United Nations troops are withdrawn. Will much of what has been done over four years be then undone? Since the United Nations Force in the Congo could be extended beyond the end of June of this year only through action of the General Assembly called in special session for this purpose—and this seems next to impossible—we may only wait and see—and hope. Not much encouragement can be derived from the barbarous raids of the Jeunesse rebels in Kikwit Province in recent weeks, which have taken many lives. The raiders have encountered only feeble opposition by the ANC. It is good to be able to say that ONUC has succeeded in rescuing many of the victims or potential victims of these youthful terrorists. The Congo operation thus displays vividly the problem which we also have with UNEF in Gaza-Sinai: how can a successfully functioning United Nations peace force ever be withdrawn without disastrous consequences?

In concluding this talk with a look to the future, it may be said that there is clear need for a critical but honest appraisal of the United Nations and its present effectiveness in peace making, not only in the Congo but elsewhere. Improvements in existing practices, even new methods, may be found. On the one hand, we see that the interdependence of countries and situations in the modern world makes the United Nations essential as a last resort in critical emergencies when all other efforts at a solution have failed, as in Cyprus now. By the very nature of things, the tough problems come to the United Nations when they have been found insoluble by others, and this is especially true when these problems, as in the case of Cyprus, may be fraught with the gravest danger for the wider peace. At the same time, it is becoming a way of life for the United Nations, though by no means a happy way, that there is a vast and increasing discrepancy between the peace aims and responsibilities of the United Nations and, on the one hand, what it is called upon to do about them by the Security Council or the General Assembly and, on the other hand, its resources, its authority, and its support, both political and material. The "tin cup" approach to financing provides a most uncertain and insecure financial basis for a peace operation. Except for a rare and exceptional set of circumstances, such an arrangement cannot fail to affect adversely the efficiency, expedition, and effectiveness of the operation.

The United Nations is a young organization in the process of developing in response to challenges of all kinds. In its peace making it operates, notoriously, not only largely by improvisation but on a shoestring. This has been seen in the Congo where a force, which is now less than 5,000 men and at its largest was only 20,000, was given the task of assisting a weak government to restore law and order out of chaos in a country the size of the subcontinent of India. This is being seen again with regard to Cyprus where there have been great difficulties in establishing an international force on that island, although failure to do so could well mean war in the eastern Mediterranean.

Serious people everywhere should cogitate on this, the indispensability of the United Nations in our present world, in situations where it alone affords the chance to avoid war, measured against its present meager resources of money and authority. It bears emphasis that, while most governments in the end give the United Nations their warm and loyal support in critical situations, the Organization (and the world) sometimes find themselves on the very brink of disaster of incalculable dimensions before the essential support is forthcoming.

Dag Hammarskjöld left a great legacy of high idealism wedded to great political and practical wisdom and imagination. The United Nations and the world have been fortunate in having a man with the devotion, wisdom, and courage of U Thant to inherit, carry on, and expand the aim of the United Nations in a strong and dynamic enough manner to meet its great challenges.

FINANCING THE UNITED NATIONS: ITS ECONOMIC AND POLITICAL IMPLICATIONS

Agda Rössel

PERMANENT REPRESENTATIVE OF SWEDEN TO
THE UNITED NATIONS, 1958–1964

Given at Columbia University, December 11, 1963

The financing of the United Nations has become a major topic of the international political discussion. The deficit in the United Nations budget has already caused some temporary halt in the normal activities of the Organization; it is a cause of great concern to the supporters of the United Nations and, naturally, provides new water for the mills of the cynics.

Let me first dwell briefly on the types of United Nations activities which have to be financed and on the methods which are currently in use for the financing. I will then try to analyze the problems which the financing poses for different categories of Member States from the economic and political viewpoints.

In the introduction to Dag Hammarskjöld's last annual report to the General Assembly, dated August 17, 1961, that is, one month before his sudden and tragic death, he pointed out that debates and events had brought to the fore different concepts of the United Nations, of the character of the Organization, its authority and its structure. He referred to the fact that certain Members conceive of the Organization as a static conference machinery for resolving conflicts of interests and ideologies with a view to peaceful coexistence, within the Charter, whereas other Members have made it clear that they conceive of the Organization primarily as a dynamic instrument of governments through which they, jointly and for the same purpose, should seek such reconciliation but through which they should also try to develop forms of executive action, undertaken on behalf of all Members, and aiming at forestalling conflicts and resolving them, once they have arisen, by appropriate means.

The rift between these different opinions concerning the role of the United Nations, described by Hammarskjöld, is still deep, and it is apparent especially in the attitude of states toward the financing of the different activities of the Organization.

The regular budget of the United Nations limits itself almost entirely to the financing of the conference-type activities of the Organization. To that extent it is approved and actively supported by *all* Member States. If the United Nations were to confine its activities in this manner there would, therefore, be no financial crisis. There are also certain parts of the regular budget which pertain to executive-type activities, for instance fact-finding and observer teams dispatched from Headquarters in connection with threatening international conflicts. The Soviet Union, which strongly resists the use of the Organization for executive purposes, has announced its intention to withhold from its contributions to the United Nations regular budget all amounts corresponding to the Soviet share of expenses for the kind of activities which have just been described, while the French government has limited itself in this respect to subtracting from its contributions to the regular budget the amount covering its share of the costs for servicing the United Nations bond issue which was launched in connection with the financial crisis resulting from the Congo operation.

The most costly enterprises upon which the United Nations has so far embarked are the peace-keeping operations which are currently being undertaken in the Middle East and in the Congo. These operations are financed through *ad hoc* and special accounts, respectively, outside the regular budget, although according to the advisory opinion of the International Court of Justice, confirmed by the General Assembly, the costs incurred for such peace-keeping operations are expenses of the Organization within the meaning of the Charter. It is the continued refusal of some Member States to pay their assessed contributions to these *ad hoc* accounts which has brought about the financial crisis of the Organization.

However, there is a third type of United Nations activity which has important financial aspects, namely, the programs for assistance to developing countries. These programs are of an executive nature and, in line with their general policy, the Soviet Union and other Communist countries wish to exclude any such programs from the regular budget of the United Nations. The vast majority of these programs, such as the Expanded Program for Technical Assistance, UNICEF, and the Special Fund, are already being financed on a voluntary basis. Voluntary contributions to these programs cannot be regarded as financial support of the Organization itself, although the very fact that funds are channeled from donor countries to recipient countries through United Nations sponsored programs tends to strengthen the role of the United Nations in world affairs.

As I just mentioned, it is the lack of support for the peace-keeping operations which has brought about the present financial crisis. I should therefore like to concentrate my remarks and observations on the political and economic implications of the financing of the peace-keeping operations.

The Charter of the United Nations gives very little guidance as to the conduct of peace-keeping operations or other executive action. The most important rules are given in Chapter VII of the Charter, which deals with action with respect to threats to the peace, breaches of the peace, and acts of aggression. This chapter provides, among other things, for the use of armed forces, made available to the Security Council by Member States, for such action as the Council considers necessary to maintain or restore international peace and security. The actions in question are to be under the direction of the Security Council itself, with the assistance of a Military Staff Committee composed of the five permanent members of the Council. The Charter contains no special provisions for the financing of these Council operations.

So far there has been no United Nations operation which has been undertaken in the manner which is thus prescribed in Chapter VII of the Charter. This is largely a consequence of the fact that the Cold War has prevented the necessary unanimity among the permanent members of the Security Council. The United Nations action in Korea was not of the kind envisaged under Chapter VII. It was taken by individual Member States acting on recommendations of the Security Council rather than under its orders and at a time when the Soviet Union was absenting itself from the Council. The peace-keeping operations in the Middle East and in the Congo, which, as I mentioned earlier, have brought about the financial crisis of the United Nations, have been even more different in nature from the military actions described in Chapter VII of the Charter. They have not been enforcement actions directed against any state and they have not been organized and directed by the Security Council itself. Instead, they have been organized and directed by the Secretary-General in accordance with mandates given him by the Security Council and by the General Assembly. The forces which the Secretary-General has dispatched to the Middle East and to the Congo operate with the consent of the states concerned and the forces in the Congo are there at the request of the Congolese government. They have been sent to the respective areas not to fight aggression but in order to prevent, by their very presence, the outbreak or continuance of hostilities. Finally, the United Nations peace-keeping forces do not consist of troops which Member States, principally the great Powers, have placed at the disposal of the Security Council in accordance with Charter provisions, but they consist of contingents from smaller, often nonaligned countries, which have been voluntarily offered to the United Nations in response to requests made by the Secretary-General.

Although none of the permanent members of the Security Council voted against providing the Secretary-General with a mandate for undertaking the peace-keeping operation in the Congo, two of these members, namely France and the Soviet Union, as well as other eastern European states, base their refusal to contribute financially to these operations on the position that such operations must be undertaken in accordance with Chapter VII in order to be binding on Member States. The question may be asked, regarding the United Nations operation in the Congo, why France and the Soviet Union did not exercise their veto when the decision to start this operation was proposed to the Council. Regardless of the answer to that question the fact remains that the two Powers disapproved of the way the operation developed and that they had no constitutional means at their disposal to exercise influence on the way in which the Secretary-General conducted the operation. When they wanted to bring the operation to a halt, for reasons which of course may be discussed, they tried to achieve this by refusing financial support and—in the case of the Soviet Union—by violent attacks against the Secretary-General. The attitude of the Soviet Union and other Communist countries concerning the Congo corresponds to their attitude as regards the United Nations operation in the Middle East. The difference is that the Middle East operation had been started by a resolution adopted by a majority vote in the General Assembly where no country has the veto.

Probably the United Nations peace-keeping operations would have been politically unpalatable to these states even if they had not been requested to contribute to their financing. We are dealing with a political problem, and not a financial one. For, if there were consensus among the major Powers about the role which the United Nations is to play, they would have no difficulty in providing the necessary funds. As long as peace-keeping operations are undertaken in an improvised manner and without explicit Charter provisions we must expect a great deal of reserve and suspicion by individual Member States, as well as attempts on their part to influence the situation by refusing financial contributions.

I have touched upon some of the political implications of the financing of peace-keeping operations. What are their economic implications? According to the latest available statements by the Secretariat, forty-seven states have failed to pay for the Middle East operation, and fifty-five have defaulted similarly as regards the Congo operation. The total deficit will soon amount to approximately $130 million. The major part of this amount represents the debt of states who refuse to pay for political reasons. Only a small portion, or approximately $9 million, is owed by the thirty-odd developing states who have given economic reasons for their arrears.

The difficulties of the underdeveloped countries in contributing to the peace-keeping operations have been given much attention by the General Assembly in the years since the Suez crisis in 1956 brought about the first peace-keeping operation. These countries have successfully contested the notion that their contributions to peace-keeping operations should be calculated on the basis of the scale of assessments to the regular United Nations budget. There has been and still is much discussion between the economically developed countries and the developing countries on this point. The developed countries have been stressing that the regular scale of assessments gives a true expression of the relative paying capacity of all Member States and that it would be logical and equitable to apply this scale to all United Nations assessments, including peace-keeping operations. Nevertheless, reductions have been granted to the developing countries, who point to the fact that the high costs of peace-keeping operations, which have sometimes amounted to 200 percent of the regular United Nations budget, confront them with a heavy and unexpected burden if their contributions are to be based on the regular scale of assessments. Undoubtedly the foreign exchange situation of some of these countries is very poor. One must also understand that these countries wish to give priority to payments which directly aid their development and that, consequently, they consider their own responsibility for the financing of peace-keeping operations to be less than that of the more developed and wealthy states. As the total amount of the contributions from underdeveloped countries—even to the regular budget—is very small, the financial benefit of insisting on full contributions from these countries is relatively small. The number of these countries lies between 40 and 50, that is, more than one third of the total membership. They can, therefore, prevent the adoption in the Assembly of financing resolutions which require a two-thirds majority. Obviously, their support is needed if there are to be any assessment resolutions at all.

Thus, the financing of peace-keeping operations has so far presented us with a picture where repeated improvisations have been necessary in order to cope with the fact that a few of the major contributors have refused to pay their assessments on political grounds, while a great number of smaller contributors, whose assessments to the regular United Nations budget are not greater than 18 percent, although accepting the principle of collective responsibility, have insisted on a lower scale of assessments than the one which is applicable to the regular budget. One cannot say that these hand-to-mouth improvisations have been successful, as they have left the United Nations with a deficit which is expected to amount to $130 million at the end of this year.

What has been done and what can be done in order to improve this situation?

The predicament of the United Nations was actually worse a few years ago, when a large number of underdeveloped countries felt that they were entitled to withhold their contributions because the United Nations expenses for peace-keeping operations seemed to be of such an extraordinary nature that they could not be automatically binding on all Member States. Other states claimed that these expenses were of the same category as those financed under the regular United Nations budget and that, therefore, in accordance with the Charter, all members were collectively responsible for them. The Assembly decided to seek an advisory opinion from the International Court of Justice on this point and the Court stated in 1962 that the expenses for peace-keeping operations were to be considered as expenses of the Organization under the Charter. This opinion was subsequently accepted by the Assembly. The developing countries have later been very active in efforts to establish a set of principles for the financing of peace-keeping operations. A resolution on this matter was adopted in June, 1963. In this resolution, the Assembly confirmed that the financing is the collective responsibility of all Member States. It also confirmed, among other things, the principle that developing countries should pay relatively less to peace-keeping operations, that the special responsibilities of the permanent members of the Security Council for the maintenance of peace and security should be borne in mind, and that, where circumstances warrant, special consideration should be given Members who are victims of, or otherwise involved in, the events or actions leading to a peace-keeping operation.

The resolution was adopted with 92 votes in favor and 11 against.

These 11 were Soviet-bloc countries and France. The resolution had the effect of isolating completely the two great Powers who for political reasons refuse to contribute to United Nations activities which lie outside the conference concept of the Organization.

The great majority of states who wish the United Nations to develop further in the direction of active peace keeping must, needless to say, continue to cooperate in order to keep the Organization going and to persuade the few remaining states to fall in line. In this connection it is very essential that the cooperation of the great number of developing states is not jeopardized by placing too heavy a financial burden on them. I have already pointed to the fact that these 40-odd countries pay only 18 percent of the regular budget of the United Nations. The sharply rising budget of the United Nations and its peace-keeping operations during late years has undoubtedly been a cause of grave concern to all those countries whose national economies are yet far from a state of self-sustaining growth. It seems reasonable to adjust in a more permanent way the scale of assessments for peace-keeping operations involving heavy expenditures in order to safeguard the interests of the developing countries. This adjustment will result in an increased burden for the wealthier states. They have already, in connection with the *ad hoc* financing resolutions, assumed such an increased burden. The economic significance thereof has for most of these countries been small. There are statistics available which, for each Member State, compare one year's assessments and voluntary contributions with the gross national product. It emerges from these statistics that the payments to the United Nations represent in most cases only a fraction of one percent of the gross national product. It also emerges that the wealthiest countries have, relatively speaking, not contributed more than the poorest countries. There is, therefore, no economic reason for the wealthier countries to take too stern a line when discussing the contributions of the developing countries. The overriding goal must be to achieve full political cooperation among those states who support the idea of peace-keeping operations, so that influence can be exerted on those big Powers who have refused to contribute.

The Charter stipulates in Article 19 a sanction on defaulting states. If they are in arrears in the payment of their financial contributions to the Organization they shall have no vote in the General Assembly if the amount of the arrears equals or exceeds the sum of the contributions due for the two preceding years. This article will be applicable to the Soviet Union as of January 1, 1964, if the Soviet Union does not make the necessary payments before that date, that is, payments which reduce its debt to an amount which may be only just below the sum of the contributions for the last two years.

Thus, in fact, the Charter permits rather substantial arrears to exist continuously. The constellation of this condition and a system of peace-keeping operations run on an *ad hoc* basis is very unsatisfactory from a financial point of view. The funds are not available when the operations are started and the Charter contains no guarantees that 100 percent of the funds will ever be provided. Even if the Assembly were in the future to adopt the necessary assessment resolutions at the time when the operations are initiated, this situation would not be changed.

One remedy would be that the United Nations build up a peace-keeping fund which is available for future operations. There is currently under review in the United Nations a proposal to establish a voluntary peace fund which could accept contributions from governments as well as from private sources. No doubt one can count on some willingness of Member States as well as of states outside the United Nations and of private associations and individuals to demonstrate by voluntary financial contributions their support for the United Nations, especially in times of crisis. The existence of a voluntary peace fund may thus serve to mobilize latent support from many quarters. However, the peace-keeping operations cannot rely on the availability of voluntary funds alone. What is even more important: peace-keeping operations cannot succeed without overwhelming political support by Member States. If they support the operation they should and could also pay for it. The very fact that governments have to pay creates a special interest in the conduct of the operations. The process of persuading governments to pay sometimes helps to foster an increased spirit of international solidarity.

It has sometimes been suggested that the United Nations should find independent means of income, such as concessions on oil from the bottom of the ocean or on resources in the polar regions, as well as rights to share fees or excises for international mail or passports or visas. Such potential new sources of income should not be needed for peace-keeping operations, for which Member States must contribute the necessary funds themselves if they want to have such operations. However, the need of the United Nations for more income is unlimited in the field of assistance to developing countries. The activities of the United Nations and its related organs for the development of the economic and social conditions of these countries are, needless to say, of the utmost importance also for the creation of stable political conditions and they are thereby a tremendous peace-keeping operation in themselves, requiring the mobilization of all available resources.

The possibility of providing the United Nations with new independent sources of revenue has not yet been seriously discussed in the Organization. It is not improbable that proposals of this nature may come up sooner or later in connection with the further deliberations on the establishment of a United Nations capital development fund. There is great pressure from the developing countries for an increased flow of investment capital through the channels of the United Nations.

For the financing of essential functions of the United Nations one should, however, count in the first instance only on contributions from Member States. The role of the United Nations Organization is to be a center for harmonizing the actions of nations in the attainment of the purpose and principles laid down in the Charter. The success of the Organization in this task has very little to do with the availability of large sums of money. Patient efforts of persuasion and a positive will by every state to support the United Nations regardless of the default of others are some of the most important elements in the process of harmonization.

There are no short cuts—and indeed not financial ones—on the road to lasting peace and security for all mankind. What the United Nations needs is the acceptance by all Members of its role as an active force for peace keeping.

DISARMAMENT AND
THE UNITED NATIONS

Alva Myrdal

SWEDISH DELEGATE, GENEVA DISARMAMENT CONFERENCE

Given at Stockholm University, March 19, 1964

I

The United Nations is the locus both for sublime resolve and for down-to-earth practice in regard to problems besetting the world of our time. This holds particularly true in the field of disarmament, where both expressions of ideals and attempts at implementation figure prominently in the records of every session of the General Assembly.

Interest in one of these aspects should not be allowed to belittle the value of the other.

The United Nations has one definite function as a forum, where objectives are set for internationalizing the action of Member States in the direction which the Charter points out in its solemn opening words "to save succeeding generations from the scourge of war." Let no one believe that resolutions adopted on disarmament could be empty words. Whatever they achieve, they are always contributing to creating a new set of norms, an international code of morals, a kind of collective superego. The more than 100 nations making up the United Nations realize "what they ought to do"—they do acknowledge that war, conquest, domination constitute no civilized way of life. This in itself is a distinct advance on earlier centuries. And even if the confessions to the ideals of disarmament have so far remained little more than lip service, they are conditioning the ways of thinking of our time and, we hope, of the future.

The very first resolution which the United Nations General Assembly adopted was a call for the elimination of all nuclear weapons from national armaments and for using atomic energy solely for peaceful purposes. That was in 1946. Since then such a massive world public opinion has formed against the "immorality" of nuclear weapons that it acts as a not negligible factor of deterrence against using them. A little more than a decade later the General Assembly was ready to proceed further and agree unanimously that the goal must be nothing less than an international agreement on "complete and universal disarmament." This meant in fact carrying the will of the nations beyond what the Charter had outlined; they were no longer content with asking just for the regulation and limitation of armaments.

It might be briefly recalled that the United Nations Charter—which has its main emphasis on maintaining security rather than on disarmament—had only this to say in relation to the General Assembly and disarmament: that the General Assembly "may consider the general principles of cooperation in the maintenance of international peace and security, including the principles governing disarmament and the regulation of armaments, and may make recommendations with regard to such principles to the Members or to the Security Council or to both" (Article 11). Nor did the definition of the role of the Security Council call for complete disarmament: "In order to promote the establishment and maintenance of international peace and security with the least diversion for armaments of the world's human and economic resources, the Security Council shall be responsible for formulating . . . plans to be submitted to the Members of the United Nations for the establishment of a system for the regulation of armaments" (Article 26).

But, at least since 1959, the expectations of the world have been raised so high that total disarmament is no longer unthinkable. Pacifists, Buddhists, and Quakers have lost their monopoly of believing in the possibility of a world without arms. Experts in many lands are busy studying the modalities of disarmament. Even the generals have begun to stretch their concern beyond problems of national strategy to the new science of international strategy just being born.

So far the bravest thinking about the strategy of disarmament has taken place outside the United Nations, in research institutions and in the brainwork of individual scholars. But the results are finding their way into the World Organization's conference rooms.

The United Nations also has to function—and that is its second role—as a market place, where nations can carry on their bargaining, their negotiations, and their settlements in order to begin implementation of the disarmament aspirations. It is only natural that the record of practical achievement should be less brilliant than that of setting goals. Still, it is hard to accept that the achievement should be a *negative* one as in fact it is: no actual disarming at all, but stupendous increases in military might and in military costs. For the purpose of illustration but one figure may be cited (one already somewhat dated but derived from a report by a group of experts from both sides of the major Power blocs), namely, that the world was, at the end of the 1950s, devoting to military purposes some 120 billion dollars annually, or 8 to 9 percent of the world's annual output of all goods and services.

Thus, between the two prongs of the United Nations approach—that of formulating objectives and that of achieving results—there is a dangerously widening gap. How long can the world live with it? Must we not have a basis for hope against hope which makes it possible to endure such a blatant discrepancy between words and deeds? Some such rock-bottom basis for hope probably does exist in our time—in contrast with earlier times. Otherwise it could hardly be explained how the United Nations could during one and the same session in the autumn of 1961 have registered two seemingly irreconcilable decisions: (1) a protest against the USSR for having resumed nuclear testing and set off a bomb of shocking megaton strength against the passionate opposition of the whole world, *and* (2) a recommendation that new disarmament negotiations should start on the basis of a set of principles on which the USSR and the United States had just been able to reach agreement and which in its eight points embodied a much wider area of concord than had ever before been approximated. This was the so-called Zorin-McCloy

"Joint Statement of Agreed Principles for Disarmament Negotiations," which the General Assembly accepted on December 20, 1961. Promptly eighteen of the United Nations Member States were formed into a committee for negotiating "general and complete disarmament" on this unexpected new basis.

The obstinate optimism which must underlie initiatives in the disarmament field derives, I believe, from observation of some powerful tendencies in this period of world history. I will mention only two which seem to have overriding importance.

One is the existence of two military super Powers with such an advantage over the gamut of all other Powers—and I do not hesitate to include France and China among the latter—that the gap seems unbridgeable. Furthermore, each of the two is in possession of what is popularly known as "over-kill capacity." Their fire-strength is such, relying strategically on their nuclear capabilities, that a situation of "mutual deterrence" has been brought into existence; everybody is aware that nuclear war would be a self-defeating policy. Add to this that they are both—as are now the majority of nations in the world— organized for defensive and not for offensive purposes. It thus seems reasonable to conclude that the level of armaments upheld by them is "unnecessarily" high: they must both be ready to reduce the level, provided they could be certain that the other one would do likewise. One might say that as long as the Cold War posture dominates our world picture—until other Powers of competitive strength appear on the arena—it would only be rational to expect the great Powers to institute quite far-reaching reductions of armaments, provided such reductions could be safeguarded by the principles of retained balance and sufficient control. It is now generally, albeit tacitly, recognized that the interests of both super Powers converge in this manner.

How far could the reductions then go? On the assumption that these two Powers retain a virtual monopoly, or rather a "duopoly," in regard to nuclear weapons, it could stretch practically to the end of a disarmament process, the mutual deterrence being assured by what has become known as the "nuclear umbrella," that is, an agreed minimum nuclear force, with warheads and delivery vehicles, to be retained by each of them. Without discussing all the problems involved—and their name is legion—and without setting any target for the reductions in quantitative terms, it is evident that considerations such as these form quite a realistic basis for hope that at least a start at pruning might be made.

It must be explicitly stressed that the favorable conditions here presumed may continue only for a fairly short time. Specific circumstances have led to a certain convergence of interests, most obviously in regard to political circumstances; what has caused the convergence is the fact that a certain lull has been reached in that Cold War which has dominated the international scene practically since World War II. But the relative harmony of interests, typical of a period of balance of deterrence through mutual over-kill capabilities, might be broken by technological advance. If one side should gain an important new breakthrough in regard to weapons development, the case for a cumulative upward spiraling may again arise. Such breakthroughs could be anticipated chiefly in two directions. One is the development, and mass production, of ultra-small tactical nuclear weapons. The other is a decisive new development in the ABM field—the antiballistic missiles. Thus, one of the most important methods to ensure favorable preconditions for disarmament is mutual understanding *not* to press forward with pathbreaking new work on weapons development. But the world being what it is, we should be aware that the period of grace may be but a short one.

The second ground for optimism lies, paradoxically enough, in the enormous cost of the present burden of armaments. Costs should, of course, always have been an argument against armaments and against wars. But today the costs involved are evaluated against some new sets of facts: first, the aforementioned one of surplus capabilities, and, second, the rising awareness of the economic plight of large groups of mankind. Not least is it important that economic problems loom large in the public discussion within each of the two super Powers themselves. There is a "war on poverty" to be fought within their own borders. And beyond them, there live the multitudes of poor people in Africa, Asia, and Latin America who are becoming more and more vociferous in claiming a share of the world's riches. The very knowledge that close to 10 percent of the world's resources are now spent on military expenditure, together with the growing awareness of the pressing needs for economic development, forces the statesmen of the world to think afresh. And when they do, they have to think not just in terms of financial resources to be devoted to other than destructive purposes but in terms of alternative uses of steel, of airplanes, of electricity, of electronics, and, most important of all, of the brain power which is now sucked up in military pursuits, in production for military purposes, in research for military development. Perhaps, or even probably, the problems looming so darkly over our world would be more possible of solution if the efforts of those hundreds of thousands of research personnel could be redirected toward solving the problems instead of toward creating more of them.

Let me with the aid of the aforementioned United Nations report give just one glimpse of a future made brighter by disarmament:

The release of scientific and technical manpower would make it possible to encourage programs of basic scientific research in fields which have hitherto been neglected. Disarmament would also open up possibilities for joint international ventures of an ambitious kind, such as the utilization of atomic energy for peaceful purposes, space research, the exploration of the Arctic and Antarctic for the benefit of mankind and projects to change the climate of large areas of the world.

II

I hope I have made it quite clear that when I point to what seem to be fairly tenable reasons for a certain optimism in regard to disarmament, these reasons relate to certain *reductions* of armaments, a beginning of a downward process. It is not possible to form a judgment now as to whether this process would lead to complete disarmament. Actually, international language is lacking in terms indicating clearly what degree of disarmament is meant. We in Sweden are fortunate enough to be able to distinguish in the process of disarmament between *av*rustning—meaning "off"—and *ned*rustning—meaning "downwards." All the optimism I can muster refers to the latter concept: first steps in a *reduction* of armaments.

For a long time international discussions of disarmament were stalling on this very problem, whether any disarmament measures at all should be taken in the absence of a prior commitment to total disarmament. The Soviet Union upheld the necessity of a prior commitment, while the United States favored "gradualism." It is perhaps one of the major achievements of the Eighteen Nations Conference on Disarmament, which has been meeting in Geneva since March, 1962, that it has found a way around this dilemma by agreeing that the bulk of disarmament measures should form part of a systematic plan, embodied in a treaty on general and complete disarmament, but that certain independent measures, called "collateral," could and should be undertaken in advance so as to build up confidence.

The Geneva Conference, consisting of five representatives each from the NATO and Warsaw blocs, including the two super Powers themselves, and eight representatives of nonaligned nations—but with the voluntary absence of France—has in this respect played a functional role. By allowing itself to carry on negotiations about collateral measures alongside an exploration of two rather elaborate drafts for the final treaty on general and complete disarmament, it has been able to survive and to some extent circumvent the two intractable problems which otherwise bedevil all international dialogues about disarmament: *balance* and *control*.

Balance of all disarmament measures was a pillar in the Zorin-McCloy Agreed Principles, which aimed at such a scheme that "at no stage would any State or group of States be able to gain any military advantage and so that security would be ensured equally for all." It is acknowledged by all concerned that such a balance must be sought. But what constitutes a criterion of that balance has never been the object of any clarifying exegesis. One interpretation is simply that the relative levels of *status quo ante* should be maintained. Such a criterion is technically easy to apply. It would, for example, be satisfied in all cases where the disarmament measure implies simply a cessation of activities: cessation of nuclear tests, stopping production of nuclear material of weapons grade, etc. A certain predilection for measures involving "freezing" one situation or another is now noticeable—evidently in order to avoid the problem of balance—as, for instance, the recent Polish proposal to freeze the number and types of nuclear warheads in Poland, Czechoslovakia, East and West Germany. However, another very different interpretation sometimes seems to be implied by the great Powers: that they should preserve not just the existing strategic balance but, despite the introduction of a certain disarmament measure, equal chances to develop further their weapons systems. But then, no fixed frame of reference can exist. And if a very wide interpretation is given to the whole phrase, not forgetting the part about "security would be ensured equally for all," nothing less than an absurdity is proclaimed, as perfect equity toward all sides, for states great and small, with or without certain types of weapons, or with widely different quantities of them, can never be assured if one factor is being changed. This would spell rigid immobility—and be absurd, as I said, since there is truly no equal security for all states to start with. In this series of lectures directed to different universities, I would venture to suggest that the academic world should make a painstaking analysis of these concepts and so place the nations, and more particularly the militarily important ones, under an obligation to declare themselves *in clara verba* on this highly pertinent problem of balance in relation to disarmament measures. While "collateral measures" might come to be introduced *ad hoc* without stringent claims on "balance" being upheld, the matter of definition must obviously be settled before any state even contemplates putting its signature to a treaty on general and complete disarmament.

The second major political problem in all disarmament negotiations is that of control. Its political character is of a more dangerous potency. In regard to maintaining "balance" the theory of the two sides appears identical, at least until we get the semantics clear, when hidden divergences might appear. In relation to "control" the approaches are most widely different. The United States has always demanded a definite verification of each disarmament step, with physical inspection not only of what is being cut away but also of remaining weapons in the same category. The USSR, on the other hand, would allow no verification of remaining weapons, and control only —but then full control—when factual elimination occurs: dismantling of production units, evacuation of bases, destruction of bombers, etc. This difference is directly linked with the difference in approach to the disarmament issue as a whole, the United States being for gradualism, for percentage reductions of existing armaments, while the USSR wants the complete elimination of one weapons system after another (each holding such views as a general principle, with some—and increasingly numerous—exceptions).

In this situation, the collateral measures again offer easier solutions, as they can be tailored to fit in with such control measures as are acceptable. A typical example is the cessation of nuclear tests. The agreement reached last year was to discontinue those tests on which there was consensus that no joint control system needed to be established. The great Powers at the same time refrained from legislating concerning the tests for which verification was a bone of contention, that is, the underground ones. In other instances collateral measures might provide a kind of "practice field" for methods of verification to find out which ones would work.

To some of us the collateral measures also have value in providing more opportunities for the nonaligned nations, or, generally, for the non-super Powers, to be active in the disarmament negotiations, to make proposals, even to participate in some actual disarmament measures, while it is more or less explicitly taken for granted that at least during the first stage of a treaty-bound disarmament process only the military establishments of the great Powers would be affected.

The opportunities for nonaligned initiatives would seem to be particularly great in relation to questions of control. As regards problems of balance, we must find it appropriate to leave to the great Powers to decide, politically, whether a proposed measure adversely affects their relative posture and to determine what the weights are of expected advantages and disadvantages respectively. But in relation to problems of control, there are numerous ways in which the nonaligned countries, as being in a way more disinterested, can be of service. Often they can point to objective methods of verification, freeing the procedures from political elements, such as, for example, the proposal to let an international scientific commission, chiefly of seismologists, collect, collate, and evaluate all observations bearing on possible nuclear tests. The neutrals could even, if that would serve to bring opposing parties closer together, reveal evidence which points to the relative fallibility of certain control methods, on which overreliance might have been placed for political reasons. Thus, if the question of on-site inspection for verification of potential underground nuclear tests had become really crucial, we—I can at least speak for myself—might have quoted chapter and verse from scientific calculations as to the enormous costs and inconveniences involved, for example, in drilling deep holes in foreign territory in order to trace radioactivity, as against a rather uncertain chance of being able to provide conclusive evidence by this method. But let me rather cite an example on the positive side: recently in Geneva it was pointed out what potentialities exist for verifying whether disarmament is in reality proceeding or not, from studies and comparisons of military budgets and of the allocation of resources for different purposes in the national income statistics.

III

It has seemed necessary to discuss first some of the burning questions which are on everybody's mind whenever the problem of disarmament is raised: the discrepancy between lofty resolutions about general and complete disarmament on the one hand and the actual acceleration, instead of deceleration, of the armaments race on the other; the question as to whether there exists any reasonable ground for optimism; the gradual approach versus the all-embracing international convention; and not least the eternally vexing problems of balance and control. In discussing those, I hope I have also painted a background which will make a description of the actual work, now proceeding, seem more meaningful.

The scene for the major efforts at solving the disarmament problems is now the Eighteen Nations Conference on Disarmament, meeting in Geneva. It is important to bear in mind that this conference is an occasion for negotiating, not for making speeches and resolutions. There are no great propaganda dividends to be won by anybody. And there is no majority to persuade, either, as negotiations are never won by votes. The atmosphere has become quite a relaxed one, marked by frankness and personal respect, relatively speaking, and with a joint fund of knowledge accumulated by the delegates which facilitates their quick understanding of positions and of shifts in positions.

Thus, an agency has been set up which I believe that all nations and not least the great Powers evaluate positively, as a useful instrument for the exchange of views and even the tentative testing of proposals. This value is perhaps enhanced by the fact that all delegations are formally headed by their respective foreign ministers, which makes it possible to transform what is usually a diplomatic conference into an *ad hoc* summit one. I regret to say, however, that it is more than a year since we had the pleasure of having Mr. Gromyko and Mr. Rusk with us in the conference room.

The achievements so far may not seem very impressive. Some agreements between the super Powers have emerged fairly directly out of the work within the conference. One is the Moscow Agreement of August 5, 1963, on cessation of nuclear weapons tests in the atmosphere, under water, and in outer space, to which more than a hundred nations have acceded. The other is the establishment of a direct, rapid communication link between Moscow and Washington, which was enumerated among the original suggestions for so-called collateral measures, and negotiated in the corridors of the Geneva Conference. A third positive result has to be registered, namely the agreement reached by the USSR and the United States during the last session of the General Assembly not to station nuclear devices in outer space, another item which had figured on the list of desiderata within our Geneva committee.

The impact of these "solutions" may seem small—yes, infinitesimal—in comparison with the gigantic problems of war preparations which still remain unsolved. Correctly speaking, they are not even "disarmament" measures, as no actual dismantling of military capabilities has taken place. But, first, it might be recalled that they are the only agreed decisions of any kind in the direction of disarmament since the London Agreement of 1930 about limitation of naval forces. Second, the cancellation of atmospheric nuclear tests has presented mankind with a relaxation of tensions and fears about radioactive fall-out, which we all were finding it increasingly difficult to live with. Third, the very fact that some agreement has been reached, that is, that the great Powers have been willing to accept some curtailment of their ambitions to proliferate indefinitely their military strength, must be a good omen. Perhaps it is a forecast that the conference can continue in what the Russians now call a businesslike manner and the Americans a workmanlike one!

On the agenda remains on the one hand the assignment to draft an international convention on general and complete disarmament, and on the other hand the self-imposed duty to proceed to new agreements on partial, collateral measures, intended to stifle the growth rate of armaments and diminish the risk of war.

On the first score, the results which are outwardly visible are meager indeed. Although both the Soviet and the Western Powers have presented comparable proposals in draft texts for a disarmament process to be pursued through three consecutive stages, all the conference has achieved so far is to produce joint texts of the preamble and the first four general articles, although not even those in final form. We have had to place in brackets—single brackets for the United States version, and double brackets for the USSR version— some important considerations, as, for example, the one on the character of the United Nations peace force by which a disarmed world should finally be protected. But in the course of the discussions and negotiations an undeniable narrowing of the original gulf between partisan positions has occurred. There now exists a whole catalogue of such concessions. Some are such that they impinge on the very dogmatism with which certain principles were earlier held. An example: the United States now accepts total cessation even in the first stage of all production of new types of armaments, while on the other side the USSR accepts a gradual percentage cut "across the board" of conventional armaments, even accepting the exact proposals of the United States for cutting 30 percent in the first stage and 35 percent in the second stage.

The most far-reaching of the modifications introduced is the agreement by the Soviet Union—forecast in speeches by Mr. Gromyko at the General Assemblies of 1962 and 1963—to allow the retention of a certain number of nuclear warheads with their delivery vehicles until the end of the third stage of the disarmament process, instead of scrapping them 100 percent in the first stage, which was the original Soviet proposal in keeping with its view that every possibility for waging nuclear war must immediately be extinguished as an initial rite. In point of fact, this concession alters the whole outlook for disarmament. It makes the hope of reaching an ultimate agreement immensely more realistic, politically speaking, because disarmament could now take place with the assurance that the two super Powers would to the end preserve their own deterrents, each against the other, a posture which has come to be characterized by the term "nuclear umbrella," as symbolizing a guarantee of security. However, it also implies an acceptance by the rest of the world of an increasing monopoly for the super Powers over decisions for war or peace. This is a consequence which is rarely spelled out. The qualification must also be made that so far no agreement has been reached between the two super Powers as to the procedure for reducing present-day capabilities to the ultimately foreseen minimum deterrence: should it be by stepwise reductions according to the well-known American model or by a decisive cut in one stroke? Neither have they agreed, or even indicated, what the size of the final forces of deterrence should be.

The prospects for success of the negotiations on a general disarmament treaty would be enhanced if more progress could meanwhile be made in regard to the so-called collateral measures. A number of suggestions have been brought forward in the Geneva Conference, although no agenda and still less any fixed order of priorities have as yet been agreed upon. In my brief comments on those partial or collateral disarmament measures I will follow neither the United States list of five points nor the USSR list of nine points, presented at the opening of the session in January, 1964, but rather deal with them in somewhat more systematic combinations.

(1) In a category by itself stands the ever-present proposal to follow up last year's partial test ban treaty with a complete one, by prohibiting underground tests as well. It would seem to be the most logical next step. But for political reasons we have to realize that this very measure is hardly negotiable for the time being, the positions in regard to verification, and particularly on-site inspection, being too extremely entrenched. It must also be recognized that while world public opinion was forcefully pressing for the cessation of atmospheric tests because of the danger of radioactive fall-out, this argument has now been removed. World public opinion is hardly wrought up about underground tests. Also, in scientific circles a hope is entertained that, if the issue rests for some time, detection techniques might improve so much that those demands for control to which the most severe objections have been raised might be relinquished.

(2) In a second category we find measures intended to bar the spread of nuclear weapons to additional countries. Under discussion

stand such proposals as the one, originally Irish, of an unconditional international agreement to make it impossible for countries who do not now control nuclear weapons to produce them or acquire control over them. Further, there are various suggestions to establish nuclear-free zones, running from the so-called Undén plan to let nations in a certain region negotiate on the conditions under which they would want to constitute themselves as a nuclear-free zone to actual proposals for the establishment of such zones in Latin America, Africa, etc. Most recently there has been the initiative taken by the Polish government to revise the so-called Rapacki plan and to suggest, for the time being, simply freezing the actual number of nuclear devices located in Poland, Czechoslovakia, East and West Germany. Without venturing to prophesy I wish to express my considered opinion that success could be achieved within this category if elements of the various suggestions were combined. I wish, however, also to pinpoint the important qualification made by the Swedish government, which may be paraphrased in the following manner: that those who are "have nots" in the nuclear armaments field should not be asked to take on obligations to refrain from acquiring nuclear armaments without some compensation on the part of the "have's," that is, some sacrifice of nuclear capabilities on the part of the nuclear Powers would seem to be a prerequisite for agreement against further spread of such weapons.

(3) Therefore it becomes logical to place in a third category measures which envisage just such a curtailment of nuclear armaments or production capacities. In the present stage of negotiations such proposals stem from the West. The United States has recently proposed that an agreement on total discontinuance of the production of fissionable material of weapons grade be inaugurated by the simultaneous shutting-down of comparable plutonium reactor plants by the United States and the USSR.[1] Inspection by adversary teams is welcomed in the initial stage; full international control is foreseen for the more advanced implementation. In this way the International Atomic Energy Agency (IAEA) might get its real chance to function accord-

---

[1] A step forward in this direction has been taken recently: in April, 1964, there was announced an exchange of notes between President Johnson and Chairman Khrushchev about an agreed closing of certain plants producing nuclear material of weapons grade.

ing to the original blueprints. Close to this proposal lies the one of transferring certain amounts of fissionable material to peaceful uses; the United States has suggested a transfer of 60 tons of U-235 from its own stockpile and 40 tons from that of the USSR. For further advance within this category the questions of control would seem manageable, the problem of balance, however, being outside the purview of a neutral observer.

(4) For the sake of convenience, proposals about reductions of military strength may be assembled in a fourth category. The more specific proposals include one, now virtually accepted by both sides, of physical destruction of a certain number of delivery vehicles, in the latest exchange of views these being reduced to "a certain number of obsolete or obsolescent bombers." A related proposal, by the United States, is that for freezing the production of strategic delivery vehicles, both their numbers and their characteristics, including intercontinental missiles, ground-to-air missiles, and certain types of airplanes. While the physical destruction of some bombing planes, a "bonfire" as we say, might have an encouraging effect on public opinion the world over, its efficacy as a disarmament measure is difficult to judge as long as there is no insight into which armaments would remain. And to gauge that would involve control methods which are, at least, not acceptable to the USSR.

(5) Finally, proposals have to be mentioned aiming at reducing tensions, the risk of war, and armaments in Europe. The Soviet Union has announced that it is reducing the over-all strength of its armed forces and that it would be prepared to negotiate a synchronized reduction of the forces on the two sides of the demarcation line in Central Europe. This, however, presupposes some measure of control. From the Soviet side the idea of establishing a number of control posts to observe major military movements at traffic centers in Europe has been connected with the last-mentioned proposal. In the proposals of the United States the same device has been given an independent role, to serve as a safeguard against surprise attack. This, one may note as a curiosity, was originally, in 1955, a Soviet proposal. In this category should be mentioned also the standing invitation from the Soviet side to conclude a nonaggression pact between the Warsaw and NATO blocs of states. I have enumerated

these proposals, without details and without comments, as they belong so definitely to the realm of great Power politics rather than that of international negotiations about disarmament. But, of course, if they were carried through their effect in reducing tensions would augur exceedingly well for the successful continuation of the wider negotiations.

It may seem surprising to some that in this catalogue I have not mentioned proposals for agreed reductions of military expenditure. Most recent among those have been suggestions of the USSR and other Eastern-bloc states that military budgets be cut by 10 to 15 percent. But to my eye such reductions would rather be the *result* of disarmament measures, which ought also to be discernible as physical phenomena. However, as I have indicated in an early part of my speech and as the Swedish delegation at the Disarmament Conference in Geneva has had occasion to elaborate on several occasions, the budget approach to the disarmament complex is a highly interesting one and worthy of further study, particularly by economists specializing in studies of national accounts who might tell us how to trace the allocation of a country's resources for various purposes, peaceful and not so peaceful.

These are, in brief, some considerations as to the present prospects of initiating a process of disarmament which I have come to hold valid during my study of this vexatious complex of problems. I cannot conceal that I would consider it within the realm of actual possibility to reach some agreement on some measure fairly soon. I might even prophesy that the great Powers will find it politically desirable to reach at least some agreement on some measure, so that we should not have to meet—or at least not leave—the next General Assembly empty-handed.

In conclusion I would point to the flexibility with which the United Nations has been able to utilize various forms of machinery for incessantly renewed attacks on these problems of disarmament. First there is the General Assembly for solemn declarations, amounting to massive expressions of the public opinion of the world, which is so adamantly pressing for disarmament within our time. Then, there are different types of committees, often negotiating bodies somewhat in the margin of the United Nations organizational structure. In recent years such efforts have been concentrated in the Eighteen Nations Disarmament Conference in Geneva. It should be noted, however, and duly emphasized to make us honestly humble, that only in the very early phase of its existence did the United Nations deal with disarmament problems through its major political organ, the Security Council. In the days of resurrected optimism after the war, the World Organization set up committees to deal authoritatively with atomic weapons as well as conventional armaments. In a later stage, or from around 1950, when it was evident that the first attempts had failed, the Security Council itself has rather been concentrating on problems of maintaining international peace and security—as one of its assignments in the Charter reads.

Finally, may I recall, in the special context of these lectures, that this latter phase of the Security Council's preoccupation largely coincides with the period of service of the late Secretary-General, Dag Hammarskjöld. When the topic revolves around disarmament, he should perhaps chiefly be heralded for his bold efforts in the direction of creating United Nations peace forces for conflicts of a kind which are continuously worrying the world while we are groping for ways to reduce the overburden of military structures.

THE GENERAL ASSEMBLY IN UNITED NATIONS AND WORLD AFFAIRS

Muhammad Zafrulla Khan

PRESIDENT OF THE SEVENTEENTH SESSION
OF THE UNITED NATIONS GENERAL ASSEMBLY

Given at the University of Leiden, May 26, 1964

I am deeply and humbly conscious of the honor of being designated to deliver a lecture in the Dag Hammarskjöld Memorial Lecture Series on the subject "The General Assembly in the United Nations and World Affairs." It was my privilege to have known Dag Hammarskjöld personally over a number of years, to have observed his activities and competence at firsthand, and to have admired his unstinting and resolute dedication to the principles enshrined in the Charter of the United Nations, to which and for which he gave his life.

The popular image of the General Assembly is both as accurate and inaccurate, as real and fanciful, as that of an average national legislature. The casual visitor to the Headquarters of the United Nations is impressed by the grandeur of the Assembly hall, its beautiful modern design, its vaulted dome and starry lights, its charming decor. It is the official place of business of the delegations representing the whole of the membership of the United Nations, whose record of attendance is as good and often better than that of national legislatures.

As a parliamentary body the Assembly bears only a rough resemblance to the average legislature. National parliamentarians serving for the first time in the Assembly sense a lack of the normal attributes of legislative action. There is no party representation in the normal sense, although there are blocs that sometimes vote uniformly. There are no visible floor leaders; there is no party whip; there are no majorities or minorities so characteristic of most national parliaments. Thus to the novice there appears to be a lack of discipline, a lack of the pressures producing a sense of direction in a debate. The Assembly debates; it differs; it disagrees and agrees; but almost always it reaches a conclusion on the matter under discussion.

While many of the accepted attributes of a democratic national legislature are lacking in the General Assembly, their very absence throws some light upon the real characteristics of the Assembly. Each delegation sitting in the Assembly represents a sovereign nation, a Member of the United Nations.

Here it might not be inappropriate to digress briefly and indicate the importance assumed by this attribute of membership in such a world body in the minds of the many newly created and newly admitted states. For these newcomers, who have hitherto played little part in traditional diplomacy and who were simply dominated by its results, to take their seats in the General Assembly is to join the world. To come, as of right, to the Headquarters of the United Nations, which in many cases itself helped former colonial territories to achieve statehood, is a symbol of sovereignty; this provides, incidentally, a unique opportunity, among many other things, for the rapid assimilation of the conduct of diplomatic business and, equally important perhaps, access to a forum where all views may be aired and heard.

Indeed, what Woodrow Wilson said of the Assembly of the League of Nations may well be thought to be largely true of the General Assembly of the United Nations:

> The underlying conception of the assembly . . . is that it is the forum of opinion. . . . It is the debating body; it is the body where the thought of the little nation along with the thought of the big nation is brought to bear upon . . . those matters which affect the good understanding between nations upon which the peace of the world depends; where the stifled voice of humanity is at last to be heard, where nations

that have borne the unspeakable sufferings of the ages that must have seemed to them like aeons will find voice and expression, where the moral judgment of mankind can sway the opinion of the world. . . .

The assembly was created in order that anybody that purposed anything wrong should be subjected to the awkward circumstance that everybody could talk about it.

Now, with respect to both older, long-established nations and the many younger states, whose admission has largely contributed to more than doubling the original Charter membership in the short space of twenty years, infusing their youthful vigor into what is still a relatively young organization, the vote of each delegation reflects the views of its government. By virtue of the principle of the sovereign equality of all its Members, upon which the Organization is based, each state in the General Assembly has one vote: old states or new states, rich or poor, strong or weak.

Critics of this system of one vote for one nation have pointed to the effects on voting of the achievement of sovereignty by newly independent states and the crystallization of regional or underdeveloped blocs or groups, arguing that the preponderance of votes by the middle and smaller Powers damages the usefulness of the United Nations. Be that as it may, it is difficult to devise an alternative system of weighted voting (based on such factors as population, area, or financial contribution to the budget of the United Nations) that would be practicable and would not have even greater defects.

In theory, the prevailing system of representation and vote would seem to imply maximum disintegration with a consequent inability to reach conclusions. In fact, the cohesive quality that exists among a large membership made up of delegations of sovereign states flows in the first place from the impulsion toward common action through adherence to the United Nations Charter with the high purposes and principles that it reflects. In this connection, the sense of responsibility is by no means limited to the powerful, rich, or older countries; the middle and smaller Powers are constantly and decisively active in the general effort to achieve the primary purposes of the United Nations. If, for example, one of those primary purposes—the maintenance of peace and security—had compelling significance in the wake of the devastation of World War II, in these years of the threat of conflict involving the extinction of the human race, the significance of this mandate for all governments and their delegations in the General Assembly becomes most urgent. It is the Charter that provides not only the framework of action but the compelling sense of direction for delegations sitting in the Assembly. In the field of substance these powerful guidelines exist, and despite heavy differences on individual issues there are always many delegations serving as catalysts on the issue who will keep the Charter obligations of the Members firmly in the center of the debate. The Charter is a safe and sure compass that provides a sense of direction for the action of the Assembly.

Secondly, in the field of procedure, the Assembly operates in accordance with a set of rules which in the main serve it well. Rules for a parliamentary body are not devised to curb or stultify debate, to prevent discussion, to focus debate into preconceived directions, but are so devised as to provide for the free play of discussion, for the expression of majority and minority views, and for the protection of the individual delegate in the judicious exercise of his right of expression. The same is the case with the rules of business of the Assembly, where, contrary to the position in a national parliament, the rules themselves are often in question and disagreement can be disastrous. The rules are intended not to slow down work but to expedite it, not to be warped in the interest of one group against another but to provide opportunity for free and full debate leading to a decision which is generally taken in the form of a resolution. It is the function of the President to apply and to interpret the rules judiciously in the interest of the whole membership and with a view to achieving timely results. Fairness, equity, and at times a reasonable degree of firmness are qualities expected of the Chair in the application of the rules.

A third factor having the effect of channeling debate into consensus reflected in a resolution is the practice whereby delegations concert their efforts actively to reach such solutions. There are two general classes of such action by delegations. One is operative in the field of political disputes or situations involving clashes between two or more Members of the United Nations. In such a setting it has long since become the practice of other Members acting as third parties to coordinate their efforts in seeking a solution. Such groups in the Assembly have sometimes been known as "fire brigades." They were actively at work and made a decisive contribution in the Suez crisis, in the Lebanon-Jordon crisis, and, although the character of the problem was different, in the case of the Congo. Third-party action was also of great importance in the development of lines of policy in that situation.

Another area in which widespread joint participation by delegations is common relates to such programs as technical assistance and economic development. The original technical assistance program was presented in its general form by the United States delegation some fifteen years ago. It was discussed at length by the Assembly and the great program that emerged was the product of the thinking of the total membership. It therefore started as a program that belonged to everybody, and the continued strength of the program as represented both by technical assistance and by the Special Fund arises in part from this very broad-based initial support.

It is well known that Resolution 1514, adopted during the fifteenth session, embodying the declaration on the granting of independence to colonial countries and peoples, furnished an impetus for the process of decolonization which is still being pursued vigorously through the activities of what has come to be known as the Committee of Twenty-four.

Third-party action in the first category of problems and the almost universal, if not universal, participation in the second category of problems arise from the obligation (indeed the opportunity) that devolves upon individual governments and their delegations. As one delegate put it upon leaving the United Nations:

I regard my experience at the United Nations as the richest in my diplomatic career. Here as Ambassador I wore two hats: one as the representative of my country, expressing and championing its views as necessary in matters of direct concern to it, but also I valued highly the opportunity of wearing the second hat, which was made possible by the ratification by my country of the Charter of the United Nations, placing it under obligations of great importance to the welfare of humanity generally, which I have regarded as my privilege to assist in carrying out.

Most delegates, indeed, have the consciousness of this dual responsibility, this dual opportunity, and it is in this capacity that the embryonic forms of world community can be seen and that the excesses of effervescent nationalism can be moderated.

In contrast with the Councils, the General Assembly consists of representatives of the entire membership, a fact which tends to increase the importance of its role and the frequency of its use. These facts, and in particular the tendency of Members to refer matters to the General Assembly, do not, however, affect, nor have they altered, the constitutional position of the Assembly in relation to other organs.

Even the Uniting for Peace resolution, adopted by the Assembly soon after the beginning of the Korean crisis, kept strictly within the provisions of the Charter with regard to the respective functions of the General Assembly and the Security Council. That resolution provided a mechanism whereby a serious dispute or situation or a threat to the peace could, if the Security Council failed to act, be brought speedily to the attention of the General Assembly. In the 1956 Suez crisis Dag Hammarskjöld was very careful to avoid the pressures which would have given the General Assembly something more of a recommendatory authority in the field of Egyptian acceptance of conditions which were thought necessary for the stationing of the United Nations Emergency Force (UNEF) on its soil. In fact, the very effectiveness of the Assembly flows largely from the respect that its Members and the Secretary-General have for its constitutional limitations and authority, as set forth in the Charter.

This authority is not inconsiderable. At San Francisco the smaller Powers engaged in various and successful efforts to extend the competence of the General Assembly beyond the terms contained in the Dumbarton Oaks Proposals. The competence of the General Assembly was widened particularly in Articles 11, 13, and 14. The last article states that the General Assembly

may recommend measures for the peaceful adjustment of any situation, regardless of origin, which it deems likely to impair the general welfare or friendly relations among nations, including situations resulting from a violation of the provisions of the present Charter setting forth the Purposes and Principles of the United Nations.

Article 13 empowers the General Assembly to

initiate studies and make recommendations for the purpose of: (a) promoting international cooperation in the political field and encouraging the progressive development of international law and its codification;

(b) promoting international cooperation in the economic, social, cultural, educational, and health fields, and assisting in the realization of human rights and fundamental freedoms for all without distinction as to race, sex, language, or religion.

The vastly important field of human rights was thus brought within the realm of discussion and of the recommendatory authority of the General Assembly. This power of the Assembly has often been challenged because of its possible conflict with the domestic jurisdiction clause of the Charter, Article 2 (7), but the Assembly has uniformly asserted its right to proceed with its debates and to act in accordance with Article 13.

It was assumed at San Francisco that, since all Members were to be asked to share equitably in contributing to the budget of the Organization and since this quasi-legislative body was the only organ to have all the Members enjoying representation, the budget of the Organization should be considered and approved by it. This provision of the Charter has been challenged in the last three years and it has been argued that the primary responsibility of the Security Council for the maintenance of peace and security carries with it the right and the obligation of that body to approve the budgets of peace-keeping operations. The Advisory Opinion of the International Court of Justice in 1962 on the interpretation of Article 17, paragraph 2, of the Charter did not adopt that view and the General Assembly in its seventeenth session endorsed that opinion.

Finally, the Charter places the responsibility for the elaboration of principles and regulations determining the organization and general functioning of the Secretariat on the General Assembly.

Each of the three Councils has a slightly different relationship to the General Assembly. Their specific functions are described in the Charter. In the case of the Security Council, which has the primary responsibility under the Charter for the maintenance of peace and security, there is a right of independent action not enjoyed in the same degree by the Trusteeship Council and the Economic and Social Council. Fortunately, however, for the peace of the world, procedures exist for the referring of disputes from one body to the other and for the making of recommendations by the General Assembly to the Security Council. Article 12 provides that while the Security Council is exercising in respect of any dispute or situation the functions assigned to it in the present Charter, the General Assembly shall not make any recommendation with regard to that dispute or situation unless the Security Council so requests.

The spirit of this article has been preserved but not always its letter. Since 1955, in the Palestine dispute, items have been placed on the agenda of the General Assembly, sometimes with a somewhat different wording, while the same general item remains on the agenda of the Security Council.

The Trusteeship Council operates under the authority of the General Assembly and assists the Assembly in carrying out the functions attributed to the Council. Responsibilities in the field of international economic and social cooperation, which belong in the first instance to the General Assembly, are delegated under the authority of the General Assembly to the Economic and Social Council.

The powers of the General Assembly are sometimes also exercised through the establishment of subsidiary organs, a power vested in the Assembly by Article 22 of the Charter. The Assembly has established some fifty subsidiary organs, most of which are *ad hoc* in character, and some of which have existed only for the short time necessary for the fulfillment of the mandate of the subsidiary organ. As in the case of the Security Council, where it is difficult to remove items from the agenda, so it is sometimes difficult to bring subsidiary organs of the Assembly to an end when they are no longer fulfilling a useful purpose. This is, for instance, true of the Interim Committee of the Assembly, the so-called little Assembly, a committee which was not supported by the full membership and never succeeded in developing a useful program of work. As a contrast, another subsidiary organ, UNEF, presumably established for a limited period of time, has continued to serve a useful purpose from 1956 to the present. Still other organs, like the Advisory Committee on Administrative and Budgetary Questions, established at the outset of the Organization, continue to perform important and useful work and deserve to be catalogued in the category of permanent standing committees.

As already stated, the effectiveness of the Assembly flows in no small part from the respect which its Members and the Secretariat have for its constitutional authority. The conclusion of the deliberative process is generally the passage of a resolution. Since the beginning the Assembly has approved nearly 1,900 resolutions. Many of these are routine in character and some deal with administrative detail, but many are of great importance to the effective impact of the United Nations upon world affairs. One need only refer to the resolutions relating to Korea, to Suez, and to the Congo as demonstrating the importance of policy and executive action aimed at bringing these crises under control.

It has been argued that the United Nations has been bypassed too often by member nations and in particular by the great Powers. There may be some measure of truth in this but it is also true that the Members of the United Nations have used its organs and in particular the General Assembly in so many emergencies as almost to overwhelm it. The new nations have looked upon the United Nations as their best protection in a world saturated with Cold War issues and other threats to security. Perhaps some problems that are now brought to the United Nations could be settled by direct action of the parties concerned, but experience shows that the resources for handling problems in the General Assembly and through the Secretariat are such as to foster the practical use of settlement through these channels.

Less dramatic, and therefore inviting less popular attention, is the work of the General Assembly in the economic field, where programs of multilateral action in economic cooperation have been devised and promoted. These efforts of partnership in growth have been making an impact on the lives of the people of scores of member countries far out of proportion to the limited resources expended on them. It is the response of the Organization to the demands of peoples everywhere who wish to raise their standard of living and provide a better opportunity for themselves and their children.

The impact of the Assembly upon the United Nations and world affairs can also be measured by the methods of action available to it. This has reference particularly to the kinds of diplomatic action which are regularly practiced in connection with its deliberations. Without a world organization such as the United Nations, most of the normal contact between and among nations would fall within the framework of bilateral diplomacy. This form of diplomacy, which can be traced back beyond the Roman Empire, was generally limited to the narrow interests of courts, matters of protocol, the rights and privileges of emissaries, rules governing commerce, and sometimes matters relating to peace and war. Whatever may be said of its negative qualities, the sometimes Machiavellian character of bilateral diplomacy, there persists the need of its continued use. For bilateral diplomacy can and does operate within the United Nations alongside multilateral diplomacy, which is the principal instrument of United Nations action. Even in collective discussions and collective efforts in reaching solutions it sometimes becomes necessary for consultation among the minimum number of parties, that is to say, two. There have been many instances in the United Nations when bilateral and multilateral diplomacy have operated helpfully together, sometimes simultaneously, sometimes alternatively. In the field of disarmament direct consultation between the United States and the Soviet Union has sometimes been assisted by group consultations involving several other Members of the United Nations.

The setting and character of the General Assembly lend themselves to public diplomacy as opposed to private diplomacy. Public diplomacy has its merits, but when delicate issues need to be resolved it is also important that it operate in conjunction with private diplomacy. There is a place for quiet corridor or office consultations, the results of which do not see the light of day until they become part of the ultimate solution. Lester B. Pearson, a former President of the United Nations General Assembly, put the matter this way:

> The United Nations is a place where we can meet either to settle problems or to make settlement more difficult. It is a place where we can try to find collective solutions, or one which we can use to get support and publicity for purely national solutions. It is a place where we can talk to each other with a view to securing general agreement, or to television and radio audiences in order to explain that disagreement is the fault of somebody else. . . .
>
> But the United Nations has, or it should have, a private as well as a public face. There should be opportunities here for other than public appearances. . . .
>
> It is, of course, essential that all free peoples should know and understand the great issues of policy which may mean life or death to them. But it is not essential, as I see it—indeed it is often harmful—for the negotiation of policy always to be conducted in glass houses.

Before we deal with the ever-present need for strictly private nego-tiation, it should be noted that in and around the General Assembly is practiced a modern and very special form of diplomacy which has been called "parliamentary diplomacy" (a term first suggested, it is believed, by Mr. Dean Rusk, then Assistant Secretary of State for United Nations affairs in the United States Department of State) and which has been described by Judge Philip Jessup as

the negotiation of solutions of international problems within the frame-work and through the procedures of an organized body acting under estab-lished rules of procedure, such as the General Assembly of the United Nations. The General Assembly, and indeed the whole United Nations complex with its permanent missions and its special committees, are today a part of the normal processes of diplomacy, that is of negotiation.

But there is more to it than that. Parliamentary or conference diplomacy conducted in or around the General Assembly may use-fully be supplemented by more quiet diplomacy within the United Nations, and it is one of Dag Hammarskjöld's outstanding contribu-tions to have insisted as he did that the one should not exclude the other. In his words:

The legislative process in the United Nations is not a substitute for diplomacy. It serves its purpose only when it helps diplomacy to arrive at agreements. . . .
It is diplomacy, not speeches and votes, that continues to have the last word in the process of peace-making.

Indeed, public diplomacy without private diplomacy can easily be-come frozen diplomacy, limiting the capacity of the parties directly concerned to maneuver freely toward a solution.

It would be wrong to take the line that certain forms of diplomacy should be used exclusively on the assumption that other forms belong to an outworn past. It contributes greatly to the strength and effec-tiveness of the General Assembly that all forms of diplomacy are used in their proper place and proper relationship.

Reference has been made to the General Assembly as a magnet drawing many questions to its attention on the initiative of its Mem-bers. There is another aspect of the work of the Assembly which represents a contribution to peace that was hardly anticipated at the time of the San Francisco Conference. An increasing number of top governmental representatives attend the annual session of the General Assembly, particularly in its early stages. Apart from frequent visits by heads of state and government, the opening weeks of the General Assembly session are now marked by the presence of more than seventy foreign ministers out of its total membership of one hundred and thirteen. Many of these foreign ministers participate in the general debate and play an active role in major questions on the agenda of the Assembly. The existence of the Assembly also provides an opportunity, seized by many foreign ministers, to carry on an exchange of views with other foreign ministers on matters outside the agenda. Some of the foreign ministers have stated that as much as 25 to 50 percent of their time is spent on the furthering of interests not related to the agenda but of importance to the direct relationship between their own and other countries. This "extracurricular" activity would not be possible if it were not for the annual sessions of the Assembly, and while the Assembly benefits from their presence, the world generally benefits from this exceptional opportunity that foreign ministers have of exchanging views with each other.

The role of the General Assembly can hardly be understood without reference to the existence at the United Nations of the permanent missions.

It is natural that the permanent and other members of the Security Council, which, under the Charter, "shall be so organized as to be able to function continuously," should be required to be represented at all times at the seat of the Organization. However, the variety of roles assumed by the General Assembly and the multiplicity of the activities conducted in and about it has led all other Member States as well to establish permanent missions in New York, the head of which usually has ambassadorial rank and is assisted by a number of foreign service officers and other civil servants.

The functions of the permanent missions have developed considerably; some of the newer nations find it more convenient to keep in touch with many governments through their permanent missions at United Nations Headquarters. In the absence of diplomatic relations between states and indeed even where such relations may have been severed, these states can engage in informal discussions through their representatives in New York.

Between sessions the permanent missions do much to help implement resolutions of the preceding session and to engage in thorough preparation for the next session. In general they carry the main burden of representation in the sessions of the General Assembly. Without them, sessions of the General Assembly would be much more *ad hoc* in character, far less well prepared, and more lacking in substance and thoroughness than we know them to be. The heads of the missions make up practically all of the personnel participating in the so-called fire brigades in times of crises. They also do more of the sustained and other tedious work in the long-range planning for the launching of major programs of the United Nations.

All in all, over six hundred members of the various diplomatic corps are permanently in New York, thus constituting what Dag Hammarskjöld has called a "standing diplomatic conference."

This results in continuous negotiation on a variety of questions, quite apart from the importance of personal intimacy and understanding among the staffs of these missions, even across substantial political barriers. In the words of Lord Hankey, "Perhaps the most important result of conducting diplomacy by conference is the knowledge responsible statesmen acquire of one another." The close personal contacts and the understandings that develop among the permanent missions facilitate negotiation and the arrival at conclusions on matters under debate.

No evaluation of the General Assembly would be complete without consideration of the role of the Secretariat. The existence of this organ with its chief, the Secretary-General, represents the difference between an Assembly as merely an *ad hoc* conference as opposed to a quasi-legislative body possessing an executive arm capable of carrying its recommendations into effect. In Dag Hammarskjöld's introduction to his last annual report for 1961, he elaborated at length the difference between the conference concept of international organizations and the type of organization provided for in the Charter of the United Nations. The overwhelming majority at San Francisco felt that the Secretary-General should possess adequate powers to serve as the executive arm of the organization and formulated Articles 97–101 in such terms as to provide the basis of an effective and independent Secretariat. While there should be an avoidance, as Dag

Hammarskjöld warned, of excessive dependence on the Secretariat, a proper balance can and should be maintained between the responsibilities of Members for the implementation of resolutions and the utilization of the Secretariat for the staging of important administrative programs or for the taking of diplomatic initiatives when such initiatives can best be undertaken by the Secretary-General. Sometimes, as in the case of the Congo and to a lesser extent in the Suez crisis, an exceptionally heavy responsibility has fallen upon the Secretary-General, not only because of the character of the administrative problems that flow from resolutions, but also because of differences of policy existing among the membership which could be overcome most readily by placing increased responsibility upon the Secretary-General. As in executive posts anywhere, the effectiveness of the office of the Secretary-General is determined not only by Charter authority but by the ability and qualities of the occupant of the post. It is obvious that, if the United Nations is to remain effective in a world where serious problems will emerge unceasingly, the role of the Secretary-General will always be one of great importance, both in administration and in negotiation.

Any consideration of the General Assembly must have regard to its increasing membership, to which some reference has already been made in the course of this lecture. Today the General Assembly Hall in New York is undergoing its largest renovation to take care of the increased membership. Someone has said that some years ago the friends of the United Nations favored universal membership and that now the enemies of the United Nations favor universal membership. The fragmentation of territories and the emergence of new independent nations with membership in the United Nations can, of course, be carried to an extreme, but the enlargement of membership since 1955 demonstrates that some of the fears expressed at that time have not materialized. This is partly due to the influence that the Assembly has upon its Members and the opportunities that it provides for the mutual exchange of views to the benefit of all. In 1960 there was a large influx of new Members; at this time some of the delegates representing the older national communities said in reference to the new African nations: "They will have much to learn from us." This observation at the time seemed quite natural and justified. Representatives of older communities with strong governments and established parliamentary institutions, with well-observed traditions and efficient administrations, would seem to be in a position to transmit much knowledge to representatives of the new nations. Yet in 1964 these same delegates put their experience of contact with the representatives of new governments in a strikingly different form: "We are learning much from each other." This new phrase is as logical and meaningful in 1964 as the other seemed to be in 1960. It demonstrates one of the great values of the United Nations and particularly of the General Assembly. It proves that the General Assembly is a most valuable school for top-level political education in the world today. Each group is learning much from the other. Representatives of older countries have often been saved from error by the long and sustained discussions that they have had with the representatives of the new nations. Mistakes in national foreign policy relating to the new countries have thus been largely avoided and a pattern of sounder relationships between the new and the old nations has been established as a result of the existence of this forum. Representatives of the older nations have discovered vital areas of wisdom and understanding among the leadership of the new countries and have been able through the presence of this leadership to evaluate their own policies and provide the basis of sound relationships.

The representatives of the new nations in turn have learned much from the old and have often merged their skills with the old as members of the third force working toward the solution of general problems on the General Assembly agenda.

In many areas the representatves of the new countries have combined wisdom and moderation; they have contributed much to the teamwork necessary for effective United Nations action. In the case of colonialism, where their concerns are understandable, they continue to press for its final elimination. As the yoke of colonialism disappears they may look to the future with a combination of anxiety and hope but dedicated to the task of building their nations in strength and in peace.

For both old and new Member States of the United Nations, the

DEVELOPING NEW ATTITUDES IN INTERNATIONAL ECONOMIC RELATIONS

Philippe de Seynes

UNITED NATIONS UNDER-SECRETARY FOR
ECONOMIC AND SOCIAL AFFAIRS

Given at the University of Strasbourg, March 18, 1964

I

In the grave and important message which he addressed to the General Assembly shortly before his death, Dag Hammarskjöld shared with Member States his final reflections on the nature and role of the United Nations as he had come to see them in the light of the Congo crisis. It was on the principle of the sovereign equality of all Member States that he based his concept of a dynamic instrument capable of acting on behalf of the weak, as contrasted with the traditional idea of a conference machinery directed solely toward solving conflicts of interest or ideology by means of conciliation.

During the fifteen years that elapsed between the San Francisco Conference and Dag Hammarskjöld's political testament, the principle of equality, proclaimed in the preamble of the Charter as an act of faith in a *higher law,* had gradually revealed some of its more far-reaching implications and, through the deliberations of a universal and virtually permanent forum, was already finding expression in a number of practical imperatives.

Although inspired mainly by the political and constitutional crisis through which the United Nations was passing, Dag Hammarskjöld's message also referred, in eloquent words, to the economic consequences of the principle of equality. This was only natural. Within the United Nations, probably more than anywhere else, economic inequality had manifested itself in a dramatic and tangible manner, against the background of formal equality conferred on all by the right to vote, and, in the full light of the public debates, had emerged as one of the basic determinants of the contemporary world.

Gunnar Myrdal speaks of a class phenomenon and emphasizes its lasting character, pointing out that the group of rich nations and the group of poor nations have remained virtually unchanged in composition for nearly a century, except possibly in the case of the present-day socialist countries which, having started from a precarious middle-class position, are rapidly joining the group of rich countries.

When World War II ended, the phenomenon of inequality was still only sensed, rather than clearly perceived in its consequences. Inequality in existing *situations* was, of course, recognized and, indeed, provided the basis for a certain amount of international action. But inequality of *opportunity,* as a basic and lasting factor accounting for some of the major trends and events, had not found its rightful place in the conventional wisdom of the day. This lack of perception accounts very largely for the setbacks encountered in the efforts to build, on the ruins of the old system, a new international order that would meet present-day requirements. Nowhere perhaps is this gap in postwar thinking more clearly revealed than in the Havana Charter on Trade and Employment and the General Agreement on Tariffs and Trade. It could not be said that the conceptual system prevailing at that time was still imbued with an unshaken faith in the equalizing effects of international trade on the return from the factors of production. Belief in the power of free international trade to ensure by itself an optimum redistribution of resources and maximum capital accumulation was no longer very widely shared. Yet, for lack of a coherent alternative assumption, such presuppositions still seemed to serve as the underlying concepts of the most important postwar documents.

Gradually, a new set of premises, a new intellectual climate, emerged from the mass of statistical data and analytical studies. Emphasis was henceforth placed on structural defects affecting the position of the underdeveloped countries, even when their policies were free of errors and weaknesses. Attention was focused on the difficulties encountered in raising exports to the level required for a politically and socially desirable growth rate and on the relative inelasticity of international demand for primary commodities, particularly its slow expansion compared to the growth of national income in the great industrial countries, as a result of seemingly irreversible factors deriving from both technological advances and changes in consumption patterns of the affluent societies. There came a gradual recognition—for many a revelation—of adverse trends which appear to be lasting, if not secular.

New propositions emerged from these observations; they were expressed in many forms, most prominently, and in some ways most strikingly, in the thesis of the "inevitable deterioration of the terms of trade," based on the unfavorable trend noted in the relationship between the prices of commodities exported by the developing countries and those of manufactured goods imported by them. This price ratio came to assume a preponderant role in contemporary economic thinking. The statistical evidence relating to the phenomenon, in itself impressive, was built in an analysis with strong ideological overtones. Mr. Raul Prebisch and the economists of the Economic Commission for Latin America were prominent in expounding the view that gains in productivity in the commodity sector of the developing countries could not benefit the producers, as they were automatically transferred, in the form of lower prices, to the consumers, that is, essentially to the industrial countries. Such a proposition, in a concise way, epitomizes a permanent and quasi-inexorable process of spoliation and exploitation, with an emotional content of great historical significance.

In this context it is of rather secondary importance that the statistical evidence is often a matter of controversy, that one can endlessly argue about the selection of a reference year, that any extrapolation, based on past trends which may incorporate accidental or temporary factors, is arbitrary, that there may be flaws in the theoretical reasoning, and that, after all, history offers examples of sustained growth taking place despite a deterioration in the terms of trade. What matters is not so much the scientific validity of the thesis as its psychological content and its sociological and political implications.

Moreover, it is evident that if an effort is made to broaden the scope of the analysis and to replace the phenomenon of the terms of trade in a more general context, taking into account all the technological, economic, and sociological factors characteristic of underdevelopment, the resulting outlook will not be very different. Whether attention is focused on the social stratification, the archaic scale of values, the population explosion, the small propensity to save, or the low "technological density," the mind is caught time and again in a maze of problems so formidable that it is not naturally inclined to trust the spontaneous interplay of economic forces. Rather it finds itself in a world of vicious circles, perverse relationships, and asymmetrical situations, which determine a new outlook.

Through such analysis, awareness of inequality in its least acceptable form, that is, inequality of opportunity, is intensified. Daily grievance and frustrations tend to become sublimated in the concept of an iron law which provides the transcendental philosophical element so vital to any movement for redress and reform, and to which the "Third World" already owes some of its early successes.

There are, of course, important correctives mitigating the pessimism inherent in such an intellectual outlook, and providing incentive for hope and action. While still the subject of acute controversy, W. W. Rostow's analysis outlining successive and almost inevitable stages of growth—with its by now classical terminology—uncovers brighter horizons. Disappointments and privations, and even marking time, are more easily accepted if they are viewed as a necessary part of an initial stage, if it is realized that the "take-off" is being prepared and that self-sustained expansion will follow.

Moreover, in some cases, hopes are already confirmed by tangible results. The experience of at least a few countries shows that a systematic development policy based on judicious planning and a vigorous public investment program can succeed in creating an expansionist climate which attracts capital, public and private, domestic and foreign. One need only think of India or Pakistan to see how far we have traveled from the prophecies of doom which were current some fifteen years ago.

Above all, the awakening of a new sense of partnership within the international community, a commitment, still somewhat vague and hesitant, but surely irrevocable, of industrial countries to accept some responsibility for the progress of the "Third World," the resulting actions, individual and collective, undertaken in this spirit—all these elements, still scattered, but generally convergent, are helping to form a perspective in which new nations can hope to pursue their destinies without a violent break and with less danger of upheavals.

Such confidence in at least a minimum of stability is still precarious and constantly threatened. Pessimism may still prevail if hopes placed in adequate international action are not fulfilled. We should listen to Mr. Julius Nyerere, a statesman universally hailed for his moderation and his aversion to violent solutions:

If we have exports for which no one can pay we shall have to go back to barter between ourselves. We shall live and begin to prosper by taking in each other's washing. Through these means we may find that even if we cannot buy exactly what we would like with our produce, at least it does not rot on the ground without any benefit to ourselves or others. Even a completely closed market which is restricted to the poor of the world would be better for us than the present system in which the poor are at the mercy of the rich.

It would be a mistake not to take such statements seriously, to toss them aside lightly as mere rhetoric. In societies which are still in so many ways primitive, enmeshed in a subsistence economy and in the cultural forms which are associated with it, the temptation of introversion and withdrawal is not necessarily a figment of the imagination, and one can only wonder anxiously where it could lead.

II

An economic doctrine for the developing countries is gradually evolving. As always in the history of ideas, it is compounded of many different, and often disparate, fragments: the findings of an imposing mass of statistical and analytical studies, bold simplifications and extrapolations, as well as emotions, aspirations, and frustrations.

Thus equipped with what is a prime prerequisite of any claimant, the "Third World" is beginning to organize in pursuit of its objectives.

Efforts in that direction progress through the Bandung, Cairo, and Belgrade conferences. The United Nations affords them a unique field of operation. In the light of the egalitarian philosophy of the Charter, the special objectives of the "Third World" naturally rise to the level of universal principles. The accession, within a short period, and like a tidal wave, of some seventy new states, all endowed with equal votes, upsets the traditional relationship of forces, still prevailing in other international bodies. To be sure, governments are sufficiently realistic not to take advantage of a majority position for the sake of short-lived victories. They accept the fact that in matters of economic cooperation majority may be the law, but is not necessarily the golden rule. Nevertheless, they are aware of the potentialities of the instrument afforded to them as a center of influence and pressure through which they can hope to affect the major economic decisions on which their future depends. The need for such an instrumentality becomes more urgently felt as a new and formidable center of economic power develops at Brussels, within the European Community, asserting more clearly every day a vocation to organize the world economy along lines which, although they reveal a genuine awareness of global problems, cannot be expected to reflect fully or precisely the requirements of developing countries.

Thus, the very success of the United Nations as an economic institution is inextricably linked to the cause of the "Third World." What was at the outset, notwithstanding the aims proclaimed in the Charter, only a marginal economic institution is gradually transformed into a major one. Its infinitely varied activities, carried on simultaneously in so many directions, show an astonishing capacity to survive failure and to reemerge in new forms. Even though the most ambitious objectives are not attained, the sum total of the by-products gathered along the way is by no means negligible. Efforts to establish a United Nations capital development fund may repeatedly prove unsuccessful, but the unremitting pressure directed toward that end leads to the establishment of the International Development Association within the International Bank for Reconstruction and Development. A plan for international insurance against commodity price fluctuations is rejected after exhaustive study, but the International Monetary Fund decides to increase and systematize its efforts to mitigate the harmful effects of such fluctuations. Furthermore, who can say that the remarkable changes recently evident in both the spirit and the machinery of the General Agreement on Tariffs and Trade (GATT), soon perhaps to be reflected in its statutes as well, owe nothing to the efforts of the United Nations to take hold, in spite of any resistances, of the problems of world trade? A new channel—or circuit—is being established through which gradually all problems are being routed, even those whose consideration was previously reserved for more antiseptic and reassuring forums; a channel characterized by a different combination of forces and a special ideology, one in which new criteria are applied to national policies and through which the world community is constantly confronted with proposals which the major centers of economic decision making cannot indefinitely overlook.

With the decision to convene a United Nations Conference on Trade and Development, this process has made decisive progress and has probably become irreversible. The conference, at first accepted by some as an isolated event which it was best to have over and done with, has virtually developed, within the space of a few months, and even before it met, into a structure whose permanence is scarcely questioned, even though its outlines are still indistinct. The United Nations, as an economic institution, is thereby taking on an added dimension. It is almost a case of what the biologists call mutation.

The event gives a new sense of urgency to the aspirations of the developing countries and stresses the need to organize their interests, which have too often been expressed and promoted in an improvised manner. Efforts to forge a "common front" are being pressed more insistently, with the will to take advantage of all the various resources of a complex institutional machinery. The immediate opportunities thus afforded vary from continent to continent. In Africa, the process is retarded and complicated by the existence of preferential systems and the resulting cleavage between two groups whose immediate interests diverge on important points when specific proposals are considered. In Latin America, however, a measure of homogeneity, a tradition of regional cooperation through long-standing institutions, and the recent efforts toward economic integration create conditions conducive to the formulation of a concrete and detailed common program.

In the global forum of the General Assembly, with the industrial countries present, the sense of the group's special interests tends to be merged and transcended in the broader concept of a world community. Nevertheless, the assertion of "separate" interests is not excluded as part of an over-all strategy. Thus appears a "seventy-five Power resolution" setting out a minimum plan of action in the field of trade, with a sponsorship deliberately limited to the developing countries. Such assertion of "distinctiveness"—which is rare—takes its full significance only in the light of the basic inequality of conditions and opportunities, as it reflects a determination to base a body of international law on the very sense of that inequality.

III

So the context in which the major problems of the world economy are to be tackled has in a way been profoundly transformed. If we are to embark on the long and difficult period of negotiations before us with the best possible chances of success, we must be fully aware of the scope of these changes and the impetus they provide—but also of their limitations.

Basic premises, or assumptions, have been revised, in some cases to the point of an agonizing reappraisal. An institutional system has been developed which has steadily grown in authority and prestige, and has perfected its machinery, so that it is henceforth able to act as a powerful center of pressure and influence.

When it comes to trade, these weapons have still to be tested against the apparatus of economic nationalism, which emerged among modern nations from the major crisis of the interwar period. One should not underestimate the power of resistance of that apparatus; it has grown in strength, effectiveness, and refinement with the requirements of the welfare state, and as the new disciplines of national planning within the modern states tended to confirm rather than counteract the protectionist bias.

It is one thing to admit the existence—and the probable persistence—of structural defects in the world economy and the need for new rules of conduct, to recognize international trade as an instrument of development, and to examine its rules and policies against the background of existing or foreseeable import needs of the developing countries, even to forsake the principle of reciprocity in situations of too great inequality. Such broad propositions find a wide measure of acceptance. But it is a far cry from them to the adoption of workable solutions. Changed circumstances preclude a simple return to classic free trade, and yet the basis necessary for a genuine coordination of national policies has not been built up. So we have to venture on unknown and unsure ground, to explore and exploit to the utmost all opportunities to overcome the power of resistance of nationalism, to make a frontal and undogmatic attack on all problems, taking advantage of all possibilities, whether liberal or *dirigiste,* cutting our coats from every kind of cloth and avoiding doctrinal obstructionism. This poses an obvious challenge to the United Nations, for the mechanism and methods which have so powerfully contributed to the change in attitudes and assumptions are not necessarily those which are best fitted for the more exacting and down-to-earth task of working out and negotiating detailed policies.

IV

Difficulties do not arise just from the need to reconcile entrenched and conflicting interests. Because of the technicalities and intricacies inherent in matters of world trade, there is a need to clarify the concepts even before the battle of interests is joined.

Obscurity and confusion beset in particular the field of primary commodities, where the situation has been allowed to degenerate into complete anarchy. Here the new attitudes and assumptions may even widen the area of perplexity. At times they seem to suggest a trading system in which the chief object would be to transfer income from the richer to the poorer countries through measures incorporating in commercial transactions a more or less disguised element of assistance. To some, the traditional method of opening up markets by the removal of tariffs and other obstacles does not appear as the only, or the most desirable, method. The idea of market organization, derived from national or regional agricultural policies, is the order of the day. The proponents of liberalization clash with the proponents of organization and unfortunately tend to raise their disagreement to the level of a doctrinal dispute, which hampers progress in either direction. Prima facie the organization argument has a great power of attraction: it is more ambitious and appeals to the desire for rationality, which grows strongest in the face of a chaotic situation. It is often identified with formulas that link it to the popular theory of the terms of trade, as proposals are advanced either to correct their deterioration by price manipulation, or, more subtly, to offset it through various kinds of concerted action.

But the organization argument has its own uncertainties: the difficulty of estimating its probable effects on the volume of production or the development of synthetics, its impact on the international distribution of the assistance burden or on the very destination of the subsidies which it conceals, above all the immense administrative complexities inherent in the fixing and control of prices by international decision. The last point has very special consequences, for if the essential cooperation and discipline appeared to be attainable in a limited group more easily than on a world scale, pressure would probably develop in favor of maintaining existing preferential arrangements, at the risk of undermining efforts toward a "common front" of the developing countries.

In any event, great care should be taken lest the promotion of such ideas be allowed to strengthen and perpetuate the slogan "Trade, Not Aid," the success of which was surely premature, to say the least, and hence possibly harmful. Whatever the hopes placed in new trade policies and rules, it should be generally recognized that progress can only be gradual. Financial assistance will remain essential for a long period. During the last decade it became accepted as a new and permanent—at least within the span of present generations—feature of the world economy. It would be regrettable if the exploration of new avenues and, in particular, the interest now being taken in matters of international trade were to imperil this remarkable innovation. International assistance was able to command the support of governments and peoples because it was based on powerful motives —enlightened self-interest or the philanthropic tradition—and because it met certain criteria which public opinion deemed important, namely, proportional distribution of costs among the taxpayers and minimum guarantee of efficient spending thanks to the preparation of easily identifiable projects reflecting the absorptive capacity of recipient countries. These motives and these criteria will probably still afford the best chance of maximizing the assistance effort. In any case, it is not at all certain that a system of subsidies disguised within commercial transactions and switching the burden of assistance from the taxpayer to the consumer could command the same general and continuing support.

It does not follow that present criteria and methods of assistance cannot be further reviewed and diversified. Over-all programs rather than individual projects could be considered to an increasing extent, and the promotion of regional integration could be more directly encouraged. Some rationality could be introduced into the determination of the total amount of assistance and the distribution of its burden, by linking it in some way with the changes in economic trends and in the structure of world demand. In this respect a constructive approach, which might become more generalized, is suggested in the program of aid to diversification embodied in the new Treaty of Association between the European Community and eighteen African states, the objective being to abandon gradually artificial price-fixing and to offset the losses arising from a return to the conditions of world competition by means of an assistance program aimed at financing new lines of production. These are possible and desirable improvements but they do not basically alter the balance and norms of international assistance.

It would be odd, however, if the idea of market organization were to be altogether discarded. The notion in its broadest sense is, so to speak, inherent in the United Nations. But it is perhaps undesirable to identify it too exclusively with the valorization of commodities prices, or to exclude from it measures designed to facilitate access to markets. It would seem on the contrary that guarantees of access, as firm as possible, would be indispensable in any scheme aiming at market organization. One should also beware of simple and uniform formulas of general applicability. Individual primary commodities are affected by very diverse combinations of factors; they have different elasticities of supply and demand; they present technical features which are varyingly adaptable to control; and they are in varying degrees threatened by the invention of raw-material saving techniques and by the development of synthetics. The search for a simple and uniform solution is illusory.

If a simple rule is not feasible, then the idea of market organization could best begin to be realized through a strong institution which could act simultaneously in various directions and promote solutions adapted to each situation. The international machinery that has been gradually built up is at present dispersed among a number of practically independent commodities councils and of committees and study groups attached to three international organizations. It lacks a comprehensive and global outlook and some measure of central direction which could work for continuing and purposive action directed toward the growth of developing countries and which could gradually raise commodities policies above their present level of mere bargaining. Such central direction could probably best be vested in a council of independent experts, which would not be endowed with any supranational power of decision making, but whose high prestige and knowledge would lend influence to their findings and recommendations. A body of this kind could effectively press for the negotiation of multilateral agreements whenever they are possible. It could help in shaping them in the most effective way, with executive organs empowered to adjust export quotas and prices according to the variations in supply and demand, thus avoiding any prolonged freezing of the competitive situations existing at a given time. It could strengthen the existing machinery for confrontation and coordination, where contractual obligations are not feasible. It could warn of the dangers inherent in certain policies, work out and formulate recommendations for rational solutions on a world-wide scale which would be difficult to ignore indefinitely. It could see to it that the various actions undertaken be, as much as possible, synchronized—between themselves, and also with discussions on industrial tariffs—so that they become mutually supporting and afford to each participant the best opportunities for mutual concessions and for a profitable package deal.

Such machinery and practices are perhaps no longer out of reach today. For more than thirty years, after all, the world has been attempting to regulate trade in raw materials, and public opinion on the subject has already undergone a certain amount of conditioning which should facilitate further progress.

V

In many ways the solutions postulated by the new attitudes and assumptions can realistically be defined only in terms of gradual action, phased over a period of years and providing for transitional steps as precisely worked out as possible. The international community has as yet no experience of such a long-term program on a world-wide basis, although experiences carried out in more narrow geographical areas can serve as useful precedents.

The gradual, but planned, approach would seem relevant to any attempt at facilitating exports in manufactures from the developing countries. Given the rigidities now universally recognized in the trade in primary products, it seems indispensable for these countries to gain a significant share of the markets of those manufactures for which they enjoy comparative cost advantages. Only the long-term view will provide the necessary incentive, for the matter is of immediate concern to a small number of countries only. And yet, considering the resistance which must be expected, an immediate start should be made, if appropriate measures are to be in operation by the time a large number of countries will be affected. The prospective view, rather than the current situation, is of the essence. For industrialization in new countries is taking place; and every day investment decisions are made in the narrow framework of an import substitution policy, within closely protected national markets, and at costs which are sometimes clearly uneconomic. The system of international trade, in its present shape, does not offer a perspective in which developing nations, laboring under the handicap of a late start in industrial competition, can hope to emulate the example of Switzerland or Sweden, which, despite meager natural resources, were able, thanks to an open world market, to specialize in certain lines of production and acquire in some of them indisputable supremacy.

A readiness to weigh long-term advantages against short-term costs, and a conviction that the prospects must be changed quickly, may remove hesitations in subscribing to the principle of "one-way free trade," whereby developing countries would be granted access to the large industrial markets, while retaining full freedom to protect their nascent enterprises. But how far are the advanced nations prepared to limit the practical scope of concepts such as "unfair competition" and "market disruption," which at present obstruct the functioning of the large commercial centers, and may well discourage the vigorous efforts which an export policy would require even in more favorable circumstances? Assuming this can be solved satisfactorily, another problem arises. How many commodities would profit by the mere removal of customs barriers? If the list of exports from developing countries is to be gradually expanded, one is led to conceive of a system of preferences in their favor. Here the controversy becomes much more crucial, for a major principle, that of the most-favored-nation clause, is at stake. Whether action is suggested under the concept of a "double standard," or more simply as a "tolerable deviation" from a doctrine whose integrity is not contested, it is not easy to condone major departure from a precept which still plays an essential part in the expansion of world trade, particularly when such departure relates to situations which are likely to be of some duration. Even when the principle no longer shocks, the formulas for putting it into practice have still to be debated. There are many possible alternatives, and their various implications are by no means clearly perceived in all their details. The idea captured the imagination much before its technical aspects had been thoroughly investigated.

VI

Whatever the steps agreed upon, whether selective tariff reductions, general or limited preferences, their impact will inevitably be measured in quantitative terms.

This in itself has rather far-reaching implications and reveals an important aspect of the transformation which is taking place in the approach to the problems of the world economy. Fifteen years ago the Havana Conference was concerned essentially with the establishment of a legal framework and of administrative rules designed to ensure the stability and security needed in international trade. Today the rules have lost none of their importance and are subjected to the test of rigorous reappraisal in the light of recent experience and present-day reality. But rules are no longer enough. The burning question is: How can we, through individual or collective action, close the chronic and probably growing external deficit of the developing countries? When the problem is so stated it is no longer possible to take refuge in the generalities that characterized the most important postwar documents. The rigor and objectivity of quantification are with us, and we cannot escape them in our efforts to improve our programs and policies. Already the enormous work of quantitative analysis undertaken has greatly helped in presenting a vivid and clear picture of certain trends, in giving a realistic measurement of the consequences of the policies advocated. This has served in some cases to heighten the sense of alarm and urgency, in others to remove the apprehensions which some proposals had generated. A serious effort will from now on be made to express commitments in arithmetical terms, such as desirable quantities or ratios of imports of foodstuffs or manufactures.

Moreover, we must also learn to live with a prospective view of the world economy, defined in quantitative terms and presented as a coherent system of interrelationship. The techniques of modern democratic planning are weaving themselves imperceptibly into the fabric of international life. Even when we observe that, applied to the world economy, they will have still less binding force than they have gained in the field of national policies, they do nevertheless introduce an innovation which requires an adaptation of our methods of work.

Global targets have already been proclaimed: for the growth of the underdeveloped countries, a rate of 5 per cent in 1970; for financial assistance, a minimum of 1 percent of the national product of the industrial countries. These objectives were postulated, perhaps imprudently, before a frame of reference had been worked out which would have made it possible to assess all their implications and to deduce from them practical recommendations in various sectors. But the very logic of the step taken now prompts us to develop habits of consultation and negotiation—in short, a new international discipline —without which the targets could quickly become embarrassing, or perfunctory. In the light of the more up-to-date preoccupations of the United Nations and given the stimulus to be expected from the Conference on Trade and Development, it is logical that the prospective view designed to guide international action should be focused on the trade gap of the underdeveloped countries, one of the strategic parameters of growth, and the one for which the international community assumes special responsibility.

This task needs to be approached with extreme caution. It is not a purely technical matter which could be left to experts—although the methodological problems are paramount. Definitions themselves and the choice of a methodology are almost political acts, inasmuch as they must be assured of a wide measure of acceptability; otherwise, the exercise would remain academic. But if we can give of the trade gap and of its probable evolution a series of alternative evaluations generally accepted and regarded as useful guides—and if we do not forget that human reality is always more flexible than mathematical models—then we will begin to consider financial assistance, trade, and economic growth in an all-embracing perspective from which could emerge a comprehensive fiscal and economic policy of the world community.

VII

However prudent and realistic we may be, we are beginning to speak of "planning on a world-wide scale" and little by little we are less fearful of using such language. It is fitting at this point also to recall President Nyerere's warning that "the economies of the underdeveloped countries cannot safely venture into the stormy ocean of unplanned international marketing until they are like ocean-going craft."

These things are sensed, more or less vividly, more or less clearly, depending on the place and the environment in which the problems are aired. Because the sense of urgency and drama is perhaps greater in the United Nations than anywhere else, it is there that a real partnership of interests and aspirations between the rich and the poor nations is most likely to emerge. Dag Hammarskjöld had perceived the importance that the Organization could assume, in a period of great and rapid changes, for the new and the weak nations. His boldness and his acute vision contributed much to the initial, and still fragmentary, elaboration of a system of collective security for these nations and by these nations. He was convinced that the Organization had no less pressing responsibilities toward these same nations in their struggle for economic progress. With a situation currently more fluid and perhaps also in many respects more promising than it has hitherto been, the coming years should enable us to translate into reality some of the lessons that he bequeathed to us.

THE UNITED NATIONS
AND THE
DECADE OF DEVELOPMENT

Barbara Ward

AUTHOR AND ECONOMIST

Given at Columbia University, April 2, 1964

It is a very, very great honor to be invited to speak in this series. I did indeed have the greatest possible respect and affection for Dag Hammarskjöld—above all, I think, for the fact that he was a man of the next generation. He truly belonged to the whole world. He had passed beyond so many of our local, tribal differences. He was a man for all seasons, too—for the spring of hope, for the winter of endurance. I do not think anyone, looking back on the enormous contribution he made in such a relatively short time to the concept of a genuine world society, can ever feel that his work will be wasted, or that in any sense he lived in vain. All of us who knew him had the feeling that he was pointing the way forward for all humanity and that it is the way which we must never, can never abandon.

However, having said so much, we must also admit that the world we live in now is an incredibly difficult one to bring together in any kind of harmonious community. The fault is not entirely ours. It lies in part with the kind of age this is. It is an age in which science and technology are all the time speeding up the changes that tend to swamp social order. We cannot modify the trend. Science operates from the known to the unknown and therefore the more that is known, the more points of vantage there are for attacking the unknown. Thus there is an innate tendency for the rate of change to accelerate and for the Niagara of new techniques and technologies and consequent social changes to pour down on us in an ever-increasing flood.

This, in itself, makes creative adaptation difficult. We are always having to adapt to things which are already being readapted as we act. But this is not all. Many of the changes that are occurring are not self-regulating. If anything, they are contradictory. There seems no innate tendency in our society at the moment to get itself back to any kind of equilibrium. It follows that a policy of drift will not restore us to a functioning world order. In fact, we face the certainty of rising contradictions unless we bring to bear on the consequences of our protean science and our developing technology an element of moral judgment, rational decision, and common policy.

We are not accustomed to this notion. We in the West have a long tradition of laissez faire and belief in the "hidden hand." It is not only in nursery tales that a great many things are supposed to go right so long as you leave them until morning or put them away in a drawer. Micawberism is not unknown among us and its temptations sometimes grow stronger as the difficulties grow more complex. But we must resist such blandishments and look sternly at the number of developments which in our world lead not to harmony but to contradiction.

Let us begin with perhaps the most startling change of all—the development of medicine. Understood in the broadest sense, to include public health and preventive as well as curative services, it is leading to an enormous increase in population. The world now adds in ten years the population that used to take a hundred years to grow. In this present "Decade of Development"—the sixties—half a billion people will be added to the world's population. And they will mainly be added in lands that are still very poor.

This spurt in population cuts right across the poorer lands' need to save. Saving, after all, is not consuming. When one lives on $60 a year, not consuming is something of a problem. Not consuming on too drastic a scale simply becomes not living. Few people would accept this as practical politics, so even before the appearance of any spurt in population, saving is a real problem. Add half a billion new mouths, all hungry, and it becomes more formidable still.

Yet the only hope of getting ahead of the growth in population implies large investment in new productive technologies in farms and factories—technologies which make possible much greater output. The trouble is that all such changes are fiendishly expensive. Think of all the developments that are involved in a modernized economy, from education and training of every kind to farms transformed by modern methods, to new factories, to new research units, to every kind of new material and resource; it is not surprising that all this new apparatus will absorb at least 15 to 20 percent of national income. But if national income is no more than $60 a head, 20 percent for saving is so formidable a percentage that it is not reached. So the productive technology necessary to get ahead of the growing need for more consumption is not acquired. Thus we find a built-in contradiction between a spurt of growth in population due to the new medicine and the need for capital which would enable society to cope with the growth.

Meanwhile—another contradiction—technology itself is growing more and more complex and hence more and more unsuited to the needs of simple economies. Some of the key elements in a modern industrial system, such as a steel mill, say, or a refinery, cost literally millions and millions of dollars worth of capital, but give employment to relatively few. The refinery, for example, being built at Port Harcourt in Nigeria will cost 33.6 million dollars and will employ only 300 people.

In most poor societies, the rapid growth of population implies a large and growing number of relatively unskilled workers, yet most of the new technologies that are being evolved today are capital-intensive. In other words, they require a lot of capital and give very few jobs— and most of these, skilled jobs. The divide between modern technology and the simple technological needs of the nations who are being left behind is steadily widening and becomes more difficult to cross.

One can see these contradictions even more vividly at work in the critical area of world trade. In the nineteenth century there was a certain comfortable circuit underlying international trade which did much, I feel, to make people believe that the system was safely self-regulating. Laissez faire can always be relied on, provided the trade circuits close in a tidy way and do not lead on to intensifying contradictions. In the nineteenth century, the circuits worked. At the center of the system was Britain, pioneer in the new arts of manufacturing. And as somebody once said of Britain: "It is a cozy little island. It is built on coal and surrounded by fish. But otherwise it is largely without resources." I suppose they might have added the Scots whom the British used extensively—until they took over. Yet Britain is not a very richly endowed island. So what was the result? As one of the first reactions to the Industrial Revolution, Britain had to thrust out overseas in search of raw materials and foodstuffs, in search of fresh areas for capital investment. There was probably no time in the mid-nineteenth century when it was not possible to find in other continents British railways being built by Scots engineers. The need to extend the system was inherent in the situation.

As a result, a very comfortable, cycle of trade began to develop on the basis of Britain's need to buy raw materials and food supplies from overseas, balanced by the ability to sell back, thanks to the British lead in technology, an increasing range of manufactures. This system gave a balance to world trade; it led, on the whole, to a fairly simple procedure for settling international debts. Since there never was any shortage of sterling, most of the debts that had to be paid in gold were marginal debts. Incidentally, gold supplies were also being replenished by new discoveries in Australia and California and South Africa. Although the world lived on the gold standard, it really had no gold problem.

However, in this century the old beautiful automatic balance has been upset. The first reason for the change is the movement of the United States to the center of world trade. The United States is that uncomfortable object, a continent that produces nearly everything it wants and can export nearly everything as well. We think of America as an industrial giant. But think of all those frozen chickens, constantly flying the Atlantic and coming home to roost. There are very few things America cannot export. In fact, it exports rather more raw materials than manufactures. The easy automatic nineteenth-century balance between exporting manufactures and importing primary products has been fatally breached.

In addition to this, a profound change in technology has also come in to affect the balance. Owing to far greater refinements in productive methods, there is much less waste in manufacture. The rate of beneficiation is much higher. I admit that sometimes, when people talk about waste in Washington, it is hard to believe that we are getting more value out of our raw materials. But this is the case; so, for any given expansion of production, we need less of them. This trend is reinforced by the remarkable development of the chemical industry. The new use of substitutes is such that the dependence of the developed industrial nations on outside suppliers of raw materials has gone sharply down. This relatively greater independence is one of the factors in the postwar tendency of raw material prices (which make up the main export incomes of developing countries) to remain, despite occasional rallies, relatively depressed.

Thus technology, as it expands, as it develops, as it changes, as it becomes more sophisticated, has once again failed to introduce new elements of balance into the world. On the contrary, it is increasing the imbalance between rich nations and poor nations, between those who have already crossed the threshold of modernization, who control a full apparatus of modern production, and who constantly increase their resources, and the others whose path toward full-scale modernization is now in fact much more difficult than it was in the nineteenth century. No one planned such a contradiction. It is simply inherent in the way in which in recent years science and technology are changing our methods of production.

It is possible that the poor nations are not the only ones to find their economic life complicated by the fact that twentieth-century technology and trade do not automatically stimulate new growth in overseas markets. The developed nations, too, may ultimately run into trouble. If the gap steadily increases between wealthy nations who can produce and poor nations who, because they do not yet produce, cannot consume, may not the developed world run into an increasing problem of surpluses? I doubt whether we have really measured the scale of our potential surpluses yet. The American farmer has shown the way. But wait until the European farmer follows suit. The air will then be positively dark with the wings of roosting chickens. Nor shall we stop at chickens. What about milk? I am told that in upper New York State every cow is attached to a computer at Cornell University by electronic devices, and through these electronic devices the butterfat content and whatever else is measured in cow's milk are systematically checked, and if the experts at Cornell notice a slight decline in volume or content they ring up the farmer and say: "Hey, George, put a little more protein and some bone meal and just a touch of tungsten into your cow." Then up goes the supply again. In fact, the farmers can get such output from these cows that they have enough milk to pour into the highways of upper New York State.

Meanwhile, the same glut has appeared on the European horizon and lies at the root of most of the vexed agricultural interests at stake in present tariff negotiations between America and Europe. We have already seen tourist roads in France strewn with surplus fruit and vegetables in the summer. I shudder to think what would happen to the tourist trade if they began covering the roads with butter—the accident rate is high enough as it is. Nor is Europe the only possibility. The tropical world is coming up behind. I have visited a number of research stations in Africa, and they can already make twenty bananas grow where one grew before; perhaps a Niagara of wheat is just conceivable, but a Niagara of bananas makes the imagination boggle. Actually, we are living on the verge of such a flood of supply that our satisfied, technologically unimprovable Western stomachs simply cannot hope to consume enough.

In fact, may not the gluts extend beyond the farm? What will the computer revolution do to us? What enormous new surge of productivity lies ahead? Within twenty years we may be able to use nuclear reactors and desalinized water to irrigate all the parched areas of the United States—or anywhere else. And when the nuclear reactors develop to the point at which, in the process of making power, they do not lose power, we shall presumably have solved the energy problem too. And I am told that such developments are not far out of the reach of our new technology.

What is *not* happening—again the contradiction—is any comparable, automatic stimulus to new markets and new demands. The surging growth of the Atlantic Powers is not bringing up the remaining two thirds of the world in its wake. We cannot even bring Appalachia along. Automation applied there to the coal industry without thought of its effect on the local miners enriches one group—the still employed miners and management and perhaps the consumer—at the price of ruin for the men thrown out of work. Similarly, increased productivity in the Atlantic world does not automatically raise standards elsewhere. How long can we continue to increase the supplies available to the rich while neglecting the deepening ruin of the poor? We have to see that for the first time in human history supplies are not the problem. I doubt if we begin to know how lavish supplies can be.

There is the familiar tale of the scientist who said: "We don't really have to bother about resources in the future because a hundred years from now we'll just have to lean down, pick up a piece of earth, put it into a little nuclear reactor, and out it will come as any shape or thing we want. We're used to the idea of margarine coming from coal. But we ain't seen nothing yet." Then he stopped and added: "I do have one anxiety; will anyone be able to lean down, given the pressure of population?"

But while our technology pours out this new possibility of abundance, I wonder whether we may not slip into the dilemmas of the Sorcerer's Apprentice? Our abundance may overwhelm us unless we keep the expansion and maintenance of demand in pace with the fabulous expansion of supply. Technology and science automatically increase the means of abundance but it takes social purpose and political skill to adapt our institutions to the change. There is nothing automatic in the process of reaching this balance—between supply and demand, between abundance and need, between rich and poor. On the contrary, the natural pressures—"To him who hath shall be given"—are all the other way. If we continue the policies we are pursuing now, we shall not bring up a vast increase in demand in the wake of our vast increase in supply. In fact, we are moving in the opposite direction. We are likely to see a small, rich, white group, composed of the 20 percent of the human race who live around the North Atlantic, getting steadily richer, while on two thirds of the human race the pressures of poverty, the pressures of suppressed ambition, the pressures of sheer anger at the disproportions and injustices of this world will become more and more pressing and more and more inescapable.

At this point, we must remember another set of contradictory changes that are brought about by our inescapable technology. All those angry people are coming nearer to us all the time. They may grow more and more alienated in feeling; in physical proximity, they are becoming daily more like neighbors. All the time our universe shrinks. Only twenty years ago, it took twenty-one hours to trundle across the Atlantic. Now it can be done in six hours. The supersonic planes are off the drawing boards and they will do it in two and a half, so that one can arrive before having left. Then comes the day when they put us in rocket sardine-tins and shoot us. And then it will be, I suppose, a 30-second trajectory.

The point is that this process will accelerate. We are inescapably destined to live nearer still to each other. We shall be nearer, too, in ideas and shared experience. In some ways, we are already rather like a village. Last summer my husband was in Delhi, then he was in Bangkok and then Pnom Penh, and he came back by way of Ghana. When he got home, I said: "Tell me about the trip. How's development coming along? What did you talk about?"

"Talk about? We talked about Christine Keeler."

Village gossip is already going round and round the world. With Telstar the village can be seen, too—possibly at times some surprising things will be seen. Meanwhile, the instantaneousness of human communication, and therefore of human experience, is bound to increase.

Last of all—perhaps in every sense—there hangs over us the risk of instant, total annihilation from the hydrogen bomb. As I have often said, if a person is not a neighbor when a man can lob a bomb into his backyard, I do not know when he is one.

The world is a physical neighborhood which is growing ever closer. And at the same time social and economic contradictions are driving the world further apart. Unless this paradox is understood, and really accepted not as fantasy but as fact, we may well face in the next decade or so a series of explosive social situations which will resemble the French Revolution, the Russian Revolution, and the Chinese Revolution rolled into one. Surely one of the inescapable lessons of modern history is that in the long run a small, immensely privileged minority cannot be confronted with a large, increasingly restive and angry majority without something giving.

In the past we have been insulated by oceans, by mountains, by distances; they are all ceasing to be barriers. Now communication is instantaneous, proximity is total, we are completely involved in a world society which is physically one yet socially, morally, and economically tending to greater divisions. This is, I suggest, the fundamental reality of politics today and we shall only begin to make sense if we accept it.

Sometimes, of course, when one talks of these facts, self-styled realists say that it is all an evasion of reality, and that the only basis of realism in politics is the independence of the sovereign nation-state. I confess I no longer follow the argument. We have not planned a physically unified planet for our pleasure. The proximity is inescapably imposed by modern science and technology. Surely realism must bear some relation to reality. I am reminded of the occasion when Thomas Carlyle was sitting at dinner next to a fine, able girl called Margaret Fuller. He was holding forth as he usually did, and he made some provocative remark. So she swept her great eyes up at him and said: "But, Mr. Carlyle, I accept the universe."

"By God, ma'am," he said, "you better had."

It is, I confess, my feeling that it is the course of wisdom to accept what is as the basis for policy.

What, then, are we going to do about it? I would like to suggest that of all the policies that are being considered these days, one of the most interesting, most encouraging, most forgotten, and most misunderstood is probably the United Nations Decade of Development which was launched very bravely in 1961 and has almost sunk without trace in 1964—as far as popular esteem is concerned. If one looks at the kind of objectives that the Decade of Development has set itself, one will see that it is more relevant to the facts of our divided world than nearly any other policy that is being pursued anywhere today. And the reasons for this are multiple.

The first is that it is a genuine attempt to bring underdeveloped and developed together to do something constructive. It is not a donor-recipient or a rich-poor relationship. It is a question of us, the people of the world, trying to do something for us, the people of the world. It provides just about the only framework within which at the moment such cooperation can take place. It represents all of us. It accepts the solidarity of the human experiment. It accepts the moral and social implications of the physical proximity in which we all live. So this is its first advantage: it really does accept the kind of underlying unity which, physically, is already here.

Secondly, it attempts to give a focus to the joint effort. It is not just a general plan to do something about something. It is an attempt to accomplish aims that are specific. It begins by establishing the rate of growth developing nations need to keep ahead of their growth of population and to achieve a small surplus for further saving. A minimum 5 percent of growth allows for a 3 percent increase in population and a modest 2 percent for investment in the whole apparatus of modernization—in education, in farming, in industrial development —which is needed to take a community over the threshold into the modern economy in which self-sustaining growth becomes possible.

I believe, in fact, that the point at which the full apparatus of modernity is achieved is the real divide between developing and developed countries. In the poor countries, supply or shortage is still the problem, because the full apparatus of production has yet to be built. But within a relatively short time of getting over the threshold and achieving the apparatus, demand becomes the problem because the machines—and the farmers—will always tend to out-produce the expected level. This problem of demand, of course, has all manner of sophisticated overtones—demand for what, at what price, with or without inflation? Yet clearly the need to cope with the embarrassments of plenty and devise enough demand to keep up with it is a much more agreeable human situation than to struggle desperately with shortages and unfillable gaps. We have constantly to remind ourselves that it is cozier to be rich than to be poor.

To go back to the specific aims of the Decade of Development, it is estimated that, to secure this 5 percent rate of growth, the imports needed by the developing nations by 1970 will be of the order of 20 billion dollars a year. Probably some 9 to 10 billion dollars will be earned by increased exports. This assumes some increase in Atlantic purchases as Western economies expand. It also presupposes that the developing countries can recapture the modest 2 percent in world trade which they have lost since the mid-fifties and bring their share back to 28 percent.

These calculations leave a gap of some 10 billion dollars a year still to be filled, but this figure is about one percent of the combined national incomes the developed Powers can hope to earn over the next few years; and if they were prepared to "normalize" their transfers of grants, loans, and credits generally to the developing world at that level, the resources would be more or less available for the kind of productive investment that will make a 5 percent rate of growth possible among the developing nations.

Thus, the Decade of Development is not a sort of "let's do good to everybody" program. It has its aims, its calculations, its frame of reference, and a number of specific goals.

The next great advantage of the Decade of Development is that it does not expect world poverty to be conquered by any one single nostrum. In its scope, its layout, and its strategy, it assumes that the problem has to be attacked from many different sides simultaneously. One of the first steps is to look at the pre-investment problem. This is the particular responsibility of the United Nations Special Fund, using as its agents all the specialized agencies, such as the Food and Agriculture Organization, UNESCO, the World Health Organization, and others.

The basic idea behind pre-investment is very simple. It is that in nearly every country, however poor, a very large part of its local resources, either physical resources or human resources, are not yet used. Even when the outlook for local resources looks rather unpromising, we have to remember that most nations have quite large reserves of their own, if only they can mobilize them. For example, after a recent survey made by a group of scientists, the estimate was made that in the developing world not more than 25 to 30 percent of the resources of earth, water, and potential power are utilized. For manpower, the percentage is even lower. Perhaps not more than 10 percent of the basic intelligence of the people is trained enough to permit them to be drawn into the modern economy.

The basic idea of a pre-investment program is, first of all, to find out what the physical resources are. Water surveys have to be made and mineral surveys and, perhaps most vital of all, soil surveys. If I may digress, I wish there were some way of making the children of the world excited about soil surveys. I have sometimes thought that if we could only arrange it, all school dropouts should spend two nights up with the astronauts. (It ought to be possible to arrange this quite soon. We may have to spend a lot more on space if we are to solve our demand problem. So why not numbers of small spaceships for school dropouts?) Up they go. Then they look down and what would they see? They would see a little planet, floating in infinite space, and on it they would see the thin little envelope of earth on which the entire nourishment of our planet depends. And around it they would see another tiny envelope—the envelope of atmosphere—upon which all breathing life depends. Then perhaps they would find our narrow home a little more precious than they do today. We might send up some governments, too. It might help. And one or two governments need not come back, so far as I am concerned.

This picture of one tiny planet in the infinity of the universe—yet, to our knowledge so far, the only planet on which sentient life can exist—such a picture would perhaps make the earth valuable and unique in a way which just reading about it cannot do. If the children could see it, see how small it is, how vulnerable, then the idea of blowing it up would become the ultimate sacrilege. Perhaps generations would grow up thinking about war the way people think about incest—as something that outrages the moral will of God and man.

Now to go back to soil surveys. They are particularly necessary before anyone undertakes large agricultural programs. The classical example, of course, was produced by the British—the groundnuts fiasco. The groundnuts scheme cost £30 millions and Britain did not even get one groundnut. The reason was very simple. Nobody had found out if the soil was suitable for groundnuts. And no one had found out if heavy tractors might not turn the poor laterite into a very good imitation of brick. The heavy tractors did, and so Britain spent £30 millions on a project which a survey costing perhaps half a million pounds would have proved useless in advance.

But perhaps it is when combinations of soil and water are in question that the worst mistakes are made, unless proper preliminary studies are undertaken. What can happen if irrigation is launched without a soil survey beggars description. Seas of unusable mud can be produced, or if there is no proper control of soil and water use, major schemes can be lost because of rising salinity or because erosion is silting up the dams. Soil surveys enable us to develop a proper respect for the living physical envelope of the world and to avoid the costly mistakes that can occur when enormous dam sites are developed, concrete monsters are built, and everyone has a tremendous time cutting ribbons and banging drums. But since nobody has bothered to anchor the soil by planting little trees round the top of the watershed, thirty years later there is no dam because it has been silted up. It is precisely this kind of error that pre-investment surveys are designed to check. Instead, they give each country a sort of physical map of where they are and of where they can go and how they can make the best use of their resources—all their physical resources—as they go along.

The human element is even more important. Before it can begin to develop, a country must have some strategy to produce the key skills that are needed. Possibly as much as 60 percent of development comes not from capital but from trained intelligence, the trained intelligence of the managerial type, the honesty and steadfast dedication of the civil servant, the professional capacity of doctors, lawyers, and engineers, and then the skills at intermediate levels—young technicians who can help the fully trained engineers, the nurses and medical orderlies who help the doctors—and, at every level, the teachers, on whose work all else depends. These are the people who will make all the difference between the use and misuse of funds. In fact, I think that one of the reasons why over the last ten or fifteen years a great deal of money has been wasted has not always been because it has been diverted to political or trivial ends—the dancing girls and the elephants. Waste has come, too, because there were not yet enough competent officials to spend it and not enough basic information about where it could best be spent. In other words, there had not been enough pre-investment in men and in research.

Pre-investment is thus an essential preliminary—but it still chiefly provides the recipe for the development cooks. How they cook the meal depends upon securing all the raw materials, home-grown and exotic, on the one hand, and upon a strategy for the whole banquet and for each course, on the other hand. Strategy—the country plan —is coming to be recognized as an indispensable method of establishing priorities and of deciding what to leave out. This is a matter in the main for each country and each government, though many micro-countries, as in Central America, are sensibly deciding to plan to-gether with their neighbors. There are few generalizations that can be usefully offered to cover all possible types of country or resource, save, perhaps, the plea that investment in argriculture should not be neglected and that industrial projects—public or private—should be tested for profitability and not regarded as expensive monuments to national grandeur.

But whatever the content of particular country plans, two points seem to hold good for all. There are not enough development planners or strategists available today for all the work that needs to be done. The World Bank is working on this problem. So are a number of universities, notably Harvard. But more training in this field is urgently needed.

The second point is the added effectiveness of outside aid if it is coordinated through a country plan and all donors accept its disci-plines. In the case of a variety of donor-governments, their assistance is likely to go further and do more if it is given, as Indian aid is given, through a consortium under the chairmanship of the World Bank. Such procedures also help to keep the laggards among the wealthy governments under the critical eye of their peers.

The next point to notice about the Decade of Development, is that, for the first time, aid and trade are being considered together. The United Nations conference on trade and development at Geneva is the first attempt to bring home to the entire world society just what has been happening in trade. Let us briefly look at it. I covered some of the field when I referred earlier to technological contradictions and men-tioned that the use of substitutes and the enormous productivity of developed societies have reduced their need to buy raw materials abroad. But this is only one part of the problem. In addition to the tendency of raw material prices to remain depressed, other factors all cumulatively discriminate against the trade of developing coun-tries.

For instance, the tariff structures of the developed world are de-signed to prevent local processing and local manufacturing in the developing world. In every case, the lowest tariffs, or zero tariffs, are imposed on raw materials. As soon as those raw materials are worked up a little locally, up go the tariffs. And if by chance local industry develops so far that it can produce manufactures, then the tariffs rise further still, and if tariff barriers are still insufficient, on go the quotas.

Thus, by a series of steps, which begin with the depressed condition of the many primary prices and go on through discriminatory structures up to the quota system, international trade is, as it were, always biased toward the interests of those who are already rich, and biased against the interests of those who are really poor.

There are further examples of this tendency. How often is it realized that nearly all the middleman services in world trade are run by members of rich nations? Whether it is insurance, brokerage, shipping conferences, organized markets—nearly all the intermediate earnings in international trade go back to the developed world.

It is, of course, one of the laws of unregulated economics that if a person is well off already, he is likely to grow more so. As somebody said—apropos, I believe, of Senator Goldwater—"the very best recipe for a fine, upstanding life, without slavish dependence upon Big Government, is to be born intelligent, lively, able, and to inherit a department store." In nations, as in families, it is simply good luck to be born into the wealthier groups. The danger is to take the good fortune for granted. Wealthy Western nations do take for granted a wide range of built-in advantages in the field of trade and do not realize how much of the gain from this trade is siphoned off from the poor to the rich. Now, at the United Nations conference at Geneva, these problems are being put, for the first time, into a development context. The wealthy nations are learning the degree of discrimination from which they have profited and its effect on poorer communities' hopes of being able to get their own development started.

To offset the trend, a number of possible solutions are being put forward: one-way free trade for tropical products; the revision of tariff structures, so that local manufacture is actually encouraged; permission to have infant-industry protection in developing countries. More ambitious steps, for example, tariff-free entry or preferential entry for some manufactured goods into Western markets, are also under discussion—although some governments are understandably uncertain about the trade-diverting effects of elaborate preferences. But one may hope that this legitimate concern will not be used as a cloak to cover a wider unwillingness to accept manufactures from developing countries. After all, developed nations gain from cheap goods, especially when inflation is one of their nightmares. Moreover, they have no long-term interest in bolstering up uncompetitive industries at home. In a recent survey, it was pointed out that, in the 14 major exporting industries of America, wages and profits ran at a level about 50 percent above the returns earned in 14 other industries coming under strong competition from cheap imports. In fact, any country that can switch from the kind of industry which is threatened by cheap imports to the kind of industries which are exporting briskly has, by that fact alone, made a step forward in its own standard of living.

The only trouble is that, although the advantages of such a shift are more or less accepted inside a national market, internationally we still do not recognize them. Nor have we set up, in our international market, any of those measures for cushioning the short-term effects of competition such as development grants for new industries and for retraining—measures which, for example, have made it possible for Lancashire to switch very largely from textiles to engineering, or for an area like the Borinage in Belgium to abandon marginal coal mining for modern industry.

There is not time to bring up in any detail other forms of support to developing trade. More stable prices for raw materials, through a variety of commodity schemes, are under discussion. Here I would only like to mention in rather more detail one method of support which, I think, makes an even more direct link between trade and aid. This is a more ambitious system of compensatory finance.

The International Monetary Fund has a relatively modest scheme already in being to offset falls in export income which follow from any decline in primary prices. The developing nations feel that the scheme should be enlarged and more of the loss of income covered and over a longer period. Other suggestions include a world-wide insurance scheme against the daunting fluctuation in the prices paid for primary materials. I would also like to mention a further possibility since it seems to me to do more than simply offset losses in income. It could become a sustained stimulant to the development of a much bigger market among the two thirds of the world's peoples who need it most. In the first place, we should steadily plan for a 4 to 5 percent annual expansion in world trade. At the same time, we should provide the necessary working capital for this growth by granting the International Monetary Fund power to make available to the developing countries an agreed amount of purchasing power, say, in the shape of International Monetary Fund certificates issued to the International Development Association, which they, the poor nations, could use to buy the development goods they need on a nondiscriminatory basis—and the developed countries could compete with each other to make secure, at one remove, the extra purchasing power for themselves. This would entail an adaptation to the world economy of steps we have more or less accepted inside our economy, where we regard bank credit as a flexible means of providing the market's working capital and attempt to use it as a sensitive instrument for keeping demand and supply in step.

Now, leaving trade, we come to another great area of work in the Decade for Development—the transfer of skills. There is no time even to outline the number of policies that are being carried on in this field by all the specialized agencies. What I can do is to underline all over again the absolutely essential need to train people for the job of development. They are extremely scarce at every level. A number of countries in Africa can hardly put together an economic secretariat in the prime minister's office. The full apparatus of development planning is quite beyond their scope. Yet their ambitions already aim at planning and disillusion will grow as hope so far exceeds performance.

I am not sure that first priority should not go to the training in each developing country of a group of top civil servants who can hold the fabric together during the troubled years after the departure of the old colonial officials and before the emergence of the young graduates of the new nation. The Special Fund is at work on this task with its Institutes of Public Administration. Private agencies such as the Ford Foundation have done excellent work. I would hope that the United Nations Training and Research Institute would be quickly launched to act in this vital area. It is essential that we should realize, throughout the whole field of development, that no policies will be pursued, no jobs done, unless men trained to do them are available. It may be a truism but it is forgotten. How, otherwise, can one explain the plethora of advisers? What is rather needed from the specialized agencies is a cadre of specialists who do the job and train the successor. This is the essential investment in trained minds that has to be achieved.

These necessities point to a further advantage of the Decade of Development. It can ideally provide a certain amount of coordination. I recall the pathetic story of the early days of the Indonesian Plan, when the Indonesian government applied to the American government for an expert to help them to deal with their experts. There were so many specialists, and so many advisers, that finally ministers could do no work; they were always trying to explain to a new team of advisers what they were trying to do.

Now, no one would claim that, as a result of the Decade of Development, coordination is perfect; but, at least, for the first time there is a certain framework within which discussion, the development of strategy, and the concerting of policies can take place at every level. At headquarters, between the top agencies; in the regional United Nations commissions—for Europe, for Africa, for Latin America, and for Asia and the Far East; and then, hopefully, at the local level, where the United Nations Resident Representative can keep in touch with people in the field, and actually find out who is digging two wells in the same place, for two different agencies. It may still be very far from full and effective coordination, but the concept of the Decade of Development provides the first context yet attempted for a genuine effort at joint strategy.

The last advantage I want to mention is the opportunity to bring to focus on the problems of development at least a part of the knowledge that has been acquired in fifteen years of effort. After all, the beginning of any development process is very messy. The number of the bankruptcies in Britain in the early years; the number of bonds on which cities and states defaulted in the United States; the financial collapses and panics; the sheer waste of the whole process—these are simply facts. If anyone had demanded in the early stages of Atlantic development the rigorous procedures of accounting which are being suggested for the poor countries today, we might not have developed at all. From the South Sea Bubble onwards, we have grown by the most unorthodox methods. If there is waste now, there was waste then, and really rich nations should try to avoid the hypocrisy of suggesting their origins were pure. But, having said that, I would also claim that, in spite of the waste, a great deal is being learned. The whole concept of a strategy of development is now better understood than ever before. This fact does not mean that we shall make no more mistakes. How many Polarises blow up? But we do not then throw the launching pad into the sea. We learn from the mistakes and evolve better policies.

When I think of the sophistication of the approach to some of the key problems in development now, compared with the stumbling and fumbling of fifteen years ago, I sometimes feel that, if only we will stay "with it," we could be on the verge of a breakthrough in our knowledge of how to develop comparable to the advances that are being so conspicuously made in science and technology. Of course, the process is infinitely more complex, because it involves men; it involves their motives; it involves reasons why they will or will not do things. But if we were to add up all that has been learned, and if we looked confidently at the really successful examples of lands ready for the "take-off"—Greece, for instance, or Israel or Formosa—then I maintain that there is now a body of knowledge to be deployed and that it could very greatly accelerate the processes of change in the next ten years.

But if I were asked whether all the promise of the Decade of Development is going to be fulfilled, I fear I would be much more dubious. Some countries—and America is one of them—are going through a sort of antidevelopment jag; one can hardly open a paper now without reading of somebody who has made a speech declaiming: "Foreign aid is a lost cause. The whole idea is a waste. It is 'operation rathole.' We are pouring good money after bad and all of it down the drain." Take one fantastic example of this way of thinking in the past two years. A number of people go around Washington saying with perfect seriousness: "The Alliance for Progress? It is a continental catastrophe." The Alliance has only been going eighteen months. Most things look pretty catastrophic at the start—even a newborn baby; but at least you give it time. This feeling that everything is bound to be a failure, that everything has gone wrong, that one can start a program on this scale and judge it a failure within a few months, this fashion of derogation may be superficial; yet it could prove excessively dangerous. Although some other nations have now surpassed America in the amount of aid given per head of population (France heads the list), the American contribution, simply because America is richer than everybody put together, still accounts for 50 to 60 percent of the transfer of capital. If, therefore, the Americans lose heart, few of the developments we have mentioned will happen.

I ask myself, again and again, how this disillusion has taken hold in a country with the fabulously generous record of America in the postwar world—from UNRRA to AMGOT to Marshall Plan to Point Four to AID? How is it that, just when so much of the experience is beginning to show promise, just when some of the experiments, far from looking disappointing, are beginning to show that first touch of spring, how is it that, at this moment, such disenchantment has set in—a disenchantment which will certainly make nonsense of any Decade of Development, or of any other sustained effort to bridge the appalling, growing gap between rich nations and poor?

I hasten to say that it is not only in America that one meets this mood. There is M. Raymond Cartier in France, who says, in effect: "Why don't you put all that aid money into the Dordogne?" There are quite a few Germans with an innate tendency to call commercial loans for five years at 8 percent "aid." The British, too, talk about the 1 percent of national income as a yardstick—but have not reached it yet. But the fact remains that there is a more articulate disillusion in America. French aid—amounting to nearly 2 percent of national income—still goes through the Assembly without a murmur. A man like Mr. Reginald Maudling, fighting for his life to become prime minister, put aid to the developing countries among his priorities, which he would certainly not have done at such a juncture if he had not believed it to be fairly popular. Yet in the American Congress, the mood of disillusion is now almost the majority mood. Why is this?

It is important to try to understand the trend. If it continues, all the constructive possibilities contained in the Decade of Development will not occur. By default, we shall choose the other way: the drift toward a steadily widening gap between rich and poor, steadily increasing violence, a proletarian world in flames, and ourselves sitting precariously for a time on top of the trouble and, in the end, engulfed in it. Let there be no mistake about it. There is no evidence from modern history that a minority privileged as we are now can continue to "get away with it." This is the mild, peaceful lull before the storm. Wait until most nations have their own atom bombs, for instance. Will the envied rich at that time enjoy some divine immunity? No. The choice is quite clear; we either do something about the world's great split or the writing is already on the wall.

The reason, therefore, why people inside and outside America are disillusioned with economic assistance goes to the heart of the issue of the world's survival. It is not a matter of trivial, passing interest. It is much more nearly a matter of planetary life or death.

The first explanation is not very attractive but we had better face it. The Atlantic Powers today are very, very rich, and there is an innate tendency on the part of the rich to despise the poor. This is not one of the pleasanter attributes of human nature. But it is a fact. When one reads what respectable people in Victorian times said about the working class in Britain, one sees much of the same mentality as can be observed in current reactions to the developing countries.

It was useless, they said, to help the working class in Britain or pay them higher wages. If one did, they simply had more children. Why were they called "proletarians?" They were always producing *proles* —those thousands of little pattering feet and greedy little mouths waiting to gobble up anything one might have given their parents. Why help people incontinent enough to produce more children than they can support? Is this not exactly what we hear about Latin America or Asia today?

Then there was the universal complaint: "They put coals in the bath." Now it takes the form of: "They take their tractors out duck-shooting." Yet the feeling is the same, the feeling of contempt, often even amiable contempt, which the competent feels for the so-far in-competent.

Again: "They are lazy; they are idle. If you give them more pay, they do less work." All these things can be found, word for word, in the Victorian blue books. The ideas behind them obsessed the Poor

Law Commissioners for half a century. The Victorians felt they could not do much to help the poor because, shiftless, lazy, and child-ridden, they were held to be incapable of helping themselves or profiting from others' assistance. It was really only toward the end of the century, after Lord Shaftesbury's crusades and Disraeli's reforms, that, by way of income tax and welfare and compulsory schooling, a larger effort began to be made. Then, little by little, it was discovered that these same degraded proletarians had become fine, upstanding consumers, on whom mass affluence depended. In short, they were no longer poor, and so they no longer had to be despised.

If this analogy is accepted—and I think it is a sound one—by the time the wealthy nations have done something really sustained about world proverty—after all, the transformation of the Atlantic working class took nearly one hundred years—they will find that developing countries, too, have become fine, upstanding consumers, like the Japanese, for instance, who only seventy years ago were being despised in just the same way.

A second reason for our difficulties is a faulty sense of time. Too many people, it seems to me, know no history in this field of development. No country, not even that of the fabulous Japanese, modernized its economy in less than forty years; usually it has taken nearly a century to acquire the modern apparatus of science and technology, to begin to accumulate capital, and to transfer the problem from the side of supply to that of demand.

Even countries with resources as vast as those of the United States took at least seventy years to make the transformation. Think of the advantages: unlimited land, a great deal of water, a long growing season, European capital streaming in, and, in the migrants, not only labor but another form of capital—because Europe trained them until the age of eighteen and then sent them to America as a brain-and-brawn drain, so to speak. Yet modernization still took nearly a century. And America's development is a reminder not only of the time factor but also of the need for external assistance. In addition to European loans, these millions upon millions of migrants, nourished and semieducated, were a vast factor of external assistance to America's growth and development.

No, the historical evidence is quite conclusive. The drive to modernize takes time. It probably takes two or three generations, and this for a good specific reason. There is no development without trained, competent minds. But the experience of Africa suggests that, although a child straight from the bush can do well, he does better quicker if he has had an educated mother. Incidentally, if a drop in the population is desired, educated mothers are quite important from this point of view, too.

Two or three generations have to pass before the full processes of modernization can be completed. Yet this is a fact that is normally forgotten. Otherwise how could anyone say anything as big as the *Allianza* was a failure in eighteen months? Let us keep our perspective. Babies take nine months; elephants take eighteen. Full development takes several decades and cannot be much accelerated, not even by the most ambitious "crash programs." It is like a man having an affair with nine ladies at once, hoping to have a baby in one month. Sometimes I think our whole approach to development resembles this anatomical absurdity. And as a result when, as is human, we "grow weary of well-doing," we have no rational convictions to offset our dangerous backsliding.

There are, of course, other reasons. I doubt if we realize the degree to which the cards in the world's game of growth are stacked against the poor. All the trumps are in our hands, all the low cards—poor climate, tropical extremes, leached soils, debilitating heat, no spring, no autumn—lie with the developers. And all this is quite apart from such man-made biases as we have introduced into trade.

Again, I doubt whether enough of us realize the common interests which unite rich and poor in the pursuit of development. The advance of two thirds of the human race toward the status of "fine, upstanding consumers" has a direct relevance to the likely continuation of very considerable advances in Atlantic technology. Where are we to find our future markets once most citizens in the West have two chickens in every pot and two cars in every garage? We cannot dispose of the chickens now. In part, the new markets are to be found among the 30,000,000 Americans who are still poor. But may they not lie, at the next stage, among the two billion and more who are poor in the world at large? They are the people who, with skills and opportunities, can enter into market relationships with us and provide the fresh demand needed to sustain our ever-expanding productivity. They can become partners in a genuine world economy—an economy of mutual interest, not split down the middle as our world economy is today. We should then repeat at the world level what, to an extent, we have already done inside our domestic society—by the building up of skills, the maintenance of consumer demand, the creation of affluence, and the transformation of at least seven tenths of the population into the middle class. It would have looked pretty inconceivable to have done this, even in the United States, only twenty-five years ago; it looked pretty inconceivable in Britain as recently as 1947; it looked fairly inconceivable in France as recently as 1954. I am not suggesting anything as sensational or as rapid for the developing world. But the ultimate process is the same: drawing workers into the economy as skilled and well-paid producers so that they become consumers too and lay the basis for the mass demand needed to absorb our fabulous productivity.

These, then, are the reasons for our contemporary "weariness in well-doing." They are understandable, no doubt. But I must confess that I find them infinitely discouraging—for two reasons. The first is that they betray a truly startling lack of generosity in our imagination. Here we are, spending $120 billion a year on armaments; quite ready to spend $5 or $10 billion a year on space; and yet, when it is a question of giving a decent life to more and more human beings, of making the desert blossom, of making this little planet more productive and opening up more opportunities to our fellow men, suddenly our hearts no longer thaw and glow. We are not interested. It is not really very exciting. Going to the moon, perhaps; evolving a new rocket, maybe; finding some splendid way of blowing up the human race in one second instead of 30 seconds; oh, very exciting. But when it comes to giving a decent life to most of the human beings on this earth—no, apparently this is not for us; it hardly stirs a flicker of interest. What could be more disturbing than this response? If people cannot be excited and cannot be enthused, if they cannot be made alert and alive by great human enterprises, then one has to ask: What is the quality of society from which they spring?

This deadening of the imagination is bad enough. But it seems even more catastrophic if it is set in the proper historical context. The world today is virtually conquered by Western habits of thought. They may take secular forms; they may take ethical forms; they may be religious. But make no mistake about it. Communists, like Christians, like Jews, like humanists, are all carrying around the world the message of dynamic change, progress, brotherhood, resurrection—the germinal ideals of what was once in space a very small civilization situated round the Mediterranean. Yet the heritage of the Jews and the Greeks has conquered the earth. Nobody is going back these days in search of his ideals to the static, archaic societies of other times or other continents. These ideas, rational and humane, deeply rooted in the apocalyptic tradition of Jewry and Christianity, have now triumphed all round the earth. The strange thing is, however, that they could be losing all their strength with us.

I was reading during Lent some of the prophecies from Isaias, Ezekiel, and Jeremias. I must confess I can understand why they are not read on Sundays, particularly in respectable congregations. They are very inflammatory. And the point that recurs again and again and has proved a unique goad and stimulus to our society—it occurs in no other—is the extraordinary combination of compassion for the poor with a profound sense of outrage at the rich who will not accept the obligations of compassion.

The Lord is often angry in the Old Testament. But He is angry above all else with the pretensions of people who call themselves respectable, who have the resources, who are rich, and who apparently give no thought whatsoever to the people who sit at the gates without food, without clothing, the motherless, the widowed, the orphans. It is not simply the hardheartedness that makes the Lord rage. It is the appalling complacency. Take this splendid passage from Isaias (Ch. LVIII):

They ask of me. . . . Why have we fasted, and thou hast not regarded? . . . Behold in the day of your fast your own will is found, and you exact of all your debtors. . . . Do not fast as you have done until this day, to make your cry to be heard on high. Is this such a fast as I have chosen: for a man to afflict his soul for a day? . . . Is not this rather the fast that I have chosen? . . . Deal thy bread to the hungry, and bring the needy and the harborless into thy house: when thou shalt see one naked, cover him, and despise not thy own flesh.

Or this rebuke from Jeremias (Ch. VII):

Trust not in lying words, saying: The temple of the Lord, the temple of the Lord, it is the temple of the Lord. For if you will order well your ways, and your doings . . . If you oppress not the stranger, the fatherless, and the widow . . . I will dwell with you in this place.

The unique note is the note of outrage, of indignation, that people with such pretensions can be guilty of such neglect. Today, we may have lost that note—but believe me, our world is never going to lose it. For the moment, much of the old righteous indignation has been taken from us by the Communists. Wherever they go, they preach the gulf between riches and poverty and set against it the ideal of brotherhood. Of course, we know what happens later on. As George Orwell said of Communist society: "All men are equal, but some are more equal than others." They pervert the ideals. But have *we* lost them? Where is the note of passion and indignation in *our* society? Where is the realization of overwhelming wealth and its obligations? Or must we admit that we are content to cry, "It is the temple of the Lord," while leaving the hungry and the naked sitting helpless at the gate.

This is always the temptation of affluence. But we cannot evade the most profound moral insight of our society: that if the rich do not accept their obligation to the poor, but rather accept their affluence as a free gift for self-indulgence in all the good things of life, while others starve and despair, then social order is already under judgment and a Babylonian Captivity lies ahead.

There is a magnificent and mysterious phrase in the Book of Daniel, where we read of the "sentence of the watchers" (the Lord's judgment) falling on societies which fail in this deepest moral sense. We would be, I think, both lighthearted and lightheaded if we did not think a similar judgment might fall on our affluent world as well.

FORMS AND FUNCTIONS
OF DEVELOPMENT
ASSISTANCE

Paul G. Hoffman

MANAGING DIRECTOR OF THE UNITED NATIONS SPECIAL FUND

Given at Columbia University, January 23, 1964

For all of us, this series of Dag Hammarskjöld Lectures offers a double opportunity. It enables us to pay renewed homage to the memory of this great man from whom we have drawn so much inspiration. And it also enables us to consider together some of the world problems to whose solution his life was dedicated.

The problem of international economic development, which is my daily concern, is one to which Dag Hammarskjöld gave a great deal of attention. He was, of course, an economist by training. I first knew him in the early days of the Marshall Plan, when he was the Swedish representative in the Organization for European Economic Cooperation. In that post, before he ever became world-famous, he made significant contributions to the postwar recovery of Europe. I realized then that he was one of the half-dozen most brilliant and capable men that I had ever met.

As Secretary-General, he did more, perhaps, than any other individual to establish a new, active, and dynamic concept of the United Nations. He brought new strength to the office of Secretary-General —not for the sake of personal power, which was unimportant to him, but because he saw that events would otherwise overwhelm and by-pass the United Nations and make it ineffective.

Inevitably, his fame came to him chiefly because of political con-flict. But it was part of Dag Hammarskjöld's genius that he under-stood where such conflict had its roots. In particular, he understood how closely the hope for peace is bound up with the striving for economic and social progress in the less developed half of the world. He believed, as he said in one of his reports on economic develop-ment, that the United Nations would finally be judged not so much by how it overcame this or that crisis but rather "by its total contribution toward building the kind of world community in which such crises would no longer be inevitable."

He also understood intuitively that a sound spirit is just as vital in giving economic assistance as sound economics. He insisted that this spirit should not be one of charity on the part of the generous rich toward the grateful poor but rather a spirit in which all concerned are equals—what he often called the spirit of "solidarity." In this spirit, he proposed one of his most original and effective ideas, the OPEX program, through which technical and administrative personnel are recruited from advanced countries to serve in the governments of developing nations until local people are ready to take over. This idea met with little enthusiasm when he first proposed it in 1956, but today there are 78 of these internationally recruited civil servants working in very high posts in the governments of 32 countries.

Fortunately for the world, in U Thant the United Nations found a successor to Mr. Hammarskjöld who is equally aware of the vital importance of world economic development. In his recent lecture in this same hall, U Thant pointed to the emphasis of the United Na-tions on economic and social progress as one of its great advances over the League of Nations. Not long ago, he remarked that it is "intolerable" and "contrary to the best interests of all nations" that, in this enlightened and prosperous age, "more people in the world are suffering from want and hunger than ever before." During U Thant's service as Secretary-General, the work of the United Nations in the economic and social sphere has grown steadily in size and effective-ness.

However, those of us who live from day to day with the problems of world economic growth know all too well that the scale of our activities thus far is not enough. There is an urgent need for a much larger effort in this area through *all* channels, and particularly through the United Nations.

Since public funds are involved, this larger effort cannot be made without public understanding. But instead we find—especially here in the United States, whose support in all this work is so important—a growing skepticism about the value of what is still mislabeled "foreign aid." Perhaps a better designation for this would be "development cooperation" because, as I will make clear later, both the developed and the less developed countries have an equal stake in the achievement of a rapidly expanding world economy. If this were understood, there would be wide acceptance of the need greatly to increase the "development cooperation" effort. Instead, as far as the United States is concerned, we find the program once again in a struggle for survival.

What is the cause of this situation? I do not believe it comes from any lack of desire to do what is right but rather from an inadequate awareness of four things:

First, the nature of the rapidly changing world we live in;

Second, the true nature and purpose of development assistance;

Third, the positive results being achieved; and

Fourth, the actual price tag on this type of assistance.

I will try to discuss some of the pertinent facts under each of these four headings.

I

First, then, most of us have not yet really managed to wrap our minds around the fact that the world is now one neighborhood. Long-range jet aircraft have made puddles out of oceans and molehills out of mountains. As for communications, when I was a boy William Jennings Bryan was noted because his booming voice could be heard by a crowd of five or six thousand people; but today when the head of a great nation makes an important speech, international television can bring his voice, his gestures, and even the least change in the expression of his face to a world-wide audience of hundreds of millions. Centuries-old isolation between peoples is rapidly breaking down, and complete strangers are being turned into neighbors by advancing technology.

Unfortunately, our attitudes evolve more slowly. I myself find it hard to conceive of having three billion neighbors! I know with my mind that this is so; but to grasp it with my imagination is beyond me. So I try to scale it down by imagining a city with three *million* inhabitants, each individual standing for a thousand people of similar economic and social status. In this city, about a third of the people live in the better section of town. Most of them are light-skinned. They live for the most part in decent circumstances and quite a few live in varying degrees of luxury. Most are healthy, well educated, and have a life expectancy of about seventy years.

On the other side of town dwell two million people, the great majority of whom live in abject poverty from which they can see no escape. Half are hungry all the time, chronically diseased, illiterate, and destined to die at an average age of thirty-five. And one more important fact: a growing number of them are waking up to the realization that the misery of their existence is unnecessary.

No real city with such wide disparities in living standards could last for long without some kind of explosion. Yet the world today is in precisely the situation of our imaginary city. And it is now almost as closely bound together. It is therefore just as necessary to attack poverty, ignorance, and chronic ill health in Africa, Asia, or Latin America as it is to attack these same evils in New York or any other urban center of the Western world.

This is by no means a matter of pure philanthropy. It is true that all the world's great religions teach that man has a duty to help his neighbor. And statesmen agree, for as President de Gaulle has said, "It is the duty of those who are best endowed and strongest to help others—those who are in want, those who are underprivileged." But beyond this duty, we see that two vital interests of every nation are also at stake: its interest in peace and its interest in its own economic development.

We cannot hope for a peaceful world unless there is some reasonable way to satisfy legitimate popular aspirations for a better life. There is already more evidence than we need that these aspirations, when they are frustrated or misdirected, eventually turn to bitterness and violence. This, in turn, can all too quickly draw in major Powers and endanger the peace of the whole world. Conversely, a nation which acquires the ability to stand on its own feet will also be able to play a part in building a more peaceful and stable international community.

The business interest in this problem is equally clear. With the rapid growth in productivity in the most advanced countries as a result of automation, there is literally no realistic solution in sight for the problem of unemployment and underemployment, or for the problem of idle manufacturing facilities, without a rapid expansion of the world economy. The greatest potential for that expansion lies in the developing countries which are Members of the United Nations and where over a billion, 300 million people live. That is the number-one business frontier of the future.

In short, our neighborhood is now the world—politically, ethically, and economically. That is the first premise on which international assistance for the developing countries is based, and undoubtedly much of the struggle over this question stems from the reluctance that many of us feel to accept that premise. Too many of us are still dreaming of "fortress America."

II

A second reason for the trouble over development assistance is that the process itself is unfamiliar and highly complex. How does it work? What purposes can it achieve—and what can it *not* achieve? A few years ago we knew very little about these questions. We lacked competence because nobody had ever done this work before on such a large scale. Unavoidably, there have been failures as well as successes, but we have learned from both.

One lesson we have learned is that economic development is very different from economic recovery.

In economic recovery, such as that of Europe after World War II, a whole variety of economic assets, both tangible and intangible, are already present, which are normally absent in a country just beginning its economic development. To give only a few examples of these assets, Europe, at the end of the war, had extensive, although badly damaged, rail and road networks and excellent ports. It had—which is even more important—a literate population, trained and disciplined over generations by industrial work and habits. It had a store of technical knowledge and skills, a core of industrial leaders, used to taking decisions involving economic forecasting and risk. It had financial and economic institutions like banks and money markets, and a fully developed demand on the part of the public for a wide variety of industrial goods, which had only to be produced in order to be sold. Under these conditions, any investment which was made was immediately fruitful. The Marshall Plan, which had a four-year timetable, actually reached its goal ahead of time.

In most of the developing countries, the institutions and skills Europe already possessed have yet to be created. Investment must therefore take place in many fields and over an infinitely wider area. To create and operate industries, for example, developing countries must acquire essential knowledge and skills and build an industrial infrastructure of roads, railways, seaports, dams and irrigation works, hospitals, schools, colleges and polytechnics.

Development is thus much more than a repair job: it is building from the ground upwards.

We soon discovered, too, that economic development is too serious a matter to be left to the economists. I feel a little like a heretic when I say this, because some of my best friends are economists and I am at their mercy on all matters of investment, productivity, wages, currencies, commodity exports, diversification, and other subjects of vital importance. But development assistance cannot be effective unless it also takes into account a country's social and political institutions, the way people live and think, the goals they set for themselves, their attitudes toward work, and so forth. Some countries are just emerging from a tradition that frowns on manual labor as beneath the dignity of men and assigns it primarily to women. In some places, education is still looked on more as a social grace for the favored few than as a means to a better material life for the majority. In too many countries, men engaged in industry and commerce are considered as third-class citizens. Such traditions are gradually giving way in the face of the demands for progress—but they don't give way overnight. And only as certain social changes take place can development assistance be fully effective.

To inform ourselves on such matters, we depend on law, history, sociology, and many other disciplines. And as we have become better informed, our assistance has become more effective. I feel sure that as citizens of the advanced countries learn more about these complexities—just as we who have the operating responsibilities have had to learn about them—another source of confusion and frustration over development assistance will tend to disappear.

Finally, we have all had to learn one other very important lesson about what development assistance can do—and what it cannot do. Experience has shown that it cannot be used to buy friendship or to win reliable military allies. Even in the economic sphere, its role is strictly limited. It cannot supply the bulk of the resources that are needed, and it cannot supply any of the will. Those things must come from within. What external assistance can do, through the provision of both technology and capital, is to furnish the vital spark to those who are determined to help themselves.

I cannot overstress this matter of self-help. In the early days of the Point Four program in the United States, we used to hear technical assistance described as "exporting know-how." This missed the point. There is no use whatever in exporting know-how, or exporting anything, unless somebody on the other end wants to import it. To "export" development makes no more sense than trying to push a piece of string. In this connection, I should like to say that one great advantage of the United Nations as a channel for development assistance is that, because our work is insulated against politics, it need only be made available where we find a genuine desire for progress and a willingness to make sacrifices for it.

III

My third point is that the industrialized nations are skeptical and timid about development assistance because of an unawareness of what it can achieve. While regrettable, this is perhaps not surprising —most of the publicity on development assistance is focused on the failures. Little if any prominence is given to the news about successes in economic and social development which are achieved by thousands of people working in obscurity all over the world every day.

A journalist friend of mine described the situation in these terms:

"The task of helping low-income countries leap into the twentieth century just doesn't seem dramatic. It's not newsworthy. Let me put it this way: If you build a fifty-seven-story skyscraper in the heart of Manhattan, my editor would probably give it a spot mention some place in the financial section. But if you blow up a two-story building anywhere, I can get you top billing on the front page."

Yet one measure of the importance of United Nations economic and social work is that 20,500 of the 23,000 staff members employed by the United Nations and its family of related agencies (that is, 89 percent) are exclusively engaged in promoting social and economic welfare. The point can be driven home with other significant statistics. Since 1949, for example, no less than $5.75 billion flowed from the three capital-supplying institutions associated with the United Nations to help meet urgent capital requirements of developing countries. Since 1949 the United Nations family has also sent to those countries 18,000 especially recruited experts and has awarded more than 25,000 fellowships to permit nationals of developing countries to improve their professional skills abroad.

What these loans, experts, and fellowships have been able to accomplish—like much good work performed under national, regional, and private assistance programs—provides a vast amount of heartwarming evidence that substantial progress *can* be made in the epic fight against poverty, ignorance, and disease. Somehow, ways must be found to publicize the successes as well as the failures.

IV

Now I come to the fourth and last source of misunderstanding about development assistance: the price tag. I will discuss the worldwide costs in a moment, but first perhaps I may say a word to Americans about a statement which we sometimes hear that the United States has "given away $100 billion for economic assistance since World War II." This statement is inaccurate and misleading and a relic of the bad reporting of the past. The facts are that, of a total of about $103 billion in assistance which was provided, some $33 billion was military assistance. Of the remaining $70 billion, $32 billion went to the European countries and Japan.

For their part, the developing countries received from the United

States between 1946 and 1963 economic assistance totaling about $38 billion. About half of this was in interest bearing loans, most of which require repayment in dollars of both principal and interest. The remainder was in grants which, over the 17 years, averaged just over $1 billion a year.

Parenthetically, I should like to recall that not all of this "economic assistance" is truly "developmental." Much of it consists of short-term loans and credits designed to bolster exports of the industrialized countries and to support their defense commitments.

In 1962, the latest year for which estimates are available, the total of United States expenditures for so-called economic assistance was approximately 1 percent of the United States gross national product. In 1949 the corresponding figure was about 3 percent.

So much for what one advanced country has been doing in this vital matter. Now let us look at the amounts of economic assistance that have been moving from all of the non-Communist countries into the developing countries. According to available estimates, the capital flow into the developing countries in 1962 came to about $7 billion.

Of this, almost $1 billion moved as private long-term capital investment. Of the remaining $6 billion, $2.5 billion was in the form of loans, and $3.5 billion in grants of various kinds and for various purposes.

In my opinion, the most significant part of the $3.5 billion of grants was the $600 million devoted to "pre-investment" activities. Pre-investment work is indispensable to, and prepares the way for capital investment. It may take the form of technical assistance, but is increasingly concentrated on relatively large projects. Among these are surveys and feasibility studies that reveal the wealth-producing possibilities of the soil, waters, and forests of developing countries, and show opportunities for industrial development. The information provided is invaluable in two ways: negatively, in warning against unsound investment; positively, in acting as a magnet for productive investment.

Pre-investment also includes expenditures on applied research and improved development planning, both of which make greater investment feasible and more effective. In addition, pre-investment concentrates on the technical education and training that nationals require to develop their country's physical resources and to use modern machinery, tools, and techniques for economic growth and social advancement.

The importance of such pre-investment work as an essential prelude to sound investment has been recognized increasingly by governments and planners all over the world. The $600 million I just mentioned as the volume of pre-investment in 1962 represented a rise of almost 50 percent over the level achieved in 1959, and this may well reach $1 billion by 1970.

The share of the United Nations in this pre-investment work has shown a spectacular increase. In 1959, $60 million, or 14 percent, of all funds for pre-investment work were channeled through the United Nations system. In 1962 this share had gone up to $190 million, or 28 percent of the total. If this trend toward the "multilateralization" of pre-investment persists, the United Nations might well be administering $400 million of this assistance by 1970.

The United Nations program most directly associated with pre-investment is the United Nations Special Fund. It is, I think, one of the most rapidly growing programs of technical cooperation in the world today.

Despite the fact that the Fund began only 5 years ago, its Governing Council has already approved 374 high-priority pre-investment projects whose gross cost is $837 million. Toward this, the Governing Council has committed $335 million, and the recipient governments, for their part, no less than $502 million—that is, 60 percent of the cost. Of these projects, 148 are large-scale surveys of natural resources; 143 are training institutes for industrial, technical, and teacher training; 77 are applied research institutes; and 6 projects are concerned with economic development planning. The implementation of the projects in the countries where they are located is being carried out with the full cooperation of the governments of those countries and that of the United Nations and nine of its related agencies. Incidentally, each dollar contributed by the United States to the Special Fund has enabled the Fund to undertake $6.12 worth of projects, $2.05 of the remainder being paid by other industrialized countries and $3.07 coming from the developing countries themselves.

The most important finding of this work so far is what has been revealed of the richness of our planet and of the high potentialities of its human resources.

Our surveys have found huge quantities of water under the desert in Syria, and enormous potentials for irrigation and hydroelectric power in many places in Africa, Asia, and Latin America. Large deposits of minerals have been found in places as far apart as Chile, Uganda, and Pakistan, and unexpected quantities of valuable timber have been discovered, even in supposedly explored forests. Each day of work strengthens our conviction that we have only just begun to uncover the vast physical resources of the developing nations.

So far as investment follow-up of Special Fund pre-investment work is concerned, I would just mention that the eleven surveys completed to date by the Special Fund at a cost of $7 million have already produced more than $400 million in investment.

In our training programs we have found striking proof of the intelligence, the adaptability, and above all of the burning eagerness to learn which animates people in the low-income countries. The 32,000 people who have already received instruction in the various educational and technical institutes supported by the Special Fund are the spearhead of a significant attack on insufficient skills and lack of knowledge. In helping to develop their skills, we are increasing those intangible assets which are of such great importance in development. Furthermore, since a large number of our trainees are now themselves instructors, the benefits must also be measured in terms of the numbers of persons they will, during their lifetimes, help to train, in school, in factories, and in technical institutes.

It is results like these which may account for the growing amounts of pre-investment assistance being channeled through the United Nations. These results are not fortuitous. The United Nations is uniquely positioned to do this kind of work. First, its sources of contributions of both money and expert talent are not confined to one nation or one region, nor even to the industrially advanced nations, but include nearly all United Nations Members—106 out of 112 at the latest count. Second, it brings to the task the rich experience in development work accumulated over many years by the United Nations and the specialized agencies. Third, as I pointed out a moment ago, it is insulated from the political relations between individual states and thus has a much better chance of keeping everybody's mind on the job of development. Fourth, when it comes to surveys of natural resources, a sovereign nation is usually more willing to entrust this kind of work to an international organization than to a single advanced country. Finally, because we only undertake projects which the recipient countries actively desire and plan for in detail, we can count on strong participation by the recipient in the work. As already suggested, these countries' contributions to projects—in both materials and manpower—substantially exceed those of the United Nations family.

The immediate need of this United Nations family is for an increase of $100 million a year in its pre-investment expenditures. We know where this money needs to be spent to pave the way for new capital investments. As to that $100 million, I might comment that it is about one thousandth of what it costs every year to maintain the military establishments of the great Powers. Yet this one tenth of one percent is a potent long-range investment in peace and security. If it can help even indirectly to prevent some future Congo crisis or Cuba crisis or Panama or Zanzibar crisis, it will have been worth the price.

V

One final point before I conclude. To carry these greater burdens efficiently the United Nations, as the Secretary-General said two weeks ago, must streamline its organization. We are now in the midst of doing this. It should mean creating at headquarters a new, single organization to be responsible for all pre-investment financing which hitherto has been divided between the Technical Assistance Board and the Special Fund. It also means a further strengthening of our United Nations offices in the developing countries. Since 1959, the number of these offices has gone up from 34 to 62, serving 75 countries and staffed by 150 highly qualified professionals. The director of each office is the focal point for all negotiations on United Nations assistance in the country or area to which he is assigned. Since the Special Fund alone now has projects in operation, or approved for financing, in 120 countries and territories, obviously the number of our field offices must be increased.

We are growing fast. We are working on a world scale—and we

have some inkling of how rich the world is in untapped resources, and how rich its people are in undeveloped talents. We have worked out an approach to the development of those resources and talents, and our experience gives us some reason to think that our approach is sound. Therefore our hopes are high.

But I cannot close on any note of facile optimism. The United Nations effort "to promote social progress and better standards of life in larger freedom" is still in its early stages. We have much yet to learn and many difficulties to overcome. Overcome them we can, if we recognize the great truth expressed by Dag Hammarskjöld when, in his first year as Secretary-General, he said: "The ultimate challenge to us all is whether man shall master his world and his history or let himself be mastered. . . . There cannot be more than one reply to that question. Man must master his world."

As we know now, this was his categorical imperative. If we make it ours, we can, before this century ends, have a world substantially without want, a world in which prosperity provides a means to human dignity and happiness and to peace.

PROBLEMS OF THE
BIRTH OF A NATION*

Willard L. Thorp

CHAIRMAN, DEVELOPMENT ASSISTANCE COMMITTEE,
ORGANIZATION FOR ECONOMIC COOPERATION AND DEVELOPMENT

Given at The Johns Hopkins University Bologna Center,
Bologna, Italy, March 2, 1964

The speeches end. The drums roll. One flag is lowered and another is raised, and a new independent political unit has been born. The political change to independence has taken place in a moment of time. The immediate objective of self-rule has been achieved.

One may question whether or not these ceremonies and celebrations have in fact created a new nation. The dictionary defines a nation as a distinct race or people having common descent, language, history, or political institutions. The significant word is "common" and the essential requirement is some binding or unifying force. Of course, the situation varies greatly from case to case. Some of the countries newly born do not have a common descent, do not have a common language, and do not have anything which might be called a common history. They may previously have had certain common political institutions but that was only because their various component parts were contained in administrative units within a much larger empire. In fact, the common political institution may have been the very institution from which they are now separated.

* This subject was selected because Dag Hammarskjöld had discussed a number of these problems with the author in 1960 in connection with the United Nations mission of that year to Cyprus which was headed by the author and arrived on the island two weeks after its independence.

A new common and independent government must now begin the process of creating a nation. This is not a process which can be carried out quickly. To the extent that there had been a prolonged struggle for independence involving more than just a few members of an elite group, the common effort may have provided a unifying force and an element of common political experience, as in the case of India. Some unity may also have been created in cases where the achievement of independence was agreed upon far in advance so that substantial institutional arrangements could be established, as was the case with the Philippines. But many of the recent births have taken place so easily and quickly that no new loyalty had time to be established to support the new state against the newly released internal forces of local division and political competition.

Just as past struggle and effort might have created some sense of national unity and loyalty, they also would have provided an opportunity for particular leadership to emerge with consolidated support behind it. However, in cases where there has not been any such prolonged effort, the new state may start with various individuals actively competing for leadership or with a head whose authority is only partially accepted. Even where there is some unity, the leader who has been effective in achieving independence may not be the type of leader who can create a stable, functioning governmental operation. The spirit of revolution does not necessarily coincide with the spirit of administration. One is likely to forget that governmental leaders in older countries have usually had substantial periods of government service and have been in the public eye for many years. A new nation may not have had the opportunity to develop such a group of potential leaders. Those who do emerge are likely to have little experience in visualizing and enforcing "the public interest." And obviously there is no body of tradition to provide elements of stability to the new government.

The problem of establishing a common loyalty to the new state is made much more difficult if there are clear-cut divisions among the inhabitants such as diversity in race, religion, or language. There may be important cultural and institutional differences (often springing from race and religion) in such matters as law, family practice, inheritance, work habits, holidays, personal habits, and the like.

These conflicts were largely, though not entirely, submerged so long as there was a foreign Power with a strong police force which kept order. But independence involved the withdrawal of the external factor which often had succeeded in keeping any antagonism among these separate groups from breaking out into violence. So long as they were all under the jurisdiction of an outside party, each could accept the situation. For them to work together on some cooperative basis was in all probability the initial pattern set up by the departing Power, but it has often collapsed in the face of the basic group differences and conflicts of political ambitions. In such cases, for any one group to take over the position of supreme authority is not easily tolerated by the others. Whatever the cause, the old struggles between metropolitan country and colony seem often to have been much less violent and persistent than the internal confusion and conflicts of today.

In some instances, this difficult problem may be solved by migration, both voluntary and involuntary, and there is some compensation for the process, cruel though it may be, which has taken place in many countries for thus removing groups in the population which could not easily be integrated. One needs only to think of the movements of the French and Italians from Africa, the Moslems from India, the Christians and Hindus from Pakistan, the Indians from Burma, the Watutsi from Rwanda, and the Dutch and Chinese from Indonesia. In a very few cases the solution, alas, has been genocide. But many of the new countries still have major groupings which must somehow be brought together in a common effort to build the nation.

Even older countries do not necessarily avoid these internal dissensions. In history, civil wars are a familiar phenomenon (the British Isles, United States, Italy, Mexico, Spain) but most of them seem far back in the past. And it is important to distinguish changes in personal government (revolutions, coups, counterrevolutions, and countercoups) or partisan politics from the disintegrating forces noted above, although they may not be unrelated. Some difficulties are long-lived. Fifteen years after the division of British India into Pakistan and India, one reads of continuing migrations reflecting primarily religious difficulties. The recent separation of Rwanda and Burundi is largely a matter of tribal differences which have come to a tragic climax. And on the island of Cyprus, Greek and Turkish flags rather than the Cypriot continued to fly after independence. Thus, the first problem of the new countries is to achieve some sort of working unity, some binding quality, so that they can get on with the job of social and economic development. This is far from easy, and one must recognize that internal dissension may dominate the lives of some of them for many years to come.

Even if internal stability may have been achieved, another complication facing any new nation is that of achieving a satisfactory and peaceful working arrangement with neighboring states, especially when they belong to the same generation. There are bound to be various political and economic problems of jurisdiction involving people, property, and goods. In older states, these problems still arise but principles have usually been agreed upon for their settlement, and there is often a considerable body of precedent. New countries are likely to be particularly sensitive about what they believe to be their rights. Any potential source of friction is aggravated if the boundaries are either not clear or were obviously drawn with pen and ink on maps, rather than based on natural dividing points. Thus, the problem of Kashmir has been a source of major irritation to both India and Pakistan; the question of the boundary between Ethiopia and Somalia has been brought before the African states; and the disposition of water adds to the tension between Israel and its neighbors. Boundary disputes are not necessarily limited to new states—note the Bolivia-Chile argument—and, unfortunately, states are not very flexible about giving up claims to territory. At worst, this can lead to a state of war. As a minimum, the result is likely to be elements of uncertainty which disturb the normal processes of living and the maintenance of a larger military force than otherwise, which diverts resources from development purposes.

The problems of achieving political unity and international comity are only the beginning of the new state's difficulties. Unless there is a period of anarchy and destruction, it may not appear on the surface that the new political status has involved any immediate revolution in the economic and social life of the country. The same biscuits and toothpaste appear in the store windows. The branches of foreign banks continue to operate. The Governor's Palace becomes the Presidential Palace. And the elite, such as it is, continues to reflect the result of having been educated in the former metropolitan Power. If the new state had been a British colony, the lawyers would all have had the common experience of dining in the Inns of Court. If it had been a French colony, it would have a school system patterned closely after that of France itself. No matter how strong the effort to escape from foreign domination, these inherited tastes, habits, and institutions relating to the actual process of living are not easily changed.

Nevertheless, the new political status may carry with it certain changes in the rights and privileges of the citizens. To the extent that the newly born country had been part of a larger political unit, certain privileges and preferences may be reduced. Its citizens may formerly have been able to travel to and from, or even migrate to, the metropolitan Power without legal formalities. Its currency was often given respectability by being tied to that of the mother country. And in all probability the exchange of goods was unrestricted or was on some preferential basis between the two areas. These advantages usually applied also to trade with other areas associated in the same empire.

Now, the old relationship is broken and two countries have emerged, foreign to each other. To be sure, there may be some carryover from earlier arrangements. A former British colony may become part of the Commonwealth. A former French colony may become associated with the European Economic Community. And the United States and the Philippines agreed to make a gradual adjustment to foreign-country tariff status over a twenty-year period. Nevertheless, the old preferences do tend to be reduced or disappear. Part of the process of creating independence involves reducing the special relationships which formerly existed and establishing closer relations than before with a number of other countries.

In addition to the new position of the new country in migration and trade, there are certain immediate consequences which are likely to spring from independence. Limited though the new country's resources may be, a further drain upon the availability of both personnel and capital takes place. Various fears, springing from the uncertainty of performance of the new country or the probable attitude of those in political power, may result in an emigration of individuals who, for reasons such as race or religion, feel that their status, property, or even their lives may be threatened. Similarly, there may be a flight of capital related to the flight of individuals or merely to the greater risks and uncertainties in the new environment. These may not be matters directly of government policy, but the natural result of the human desire to preserve life and possessions. Nevertheless, they constitute an immediate loss of valuable resources to the new nation.

This situation usually is further aggravated by a deliberate effort to eliminate foreign elements from the country. The new nationalism is likely to carry the campaign against foreign political domination into other fields than merely the political. All foreigners become suspect as threats to full-scale independence, and the foreign element most easily removed is that of foreign personnel. Such a policy has immediate appeal, for the presence of foreigners in posts of responsibility raises questions about the actual fact of the new independence. The continued employment of foreigners may be made procedurally difficult, as in the case of Cyprus, where the constitution allocates the positions in the civil service 70 percent to Greek Cypriots and 30 percent to Turkish Cypriots, with no percentage left for other nationalities. In some countries there are special personnel boards to see that no positions are given to foreigners if natives are available. To such a policy of removal (or expulsion) by the new government is added an encouragement for former personnel to withdraw as an unplanned result of generous payments made on the part of the former colonial Power to such civil servants as lose their positions.

This loss of a substantial part of the former technical and administrative personnel, as well as persons at the policy level, may be augmented by the distrust and even dismissal of native citizens who served in the government under colonial authority before liberation. The sort of prestige which has attached in Communist China to those who were on the long march and in India to those whose passive resistance put them in jail has its reverse aspects in many countries for those who did not demonstrate their rebellion. Since in some cases the option to retire on exceedingly generous terms also applied to the upper strata of native civil servants, the new government often starts with less native skill than appeared to be available.

Even this is not the whole story of the new operating difficulties, for much depends upon the extent to which independence had been approximated in the colonial days. Whereas countries such as the Philippines, India, and Tanganyika began their independent existence with substantial experience in legislative and executive processes, the Congo became independent when it had very few university graduates and less than two hundred graduates at the high school level per year. Cyprus had not even its own legislative or judiciary in its later years as a colony. Even if the country had a substantial and experienced civil service, there were likely to be four fields in which the colonial Power had kept a strong hand—the military, the judiciary, fiscal policy and operation, and international affairs—and each of these is full of trouble even for those with considerable experience to help them.

As if the absence plus the losses described above of capital and skilled personnel were not enough, the new country suddenly finds that there are new demands upon its resources. It must establish itself in the area of foreign affairs, and this means ambassadors and all the paraphernalia of embassy operation. How many embassies should it have, how much will they cost, and who can be spared from the establishment or perhaps banished from political competition at home? These are immediate problems to which must be added the bewildering world of international organizations, each with its annual assessments, its meetings to be attended, its desire for personnel, and its secretariat's insatiable demand for information. To be sure, these all may be helpful in the long run. On a balance-of-payments basis the in-payments by foreign embassies in the country may exceed the cost of out-payments for its new embassies abroad. But the foreign embassy staffs in the country in a way are an added burden. And they cannot make up for lost domestic services of the group of native personnel which must spend time abroad, drawn from the much too small number of competent persons available. More time must be spent on foreign affairs within the country. Its representatives must be instructed as to how to vote in international bodies on matters which are quite unrelated to its life and experience. It must be responsible for its own citizens who travel abroad. In fact, there must be a new Ministry of Foreign Affairs to handle the vast amount of varied matters which never were the subjects of concern before.

Similarly, there are new manpower and budgetary requirements in the area of the police and the army. Undoubtedly the cost of such activity was borne in part by the metropolitan Power, plus what is even more difficult to replace, the ultimate responsibility for direction and policy guidance. Under these general headings of police and army are a variety of specialized matters involving selection, training, equipping, and maintenance. This is a particularly sensitive area, since the military leaders may be the only persons in the country who head an organized and effective power group. But, returning to the problem of new burdens to be carried, there are other matters related to the keeping of order. For example, the operation of prisons was usually carried out under foreign direction, often with no native personnel instructed at the policy level. And the judiciary must now be organized to operate without reference to a final review elsewhere.

Similarly, new requirements are likely to appear in the fields of fiscal policy, budget making, tax collecting, and the processes of government expenditure. Again, the shock of such new expenditures on the resources of the new government is related to the degree of foreign control which existed before, the degree of experience in these fields, and the degree to which expenses were shared in the past. In some particular instances, metropolitan Powers have made efforts to ease the transition by operating with a "shadow government" or by trying to make a gradual transfer of authority in advance of the date of birth. In other cases, the tensions were such as to make such an effort impossible. All these new or newly assumed functions are not merely burdens on the budget, but require skill and experience in areas where often the new nation has no reserve of manpower upon which to call.

At this point of new national pride, assistance from the industrial countries is likely to be suspect, although there are recent exceptions to the rule. India has gradually relaxed her initial restrictions on foreign technicians and foreign capital. After an initial outburst against the Belgians the Congo has asked for help from the government of Belgium in many fields. Certain recently independent East African countries asked for British help in keeping their own military forces in order. And nearly all the African ex-French colonies depend upon French assistance for government operations. Nevertheless, stemming out of the concept of independence there is a basic reluctance to accept foreign technical assistance or foreign capital at the same time that it is obvious that such assistance is essential to progress and development. To some extent, technical assistance provided by the United Nations has been more acceptable, although it has been limited in amount. The difference is more one of label than fact, since United Nations technical assistance consists largely of personnel obtained from advanced countries for temporary service, differing little from that which would be provided under bilateral arrangement.

The above discussion describes some of the special difficulties which may be traced directly to the birth of a nation and which vary of course from case to case. At the moment, these problems are very conspicuous, in view of the fact that the birth rate of nations has been very high since the end of World War II. Except for possible further subdivision, this population increase cannot be expected to continue much longer. But the difficulties which have been outlined above are only the beginning. The new postwar countries, almost without exception, are underdeveloped countries. Many of them have per capita incomes of less than $100 per year. Thus, to the problems of establishment described above must be added the difficult ones facing all such countries, problems associated with economic development and growth: the upgrading, mobilization, and appropriate organization of resources, manpower, capital, and enterprise; the acceptance of new technology; the development of markets; and the encouragement of the process of savings and investment.

In looking at the future of the new country in development terms we may note another special problem. The shape and size of the new country in all probability is the result of historical accident having little relationship to its economic resources and prospects. Therefore, it may have few natural resources, it may have such a small population and constitute such a small market that its productive possibilities are strictly limited, and it may have difficulty of access to the rest of the world. Thus, if it happens to suffer from one of these handicaps and unless it is fortunate in producing some much-desired export product, its prospects for economic viability on the basis of a much higher level of living are not bright. At this stage in its history, it may be difficult for it to develop those intimate, special relations with other countries which can mitigate such accidents of size and shape.

But in spite of all this, an improvement in economic and social conditions is expected. In most new countries, if he thought about it at all, the man in the street believed that political independence would result in a change of life for the better. He had been told so over and over. His leaders in the struggle for independence attacked the previous regime as one of exploitation and painted the future prospects in glowing colors. The emphasis was on the real and fancied evils in the situation rather than any careful blueprint of how the glowing future was actually to be achieved. The inevitable difficulties described above were seldom given any recognition. It should also be noted that the advanced countries did not come up with any effective suggestions as to how to achieve a better transition or to improve the prospects of some of the less fortunate new states. The conservatives did a great deal of grumbling but it was mostly in terms of the loss of empire. It was difficult for liberal groups in the advanced countries to resist the appeal of "freedom now." They were swept along by a philosophical idealism and paid much too little attention to the extraordinary problems which would be created for the new countries.

The emphasis then was on political independence and few recognized that political independence was primarily a shift of responsibility—that by itself it provided no new capacity or ability to improve the level of living and, in fact, probably reduced the resources and skills available. But once the initial objective of political independence has been achieved, the focus shifts to better social and economic conditions. And so the new government, with all its weaknesses and other difficulties of early childhood, is forced to struggle with many new and most difficult problems in the economic development area.

While some of the various difficulties which are described above were probably unavoidable, others might have been avoided by greater foresight. Because of their intimate part in the earlier political and economic history of these areas, the older nations have a special responsibility to help them in every way possible. They are already providing increasing amounts of technical assistance and capital.

In the face of the record which shows so many difficulties, it would not be hard for the more advanced countries to feel that there is little hope for progress in these new countries. But one must put the present in perspective. These are very new nations. It is important to recognize and have full sympathy for the special difficulties of the initial period of independence. Perhaps methods of cooperation and coordination can be developed which will establish more viable units. One can hope that in one way or another elements of political stability will be achieved without violence and that rapid social and economic improvement will then be possible.

FRONTIERS OF CHANGE

Douglas Ensminger

REPRESENTATIVE OF THE FORD FOUNDATION IN INDIA AND NEPAL

Given at Columbia University, May 6, 1963

It is a privilege to join in doing homage to the memory of Dag Hammarskjöld—servant and martyr of peace—great leader in the progress of man in our era.

The present lecture, on "Frontiers of Change," is offered as a tribute to this great pioneer for peace. Our lecture deals with man's continuing progress toward a better world—a world of peace and dignity for all. The subject is particularly appropriate, since it concerns the central goals to which Dag Hammarskjöld, as Secretary-General of the United Nations, devoted—and finally gave—his life.

I

In this generation, frontiers of change are not new to us. Neither new trends nor individual changes are unfamiliar. We have learned to expect them. New advances, new relationships, new problems, and new forms of old problems continuously unfold around us. On this occasion we shall look at some of these changes, present and emergent, which importantly involve the peace of the world and therefore the welfare of mankind.

It is my view that we are now participating in the movement of two world-wide *frontiers of change;* and that these are among the principal shapers of the destiny of man for all times to come. It is clear also that each of these, in turn, will create numerous lesser frontiers of change as we move ahead with manifold adjustments to these broad forces.

I shall refer but briefly to the first of these two great movements of change—the scientific and technological revolution—which is now under way in maturing vigor. It is an enormous engine for human growth, and a reflection of that growth. We marvel at it, and at its still unfathomed powers and effects. We accord it admiration, respect, even awe.

However, it will be discussed here mainly as the mother and feeder of another great forward surge that is in an earlier stage of building. This newer frontier comes from the womb of the older. It is man's dawning response to the new imperative of living together in peace—an imperative created by his science and technology.

In a sense, our modern world is the product of scientific and technological advances. Compared with a hundred years ago, or even half that, our present setting is a new planet. The advanced peoples of today live in a world as different from that of the past as the jet airplane is different from the oxcart. Even the less advanced peoples are sharply affected by the new advances; they are adopting them as rapidly as knowledge and circumstances permit. And they are aware, even as we are, that the march of man's control over nature, far from ending, is still accelerating, rushing out to boundless space and limitless horizons.

Fundamentally new resources and powers have come into being. As a result, we have the physical means for building a better world for all humanity. Compared with the past, we possess almost miraculous means of construction, production, and distribution. Science and technology have mutiplied the world's food potential and brought great and widespread improvements in living and learning. At the same time, the tide of advance has created previously unimagined speeds of communication and transportation—wiping out the world's distances and many of the old barriers of isolation, delay, and misunderstanding. And then, as a grim "enforcer" of new neighborliness, these gifts have included another: the power for cataclysmic destruction. This gift, attended by fearful peril, is imposing on us a new mutuality of discipline.

These developments, earth-shaking and world-changing, have brought forth a vast new change. This is the frontier of a new and inescapable interdependence of mankind, which brings with it the urgent necessity for increasing world neighborliness.

We are now moving ahead on that frontier, though still hesitantly and at times reluctantly. This movement Dag Hammarskjöld observed and characterized as "a growing sense of sharing a common membership in a world community."

This change embraces the broadening of mutual interests and concerns which necessarily occurs when neighbors move much closer together than before and therefore become more dependent on each other for maintaining orderly behavior, decent living conditions, and necessary community services. It does not require, obviously, that differences in philosophies and interests disappear. However, it does mean the growth of a common concern for the welfare of the community as a whole.

At present, we are able to see only a limited part of the ultimate meaning of this great frontier. But its promise is rich indeed. We can be sure even now of its vast potential for the advancement of civilization and the well-being of men.

Establishment of the United Nations was a major advance on this frontier. Dag Hammarskjöld's leadership, we know, carried its work forward by great strides, helping to build the United Nations as a powerful instrument for world peace and neighborliness. The work of the United Nations Relief and Rehabilitation Agency, begun while the guns of World War II still blazed, was an early milepost of the advance. So have been the operations of Point Four, the Marshall Plan, the United Nations Technical Assistance Board, the Food and Agriculture Organization of the United Nations, the United Nations Children's Fund, the United Nations Special Fund, and the various other United Nations organizations and regional economic commissions.

To these are added the current international assistance programs of individual countries, notably the United States. Also, organizations such as the World Bank and the International Monetary Fund have an important place; they, too, reflect the world-wide urge for peace and progress. In addition, international aid by private organizations is part of this picture and has shown unprecedented growth. It has been my privilege to be associated for more than a decade with such efforts by one of these great private institutions, the Ford Foundation.

All these efforts reflect the growing reality of a world community based on mutual responsibility. They are the opening phase, at least, of a continuing planned program for world peace and human well-being. They represent our joint recognition that, with the world more crowded together than before, the community faces the need to clear away its slums of abject poverty, ignorance, disease, and despair. These efforts face up to the fact that widespread progress, hope, and well-being are the only dependable foundations for world peace and order. They also recognize that these foundations have to be built through positive action, and as rapidly as possible.

These assistance efforts, both public and private, are seeking *intended change, planned change*. They are carefully shaped toward achieving particular development, for particular purposes, within more or less fixed periods of time. Generally speaking, I would judge that most of them are helping us move toward the desired objectives.

Building a secure world peace, with the tools and methods of peace, requires elimination of the needless and terrible poverty of peoples in the developing areas. To this end, economic and other assistance is given for the conduct of various development projects.

This assistance is much more than the building of dams and factories; it is also aid to agricultural change, community development, educational improvement, research, strengthening of administration, health improvement, urban development, and assistance with various industrialized problems.

Its scope can be large, as in the building of a great steel mill, or it can be quite small. In general, assistance is aimed at bringing about key developmental changes which will themselves be in-country "frontiers of change," serving as generators of future change in related spheres of activity.

The improvements sought in these countries are urgently needed and are costly in money, men, and materials. Efficiency, then, is essential. In my view, the only truly efficient path for such work lies in the creation of self-generating and continued changes. For this reason, I would always emphasize the value of developing the human resources, strengthening the educational base, perfecting the administrative competence, and increasing the developing country's leadership competence and motivation for change.

Efficiency in development calls for maximum attention to the key areas of concern in each country, together with a firm commitment to the full assistance which is required to bring about significant and lasting changes. Such changes will and can be achieved only if the commitment is to assist the programs in depth over a sufficient span of time. We know, for example, that it takes about a decade to develop new institutions.

We are in a hurry, yes, and we should be so. There are some who say time is running out and that we cannot afford the time to bring about changes. Yet there is no other way. There are no alternatives to hard work and patient persistence. As with growing a crop in the fields, it takes time to bring about significant changes of lasting value.

II

Economic and social development in India has been carried forward since 1951 under successive five-year plans. India's development in the past twelve years, with benefit of much foreign assistance, has made striking progress. Industrial production has doubled; agricultural output has risen some 41 percent; employment has increased; and national income is up about 42 percent. Mining, manufacturing, construction, and transportation, including air transportation, have greatly expanded. Steel output has increased over 150 percent, aluminum over 400 percent, machine tool production over 1500 percent, and nitrogenous fertilizer output over 300 percent. Many new plants for manufacture of chemicals, electrical equipment, tools, and consumer items have come into being. New state capital cities have been built or are building in the Punjab, Orissa, and Madhya Pradesh. New dams have brought electric power to wide areas and have supplied water for irrigation of added agricultural land. In addition, educational, health, welfare, agricultural extension, and community development services have expanded greatly.

These gains are very impressive. At the same time, the pace of improvement is not yet adequate to support necessary improvements in the living conditions of the people. Despite the rise in total income, population growth has held per capita income to a rise of only 16 percent—meaning that it remains at an extreme poverty level. Unemployment and underemployment are large. Also, population expansion and the low agricultural yields per acre are pinching per capita food supplies. Although food consumption per capita is about one-sixth above 1950–51, it is still very low; and agricultural productivity is now rising more slowly than population. Vigorous action is necessary to increase India's very low yields per acre and to stop the too rapid rise in population.

Continued strong assistance from abroad is essential for India to achieve the intended "breakthrough" into self-generating and self-supporting growth. Development of a productive economy in a new and extremely populous nation where productivity is low and where poverty, disease, hunger, and ignorance are widespread is no short-run undertaking. Human well-being and world stability alike call for our continuing efforts and assistance.

Even as aid proceeds, however, it must be realized that the desired progress must hinge mostly upon the actions of India's own institutions and people. They are the ones doing most of the work and who regulate its pace, fast or slow. Necessarily, progress in the change orientation of these institutions and people is a central sphere of development. In a traditional society, creation of change-mindedness and of an "action-now" view of improvement is perhaps the most important assignment of all.

In addition, let us recognize that national development planning is a complex and difficult task. Under the three five-year plans to date, India's planners have rendered outstanding service to India and to the agencies assisting her development. However, planning for changes, even when backed up with funds and national authorization for work, is not enough. There is a companion need for emphasis on getting the plans carried out, organization by organization, phase by phase, area by area, year by year. National economic and social planning is relatively new and there is still room for learning from experience. The experience to date indicates that, for over-all planning to be most effective, it should be supported by specific plans of work, yearly calendars of assigned activities, and energetic supervison and liaison at all levels of operation. These and other needed improvements will doubtless come into play in the future, as India moves ahead toward her goals.

The development of self-reliant citizens in the developing countries, with improvement of their living conditions, is the central element in assistance goals. The general levels of living in these countries are almost incredibly poor. Many of us find, in fact, that personal contact with their depressed condition calls forth feelings of discomfort and shame. To confirm this experience, I suggest that one go to an Indian village and try eating his lunch under the gaze of the village children.

Let us look at a farmer in one of these areas. He is likely to die at an early age. He and his family probably live in a mud hut or flimsy shack with an earthen floor. The family cooks its inadequate food over a cow-dung fire, eats from a common pot, and may sleep on a straw mat or on the ground. The farmer's clothing is a loose smock or loincloth, and his younger children are likely to go naked. He is most probably illiterate, and his children may be growing up the same. His body and mind are sapped of vigor by sickness and chronic malnutrition. His farm work is hard labor, produces relatively little, and he has no survival margin against crop failures.

Consider the contrast with his brother farmer in a developed country. This man may live a quarter-century longer than the other. He and his family have many comforts and amenities of living, are healthy, well fed, well educated, well housed, and well clothed. The advanced farmer's labor-saving tools remove the drudgery from his work, and his greater productivity gives him greater income and security.

For urban people, too, the same yawning contrast exists between conditions in the two kinds of societies. They can be partly described, but must be seen to be understood. In many cities of the poorer countries, for example, multitudes of the homeless are accustomed to sleeping on the sidewalks and streets and to eating only on a catch-as-catch-can basis.

III

The economic planner who is shocked by such a picture of poverty and misery receives another brutal jolt, in many countries, when he considers the rate of population increase. For example, India's population is growing by about 2.1 percent per year. At this rate, its present population of 450 millions will be *doubled* within 33 years.

With nine million extra people each year to feed, to clothe, and to try to educate and employ, how can India's living conditions be expected to improve substantially? On the other hand, without such improvements, how can the people feel that political freedom is, in fact, ushering in the other freedoms which they so much desire—freedom from hunger, disease, and ignorance? Those of us who value democracy, and who value the right of people to make free choices, must understand that democracy has little or no priority appeal to hungry and desperate people. Hunger and despair are in a context quite different from that.

In order for us to face the population problem, it is important that we look at its origins. The population overgrowth is itself a result of relatively modern advances in knowledge and tools. In India and some other countries, for example, the development of railroads, plus improvements in local administration, made possible much better distribution of the food grains that were available. In addition, a large-scale extension of irrigation works made possible absolute increases in the amount of food available. These improvements have led directly to control of the famines which regularly swept away millions of people during the last century.

As a result, more people lived longer. Death rates declined markedly, though birth rates remained high. Later, the decline in mortality received further impetus from health measures such as the use of DDT to control malaria. Paradoxically, however, the lack of an extensive, permanent health administrative network now poses a serious barrier to carrying the population control program to the masses of the people.

This population growth is part of a world-wide phenomenon. Science and technology have led us unwittingly and suddenly to a general expansion of our numbers. This expansion, as we have seen in the case of India, already threatens man's further development. It is a major problem of our time. It is evident, I believe, that, here again, the peoples of the world are being impelled to see their need for living closer together, for living with each other in peace, and for providing mutual assistance in meeting their common responsibilities.

Our species has put itself into a critical situation indeed. We are all involved, whether we wish it or not. We see the situation unmistakably. Therefore, seeing it, we must act. The response required by the challenge of excess population growth seems plain enough. Just as man has applied his powers of rationality, organization, and technology to the control of death, he must now proceed to apply these same powers, in the fullest necessary measure, to control of births.

The growth of the population control movement in India offers some useful lessons for attacking this problem. After India's independence in 1947, demographers and economists added their voices to the welfare workers who had been advocating an official program for nationwide family planning. The sensitive new government felt it must proceed cautiously, but India's leaders skillfully prepared the way for a national movement. Several small pilot projects demonstrated that people were basically receptive, and that there was virtually no opposition. In addition, Indian researchers were encouraged to apply themselves to the demographic, medical, biological, and communications aspects of the problem, so as to provide the scientific basis for a program which would be structurally sound and locally acceptable. It was also necessary to acquire a nucleus of trained and experienced workers. In pursuing these steps over the subsequent years, India has made good use of limited technical assistance resources from abroad. The Ford Foundation has deemed it a privilege to assist this work.

In 1956 came the first move toward an official nationwide program. Initially, this tended to copy the traditional family planning clinic pattern of Western countries. However, a number of states forged ahead with experimentation on newer modes of promoting contraception. Perhaps the most striking has been the surgical "camp," in which voluntary sterilization services are provided to the people of an area on a mass scale.

India has now taken the next step. It has recently adopted a plan for a truly extensive national movement, geared to its own culture and resources. This will involve strengthening of the basic administrative structure required for such a program, and development of broad-scale, community-level extension education activities. At the same time, urgent attention will be given to production of contraceptives, to their wide distribution through nonclinical channels, and to assessment of program effects in different areas.

India's current five-year plan refers to the population control pro-. gram as being "at the very center of planned development." During the years to come, it is expected that this description may indeed start to be fulfilled. The country appears to be on the threshold of a bold and rational "frontier of change," from which we can all learn a great deal.

I have referred to a slow, a very slow, rise in the levels of living of poverty-burdened people. This sluggishness of improvement is by no means confined to India. The too slow rise of levels of living in the disadvantaged areas of the world is a clear and present danger for their people, their governments, and the peace of the world.

The people of the newer nations demanded and obtained their independence from the colonial Powers precisely because they were impatient for more advantages—economic, political, and social. They were told and they believed that independence would bring such benefits in short order. In some areas it is now a political reality—even if not an economic one—that part of these expectations must begin to be realized soon. Economically sound or not, the people's expectations exist; they are real; and they cannot safely be allowed to fall to the ground. Nor can too many of them be long deferred. The rationale of sacrificing in the present for the sake of gains to the next generation is wearing thin.

The developing countries have many in-country "frontiers of change." Their governments want the people to enjoy the benefits of modern science and technology. Actually obtaining those benefits, of course, requires more from these countries' governments than may appear on the surface.

The effectiveness of such governments in bringing about change will be directly related to their readiness to begin making more or less drastic breaks with the traditions and habits of the past, to adopt unfamiliar attitudes and practices, and to move purposefully and courageously toward a better life.

Suppose such a government decides that its outmoded system of agriculture and agricultural practices need sharp improvement—and begins to act on the decision. At that moment, an "in-country" frontier comes into being. New needs and problems immediately arise;

farmers must be taught new techniques and supplied with new implements and aids to production; research is required; problems of institutional support must be dealt with, as in credit, transportation, and marketing; and widespread education as to the benefits and know-how of improvement becomes a necessity. In brief, the frontier effort in agriculture requires a formidable array of support.

IV

India provides one of the great examples to aid understanding of what is involved for a developing nation in transforming a static agricultural economy to one of dynamic development. Its progress in this undertaking within the last decade is a lesson to the world.

The over-all task required action to shift village cultivators' attitudes from unquestioning reliance on the traditions of the past to active acceptance of science and technology. It required mobilizing all the national resources related to agricultural production—in a country totally lacking experience in the mobilization and concerted use of such resources. This task had to be undertaken, even though the government at that time was unaccustomed to working with village people or helping them work together in solving their problems. And the village people themselves had long ago accepted the status quo as a way of life.

India's Community Development Program, launched in 1952, was designed to expand the people's competence to solve their problems and to help the cultivators increase their food production.

Within the year 1963 all of India's 550,000 villages will be included in organized development blocks. Naturally, this program has considerable development problems of its own, yet there can be no question of its great contribution in preparing the minds of India's villagers for the changes that are necessary.

As a result of community development, village people have now come to understand that, with freedom, they no longer have to live with the old patterns of poverty and deprivation. Village people now express hope. They have expectations for many many things they want but don't yet have, and which they never before expected to have. Throughout the villages of India, at least some new practices in health, in agriculture, and in ways of living have been introduced. The people thus have been given opportunities to see and learn better things than the old attitudes and practices.

As a student of social and economic change, I want to underscore the fact that really significant development is never easy. This is especially true in agricultural and rural development.

Before village cultivators can be expected to get excited about taking up improved agricultural practices, they have to undergo some inner changes. They must go through the steps of psychological change the village cultivators of India have taken in the past twelve years as a result of cummunity development. First, they must recognize that they no longer have to live as they have lived and they must want things they don't now have. Second, they must have become aware of the existence of better practices and of their benefits. And third, they must have seen these practices demonstrated in their villages, must have understood them, and must have realized they were possible to adopt.

Having been taken through these steps of change, they can now be educated to see the importance to them of adopting improved agricultural practices. By intensive extension education, the cultivators can be taught stonger emphasis upon carrying out the recommended improved agricultural practices. They can now be brought to see that the adoption of the improved agricultural practices will provide them the needed wealth they must have if they are to get the new things they now express as wants.

Under community development, India's cultivators have largely passed through these three initial phases. Therefore, they are now ready for the fourth step.

The Ford Foundation has been closely associated with Indian community development and food production programs for the past twelve years. To assist India in taking this fourth step in the series of changes required for full focus on food production, the Foundation is now assisting India with an intensive districts agricultural production program. In essence, this program seeks to provide to the cultivator on a coordinated basis all the essential resources—administrative, educational, technical, and physical—that are required to speed up the mass adoption of improved practices. The program actively assists the cultivators in achieving successful experience in carrying out a "package" of improved agricultural practices.

This intensive effort is now being carried out in each of India's fifteen states, on a general basis of one district per state. It is projected as a five-year program. Assuming that it succeeds in bringing India to a "breakthrough" on this frontier of change—a "breakthrough" pointing the way to substantially increasing the nation's food production—the projected time span required for its development will be seventeen years.

In creating the Community Development Program, India purposely set out to create forces for change among the village people of India. The evidence today seems abundantly clear that the village people of India are now "change oriented" and can be counted upon to follow examples of change which prove beneficial to them. They now need only to be assisted in making the change-over from traditional ways to improved ways of living and making a living.

The thing India has not fully succeeded in doing is to transform its administrative bureaucracy from its pre-independence regulatory orientation to one of forceful developmental purpose. There is need for a more universal change orientation which would permeate the administrative structure in depth.

In the beginning phases of national development, the government took the initiative in promoting change. Today, however, the pressures for change are increasingly being expressed by the people. This situation presents both a challenge and a potential crisis. The challenge is for administration to bring about far-reaching administrative reforms so that government can give more effective leadership to change. The potential crisis lies in the fact that administration has succeeded in making the people "change oriented" but now lags in meeting their needs. It has thus far lacked the necessary dynamism to force changes within itself that would enable it to move on to greater developmental leadership.

In a real sense, whether India does in fact make its desired "breakthrough" in food production will be determined by the steps it takes in administrative reform. The administrative bureaucracy will have to become more "change oriented" if it is to help village cultivators make a large-scale shift to improved practices based on the findings of agricultural science.

V

Decision to launch a development undertaking is not something to be lightly considered by either the giver of assistance or the recipient. It is a serious and costly business—one in which inadequate planning, or too few resources, or too little follow-through in operations can bring severe disappointment. It may be able to bring great benefits if well conceived and carried out, but the penalty for failure can be painful indeed.

Moreover, since development resources are scarce, and the need for progress is immediate, the recipient country must choose to focus upon the most profitable and most urgent areas of change. This may be politically difficult. Yet poor selection of development undertakings can nullify the country's chances of rapid advancement. Stern self-discipline is required. First things must be put first, in their order of developmental importance. The relative priority of an intended project should be decided on the basis of its potentiality for sparking and feeding still further development in other spheres. The lesser priority items should be made to wait.

The developing country also faces other new things. It needs to realize that, in launching a new frontier of action, it embarks on an unfamiliar course that will require procedures and activities it has never previously found necessary. Urgency becomes a key factor, and flexibility a key necessity to permit urgent action. Although the government of the country can initially select the particular "frontier of change" when work is to be done and can designate the time to start work, it cannot possibly determine in advance the details of action and procedure that will be required over time and under differing conditions. The administrators and technicians have to be allowed freedom to act. They must be able to exploit "breakthroughs" as quickly as they arise. Also, they must be able to shift quickly to new or modified approaches to meet operational needs.

These requirements are themselves new to developing countries. For most of them, such requirements make up a very tall order. But before launching upon each project toward a new frontier, therefore, both the developing country and the assisting agencies should carefully weigh these needs and provide for them. They cannot be avoided. There is no useful purpose in ever pretending that they can be dispensed with.

As we look out toward a better balanced and more peaceful world, the process of change is a matter worthy of study. This process requires understanding. There is no cut-and-dried formula for it. It cannot be bought with money, or equipment, or technical assistance —necessary though these may be.

The first requirement, I believe, is motivation. The people and their leaders have to want better conditions, and want them enough to work for them. Without this prerequisite, improvement can only come slowly if at all. The use of assistance resources can never substitute for motivation.

Economic improvement and development do require the use of economic resources. Nevertheless, these are not the whole story. The people, for example, need to feel that their government is genuinely concerned about their welfare. They need to feel a sense of achievement growing out of their own efforts. Also, they must know as much as possible about the development effort, why the work is under way, and the changes in practices and attitudes that are recommended. Above all, they must see and know that they are making progress in shedding the burdens of poverty and backwardness.

The growth of a world sense of community responsibility, with resulting assistance for developing countries, does not necessarily guarantee the success of the assistance. Many considerations—practical, down-to-earth, hard-headed—must come into play for particular projects to be really effective. Each assistance possibility has to be closely examined and weighed on its merits.

Broadly speaking, the worth of any assistance effort—no matter how attractive its promise—depends upon two key factors: (1) the willingness and ability of the recipient country to utilize such financial help and guidance; (2) the willingness and ability of the donor government or institution to provide assistance in finance and expert guidance.

The success of each development project depends heavily upon official understanding and support in the country, and also upon popular support. Undertakings launched in response to needs that are strongly felt by leaders of the recipient country have a real advantage. They nearly always move ahead better than projects which the recipient government has not fully understood but has accepted for other reasons.

Support for development is based on understanding. For this reason, adequate orientation of policy makers is essential before initiation of a project. It is vital also for officials and staff at the operating levels. Thorough advance orientation is the best assurance of official support.

Popular support is usually a necessity and is always helpful. Reasonable and thoughtful efforts to create public understanding of the need for each undertaking, and of the basic elements in it, facilitate progress and help make sure that the project will have its intended effects upon the lives of the people. Public understanding and support are valuable assets. Much greater attention than is now the case could well be given to building both official and public understanding of development tasks.

Both for the developing country and for the donor of assistance, I would emphasize the importance of the pre-investment phase of development work—that is, the phase which immediately precedes decision to make investments of capital and manpower in a particular project. This phase is required in order to help make clear to all concerned the nature of the task ahead. Also, it is here that the assisting agency has its best opportunity—and greatest responsibility —to ensure that the assistance will, in fact, achieve its purpose.

For each development project this phase should begin with a preliminary study in reasonable depth, probably extending over a few months. A study of this kind assesses the dimensions of the development problem concerned, gauges the relative importance of the project as a force for improvement, and estimates the assistance resources and facilities that will be required. It also evaluates the project's need for special administrative arrangements and expert guidance, and considers the over-all likelihood of the undertaking being conducted successfully. This survey should take into account the attitudes of the officials and people of the country or area. It should also identify any likely obstacles arising from religion, culture, traditions, laws, and administrative practices.

Ideally, the donor country or institution and the recipient country would then use the findings of this survey as a guide for final formulation of the project. Proper use of the survey can not only ensure adequate provision for the project itself but also contribute greatly to the creation of really common understandings and meaningful agreements regarding the work ahead.

Full understanding and unity of purpose is difficult enough to achieve in any area of life, even in relatively simple matters. Assistance undertakings, however, are far from simple. They involve factors regarding operations, relationships, and procedures which will present many difficulties unless there is a specific meeting of minds upon them in the pre-investment stage.

Achievement of such a meeting of minds should never be too readily or rapidly assumed in foreign assistance work. For one thing, language differences are not yet bridged as well as we would often be inclined to believe. For another, the differences between our culture, traditions, and habits of thinking and those of the officials in the newer countries are quite conducive to ineffective communication of facts and ideas. The pre-investment preliminary study, adequately discussed back and forth, does much to bridge such gaps.

The building of world peace is a lofty as well as a necessary goal. As with lesser ventures, however, good management is necessary. In undertaking each specific project, both the recipient country and the giver of aid need to insist upon suitable administrative resources. Even highly desirable aid projects should be held in abeyance unless and until efficient administration can be provided for them.

Administrative competence is essential. Some of the developing countries have at the top strata of government a very high level of competence and concern for progress. Even so, economic aid can be stripped of much of its usefulness by poorly oriented and poorly trained personnel at the lower levels. Everyone who has been associated with development assistance will be able to recall examples of this. The governments of at least some of the developing countries are themselves conscious of the problem.

Suitable education is a "must" for administrators, project leaders, and their key personnel. This is the necessary foundation on which to build. Such education must then be supplemented with intensive staff orientation as to the project's purposes and with intensive job training for the work at hand. In most development work, training of staff has to be a major part of the operation. Full attention should be given to building the understanding and cooperation of related workers in other fields.

One further matter in the administrative area should be mentioned. Let us imagine for a moment that one is preparing to help launch a foreign assistance undertaking of some kind. Let us suppose that the problem and project are clearly defined, the pre-investment survey has been made and utilized, trained administrators have been appointed, the operational staff is well oriented and trained, and the agency or institution is ready to supply necessary resources and expert help. Are these enough?

In some cases they may have to be. But I suggest that one more ingredient be added, if at all possible. This is the ingredient of "change-mindedness." In a development project, it makes a great difference whether the officials and staff are people who just follow instructions and established routines, without "change-minded" initiative in their work, or workers who desire and seek all possible ways to attain the goals of the project.

Selection of "change-minded" officials and staff is often neglected by the countries receiving assistance. The need for such "follow-through" on their development decisions may not even enter the minds of policy makers. This lack in selectivity can lead to major difficulties. "Change-mindedness" can easily be lost in the bureaucratic maze of routine selection of personnel. As a result, the development undertaking can easily find itself clamped into a mold of the past before it has even started. If "tradition-minded" administration is coupled with a resistance to foreign guidance, the project will certainly have trouble.

As we move ahead on the frontiers of international aid and the building of a better world, we meet new relationship problems. The relationship between donor and recipient is, for example, a sensitive one. A donor nation or institution, conscious of its own good purposes and generosity, is sometimes baffled by certain resistances of the recipient.

Some of these are the result of quite explainable factors. It should be realized that no nation, however needy, feels wholly comfortable in receiving economic assistance from more fortunate neighbors. In some way, the national ego is involved. The assistance can be and is appreciated, but the necessity of obtaining it is not pleasant to think about in a nationalistic context.

In addition, of course, the nation being assisted is always sensitive as to the possibility of undue influence from abroad. The new nations do not wish to become colonial outposts again, in whatever guise the colonialism might take. This sensitivity is quite understandable. It is essential, in fact, that this be accepted by all, if international aid is to serve the advancement of humanity and of peace.

In his thoughtful contribution to the "Conference on Tensions in Development" at New College, Oxford University, in the fall of 1961, Dr. C. D. Deshmukh, now Vice-Chancellor of Delhi University, declared: "It is essential that each recipient country should become a donor country, at least in a small way, as soon as it can." In fact, many governments are already appearing in dual roles, both receiving technical and other aid and—on a much more modest scale, to be sure—giving such aid.

Dr. Deshmukh gave two reasons for this need: such two-way aid enlarges the pool of available international aid for development; and it helps recipient countries to understand better the point of view of a donor country. To this I would add a third point: being a donor country will reduce the psychological strain of being also an aid recipient.

But whatever the reasons, the phenomenon of two-way aid is proceeding. It is one of the useful adjustments being continually made in development work, a part of our "frontier of change."

VI

Returning now to my earlier statement that our generation has seen and is participating in two world-wide frontiers of change—the scientific and technological revolution and man's dawning response to living together in peace—we must recognize that man's capacity to adjust to these frontiers of change will require that he be educated. If man is to apply science and technology, as he must, in freeing himself of his burden of poverty, he must increasingly understand the basis of science. This he can do only through himself becoming a student of science in its broadest and most meaningful sense. Furthermore, if we are to achieve a situation of living together in peace, the developing countries must also make their contributions to the world bank of scientific knowledge, as well as draw upon it.

But simply understanding and knowing how to apply science and technology will not bring us peace. Through education men must learn how to play their roles in free societies. They must grow in their respect for the right of others to hold views different from their own. They must increasingly understand the meaning of tolerance. They must also realize that, though peace requires the harmonizing and civilizing of our behavior, there must remain the freedom for differences in beliefs and points of view.

In discussing the means used to cope with the urgencies of the two broad frontiers of our age, it has been necessary to speak in rough detail about our specific efforts and their problems. It seems to me that these details give added meaning and depth to the canvas as a whole. It is in these detailed actions and considerations that we actually come to grips with the problem of building a better world community—a community of peace and increasing mutual responsibility.

I would conclude on this note: owing to our science and the machines, we are able to move mountains of many kinds. Mankind has and is still gaining the knowledge, the tools, and the other resources that will enable us to meet the imperative of peace and dignity for men.

We do not lack the means for this. The only question is whether we have the will, and the vision, and the wisdom required. Barbara Ward has said: "It is our imagination that has become our limiting factor, not our means and not our resources." I have faith that we are overcoming even that barrier, and that the future of man, blessed by enduring peace, will move on and on to ever new frontiers of achievement.

THE INTERNATIONAL
TRANSFER OF KNOWLEDGE

Ingvar Svennilson

PROFESSOR OF ECONOMICS AND VICE-CHANCELLOR,
UNIVERSITY OF STOCKHOLM

Given at the University of Stockholm, March 12, 1964

I

We are all aware today of the enormous economic disparities that
exist between different countries. Some are very rich and others extremely poor. It is also clear that these disparities depend only to a
minor extent on differences in climate or natural resources. Actually,
these latter conditions are often more favorable in some of the poorest countries than in the richest. In the hothouse climate of tropical
countries it would, for example, often technically be possible to get
larger yields and more harvests per year from one acre of land than
in the temperate zones. The potentialities are there, but are not ex-
ploited. Food for rapidly growing populations could be produced, but
instead we find undernourishment if not starvation. The abundant
resources of manpower in these conditions are regarded as a burden
and not as an asset. The labor force is in large part left unemployed
or is used in an unproductive way, while enormous natural resources
are left untouched.

It is true that in order to exploit the resources more completely and
in an efficient way a large accumulation of capital must take place.
This accumulation must necessarily be a relatively slow process.
However, whether we think of the utilization of natural resources and

resources of manpower or of introducing man-made instruments for using them in an efficient way, it is evident that what first of all is needed is knowledge about technology and methods of organization. In this respect, the poor countries have witnessed a stagnation that has lasted for centuries. In the meantime, the countries that have now become rich have made immense progress in technical knowledge. The disparity in standards of living largely reflects a disparity in knowledge.

It has often been assumed that the transfer of knowledge between different countries was an easy process. Economists have spent much effort analyzing the imperfections in the international markets for labor, capital, and commodities, while knowledge, and especially technical knowledge, has been assumed to form a common international asset that is available easily and freely everywhere. Some economists have assumed that industries in different countries could choose freely in their "production function." Underdeveloped countries that are short of capital but have an abundant supply of labor would choose a more intensive labor technology. Highly developed countries would do the reverse. Each group would, however, potentially have the possibility to choose the technology that the other group applies, because their knowledge about technology is assumed to be the same.

The conception of the free mobility of knowledge overlooks one of the main reasons for economic disparities in the world, the imperfections in the international market for knowledge. The idea of complete frictionless mobility of knowledge reflects conditions in the academic scientific world. We take for granted that the results of academic research are published and thus made available without restraint to everybody irrespective of national frontiers. However, this picture represents an ideal that does not correspond to the general conditions in the market for knowledge. Serious imperfections exist as regards the supply, the marketing, and the consumption of knowledge. New knowledge that is generated is not always easily available. The types of knowledge that are supplied only partly correspond to consumer needs. And the capacity of consumers to absorb available knowledge is often deficient. This is to some extent the case in the relations between highly developed countries. In the relations between them and the underdeveloped countries a gulf exists that is not easily bridged.

II

It would evidently represent an oversimplification to assume that all relevant new knowledge is generated in free and open academic research institutions. Science has today become the basis for military power. Governments have organized research in the fields of atomic science, chemistry, and engineering that serves to maintain their military potential and, to a large extent, is kept secret. More important from the point of view of underdeveloped countries is the fact, however, that scientific research has moved into the private enterprises and that its results, then, no longer are public but are instead private property. Even more important, however, is the fact that new knowledge is generated only partly by specialized research. Modern industry may be regarded as a huge research laboratory, where new knowledge is acquired in a process of trial and error.

The technical knowledge that is accumulated within highly developed public and private units may only with considerable delay and to a limited extent leak out into the general market for knowledge and become common property. It may partly be derived from products that are sold in the market. It may be marketed in the form of licenses to use patents. But patent documents usually do not disclose all the know-how that goes into a product or a process; what is disclosed is often useless, if the rest of the know-how does not become available. In any case the relevant knowledge is only partly, and often with a considerable delay, translated into literary form. In a complete form, it can only be transferred by experts who have acquired the know-how or by allowing outsiders inside the unit in which the know-how has been accumulated. Besides publications, experts have thus increasingly become a necessary medium for carrying knowledge about modern technology between different countries. Furthermore, the persons engaged in a modern enterprise as a rule form part of a team within which each has only a partial knowledge of the complete process. Transfer of knowledge has, therefore, to an increasing extent become a team operation. It is evident that this makes the international transfer more complicated.

These conditions for the supply of knowledge have formed the basis for the organization of technical assistance by the United Nations and other national and international organizations. The assistance has only to a limited extent taken the form of publication but mainly the form of sending technical experts. This form of transfer has been developed into a massive migration to underdeveloped countries. In various countries one finds thousands of these experts. It is, however, evident that in relation to the cost of the operation the result has been far from satisfactory. In most countries, both at the delivering end and at the receiving end, the system has been criticized for a lack of efficiency. There may be many reasons for these imperfections. One of the reasons, however, has often been that isolated experts have been able to carry with them only a part of the knowledge that was needed to apply the new technology or organization. They have not found a counterpart in the receiving country able to supplement their knowledge.

They have written reports in their specialized field, which soon have been filed and forgotten. The archives of underdeveloped countries must by now be filled with the products of such abortive essays in the transfer of knowledge.

In this respect, a change seems now to be under way that promises to provide a more efficient medium for technical assistance. The prototype is found in the operations of private industries that have created subsidiaries in underdeveloped countries. In such cases, all the personal resources of the mother firm have been put at the disposal of the new unit. On the whole, the result has been very effective. The method may be extended beyond the establishment of privately owned subsidiaries. Governments may make contracts with private enterprises to establish new industrial units in underdeveloped countries. Consulting firms may carry out similar comprehensive operations. It may also be mentioned that teams from many American and European universities now are assisting such countries in economic planning and the development of institutions for education and research. The fact that knowledge is invested in modern complex organizations with a high degree of internal specialization should be reflected in the methods for assistance.

III

The methods of transferring knowledge must evidently also be adjusted to the conditions in the receiving countries. In this respect, there are great variations between countries and between various fields of activity.

One extreme may, as an illustration, be represented by agriculture in the countries in Southern Asia. According to experts, the potentialities to increase the agricultural output in these countries are very large. Water control, irrigation, improved seeds and breeds, fertilizers, and new technical methods in general may in countries like India and Pakistan double or triple the agricultural output. If this could be done without too much delay, the problem of feeding the population could no doubt be solved in spite of its rapid growth. Enormous public organizations have been built and numerous foreign experts have been engaged to spread knowledge of modern technology to the numerous farms in the area. The most intensive methods of "extension service" have been used. The results have, however, so far been very disappointing. The farmers in the 600,000 villages have refused to change, even if all material supplies have been put at their disposal, often at subsidized prices. The result has been that these countries now are facing a serious agricultural crisis.

How this is possible is a riddle to which no clear answer has been found. Some lessons seem, however, to emerge from all the experiments that have been made. The farmers are to a large extent illiterate, as a rule extremely poor, bound by the social and cultural traditions of the village, and skeptical of advice given by officials and foreigners. A new social and economic framework must, therefore, first be created, where the individual farmer is able and willing to accept the technical knowledge that is offered. What is needed was expressed in a brilliant way by Dag Hammarskjöld in a speech about "Science and Human Relations." He drew attention to the relationship between men, their relationship to environment, and the relationship of one group to another as dominating problems of our time that must be solved in order to create an atmosphere in which science and technology will yield results which will enable us to satisfy the demands that science itself has created.

In other words, knowledge cannot be transferred, if the potential consumer does not actively desire it. His interest may not be awakened if he lives in depressed conditions, immobilized in a net of antiquated social relationships. The first condition for an effective transfer may, then, be political, social, and economic reforms. The most successful experiments in the modernization of the Indian and Pakistan villages have combined such reforms with the supply of material equipment and of information about modern technology.

An essential element in such a comprehensive approach is evidently education, in the first place an elimination of illiteracy. One of the most encouraging features in the development of the poor countries is the impressive drive to extend education on all levels. Primary, secondary, and high schools, practical polytechnical institutes, and new universities are established on a large scale. Certainly nobody would deny the importance of education for increasing the capacity to absorb new knowledge. We should, however, not assume that formal education forms a sufficient or even always a necessary condition for the transfer of knowledge. Learning by doing is often the only way to acquire a specialized know-how. Experience shows that even illiterate people can learn to drive a truck or handle a boring machine in a mine. General education may be an important long-term target. If we want to make rapid progress, it may, however, be more important to educate a leading highly qualified elite than to spread education too thinly over the broad mass of the population. This elite can serve as qualified leaders of others and become the innovators who set examples that demonstrate how modern knowledge can be applied and that others may be willing to imitate. In India and Pakistan, a new policy is now being developed along these lines. The extension of new technology to all farmers by broad systems of organization has failed. It has now been decided to concentrate efforts on a limited number of "model farmers" in each village. It is hoped that they will exercise a demonstration effect on their neighbors.

Learning a new technology by demonstration may be a more effective way of transferring knowledge than textbook teaching. This also applies to industrial technology, which may be transferred most effectively by letting a team of experts, from top managers to engineers and trained workers, come from a more developed country to lead an inexperienced labor force. This method has been successfully tried in new steel works and other types of factories. As the new labor acquires the necessary knowledge and skill by demonstration and training, the team of foreign experts can gradually be withdrawn.

Teaching by demonstration and learning by doing make it possible to gain time in the transfer of knowledge. And the main problem is to speed up the transfer process, if the population increase is not to swallow up the gains that are made. On the other hand, such methods will demand a very large increase of the groups of experts that must be sent to underdeveloped countries or of the number of persons that must be sent to modernized units in developed countries.

IV

I have so far been assuming that the foreign experts master the knowledge that is needed to modernize activities in underdeveloped countries. To some extent this is a correct assumption. In most cases, there are few possibilities of deviating from the technology that is used in the manufacturing industries of the developed countries without losing too much in efficiency. However, in some fields and especially in the field of agriculture that depends on local natural conditions, the technology that foreign advisers can provide is not always adjusted to the special climatic and soil conditions, to the often small sizes of farms, and to other economic and social conditions. The skepticism of farmers about expert advice is often well founded. Artificial fertilizers applied to local types of seeds have, for example, not yielded the results that were promised. The research and experiments that are needed to adjust agricultural technology to local conditions in underdeveloped countries present an enormous task that has been taken up only on a very limited scale and with far too poor resources. The research and experimental institutions that have grown up in underdeveloped countries as a rule have a very weak research capacity. It is symptomatic that in Southeast Asia, with its very diverse natural conditions, only one large highly qualified research institution exists for the improvement of the strains of one of the basic crops, rice. The research that is needed to make more rapid progress will demand much greater assistance from foreign experts if enough progress is to be made within a short time. As it now is, the disparity in agricultural technology between poor and rich countries is probably increasing in spite of the fact that the potentialities for technical progress in the poor countries, which start from scratch, probably are comparatively great.

V

My preceding remarks about the conditions in the international market for knowledge show that the transfer problem can be solved only by establishing a very complicated market mechanism. The knowledge that is needed can only partly be standardized. To a large extent it must be tailor-made. And the exact specification is often unknown in advance. It often has to be found by new research and experiments at the point of delivery. It can only partly be delivered by mail. To a large extent it has to be transferred by migration of people or by teams with a specific composition as regards their specialization. Their task is not only to deliver the right type of product but also to find out on what conditions the knowledge they carry or produce on the spot may be accepted by the recipient. A precondition for acceptance may be radical political, social, and economic reforms. And the methods of transfer may have to include not only information and formal teaching but also teaching by demonstration and learning by doing. The bearer of the knowledge or the capacity to create knowledge must engage himself in the social and economic life of the country that receives him and this often for a long period. He must himself learn about the people and from the people whom he encounters. This was probably one of the reasons why Dag Hammarskjöld took the initiative to establish a corps of international civil servants, who would more or less permanently serve in the administration of underdeveloped countries.

It is no wonder that the transfer of knowledge by technical assistance has to a large extent been wasteful and inefficient, even where it has not completely failed. Lack of knowledge about what in the first place is needed, failure to select persons suited to solve the complicated transfer problems, sending isolated experts where teams were needed for a comprehensive approach, these are some of the reasons for failure. The delivering countries face a difficult problem of organization that must be solved before a more efficient transfer can take place. The problem of organizing for the transfer of knowledge does not concern only the public organs for technical assistance, which in the first place have been severely criticized. Their activities must be supported by organizational reforms of all institutions that may contribute to the development of an effective assistance, public administration in general, private industry, education and research units. Our universities, which must form the backbone in a system adjusted to the big task of transferring knowledge, have in a regrettable way lagged behind. Dag Hammarskjöld, who once was a scholar of Stockholm University, would no doubt have been the first to support the efforts that now are being made in order to repair what has been neglected.

It has rightly been said that the people in underdeveloped countries know more about us than we about them. This lack of balance must be corrected before the transfer of knowledge can become effective. It has to be done by extending our research and studies of cultures and social systems in the underdeveloped parts of the world and by spreading the results of this research to all who take part in the transfer process.

THE ROLE OF EDUCATION
IN THE
ECONOMIC DEVELOPMENT
OF LATIN AMERICA

Galo Plaza

FORMER PRESIDENT OF ECUADOR

Given at the University of Wisconsin, May 5, 1964

In the world today we are witnessing the disintegration of a whole system of relationships which in the past provided nations with some degree of political and economic stability. Great transformations in human aspirations, in the structure of societies, in science and technology, have reshaped events to an incredible degree.

In Latin America, economic and social conditions that had been taken for granted for centuries have come to seem intolerable. There is a demand for change, with a sense of urgency, that goes far beyond our present possibilities. Ours has been labeled rightly the "Revolution of Growing Expectations."

The Alliance for Progress, which is based on the premise that progress and well-being are meaningless unless they can be shared, proposes to provide the necessary resources and know-how to accelerate the process of economic growth in Latin America and prove that prosperity and social justice can flourish in an open society, where free men have an opportunity to make the best use of their possibilities as human beings.

Lack of education is a more serious limiting factor than lack of money in the effort to achieve these goals. The Indian farmer on the remote slopes of the Andes must be taught better management practices in order to double or even triple the meager wool production from his flock. The investigator in a research laboratory must learn how to make the best use of the region's resources. The engineer, the physician, the economist, the factory manager, the veterinarian, the extension agent, the trained nurse, the teacher, the foreman, the mechanic, the electrician, the specialized worker, the whole army of technical personnel needed to move a modern economy—all must be trained over a short or a long period of time, depending on the complexity of their respective skills. Latin America does have a growing technical force at all levels, but it is not large enough to meet the expanding needs of economic development. We need more and better trained personnel if we are to move ahead at a faster pace and this is why education should have a priority rating as an essential part of any development plan.

In Latin America, deep and significant changes must take place in the field of education whether education is regarded as a universal basic right or as explicitly designed to serve the needs of economic growth in order to increase national income and human well-being. If education is to serve social development, planning is a prerequisite, and as development generates demands for change, educational planning requires a spirit of innovation and, in some cases, the abandonment of traditional attitudes.

Within our hemisphere, education has played a major role in developing a free and prosperous society in North America. If we compare the major characteristics and trends of the educational systems in Latin America and in the United States, we will find differences that stem from our historical backgrounds. Although both our cultures have their roots in Europe, the differences in value systems and philosophy of life between the people of the North and those of the South of the hemisphere have created wide divergencies in the conception and purpose of education from the very beginning.

The semifeudal, absolute system of government in Spain and Portugal, in which Church and State were closely united, was transplanted by the Spaniards and the Portuguese, after the conquest, to their colonies in America and Catholicism was imposed as the only religion. The English colonists to the North had fled from religious persecution in Europe and organized their new communities on the basis of freedom and tolerance. They were governed, for the most part, by charters which were democratic constitutions that served to bring forth democratic government at the time of independence. In the South, colonial despotism bred military dictatorships. The North benefited greatly from the full impact of the Reformation and the Industrial Revolution, which served to extend education to the masses as a means of improving their conditions of life. In Latin America, the political and social environment produced a system of selective aristocratic education dominated by the Church, for the purpose of preparing for service to the Crown or the Church. In the North, education was greatly influenced by the scientific achievements in Germany and England and acquired a sense of social responsibility, while in Latin America, French culture, which was the highest expression of Latin culture, became the dominant influence, with its emphasis on culture for culture's sake.

Today, these differences are not quite so clear-cut. Crosscurrents of influence, particularly during this century, have been growing in both directions. However, the differences are still much in evidence.

A distinguished Chilean educator, Irma Salas, has ably stated some of the differences between education in Latin America and the United States thus:

a. Education in the United States is democratic in purpose, while education in Latin America has been, and to a large extent still is, aristocratic in purpose.

b. Education in Latin America is characterized by centralization of control, in contrast to the local control which is characteristic of North American education. While in the United States, education is a community enterprise, responsive to the interests and needs of the people, in Latin America it is a state enterprise, imposed on the people.

c. Education in Latin America, in general, follows a pattern of uniformity, in contrast to the diversity which characterizes North American education.

d. The Latin American secondary school, like the French *lycée*, imparts general education and prepares for the university, while North American education is more concerned with usefulness, with preparation for practical life.

e. The administration of the schools in the United States is unified for all grades and branches. The superintendent of schools will have under his administration all public schools, elementary, secondary or vocational in his city. In Latin America, the different branches of education, elementary, secondary and professional, are usually administered separately. Therefore, the articulation, co-relation, continuity, and unity of the school system is greatly impaired.

Advocates of the Latin American philosophy of education find fault with the United States system for being too pragmatic, materialistic, and utilitarian in its characteristics, without sufficient interest in and appreciation of the higher values of the spirit; while critics from the North find our system humanistic, purely cultural, highly impractical, and remote in time and space. In certain quarters in Latin America it is argued that our mentality, used to the humanistic conception of life, does not yield readily to pragmatism and that an education aimed at answering practical questions does not fit well with the Latin American tradition. These arguments for resisting change, which stem from dangerous generalizations, could hardly stand up under careful analysis. But the fact that such views are expressed is proof of the existence of conceptions, deeply embedded in cultural traditions and historical background, that must be reoriented for learning to live in the twentieth century.

A brief review of the problems of education in Latin America, at the different levels, will be helpful in pointing out the principal issues involved.

The principle that elementary education should be universal, that all children, whatever their sex, color, creed, or social status, should have access to free primary education, is written into every constitution in Latin America. Unfortunately, this consecrated principle has not always been carried into practice to the full extent implied.

Our countries, with limited resources at their command, have had to serve many other vital needs of the people as well. Consequently, public education has suffered from all kinds of limitations and what it has accomplished, sometimes under the most adverse conditions, is a tribute to all those dedicated to the cause. Private schools, mostly run by the Catholic Church, have helped the state carry this great responsibility to a substantial degree. Unfortunately, not enough has been done, or could be done, and an alarming percentage of children of elementary school age—in some countries more than in others—are deprived of the privileges of an education.

If the number of schools is insufficient, the quality of the education also needs improvement. Although new ideas have been brought into play and are already influencing methods and programs of study, traditional ideas still prevail in a great majority of elementary schools, particularly in rural areas, where the student takes dictation or copies from the blackboard and memorizes his lessons day in and day out, with little opportunity to develop his creative talents or to learn important characteristics of his home and community environment. Besides, physical facilities are usually meager. The relationship between teacher and pupil is quite formal and not much recognition is given to the different abilities and interests of the developing child as he moves from infancy to adulthood. Many children go no further than the third or fourth grade.

As a consequence of the inadequate coverage of the school age population, adult illiteracy is a major problem in Latin America. Even those who have had some schooling need additional training in order to be effective in their jobs. A very small fraction of the labor force possesses the training necessary to play its part in operating a modern economic system. The rapid rate of change in underdeveloped countries and the time involved in setting in motion programs for universal primary education and extensive secondary education demand special measures to raise the educational level of the existing labor force.

In Latin America we all realize that our very future is at stake on this issue. Governments are increasing their budgets for education, successful methods from abroad are being studied and adapted to national realities. The school is becoming, every day, more and more a living part of the community. But if we are to lower those menacing statistical figures for illiteracy, we have to treat the problem on an emergency basis. The need for more schools is more urgent now than the need for better schools. Most likely, a policy of sufficient schools for all children rather than improved schools for some children is the answer to this problem.

Secondary education is by far the weakest link in our school system. Its weakness stems from deep roots in the past that go all the way back to colonial times when it was almost exclusively in the hands of the Church for a selected minority. After the wars of independence the French concept prevailed. The aim of secondary education was to develop an intellectual elite, capable of appreciating the arts, letters, and sciences. The task was to select and train the best minds for positions of leadership in social, economic, and public life. The secondary school imparted general education with a heavy emphasis on classical subjects and with little attention to teaching applied sciences and vocational subjects. Its goal was to prepare for the universities.

Rapid economic development after World War II and a certain degree of industrialization in some regions of the continent are now slowly bringing to Latin America a new way of life, a new set of cultural values which are helping break down many traditional patterns. Leaders in the field realize that the task is to bring secondary education to all the elements of a heterogeneous population, who must be trained for living and educated for life in a democracy. The necessities of today demand that secondary education should develop vocational skills and offer a terminal education for those not going on to the universities. It should also emphasize the development of the personality, not just training of the mind or the acquisition of knowledge.

At no other level of education is there a greater struggle between traditional ideas, with their heavy emphasis on the humanities, and new concepts that insist on confronting theory with practice and ideas with realities. Programs of study are being continuously revised in the search for improvements, but the results have not always been encouraging. The pull of tradition, in some cases, has been too strong. Traditionally the secondary school has been conserved as an institution with identical requirements for all students. The concept of its aims is not yet sufficiently clear to satisfy the needs of either the student or society at a time when it should be equipped to guide the student either into professional training or university studies, or to immediate participation in the life of the community.

Vocational education in Latin America has, on the whole, been neglected and viewed as a poor alternative for academic secondary education. Industrial and commercial training is given in schools that are completely separated from the academic high schools. Vocational education has yet to become an integral part of the total educational picture and consequently will remain the most neglected sector in the educational system until it becomes articulated with other levels and types of education.

At least a score of universities in Latin America are older than Harvard. The University of Santo Tomas de Aquino, in the Dominican Republic, was founded in 1538, a century earlier than Harvard; Mexico, Bogotá, Lima, Quito, Santiago, Sucre, and Córdoba had universities before any such institutions were founded in the English colonies to the North. The universities reflected the prevailing mentalities of those times. The teaching was academic and abstract, although in a few instances enlightened educators with ideas far ahead of their times introduced studies such as mathematics and natural science. All these schools were Church-controlled and -dominated.

The birth of the republics brought about the nationalization of many institutions of higher learning and the Church lost, in many cases, its absolute hold on higher education. The old struggle against the Crown and clerical power continued against tyrannies and all forms of oppression. The universities gradually became politically and intellectually autonomous to a certain degree, a status which they have always defended and protected with great zeal. They are proud of their spirit of liberalism, their record of resistance to dictatorships, and their continued concern with social reform. All this makes for a politically charged atmosphere on the campus, but has not contributed to improve academic standards. Because of grossly inadequate budgets and administrative organization, because of part-time professors whose main source of income and interest is outside the university, and because of excessive student influence and control, the universities in Latin America as a whole are not prepared to play the role they must assume in shaping the future of the continent. The students are not learning the necessary intellectual and moral disciplines that would equip them to assume in the future the responsibilities involved in the management of the more complex socioeconomic structure which is necessary to meet the urgent demands of the people of Latin America. The students, in their efforts to protect the university from the political instability that surrounds it, have achieved the opposite effect by bringing politics into the classroom.

Graduate work, research, and extension are particularly weak. There is an incredible waste, by dispersion or duplication, of already very limited resources. In many cases there are separate laboratories and staff in each school or department to teach the same subject. There is a shortage of qualified instructors for technical training and there is insufficient correlation between the instruction being given and the real needs of the economy.

Leaders in Latin America agree that training for leadership to improve technology and to achieve economic development should be done in the universities and that research designed to yield results directly applicable to local problems and conditions should be carried on there. Ways of transmitting accumulated knowledge to the people and translating it into action should be developed at the universities. The institutions of higher learning must become a living part of the community and should not remain, as in the past, ivory towers of erudition.

Possibly this may seem a bleak picture of higher education in Latin America. Fortunately there is a brighter side, but what I have said may help in visualizing the uphill struggle which a growing number of institutions have had to go through in order to achieve a remarkable degree of progress. Such establishments, among others, as the Institute of Technology and Higher Education of Monterey, Mexico, and the Medical School at the University of Cali, Colombia, meet the highest standards for education. The University of Concepción, Chile, with a pioneering spirit of innovation, has upgraded its standards to a level that caused UNESCO in Paris in 1958 to recommend the "Concepción Plan" as a pilot project for university education in Latin America.

The Conference on Education and Social Development, sponsored by several regional organizations, which took place last year in Santiago, Chile, reached the following dramatic conclusions after reviewing education in Latin America: 40 percent of the children of school age in Latin America are not in school; only 17 out of 100 children who enter school finish their primary education; and only 4 percent of the young people of university age reach the universities. The conference recommended that each country should earmark 4 percent of its gross national income for education and that 15 percent of all Alliance for Progress funds should be dedicated to the same purpose.

Although education has uses and values that go beyond those of economic development, the bottleneck to rapid social and economic growth is education. The interdependence of the Western Hemisphere is a recognized fact. Unless Latin America is able to accelerate its development process the economy of the whole hemisphere—North as well as South—will be diluted. This is why our growing pains and problems are of concern to all within our hemisphere.

DIVERSITY AND UNIFORMITY IN THE LAW OF NATIONS

Philip C. Jessup

JUDGE, INTERNATIONAL COURT OF JUSTICE

Given at the University of Leiden, February 20, 1964

It is a privilege to deliver this lecture in tribute to the memory of the late Secretary-General of the United Nations, a man rich in resources of intellect and of spirit which he spent freely in the service of mankind. He added new luster to a name already notable in the annals of international law. As his annual reports and occasional addresses demonstrate, he cared deeply about the international rule of law as a fundamental tenet of the United Nations and was convinced that lawless policies were unsound policies. It has been well said of Dag Hammarskjöld that he was "imbued with the spirit of law." One may appropriately dedicate to his memory a lecture on the law of nations.

In addressing oneself to the subject of "Diversity and Uniformity in the Law of Nations," it is well to suggest at the outset that these two attributes are perennially present not only in the international legal system but in many, if not all, legal systems. This is a statement of the obvious, but it merits some attention at a time when there is such a spate of writing about the changes in international law which are said to be required to meet the needs of an international society which is itself experiencing great changes.

Back in 1931 Maurice Bourquin gave a description so applicable to the situation today that it merits quotation at some length:

C'est devenu une banalité de dire que le droit international est en pleine transformation. Non seulement ses emprises sur la vie des peuples se multiplient, mais les conceptions qui l'inspirent subissent un profond renouvellement. Certains juristes, par attachement à la tradition, s'efforcent de minimiser la portée de ce mouvement, de la présenter comme un simple prolongement du passé, dont les assises resteraient intactes. Assurément, tout s'enchaîne plus ou moins dans le développement des sociétés, et les révolutions elles-mêmes, malgré certaines apparences, se soudent à l'état de choses qu'elles ambitionnent de détruire. Mais s'il n'y a point, à vrai dire, de solutions de continuité, il y a des phases d'évolution rapide, où le paysage ancien désagrège sous les regards du spectateur, pour laisser apparaître l'ébauche d'un paysage nouveau, dont le temps précisera les contours et qui finira par régner sans partage. Que nous soyons dans une telle période, trop de signes l'attestent pour qu'il soit permis d'en douter.

C'est ce qui fait aujourd'hui l'intérêt passionnant du droit international. C'est ce qui fait en même temps la difficulté de son étude. L'image qu'il offre est complexe, pleine de traits contradictoires, de plans qui ne s'alignent pas dans une même perspective. Ceux qui le contemplent et cherchent à l'exprimer courent un double risque: fermer les yeux sur les innovations qui brouillent le dessin des institutions anciennes, ou bien, au contraire, ne s'attacher qu'aux indications qu'elles fournissent et construire, avec ces points de repère, un avenir plus ou moins imaginatif.

Similarly stimulating is Baron Frederik van Asbeck's vision of the purpose of the study of international law:

To explore how the present law has come to be what it is, how it is involved in a process of reform and extension and intensification, in order that we may be able to assist in the building, stone upon stone, in storm and rain, of a transnational legal order for States and peoples and men.

I shall not dwell upon the myth that change in international law is disastrous or even novel. I shall call attention to a few examples of the way in which new legal rules or doctrines have been advanced by states—some successfully, some unsuccessfully. Attention will then be drawn to what may be called regional law, with first emphasis upon the developments in the European Community both in the creation of new law and in the unification or assimilation of existing laws. Then aspects of the development of maritime law, in what one may call a functional rather than a regional community, will preface a brief reference to the origins of international law and to some of its evolutionary characteristics. Again, attention will be turned to law unification, taken as a symbol of the fact that, while diversity of law among interacting groups has been tolerated, uniformity has often been sought as an end in itself in federal states, in Europe, in Africa, and on the international level especially again where we find an international functional community.

Granted that some law has geographical, personal, or temporal limitations upon its applicability and binding force, and granted also that certain courts are limited to the application—as law—of certain defined or prescribed bodies of rules and principles, nevertheless law in the large has a certain unity, and no body of law is an island complete unto itself. That is why it is pertinent for the Statute of the International Court of Justice to list the general principles of law among the sources of law which the Court is to apply. That is why the system of private international law is a system of tolerance, particularly in applications of the doctrine of comity. The Chief Justice of the Federal Supreme Court of the Federation of Rhodesia and Nyasaland pointed to the need for tolerance of legal rules strange to the *lex fori,* since, without such tolerance, "the effectiveness of private international law, the system without which it would be impossible to maintain the legal relationships existing between the inhabitants of the various countries . . . would be most seriously impaired." I would go on to say that the effectiveness of *public* international law, the system without which it would be impossible to maintain the legal relationships existing between the various states of the world, would be seriously impaired if there were no tolerance of certain differences stemming from various legal systems. "Nations are, and should be, different from one another," writes Margaret Mead.

Within the bounds of this lecture, it would be impossible to inventory and even more to analyze all the interesting current views about change in international law. There is no pretense that references which follow are exhaustive. It will suffice if some realms of legal interest worth further exploration are identified by brief illustrations.

Among the changes in the international society to which current books and scholarly journals keep calling our attention are certain prevalent differences in ideological approaches and the entry into the family of nations of many new states in Asia and Africa. One may pertinently recall that with reference to many of the newer states there has been an evolution in the terminology—an evolution which was due to certain important psychological and political factors. A few years ago one found references to the economically "undeveloped" countries. A seeming pejorative connotation of that adjective led to the use of the term "underdeveloped," which has now been widely supplanted by the adjective "developing." Perhaps international law suffered from the fact that, in many quarters and over decades, it was considered to be the law of an undeveloped or underdeveloped international society. Let us assert that international law is—and long has been—a *developing* legal system.

"I am certainly not an advocate for frequent and untried changes in laws and institutions," Thomas Jefferson wrote to a friend in 1816. "But I know also, that laws and institutions must go hand in hand with the progress of the human mind. As that becomes more developed, more enlightened, as new discoveries are made, new truths disclosed, and manner and opinions change with the change of circumstances, institutions must advance also, and keep pace with the times." So, too, Bynkershoek in 1737 told his readers, "As customs change, so the law of nations changes."

Each generation imagines it is confronted with stupendous unprecedented novelties. One might read in a dozen sources today an analysis like this: "Prosperity never before imagined, power never yet wielded by man, speed never reached by anything but a meteor, had made the world irritable, nervous, querulous, unreasonable and afraid." Actually this is what Henry Adams wrote in his *Education* during what we are apt to consider the tranquil era of the first decade of the century.

It may well be said that one cannot posit the coexistence in international law of two mutually contradictory rules or principles both of which would be legally valid. States may disagree as to the rule itself or as to some factual application of the rule. One or the other view may eventually prevail and be blended into uniformity, as the result of the abandonment of one view, the negotiation of a treaty, the decision of a duly empowered tribunal, or a process such as any one of those taken into account by the United Nations International Law

Commission. One may examine a few historical samples which illustrate different types of legal diversity. And since uniformity of law is sought and achieved at various levels, we may examine how this comes about. We may find that many of the processes, even in the private law field, can make their contribution to that international harmony which it is the function of international law to promote and which may best be attained by gradual stages.

When the United States of America became a new member of the society of nations toward the end of the eighteenth century, there had been some two centuries of experience with the law of neutral rights and duties. Certain rules and principles had become clearly enough established by customary practices embodied in national ordinances, prize court decisions (jurisprudence), the customs of merchants, and a very large number of treaties, chiefly bilateral. There was general recognition of certain rules applicable to blockades and blockade running, and of the principle that a ship taken within the waters of a neutral state was not good prize if the neutral state objected. The basic notion that certain goods were contraband and that under some circumstances they were forfeit to a belligerent captor was not controverted, but there were vast differences in national definitions of contraband and on such issues as whether free ships made free goods. The principal maritime carriers—at one period the Dutch and the Hansa towns, for example—naturally sustained rules which provided the maximum protection to neutral shipping. The Scandinavian countries, as suppliers of masts, timbers, pitch, and tar, maintained that these products were at least no more than conditionally contraband. The United States, espousing the role of a neutral as a matter of political and economic policy, long favored total freedom for neutral trade at sea, so consistently indeed that it refused to ratify the 1856 Declaration of Paris, even though that declaration contained the major concession of free ships, free goods, because it did not go all the way toward meeting the American desideratum. A few years later, during the Civil War, the same government eagerly invoked every possible belligerent right against neutral shipping. But the geographical and naval situations of the end of the eighteenth century led the new western republic to a novel emphasis upon neutral duties in addition to neutral rights—a position which stood it in good stead when it came to arbitrating with Great Britain the Alabama claims. The contention for total freedom of neutral trade at sea was never embodied in international law, but much of the American doctrine of neutral duties did become part of that law.

The basic general concept of the rule of continuous voyage (but not the extreme extensions to "ultimate destination"), against strong opposition from whatever countries happened to be neutral during certain conflicts, was eventually accepted as law probably because it was essentially realistic and reasonable, but not because it could be supported by logic, since rules historically evolved by compromise cannot be extended by logic.

This whole branch of law affords numerous examples of the way in which national interests dictate national views on what are the rules of international law. The diversities were often met by impartial adjudication (whether in national prize courts or in international arbitrations), by bilateral treaties, or by more general agreements reached in international conferences. From the point of view of our present consideration, it is most interesting to note over centuries how rare it was for a government, whether belligerent or neutral, to take the anarchic stand that no law of neutral rights and duties existed. In other words, there was a basic uniformity on a legal principle. Moreover, in numerous instances, states small in military power could still, as neutrals, exercise important international influence through the disposal of access to their ports, by their economic resources, or by adopting with other small neutrals a solidary posture.

There is another set of legal rules applicable in time of war (although it may be a matter of debate whether or not these rules are part of the corpus of public international law), which reveals an interesting diversity, this time between the Anglo-American common-law systems on the one hand and the civil-law systems of Europe on the other. Both systems agree that the outbreak of war has certain legal consequences in its effect on preexisting legal relationships. In the common-law system, on the outbreak of war it immediately becomes illegal to have intercourse with the enemy, even in the carrying out of private contracts or personal correspondence; all these contracts are illegal unless specifically licensed. Under the civil-law system, private commercial and personal contracts continue to be legal unless specifically prohibited. Over the years, neither concept has prevailed over the other, but in any protracted war the end results can scarcely be distinguished.

To illustrate further a kind of uniformity in practice despite diversity in doctrine, one may refer to the question of what criminal jurisdiction a state, under customary international law and in the absence of treaties, is entitled to exercise over foreign ships in its ports. Traditionally, under what has been called the French doctrine, the local state is not entitled to exercise criminal jurisdiction over events on a foreign ship in port unless there is some felt consequence on shore— disturbance of the tranquillity of the port, involvement of shore personnel, or an appeal to local authorities for help. Yet under the French practice, a murder, no matter how quietly committed below decks on such a ship, may be considered a disturbance of the tranquillity and jurisdiction may be exercised. Under the United States doctrine, the local state's sovereignty is supreme, and a foreign ship in port is considered fully subject to that sovereignty. In practice, American courts will, in the exercise of their discretion, generally refrain from exercising jurisdiction except in the three types of cases admitted by French doctrine, including the liberal French interpretation of what constitutes a disturbance of the port's tranquillity.

A more serious clash has historically sprung from a United States doctrine, espoused when the country loomed small on the world stage, and opposed by most other countries. This was the United States doctrine of the right of expatriation, which was obviously in the interest of a young country needing and welcoming immigrants, but which was flatly opposed to English and European doctrines of indelible allegiance. The United States Congress in the mid-nineteenth century eloquently stated the American claim in terms of what today we call human rights, although actually the issue was whether the automatic legal effect of naturalization was the termination of the prior nationality, even when the individual's former sovereign insisted that he could not lose his nationality of origin without his sovereign's consent. After decades of incidents on land and sea and long diplomatic arguments, treaties which struck a compromise between the just interests of both sides eliminated most controversies, but many authorities would insist that the United States never succeeded in establishing its doctrine as a part of international law.

One doctrine, although it still does not pass unchallenged, which came to be established in international law in derogation of a preexisting rule, sprang from the national jurisprudence of the Belgian and Italian courts rather than from diplomatic asseverations. This was the holding that a state is not entitled to the usual sovereign immunity from proceedings in the courts of another state, if the activity in question is pursued *jure gestionis* rather than *jure imperii*.

Still another doctrine, now uniformly accepted in principle but diversely applied in practice, was widely admitted so rapidly that one can scarcely detect a period of diversity as to the doctrine itself, which one might therefore describe as merely an acceptable formulation of existing customary international law; this is the doctrine of the continental shelf, quickly imitated—and sometimes misunderstood or distorted—after its enunciation by the United States government in 1945.

On the other hand, the British government's espousal of Sir Hersch Lauterpacht's proposition, that under international law there is an absolute duty to grant recognition under certain circumstances, does not seem as yet to have commanded general support. On the question whether the proposition itself was soundly based in law, I do not venture to express an opinion.

In another geographical region, states of South and Central America and Mexico have evolved and contended for various doctrines suited to their national interests—doctrines bearing such names as those of Calvo, Drago, Tobar, and Estrada. The Calvo Doctrine, for example, was clearly designed to meet conflicts with governments of states in other parts of the world whose citizens made and followed investments. On the other hand, the familiar and distinctive *uti possidetis* doctrine has developed chiefly for the solution of territorial disagreements among the states themselves of the Western Hemisphere south of the Rio Grande. The name of the late Judge Alvarez will always be associated with the idea of an "American international law," considered to have a regional applicability.

But what is a "region"? It may never be necessary to suggest a definition in applications of Chapter VIII of the Charter of the United Nations, but in the development of law the identification of regional interests or concerns may have an importance. On a previous occasion I have tried to explain why I thought that "one's idea of what constitutes a 'region' is apt to be artificial and highly subjective," and I ventured to suggest some parallels between national and international regional situations especially from the point of view of human welfare.

Professor van Panhuys wisely entitled his inaugural lecture at Leiden "Regional or General International Law? A Misleading Dilemma." In one sense it is a misnomer to speak of regional international law, since it seems to deny the universality of the applicability of the law of nations. On the other hand, even without utilizing the concept of "transnational law," one is bound to recognize that substantial portions of what is with precision denominated "international law" are regional in character. The example just noted of the Latin American doctrine of *uti possidetis* is a case in point. The most notable instance is the rapidly growing law of the European Communities. The basic treaties are pure international law, as is the rule which makes these treaties binding—*pacta sunt servanda*. But the jurisprudence of the Court of Justice of the European Communities shows that to a great extent the law of the Communities is something different—something which I would call "transnational," which may be in part international law in the sense in which that term is used in Article 38 of the Statute of the International Court of Justice, and partly law which has certain other characteristics.

None of the Community treaties specifies the sources of law which the European Court of Justice is to use in the interpretation of treaties. The Court has said: "Notre Cour n'est pas une juridiction internationale mais la juridiction d'une Communauté créé par six Etats." But again: "Quant aux sources de ce droit, rien ne s'oppose évidemment à ce qu'on les recherche, le cas échéant, dans le droit international, mais normalement, et le plus souvent, on les trouvera plutôt dans le droit interne des divers Etats membres." Moreover, the Avocat Général, while modestly protesting that he was not an international law specialist, in one case supported his arguments by showing the similarity between the approaches of international law and of national law in determining norms of interpretation. The Court, in turn, invoked the common approach as part of the justification of its decision.

But the Court revealed how it stands on new frontiers of international law when in 1963 it said that the Community constitutes "a new juridical order in international law" and that Article 12 of the Rome Treaty must be interpreted in the sense that it produces immediate effects and creates individual rights that internal jurisdictions must safeguard.

More broadly, the European Communities are engaged in a process of attaining uniformity at a different level, that is by assimilating —at least in some aspects—the legal systems of the member states. Although this effort has much in common with the uniformity and unification of law movements (which we may consider in turn), it differs, as Professor Eric Stein writes, in at least two important respects:

First, assimilation of national laws in the Community is an integral part of an intricate plan for a progressive coalescence of the national economies of the six member States. . . . Second, the assimilation takes place within a new and unique institutional framework; the institutions of the Community have the legal power to order the national governments to make the adjustments in their legal systems necessary for the accomplishment of the assimilation.

One may recall that, with the creation of the International Labor Organization, the—by comparison, extremely modest—governmental obligation to submit to the appropriate local authority for approval agreed proposals for what one may call the assimilation of labor standards was hailed as a tremendous advance along the road to the establishment of an effective international community. If the progress in the entire international community is slower than that in the more limited European Communities, it is because, as Professor Stein says:

Even within a nation-state, a legal norm is the ultimate expression of the will and values of the society; only after the conflicting economic and social forces have been composed may the resulting consensus crystallize into a general norm.

Although progress in law assimilation within the European Communities may be achieved in certain areas with relative speed because of supranational characteristics, including the powers of the Council of Ministers under Article 100 of the Treaty, the Community still must rely at times on the traditional international process of concluding a multilateral treaty. This was the case in connection with the important establishment of a uniform rule within the Community for creating patent rights which would be valid throughout the Community. The same need for the use of the treaty process has been evidenced in connection with the recognition and execution of judgments of the national courts of the several member states.

Within the limits of this lecture, one can go no further in considering the development of the European Community law except to recall in passing the important provision of Article 177 of the Rome Treaty which empowers the Court of Justice of the Communities to give binding interpretations which a national court of last resort under certain circumstances is bound to seek. Thus uniformity of interpretation is assured. Although in general practice there are numerous clauses in multilateral treaties conferring jurisdiction on an international tribunal to interpret the treaty on the application of one of the parties thereto, such clauses are rarely invoked because, as Mr. Wilfred Jenks has pointed out, "the disadvantage of the existence of divergent views regarding the interpretation of a general international convention of a technical character is rarely regarded by those responsible for the foreign policy of a State as a sufficient reason for accepting the political responsibility involved in instituting contentious proceedings against another State." Perhaps this difficulty, which has been referred to as "the psychology of the litigant," might be dissipated if, through an appropriate international convention, a wider circle of states than those which are members of the European Communities were to agree that in given circumstances a national court would refrain from passing final judgment on a question of treaty interpretation (or indeed of the scope of a rule of customary international law) until an international jurisdiction, appropriately empowered, had given at least an advisory opinion on the question at issue. Such a step would be far short of all of the obligations already accepted by the members of the European Communities, but it would mark a spectacular advance toward uniformity in the field of public international law.

As already noted, Stein points out that a basic plan for a progressive coalescence of the national economies of the six member states is the motive force for the assimilation of national legal systems. Without such a deliberate plan, the needs of trade and commerce have in the past afforded examples of international processes by which legal diversity has been supplanted by uniformity in regard to maritime law. It might be said that, even though the seas do not constitute a "region," the maritime interests of the world have long given evidence that to a degree they constitute a functional international community. The customs of merchants and seafaring men tended to unify maritime law as far back at least as the seventh century B.C. In the 1860s, modern shipping interests, including prominently underwriters, felt the need for more precise agreement upon some of the applicable rules of law. First steps were nongovernmental and directed toward producing uniformity in various national applications of the law of general average. Preliminary consideration was given to the device of drafting a uniform law to be enacted voluntarily by the legislatures of all maritime states. This procedure was discarded in favor of the device of voluntary private agreement. As the final result of numerous nongovernmental conferences, agreement was reached upon the text of the York-Antwerp Rules, which today constitute uniform law by virtue of the fact that they are incorporated by reference in bills of lading and charter parties throughout the world. This is one of the situations where a new member of the international society would have no occasion to debate whether or not the existing rule seemed to it the most desirable; the necessities and the conveniences of international shipping point to but one conclusion.

The method discarded in connection with unification of the law of general average, namely, the adoption of identical legislation in many states, was, at about the same time, successful in bringing about uniformity in the rules of the road at sea. Within the comparatively brief span of a dozen years, more than thirty maritime states had enacted identical rules in their respective legislation. On various other subjects of maritime private law, the international maritime community has utilized the time-honored method of multilateral international conventions. This is the method used also in connection with other maritime interests, such as fisheries, and still more broadly in the recent Geneva Conferences on the Law of the Sea, when the international community made use of another useful process which is itself the product of general advances in international organization, namely, the United Nations International Law Commission.

We have invoked the most recent interstatal or transnational experience with uniformity in the circle of the European Communities and we have referred briefly to some of the modern portions of the history of one of the oldest bits of transnational law—the law of the sea. We might have gone back of the Rhodian law to the earlier potent influence of the Phoenicians and thus have suggested a bridge from Middle Eastern to European origins of various concepts. Sometimes one notes that the origins of modern international law are traced to Europe or to Judaic-Christian precedents which already move one geographically off the European continent, whatever may be the continuity of thought.

Any identification of a specific limited geographic or civilizational origin in Europe of those basic legal concepts which came to be accepted by the whole international community is a myth. International law, as we commonly think of it, probably cannot trace its origins back of the sixteenth century, but we are familiar with the fact that many of its particularities reflect practices of much more ancient times, as Grotius was assiduous in pointing out. Even when we find maxims of the Roman law quoted as applicable to the solution of international law problems today, we are aware that law did not begin with Rome. Professor Speiser makes a persuasive case for finding the origins of many of our legal concepts in ancient Mesopotamia from the middle of the third to the end of the first millennium B.C., where he finds the "initial chapter in the history of jurisprudence in general." Pertinent to the theme we are now exploring is his observation that "the legal tradition concerned is closely integrated in spite of the underlying differences in date, geography, political background and language." *Inter alia,* he reminds us of Mesopotamian legal precepts that laws reflect truths which are timeless and impersonal; that the interpretation of laws must be entrusted to professional judges and that these judges must look to precedents. In this law the written document found its high place, and this was but one of the legal concepts passing on with trade and the shifts in political influence through the Phoenicians, the Hittites, the Egyptians, and so on into Greece and Rome. Professor Speiser writes:

Today, though we freely acknowledge our manifold debt to Greece and the Bible, we do not always appreciate the extent to which Israel and Greece contributed to one of our fundamentel affirmations, namely that truly constructive power is power vested outside the agent who wields it. This abiding truth, however, was discovered long before the start of the Biblical and Greek experiences. It was first glimpsed in ancient Mesopotamia; and once glimpsed, it was held on to tenaciously as a source of strength at home and an example to others abroad.

May it be said that the truly constructive power of *international* law is to be found in the fact that, being the law of all the nations in the international community, it cannot be wielded to fit the interest or the whim of any one member of the community which seeks to invoke it?

I agree, too, that it was a myth which perpetuated the "falsely mechanical image of the legal process that conceived of law as a method for achieving the objective application of the single rule that alone properly governs the outcome of the legal controversy," and I pay tribute to the service which Professor Myres McDougal and his school have rendered in destroying such myths. In more conventional language, Wilfred Jenks has remarked that international law is not a set of rigid rules inherited from the past and allowing no scope for development but a body of living principles in the light of which new problems can be resolved as international relations develop.

Wolfgang Friedmann, with his usual insight, points to the applicability to international law of an analysis which Professor H. L. A. Hart had applied to law in general. Hart in his *Concept of Law* pointed out:

The power . . . conferred on individuals to mould their legal relations with others by contracts, wills, marriages, etc., is one of the great contributions of law to social life; and it is a feature of law obscured by presenting all law as a matter of orders backed by threats.

So, writes Friedmann, the "developing 'cooperative' law of nations" has "a fundamentally different character" from traditional international law—"the steadily increasing scope and variety of international conventions, agreements, or, in some cases even new customs, which bind the nations, not in the traditional rules of abstention and respect, but in positive principles of cooperation for common interests."

Starting from such premises, it is by no means irrelevant to note how consistently human societies, as they enter upon more complex relationships, are impelled to seek greater uniformity in the legal system which theretofore had been traditional and perhaps unquestioned. I find it convenient, with a glance back at the contemporaneous developments in the European Communities to which reference has already been made, to note the experience of other federal groupings.

We tend to assume that any diversity in the views of states concerning some particular rule of international law proves that one of the states must be repudiating the rule of international law. In some cases this is true, but we have already noted some national peculiarities which certainly did not constitute repudiations. Thus there may be agreement that international law authorizes a state to claim a belt of territorial waters, but disagreement on the base line from which the outer limits of the belt are to be measured. So it is in national legal systems. In the United States, for example, that a contract is concluded by offer and acceptance is a common principle, but the courts of different states of the Union have different views as to whether the contract is made at the moment when a letter of acceptance is posted or at the moment when the letter is received. The doctrine of contributory negligence, as distinct from comparative negligence, persists in the great majority of United States jurisdictions, although comparative negligence is the rule in admiralty, as it almost universally is in civil-law countries.

One of the most striking illustrations—and one which is not without pertinence to an evolving branch of international law—is the principle of strict liability when a person "damages another by a thing or activity unduly dangerous." In 1955 it was reported that the doctrine was still rejected in ten American states and approved in twenty. *Mutatis mutandis,* the explanation of the rejection describes the frame of mind of some governments in considering rules of international law:

One important reason often given for the rejection of the strict liability was that it was not adapted to an expanding civilization. Dangerous enterprises, involving a high degree of risk to others, were clearly indispensable to the industrial and commercial development of a new country and it was considered that the interests of those in the vicinity of such enterprises must give way to them, and that too great a burden must not be placed on them.

Similarly, local conditions have influenced the acceptance or rejection of the common-law rule of strict liability for animal trespasses. In western parts of the United States, where cattle grazed at large on the range, some states by statute enacted that the duty lies rather with a crop grower to fence the cattle out than with the cattleman to fence his cattle in. (I interrupt a consideration of United States experience to suggest that, just as law in some American states reflects the invasion of cattle ranges by crop farmers, so in a West African district, where the scant population in a large forested area formerly made it unnecessary to delimit tribal boundaries by specific metes and bounds, the construction of a highway through the district made it of immense practical importance to know which tribe or whether both tribes had proprietary rights to the roadsides.)

Returning to a consideration of United States experience, to prevent misunderstanding of the meaning behind what some may consider a juristic minuet in which national and international law are ill-matched partners, I hasten to note that the states of the United States, in regard to such legal matters as are not regulated by the Federal Constitution, are under no obligation to maintain a rule of the common law but are quite free to adopt by statute a directly contrary rule. Quite different is the position of a state member of the family of nations, which has no right to enact by statute a rule contradictory to international law; for example, to enact a law denying all immunities to foreign ambassadors.

While legal diversity thus continues to prevail among states of the United States, in many respects, particularly in commercial and financial matters, it became evident that diversity in legal rules was distinctly disadvantageous, and measures to secure uniformity were adopted. When the American Bar Association was founded in 1878 it dedicated itself in part to securing "uniformity of legislation . . . throughout the nation." Twelve years later the Association appointed a Special Committee on Uniform State Laws, and in 1892 was held the first National Conference of Commissioners on Uniform State

Laws, in which all states of the Union now participate. Over one hundred of the uniform laws which the Conference has drafted and approved are still current, although the number of states which have enacted them varies from one subject to another. For some forty years, the American Law Institute has pursued an additional process for securing uniformity by preparing *Restatements* of various branches of law. These *Restatements,* by reason of the excellence of the *rapporteurs* and the painstaking process by which the drafts are examined, reexamined, and finally approved after debate by the most distinctively qualified group drawn from Bench, Bar, and law faculties, have become standard authority, gaining still more authority from year to year as they are cited by the courts throughout the United States.

Somewhat comparable developments have taken place in Canada through a Conference of Commissioners on Uniformity of Legislation, although it has not been easy to unify the law of Quebec and that of the other provinces. So in Australia, the individualism of the six states long hampered the adoption of uniform laws, although today considerable progress is made through a somewhat different type of body—the Standing Committee of Commonwealth and State Attorneys-General.

In Europe, more broadly than in a federal context, the activity of the Institut International de Rome pour l'Unification du Droit Privé has had the support of the League of Nations and subsequently of many individual governments. The Consultative Assembly of the Council of Europe in 1962 invoked the aid of the Rome Institute as well as that of the Max Planck Institute in Hamburg in an opinion which endorsed the view of the Austrian Minister of Justice "that the unification or harmonization of the legislation of member States is already possible not only in special branches of law, but also with regard to fundamental legal concepts."

Again more broadly than in a federal context, and at times more narrowly within the confines of a unitary political state, but with abundant variety, past, present, and future, the experiences in Asia and in Africa present to the nonspecialist a bewildering fascination. A former Chief Justice of India (Vivian Bose) has referred to the problem of "how to weave tribal customs and institutions into the fabric of a modern state without disrupting the lives of the people too deeply." He identified the problem as still existing widely over the African continent and in parts of Asia, but already faced and solved in India, Pakistan, Burma, and Ceylon.

We are reminded of the prevalence of Islamic law throughout the Arabian peninsula and its position as a fundamental unifying source of legal rules in numerous other countries of Asia and Africa. Much recent attention has fortunately been paid to expounding the lessons to be learned from the law of ancient India. Some of the recent writings about African law seem to have a somewhat defensive tone, as if the writers were conscious that they needed to dispel the uninformed assumption that African law cannot be identified in such way as to afford a basis for comparison with legal systems of Europe and the Americas, for example. But Herskovits insisted that the evidence showed that, throughout the East African area, despite tribal variations, the dispute-settling process has a logic that makes it "as a whole comparable, in terms of ethical assumption and procedural regularity, to Euro-American legal thought and procedure, however different the forms in which they are cast may be."

To the same effect, and with special reference to the law of Ghana, Allot writes:

African law has a certain unity, deriving principally from its being customary and unwritten in character. . . . There are many coincidences of legal rule in different systems; but the wider unity is more a question of spirit, approach and the legal complex than of detailed resemblances.

And again in writing on Basuto law he describes their concept

that the law derives ultimately from God and the fundamental conscience and ethical beliefs of mankind, so that it is the expression of, or linked with, *morality, reasonableness,* justice between man and man; that law is *flexible* in its application, the traditional norms merely establishing a broad framework within which justice is done in the particular dispute. . . . All these features and attitudes are widespread in negro African legal systems.

But the existence of common philosophical or religious basic tenets does not eliminate the need for unification of law, as is apparent in the Euro-American experience. In geographically and politically complex situations, active steps are being taken to collate and to synthesize customary law. The outcome of a representatively attended colloquium organized by the Fondation Giorgio Cini and the Société Africaine de Culture, in Venice in October, 1963, to consider the development of traditional African law to modern law, was a final resolution which registered agreement

que le relevé systématique des coutumes et leur rédaction dans une langue et sous une forme juridique appropriés, constitue une étape importante dans la connaissance du Droit africain et une condition essentielle de son évolution; . . . que l'harmonisation des législations nouvelles des Etats Africains est, dans le mesure où elle est possible, de nature à faciliter des échanges humains, culturels et économiques entre ces Etats et l'évolution de l'Afrique vers l'unité.

From these excursions into the domain of attempts to unify private law, I would divert attention to another legal phenomenon, this time on the international level, which does not have a regional basis but which again recalls that functional bonds may be just as dynamic, may have just as much, if not more, motivating power. The story is a familiar one and details may be omitted as one recalls how members of the international society of states have organized themselves from time to time on the basis of common economic interests—interests which arose, for example, from the common concern with transportation on great Euorpean river systems, shared interest in the production and consumption of commodities such as wheat, sugar, coffee, tin. As is often pointed out, the degree of importance and of voting strength in organizations formed on such functional lines is not based upon the traditional symbols of military power but upon economic interest resulting from geographical, economic, agricultural, or mineralogical facts. One of the lessons to be learned from such groupings and the ensuing "cooperative law of nations," to return to Friedmann's phrase, is the fact that it has been found possible to design and to use new methods of settling disputes. It has been said that "the legislative process of compromise, rather than the judicial process of victory-defeat, is considered more suitable to the resolution of disputes in . . . relatively new and uncharted paths of economic cooperation among nations." But this is not universally true, as is shown by some of the experiences in the European Communities, and there is the significant point that it has often been agreed that questions of fact may be determined by an international body, as by the Permanent Sugar Commission under the Brussels Convention of 1902.

The "legislative process" is indeed a process of compromise and the international community has produced a vast amount of international legislation, as Hudson's great collection shows. It would be safe to say that at least a very large number, if not all, of the great multilateral lawmaking treaties were finally drafted in and out of international conferences with much give and take in the common interest of finding a uniform rule for some particular activity—a rule which had to be a compromise among conflicting interests and positions, since, if this were not true, the need for concluding a convention to establish a uniform rule would not have arisen.

The same observation is applicable to what is often called the codification process in international law. The process is different from the legislative-conference method. Just as the uniform law movement in the United States is aided and abetted by the nongovernmental *Restatements* of the American Law Institute, so in the international field, numerous private institutes and associations have provided invaluable aid to the intergovernmental process, which can be traced from the creation of the International Commission of Jurists at the Third Inter-American Conference of 1906, on through the Preparatory Commission of the League of Nations, to the present vital activity of the United Nations International Law Commission in gradually transforming into uniform law clouded areas in which the General Assembly decides that it will be in the common interest to eliminate diversity. If the process seems slow, one must think of the present size and variety of the international community and recall that in a single national entity the preparation of the German Imperial Civil Code began with the appointment of a preparatory commission in 1874, which reported in 1887, and whose work as revised did not finally become law until 1900. At conferences convened to transform drafts of the International Law Commission into multipartite conventions, diversities of view are inevitably revealed, but one has had occasion to point out that in the conferences on the law of the sea the national differences did not follow any pattern of alignment among Powers great and small, new and old, East and West, or North and South. Without attributing to the fact undue significance, one notes illustratively that, after a variety of views had been argued on one or another detail, the Vienna Convention on Diplomatic Relations was adopted as a whole on April 14, 1961, by 72 votes to none, with 1 abstention.

In the conclusions to his penetrating study of "International Law in a Divided World," Professor Lissitzyn makes a statement to which one gives full agreement:

The absolutist dichotomy between the presence and absence of worldwide agreement on values is false. In the world community, as in national societies, there is a broad spectrum of values and of degree of consensus on them. A large measure of agreement on values, does, of course, strengthen the cohesiveness of a community and the efficacy of its legal order. But it is not a question of all or nothing.

It is indeed true that "no one is asking for a complete rejection of what we know as international law. No one is asking that the books be burned and that we start afresh in rejection of the lessons history has given as to the rules which minimize friction." In his distinguished contribution to the series of lectures in honor of Dag Hammarskjöld, Secretary-General U Thant made a plea for a world "made safe for diversity," and the same plea was echoed by the President of the United States in his State of the Union Message. In a world so oriented, none need despair that there will be general international realization of the common interest or that the timeless tide will still flow toward uniformity in the law of nations.

This lecture was also published in the *American Journal of International Law,* April, 1964, with detailed reference footnotes on sources. These have been omitted in this volume.

HUMAN RIGHTS: A CHALLENGE TO THE UNITED NATIONS AND TO OUR GENERATION

Jacob Blaustein

MEMBER OF THE UNITED STATES DELEGATION TO THE
TENTH SESSION OF THE UNITED NATIONS GENERAL ASSEMBLY

Given at Columbia University, December 4, 1963

In one of my many talks with Dag Hammarskjöld, which I hold in precious memory, he accepted my invitation to address the 50th Anniversary Dinner of the American Jewish Committee of which I was chairman. We agreed that his topic should be "Human Rights," the field to which we are directing our thoughts in this lecture.

In that address—so full of wisdom and understanding—he made a basic and fundamental statement. He said:

We know that the question of peace and the question of human rights are closely related. Without recognition of human rights we shall never have peace, and it is only within the framework of peace that human rights can be fully developed.

Again, with reference to the method for the broadened attainment of human rights, he said:

The United Nations cannot lay down the law for the life within any national community. Those laws have to be established in accordance with the will of the people as expressed in the forms indicated by their chosen constitution. But just as the United Nations can promote peace, so it can, in joint deliberations, define the goals of human rights which should be the laws of the future in each nation.

Human rights are realized—either in their plenitude or often inadequately—within the confines of the national community. Among the legacies left by our late and lamented President Kennedy was his valiant struggle for civil rights. In his last speech from the forum of the United Nations on September 21, 1963, he said:

The United States of America is opposed to discrimination and persecution on grounds of race and religion anywhere in the world, including our own nation. We are working to right the wrongs of our own country. . . . Our concern is the right of all men to equal protection under the law —and since human rights are indivisible, this body cannot stand aside when those rights are abused and neglected by any member state. . . . Those rights are not respected when a Buddhist priest is driven from his pagoda, when a synagogue is shut down, when a Protestant church cannot open a mission, when a Cardinal is forced into hiding, or when a crowded church service is bombed. . . . New efforts are needed if this Assembly's Declaration of Human Rights, now 15 years old, is to have full meaning.

Dag Hammarskjöld and John F. Kennedy, those two great champions of human rights, of justice for peoples and among peoples, of freedom in a responsible society, reflected aspirations which have been gaining wider articulation and acceptance during our generation.

I

In contrast to the League Covenant, which was silent on human rights, the United Nations Charter mentions human rights no less than seven times. Indeed, in Article 1, which defines the purposes of the Organization, the promotion of human rights is placed on the same level as the maintenance of international peace and security and the development of friendly relations among nations.

The impressive place given to human rights in the Charter is paralleled by the time and effort which the United Nations devotes to those questions. In the General Assembly, in the three Councils, and in various commissions and committees, as well as in diplomatic conferences convened by the United Nations, human rights are a constant item of discussion and decision. Some of these organs, like the Commission on Human Rights, the Commission on the Status of Women, and the Sub-Commission on Prevention of Discrimination and Protection of Minorities, devote their full and undivided attention to these questions. To an increasing extent, the same thing can be said of the Third Committee of the General Assembly, which is becoming more and more a human rights committee.

It is not surprising that, in a world where the rights of individuals are in almost constant jeopardy, the United Nations should be so concerned with them. The United Nations responds very quickly to events; and when, for example, whole populations in Africa are denied even the most elementary rights, it is natural that there should be repercussions in the World Organization. It would be a mistake to think, however, that it is only in these highly publicized cases that the United Nations exhibits its concern for human rights. It is no exaggeration to say that this concern is manifested almost daily at every level in the United Nations Organization—a concern which reflects what is actually happening in the world at large.

The vital reason, if not the exclusive one, for this concern which is reflected by the Charter was the cynical and wholesale violation of the most sacred human rights immediately before and during World War II in certain countries where the violation of human rights became part of public policy.

It serves no useful purpose to reopen the sores of history, and I will not, therefore, attempt to describe again the horrors of Nazi concentration camps, the brutal murder of thousands, indeed millions, of men and women for no other reason than that they professed a religion, were of a race, or held political opinions different from those of a dominant group which had taken possession of the powers of the state. Nor will I reopen again the sores caused by the other proscriptions, indignities, hardships, and insults which, to the shame of the twentieth century, were imposed on their fellows by so-called civilized men in an age that we had been pleased to call enlightened.

Suffice it to say that to obtain the total defeat of those criminals was the principal reason for which the war was fought, and that the establishment of some means for preventing a repetition of these events became one of the goals of the peace settlement. We knew then, as we know today, that it is our duty to work for a system under which the rights of every man everywhere will be respected, honored, and upheld in essence and in spirit, in principle and in practice.

This was reflected in the Dumbarton Oaks Proposals for the Establishment of a General International Organization which were published by the great Powers in the fall of 1944. The Dumbarton Oaks Proposals said that "with a view to the creation of conditions of stability and well-being which are necessary for peaceful and friendly relations among nations, the new international organization should, amongst other things, promote respect for human rights and fundamental freedoms."

The generality of the language used in the Dumbarton Oaks Proposals failed to satisfy the expectations of an aroused public opinion which, in this country and other countries, was insisting on something far more concrete. So when in May and June, 1945, the representatives of the countries which had been associated in the war against the Axis met in San Francisco to draft the Charter of the United Nations, there followed one of the most interesting phenomena in the history of international relations.

Let us recall that the leaders of the principal national, nongovernmental organizations—comprising a cross-section of the population of the United States from its important fields of endeavor—had been called by the State Department to serve as consultants to the United States delegation. And permit me in this connection to make a personal reference. I shall never forget the talk my colleague, Judge Joseph M. Proskauer, and I of the American Jewish Committee had with President Roosevelt, a month before his death. The Committee is an organization deeply concerned with human rights, and several years before it had commissioned Professor Hersch Lauterpacht of Cambridge University to write for the postwar era perhaps the first definitive treatise on "An International Bill of Rights of Man."

The year, as was said before, was 1945—when fifty-one nations were sending their representatives to San Francisco to forge the United Nations Charter. The President said to us: "Go to San Francisco as consultants. Work to get those human rights provisions into the Charter so that unspeakable crimes, like those by the Nazis, will never again be countenanced by world society."

And it was those consultants, along with equally concerned representatives of the smaller countries, who were able, by bringing pressure on the great Powers, to obtain a significant strengthening of the Charter in the matter of human rights.

In the long pull, in the day-to-day attention given to human rights in the last seventeen years, the nongovernmental organizations (which now have consultative status at the United Nations) have often seemed less effective than in that period of intense consideration of the drafting of the Charter. It is to be hoped that these nongovernmental organizations—whether American or international —will in the future, because of their political disinterestedness, bring their full influence to bear upon Members of the United Nations, Members who are often motivated by purely political considerations.

The Charter, as finally drafted, provided for the establishment of a Human Rights Commission, and placed certain duties in the matter of human rights on the General Assembly and on the Trusteeship and Economic and Social Councils. On Member States, too, Articles 55 and 56 placed an obligation to take joint and separate action in cooperation with the Organization for the achievement of universal respect for, and observance of, human rights and fundamental freedoms for all without distinction as to race, sex, language, or religion.

The task of securing acceptance of these provisions was not easy. At one point early in the San Francisco Conference the cause seemed lost. Let us go back to a scene in the conference room at the Fairmont Hotel in San Francisco, the headquarters for the United States delegation. It was the morning of May 2, 1945. The consultants to the delegation were meeting with Secretary of State Edward R. Stettinius when we were shocked to get the news that our recommendations bearing on human rights and fundamental freedoms were not to be incorporated into the Charter.

As a last desperate measure, the consultants appointed a committee of five to prepare an eleventh-hour plea to Secretary Stettinius and his adviser on the subject, the late Dr. Isaiah Bowman, President of The Johns Hopkins University.

The statement completed, we then, with the other consultants, met again the same day with Secretary Stettinius and Dr. Bowman. Dr. Fred Nolde, Director of the Commission of the Churches on International Affairs, opened forcefully with a presentation of our statement.

We could feel the door come somewhat ajar. It swung wider after Judge Proskauer delivered an eloquent appeal that combined logic and deep concern; Professor James T. Shotwell, historian and then President of the American Association for the United Nations, drew on his own vast knowledge of international affairs to consolidate our gains; Clark Eichelberger, Executive Director of the American Association for the United Nations, spoke very effectively; and then to remove the practical objections of the American delegation who stated that it would be impossible there in San Francisco to work out with the other delegations, and agree upon, the many provisions of a human rights declaration, I proposed that the Charter merely state the general principle and provide for a Commission on Human Rights to set up the particulars. This was accepted as possible by the Secretary and Dr. Bowman.

Our proposal was taken up the next day by the American delegation as a whole, then by the Big Four, namely Britain, China, Russia, and the United States. And finally, the "Voice of the People," as personified by these nongovernmental organizations, was recognized —the human rights provisions were written into the Charter—and the way was prepared for setting up the Commission on Human Rights.

It will be noted that nowhere does the Charter place a duty on the Organization or on Member States to guarantee human rights. There were some governments represented at the conference which would have gone that far; the delegations of Chile, Cuba, and Panama all put forward proposals that would have had the Organization not only promote but also protect or guarantee the observance of human rights. These proposals were not adopted because the great majority of the governments represented at the conference, including the United States, were not willing to give such wide powers to the World Organization.

II

It was generally understood that one of the first tasks of the Commission on Human Rights, which by Article 68 of the Charter the Economic and Social Council was required to set up, would be to prepare a draft of an international bill of rights.

The Commission on Human Rights was duly established and in

February, 1947, began to work under the chairmanship of that great human being, the late Mrs. Eleanor Roosevelt. As expected, it gave priority to an international bill of rights which it decided would have three parts: a declaration, a multilateral convention, and measures of implementation.

The Commission worked so well that within a little over a year it had completed its draft of the declaration and part of a convention, which were sent up to the General Assembly in the fall of 1948. After a long and difficult debate, the General Assembly adopted, on the night of December 10, 1948, the first step toward an international bill of rights under the name of the Universal Declaration of Human Rights. The Universal Declaration of Human Rights consists of thirty articles in which are defined all the traditional civil and political rights, as well as the more newly recognized and more controversial economic, social, and cultural rights.

The Declaration, which was adopted as a resolution of the General Assembly, was never meant to be legally binding; instead, it was to be, as its preamble says, "a common standard of achievement for all peoples and all nations." Nevertheless, in the fifteen years since its adoption, it has acquired a political and moral authority which is unequaled by any other international instrument with the exception of the Charter itself. It is no exaggeration to say that no international instrument has ever received the same acceptance on all levels of society.

In the United Nations itself it has an authority which is surpassed only by the Charter, and it is constantly invoked not only in the General Assembly but also in the Security Council, in the Trusteeship Council, and in other organs. It has found its way into various international conventions, including the Japanese Peace Treaty and the European Convention on Human Rights. Many of its provisions are reproduced, sometimes textually, in the many national constitutions that have been adopted, particularly in the so-called new countries, since 1948; and it has inspired and sometimes become part of the national legislation of many countries. It has even been cited with approval by national courts. It is, as the late Pope John XXIII said in his encyclical *Pacem in Terris,* "a document of the very greatest importance."

The next step toward an international bill of rights was to have been a multilateral convention which would be legally binding on those states which ratified it. Later it was decided—largely on the initiative of the United States—that there would be two conventions: one on political and civil rights and the other on economic, social, and cultural rights.

The reasoning given for this division was that the two categories of rights required different modes of implementation. Governments can be expected to ensure respect for political and civil rights, but the implementation of economic and social rights can only be progressive, particularly in the economically underdeveloped countries. There is something to be said for this position, but I believe that the main reason for supporting this distinction in the United States was the fear of the Administration that the Senate might refuse to ratify a convention on economic, social, and cultural rights.

The Commission on Human Rights finished its work on these two conventions, which it decided to call covenants, in 1954 and sent them to the General Assembly, which has been working on them ever since; nor is the end yet in sight. Nine or more years may seem like an unconscionably long time for the General Assembly to have been working on these drafts, but the work is extremely difficult and often highly controversial. Some of the articles of these covenants are as intricate as the whole texts of other conventions that have occupied the whole time of international conferences after careful diplomatic preparation. And they involve an attempt to achieve a synthesis of the ideals of 111 sovereign states reflecting very different religious, philosophical, and political backgrounds and cultural traditions from the Western, Asian, and African worlds.

It should also be noted—and this is helpful—that the debates on the covenants have provided the context for the ventilation of a number of such questions as anti-colonialism and the self-determination of peoples which are directly related to basic human rights and are also highly political.

The fact remains, however, that eighteen years after the San Francisco Conference the United Nations has still to justify the hopes which, in this particular matter at least, men and women everywhere have placed in it; and it is not difficult to understand why there should be some dissatisfaction with the performance.

The main differences between the covenants and the Universal Declaration of Human Rights are: (1) the covenants, when adopted, will have a binding force in international law not possessed by the Declaration and (2) the covenants are to be supported by measures of implementation. This is indeed their chief justification.

The question of implementation is therefore most important. Indeed, this is the test of the sincerity of governments in this matter. As to the mode of implementation proposed for the Covenant on Economic, Social, and Cultural Rights, ratifying states will only be asked to report to the United Nations on the progress that they make toward the achievement of these rights. These reports would be reviewed sympathetically by the Economic and Social Council with a view to assisting the states, if necessary, toward achievement of the standards laid down in the covenant.

In the matter of civil and political rights, however, the measures of implementation that have been suggested—they have not yet been discussed by the General Assembly—are more complicated. According to the plan, a fact-finding and conciliation organ known as the Human Rights Committee would be established to which States Parties could complain that other States Parties had violated their obligations under the covenant. The Human Rights Committee would attempt to bring about a settlement and, failing this, would publish a report indicating whether in its opinion there had been a violation of the covenant. There would also be a right of recourse to the International Court of Justice.

Now the main feature of this system is that only states could complain to the Human Rights Committee, and therein lies its weakness. For experience has shown that states are unlikely to complain about the conduct of other states toward individuals unless they have a political reason for doing so. That they would not complain against their own conduct seems pretty obvious. A similar procedure in the constitution of the International Labor Organization has been invoked only three times in forty-three years.

III

It is mainly for this reason that many people think that the Covenant on Civil and Political Rights should recognize a right of petition by individuals or, at the very least, by selected nongovernmental organizations. It has been suggested that these petitions might be sifted by a kind of International Attorney-General, who would be responsible for instituting proceedings before the Human Rights Committee. There is little reason for believing that any appreciable number of governments would be ready to vote for such a solution in the General Assembly, let alone ratify a treaty which would subject them to the possibility of being haled before an international tribunal by an individual or nongovernmental organization. And yet the time has come when the United Nations should face the immediate problem of transition from mere promotion of human rights to implementation of human rights.

It has been clear for the past ten years that the United States government has not been prepared to assume any such obligation. Indeed, the official position of the government of the United States in the matter of the convenants on human rights has been that it does not favor them and will not ratify them. Just over ten years ago the late Secretary of State John Foster Dulles appeared before the Senate Committee on the Judiciary and said that the United States government "did not intend to become a party to any such covenant or present it as a treaty for consideration by the Senate."

I do not agree with the position that our government has taken in this matter, and I think that it should be changed. Indeed, from statements by our late President Kennedy and by President Johnson, one is encouraged to feel that perhaps, at least as far as the executive branch of our government is concerned, it may be in process of some transition in its position.

The policy of the past ten years has been a complete reversal of previous policy, a retreat from the position of leadership which this country had assumed in the matter of the international protection of human rights ever since the San Francisco Conference. It is a denial of express promises made when this country took the leadership in obtaining the creation of the United Nations Commission on Human Rights for the express purpose of drafting these covenants, and a capitulation in the face of agitation by a minority which comprises some of the most reactionary elements in the country.

In this connection, it is encouraging to note that in a recent speech Justice Arthur J. Goldberg of the United States Supreme Court called for the United Nations Members to adopt a treaty to implement the Declaration of Human Rights and also to establish an International Court of Human Rights to implement the essential civil rights of the Declaration. He said the court and the treaty would seek to guarantee individuals speedy and public trials, legal assistance, freedom from coercion, the presumption of innocence until proven guilty, and security from cruel and excessive punishments. He reminded his listeners that the idea of an International Court of Human Rights is neither new nor impractical, pointing out that the Council of Europe set up a European Court of Human Rights in 1953.

Well, it is an ill wind indeed that blows no good. And when in 1953 the United States government took the position which I have described, it recognized at the same time the need of alternative positive approaches by the United Nations in this field. So in that same year, the United States delegation, in a meeting of the Commission on Human Rights in Geneva, proposed that the United Nations should engage in a so-called Action Program for the Promotion of Human Rights.

The other nations were somewhat skeptical about this program at first and not at all prepared to accept it as an alternative to the covenants. On the understanding, however, that it would be treated not as an alternative, but as complementary to the covenants, the Action Program was eventually adopted. It consists of three operations: first, the Economic and Social Council has invited all Member States to report periodically on the progress that these states have achieved in the matter of human rights; second, the Commission on Human Rights has undertaken a series of global studies or surveys on human rights; and third, the General Assembly has authorized a program of advisory services in the matter.

The first feature of the program—the new reporting system—is a most interesting development. For one thing, it has anticipated one of the systems of implementation of the covenants to which I have already referred, broadening it to apply to all states whether they ratify the covenants or not. It may be objected that states are under no legal obligation to report. In such a matter, however, there is a strong moral and political sanction; and, as a matter of fact, the great majority of Member States do report.

It is pretty obvious to me, however, that the success of this particular operation will depend upon whether there exists an alert and informed public opinion in the matter. Governments—all governments—particularly in free societies—are sensitive to public opinion; it is the most powerful weapon in political life. If the public insists, governments will report, and they will report accurately. What is more, public opinion can influence governments to remedy any abuses which the reports may disclose.

The real difficulty is that public opinion is often too inarticulate, too loosely formed. I must confess that I have never read a newspaper account of any public protest based on these periodic reports; and again, I wonder whether the nongovernmental organizations are sufficiently alert. It is most important they should be.

The second innovation in the Action Program was the initiation of a series of global studies on various human rights. The Commission on Human Rights has now undertaken a number of these studies, and even more have been conducted by its Sub-Commission on Prevention of Discrimination and Protection of Minorities. The studies have dealt with all aspects of human rights; such matters as discrimination in education, political rights, religious rights and practices; the rights of illegitimate children; the right of everyone to leave any country, including his own, and to return to his country; the right to be free from arbitrary arrest, detention, and exile; the right of arrested persons to communicate with friends and counsel; and equality in the administration of justice.

These studies can have important repercussions. Thus, the study on discrimination in education resulted in the adoption by UNESCO of an international convention on the subject. Possibly the most important consequence of the studies is that, since they are carried on in cooperation with governments, the latter are encouraged to review their legislation and practice in the matter under review. But again, the usefulness of these studies is diminished by the fact that there apparently exists no organized public opinion, no "public watchdog," as it were, in the matter. *And one recommendation I now make is that, in the United States at least, a committee of independent and distinguished citizens be set up which could act as a kind of a "public watchdog" in this situation.*

The third new operation introduced by the so-called Action Program is the advisory services in human rights. This was undoubtedly inspired by the technical assistance which the United Nations offers to economically underdeveloped countries. In the case of human rights this analogy does not always apply. An economically underdeveloped country is not necessarily backward in the matter of human rights; nor are economically advanced countries necessarily the ones in which human rights are most respected. If any proof of that statement is needed, I need only revert to the example of Nazi Germany, which was very well developed economically.

In any event, the Secretary-General has been authorized by the General Assembly to extend certain services to governments which request them; these services consist of the provision of experts and fellowships and the organization of seminars. The most successful part of this advisory services program seems to have been the series of human rights seminars which have been held in various countries in recent years, bringing together key persons from various countries for short periods of time and giving them an opportunity to exchange their views and experience. These seminars have been held in all parts of the world—in the Americas, in Europe, in Asia, and in Africa—where all aspects concerning the protection of human rights have been discussed: the administration of justice, remedies against the abuse of administrative action, freedom of information, the role of the police in the protection of human rights, rights of minorities, human rights in developing countries, and various aspects of the status of women. These seminars have had a considerable impact on public opinion in the areas in which they have been held, and they have also been helpful to the participants and to governments.

The advisory services program, however, is still so small in relation to the magnitude of the problem of human rights in the world that, while useful as far as it goes, it can hardly be considered as anything more than an interesting experiment. This is, it seems to me, one of the programs that, if we are really serious in this business of the international promotion of human rights, should be considerably expanded.

IV

The future of human rights was left on the doorstep of the United Nations at San Francisco. What has been the response of the United Nations to that challenge? Has the response been adequate?

I will say this. The United Nations has many achievements to its credit. The Universal Declaration of Human Rights is undoubtedly one of the most important international instruments ever adopted, and it has already had a significant impact on events. The United Nations has also adopted a number of important conventions, including the Genocide Convention which our country should have ratified long ago. As to the two covenants on civil and political rights and economic, social, and cultural rights discussed here, the future is more uncertain; but if they include an adequate system of implementations, then all the time and effort devoted to them over a period of nearly two decades will be justified—provided a significant number of countries, including the United States, ratify them. The Organization is also engaged in the token program of advisory services which I have mentioned and, if developed, this could be useful.

Perhaps most important, the United Nations has provided an international forum for the ventilation of a number of great issues affecting human rights in many parts of the world, and has helped as earlier indicated to crystallize the formation of international opinion. This in the final analysis, I would emphasize, is the strongest weapon that can be used for the promotion of human rights.

Merely to establish this inventory is, I think, to answer the question whether the response to the challenge has been adequate; for we must put at the other side of the ledger the urgent and tremendous need for action; and when the balance is struck, we must conclude that much remains to be done—indeed, that an effort is required significantly greater than any that has been made until now.

With the above in mind, I offer a positive proposal. It may well be that the time has arrived to strengthen the executive powers of the United Nations in the matter of human rights. *Thus, the General Assembly or the Secretary-General might appoint an independent person who would be a kind of international commissioner dealing with human rights, bearing perhaps the title of United Nations High Commissioner for Human Rights.*

Such a High Commissioner could, among other things, lend his good offices to governments and be available at their request to investigate situations where there have been alleged violations of human rights; he could assist underdeveloped countries in the organization of various institutions for the promotion of human rights; he could advise the Economic and Social Council on the human rights aspects of the Development Decade; and he could assist the Commission on Human Rights in its review of the periodic reports from governments on human rights to which I have already referred.

Creating such a position would not require a treaty. It would be in the same category, for example, as the office of the United Nations High Commissioner for Refugees. Therefore, it should also have the ready support and cooperation of those Member States, like the United States and some others, which have not been willing thus far to enter into treaties.

It would seem to me that this proposal is practical and the very minimum that should be done at this time. If the human rights commitment in the United Nations Charter is to be really effective, the trend of development must be in the direction of greater capacity to deal with—initially, at least, to expose and air, if not to "judge"—specific violations. I say this is the very minimum.

United Nations concern with human rights is a reflection of a deep social malaise in our own time. On what the United Nations does, on what we in our own country do, to find and apply a cure for this malaise depends perhaps the future of the human race on this planet; just as much as on the elimination of war and the control of armaments depends whether mankind will continue to inhabit it. That, in my opinion, is the challenge to our generation, to our times, as well as the challenge to the United Nations.

THE PROMOTION OF HUMAN RIGHTS THROUGH THE COUNCIL OF EUROPE

Sture Petrén

PRESIDENT OF THE EUROPEAN COMMISSION OF HUMAN RIGHTS

Given before the Stockholm Branch,
Swedish Bar Association, April 27, 1964

Human rights have been in the forefront of efforts toward building up a new world order ever since the end of World War II. Thus the United Nations has had the promotion of human rights on its program since it came into existence and the promotion of these rights was something Dag Hammarskjöld always had at heart.

In conjunction with the work being done by the United Nations in this sphere, the Council of Europe has also placed on its program the protection of human rights. In the circle of closely related states combined in the Council of Europe it has been possible to create real legal guarantees for these fundamental rights of the individual, a thing which has not yet been universally possible.

In Sweden, the question of inserting a list of the citizens' fundamental rights in the Constitution has become topical in connection with the revision of the Constitution now in progress. Between what is done on the international plane and what is done on the national plane there are, of course, bridges, since today efforts on the international plane are aimed at obliging states to accord to all individuals in their jurisdiction, nationals as well as non-nationals, certain fundamental freedoms and at creating an international system of supervision to check that the individuals are actually enjoying these rights and freedoms.

With regard to the individual's legal position, international law was formerly interested, as a general rule, only in how the states treated the nationals of other states. Thus aliens were protected by a series of customary rules and a developed system of international treaties. On the other hand, international law did not, generally speaking, concern itself with how the states treated their own citizens. In this respect developments after the war led to an extension in the domain of international law, which should cause the states to check whether their internal judicial system meets the international standard, as regards the fundamental rights and freedoms of the individual. These rights and freedoms have either been laid down by the Council of Europe or are taking shape in some other international context, as in the work of the United Nations.

In other respects the actual concept of human rights goes back, of course, to much earlier times than the present day. It may nevertheless be sufficient here to recall the form taken by this concept in the Age of Enlightenment and the two important constitutional texts arising from it—the Bill of Rights in the American Constitution and the Declaration of Human Rights adopted by the French National Assembly in the early days of the Revolution of 1789. These two basic texts have inspired a large number of liberal constitutions in different countries, constitutions which came into existence during the nineteenth century and the first half of the present century and which also guaranteed the citizens a series of stated basic rights. A common feature of these lists of rights with roots in the American and French Revolutions and dating from the period before World War II is that they included only what are usually called political and civil rights, that is, rights such as freedom of opinion, freedom of speech, and freedom of assembly, which, from the point of view of action by the state, only assume that it will not place restraints on the freedom of the individual in these respects. Later developments led to the list of human rights also coming to include the individual's right to material security in various respects, such as the right to work, to medical care, and to provision for old age. Thus, along with the political and civil rights, there are also appearing at the present time the social rights, which presuppose positive efforts on the part of the state.

Even at the end of World War II it was still primarily the time-honored political and civil rights which appeared to be the most urgent subjects of international lawmaking. The reason for this was a twofold one. On the one hand, during the previous few years these basic human rights had been trampled underfoot and outraged in a way and on a scale which had no counterpart in modern times and which made it appear to the world's conscience as an imperative duty to create the means of preventing a repetition. On the other hand, a strong conviction had grown up that the maintenance of the basic democratic rights in a country was a safeguard against its becoming a hotbed for international conflicts. On this account the protection of human rights came to appear as obligatory in the interests of world peace. By way of summary, we may consequently say that the victorious democratic Powers came out of the world conflict with a strengthened consciousness of their principles and were resolved to secure their position in a new world order.

It was against this background that it was laid down in the preamble of the United Nations Charter that the peoples united in the new world organization were determined to reaffirm their faith in fundamental human rights, in the dignity and worth of the human person, and in the equal rights of men and women and of nations large and small, and that in Article 1 of the Charter one of the purposes of the United Nations was stated to be to achieve international cooperation in promoting and encouraging respect for human rights and fundamental freedoms for all, without distinction as to race, sex, language, or religion. These guiding principles are further spelled out in Articles 55 and 56 of the Charter. Thus Article 55 states that the United Nations shall promote universal respect for and observance of human rights and fundamental freedoms for all, without distinction as to race, sex, language, or religion. Under Article 56 all Members pledge themselves to take joint and separate action in cooperation with the United Nations for the achievement of the purposes set forth in Article 55. Furthermore, Article 68 provides for the setting up, under the

Economic and Social Council, of the Human Rights Commission, as a permanent organ of the United Nations, charged with the basic preparatory work in this field.

The above-mentioned provisions of the Charter—their origin has been ably described by Mr. Jacob Blaustein in his Dag Hammarskjöld Memorial Lecture—accordingly lay down the aims of the United Nations as regards the promotion of human rights, while their implementation has remained dependent on further endeavors, primarily on the work of the Human Rights Commission. As one of the first fruits of these endeavors the General Assembly was able in 1948 to adopt the Universal Declaration of Human Rights, which enumerates a series of rights, both of the earlier type, belonging to the category of political and civil rights, and of the more modern type, classifiable as economic, social, and cultural rights. The frequency with which the Universal Declaration is quoted bears witness to its great moral significance and this must not be underestimated. However, the Declaration does not impose on the Members of the United Nations any definite, binding, legal obligations. The intention is that such legal obligations shall be brought into being by the two covenants on the subject, for which the Human Rights Commission has drawn up proposals. These have been under discussion in the General Assembly since 1954. One of these covenants is designed to cover political and civil rights and the other one economic, social, and cultural rights. In his lecture Mr. Blaustein has explained why the important work being done in this connection has not yet yielded any definite results. The patient detailed work on the definition of various rights which is going on can in a certain sense be said to amount to a definition of the democratic system of government itself. With the different ideas of the democratic system that are held today no one is likely to be surprised if at many points it turns out to be difficult to reach agreement. In addition there are the difficulties which arise as regards agreeing on the machinery for international supervision to make sure that the individuals concerned really enjoy the rights included in the two covenants.

It is therefore natural that it should prove to be easier to regularize the protection of human rights on the regional level, within a group of states with similar political and cultural traditions. The European Convention for the Protection of Human Rights and Fundamental

Freedoms offers an example of such a regional convention in close accord with the Universal Declaration of Human Rights.

The origin of this Convention is explained by the fact that the Council of Europe, founded in 1949, also laid down the promotion of human rights as one of its principal aims. This is already clear from Article 1 of the Statutes of the Council. The aim of the Council is here stated to be to achieve a greater unity between its members for the purpose of safeguarding and realizing the ideals and principles which are their common heritage and facilitating their economic and social progress. According to the same Article, this aim shall be pursued through the organs of the Council by agreements and common action, *inter alia,* in the maintenance and further realization of human rights and fundamental freedoms. Therefore, from the very beginning of the Council's life, the conclusion between its members of a convention for the protection of human rights and fundamental freedoms was considered as one of its most urgent tasks. The Convention was signed in Rome in 1950 and entered into force in 1954, together with its first Additional Protocol of 1952. It has been ratified by all sixteen members of the Council, except France and Switzerland.

The Convention and the Additional Protocol together guarantee the following rights: the right to life; the prohibition of torture and inhuman and degrading treatment; the prohibition of slavery, servitude, and forced or compulsory labor; the right to liberty and security of person; the right, if arrested or detained, to be informed of the reasons for such arrest or detention, to be brought at once before a magistrate, and to have the case tried within a reasonable time; the right, in both civil and criminal cases, to the fair and regular administration of justice; the prohibition of retroactive penal laws; the right to respect for private and family life, home, and correspondence; the right to freedom of thought, conscience, and religion; the right to freedom of expression; the right to freedom of peaceful assembly and to freedom of association with others, including the right to form and to join trade unions; the right, for men and women of marriageable age, to marry and to found a family; the right to respect for property; the right to education and the right of parents to ensure that their children are educated according to their own religious and philosophical convictions; the right to free elections of the legislative body; and, lastly, the right to make an effective appeal to a national court in the event of a violation of one of the rights or freedoms guaranteed by the Convention.

This list shows that the rights guaranteed by the Convention are mainly political and civil rights or, in other words, rights concerning which the state's obligation is to refrain from interfering in the sphere of liberty guaranteed to the individual. The administration of justice obviously calls for some positive action on the part of the states, but otherwise, among the rights written into the Convention, there is scarcely more than the right to education that presupposes, at least ultimately, an activity on the part of the state aimed at meeting certain needs of the individual. Other rights of the same type, especially social rights, are likewise protected by the Council of Europe, but the method chosen is that of other instruments than the Convention we are now discussing. For example, we may refer to the European Social Charter, signed at Turin in 1961, which, however, has still to come into force.

Thus fifteen of the Council of Europe's member states, by adhering to the European Convention and its Additional Protocol, have exchanged reciprocal pledges to guarantee to all individuals under their jurisdiction the rights and freedoms just enumerated, irrespective of whether these individuals are their own nationals, the nationals of other states (whether these states have adhered to the Convention or not), or stateless persons. Thus the Convention makes it possible for each state adhering to it to lodge a complaint against another contracting state regarding an infringement of the Convention, even though the victims may be the nationals of the state accused.

This involves, as I said before, a new principle in international law. Experience has shown, however, that a state cannot, except under very special circumstances, be expected to take such action against another state on account of the latter's treatment of its own nationals. The only cases of complaints lodged under the European Convention by states against states have accordingly been concerned with situations in which there has been an ethnical connection between the state that made the accusation and the victims of the alleged violation of the Convention. Thus, some years ago, Greece lodged a complaint against the United Kingdom on account of certain measures taken by the British government, which was then administering Cyprus, and recently the European Commission of Human Rights has dealt with a complaint lodged by Austria against Italy concerning the trial of some members of the German-speaking population of South Tyrol– Alto Adige who were charged with having caused the death of an Italian customs official.

Apart from quite special cases like this, however, it is not to be expected that states will show themselves to be disposed to lay complaints against each other regarding a state's violations of the Convention in relation to its own nationals. This is why the Convention is only of true significance for the individual in so far as it allows him to lodge a complaint against his own government. The Convention has established such a right of individual appeal, but it cannot be exercised except against contracting states which have declared that they recognize this right. Up to now, such declarations have been made by ten states: the Federal Republic of Germany, Austria, Belgium, Denmark, Ireland, Iceland, Luxembourg, the Netherlands, Norway, and Sweden.

Disregarding the very rare cases of state petitions mentioned above, it is the individual petitions originating in the ten countries named which have put the Convention to the test and given employment to the two bodies established to secure respect for it, the Commission of Human Rights and the Court of Human Rights.

All petitions must be addressed to the Commission. They are first examined as regards their admissibility. The aim of this examination is to enable the Commission to reject all petitions presented too late or presented without the petitioner having exhausted the legal remedies available to him in his own country and all other petitions in respect of which it can be stated already at this stage that they could not show any violation of the Convention. This preliminary sorting is therefore intended to eliminate useless petitions and to allow the Commission to concentrate on petitions deserving a closer study.

However, it may be that even at the stage when the admissibility of a petition is being examined, an exchange of views may take place with the government of the state implicated in the case and there may even, sometimes, be a hearing to which both parties are summoned.

The fact remains that of the approximately 2,000 petitions dealt with up to now by the Commission only about 35 have been declared admissible.

This result, which inevitably gives a large number of the Commission's decisions a certain monotony, is explained in part by the fact that many of the petitioners do not realize the limitations of the Convention's sphere of application. Thus numerous petitioners have complained about acts which occurred before the Convention came into force, particularly in Germany under the Hitler regime. Others have failed to exhaust all the possibilities of internal legal resort and many do not understand the function of the Commission, believing it to be called to act as a kind of supreme court, invested with the power to correct all the alleged errors of judgment committed in the national courts. As regards the working of the national courts, the Commission has been given the task only of ensuring that the decisions reached by these courts are made under a procedure which conforms to the requirements of the Convention.

The decision by which the Commission declares a petition inadmissible is therefore of a distinctly judicial character and definitely settles the matter. On the other hand, the petitions declared admissible give rise to a thorough scrutiny and rigorous examination of the alleged facts and the legal argumentation of the two parties. Afterwards the Commission's first task is to place itself at the disposal of the parties, with a view to reaching an amicable settlement of the matter, a settlement which must be imbued with that respect for human rights proclaimed by the Convention. If this attempt at mediation fails, the Commission drafts for the Committee of Ministers a report, in which it must state the facts and present an opinion as to whether the facts stated disclose, on the part of the state implicated, a violation of the obligations incumbent upon it under the terms of the Convention. Here again the Commission's task is to express a purely judicial opinion.

After the Commission's report has been transmitted to the Committee of Ministers the subsequent procedure may take two different courses. If the state implicated has accepted the jurisdiction of the Court of Human Rights, the matter may be referred to the Court by the Commission, by the state concerned, or by another state which is interested in the matter, but not by the individual from whom the petition has emanated. Up to now, nine states have accepted the compulsory jurisdiction of the Court.

If, on the other hand, the matter cannot be referred, it is the Committee of Ministers that will make a decision on whether there has been an infringement of the Convention or not. If the answer is in the affirmative and if the state implicated does not, within the time fixed by the Committee of Ministers, take the measures entailed by the decision, the consequences of the decision will be prescribed by the Committee of Ministers.

This last provision of the Convention leaves a certain scope for considerations other than those dictated by strictly legal points of view. However, the fact remains that, as in the case of the Court's decisions, the Convention obliges the contracting states to respect the final decisions of the Committee of Ministers in the matter.

Obviously the Convention will not produce its full effects until all the contracting states have recognized the individual's right to have recourse to it and have accepted the jurisdiction of the Court. Meanwhile the effects of the Convention are not to be measured only by the number of petitions dealt with and by the fate they meet. In eight of the states which are parties to the Convention, its provisions have been directly incorporated in the internal law. The other contracting states have to employ other means in seeing that their internal law conforms to the Convention. There is no lack of examples of internal law being amended in order to bring it into better agreement with the Convention. In certain cases there has been a relation of cause and effect between the matters brought before the Commission and such amendments to the national laws.

Thus the influence of the Convention makes itself felt primarily through the internal legislation and the jurisprudence of the national courts of the contracting states, above all when these courts have to apply directly the provisions of the Convention.

As a small illustration of how the Convention operates in the internal judicial systems of different countries, we may mention the case of a national of the United States who was recently fined by a German court for a minor offense and was also ordered to pay the costs of the legal proceedings. These costs included a sum representing the remuneration of the interpreter who had to be called in to interpret between the accused and the judge. However, Article 6 of the European Convention on Human Rights prescribes that everyone charged with a criminal offense has the right to have the free assistance of an interpreter if he cannot understand or speak the language used in court. In consequence the American was released by a decision of a higher German court from the obligation to repay the interpreter's remuneration. Here we see how the Convention, by being observed in the internal legal system of a state subscribing to the Convention, also acts in favor of a national of a state which is not a party to the Convention. Thus, if this foreign national had not had the matter rectified within the Federal Republic of Germany, he would have been at liberty to bring the matter before the European Commission of Human Rights, since the Federal Republic of Germany has accepted the individual's right to refer complaints to the Commission.

In the light of what has just been said, there is therefore nothing surprising in the fact that the percentage of petitions retained by the Commission should be so low. Like the Court, the Commission seems particularly to be called to play a part when it is a matter of stating precisely the meaning of the rights whose definition in the Convention has been drafted in rather general terms. Here the task of the two supervisory bodies is to go more deeply into the analysis of the concepts of law, by drawing on the legal tradition common to the member states of the Council of Europe. Thus, for example, the Commission has had to express its opinion several times, with reference to Article 6 of the Convention, on questions concerning the definition of the right of every person to a fair hearing in the determination of his civil rights and obligations or of any criminal charge against him.

A similar task is imposed on the Commission and the Court in relation to the restrictions permitted by the Convention on the rights and liberties which it guarantees. In the case of such rights and liberties as the right to respect for private life and freedom of expression, these restrictions are only defined by reference to the imperative requirements of democratic society, for example, in matters of national security, public safety, and the protection of health or morality. It is clear that in many situations the existence of such an imperative requirement may be subject to debate. Thus, in the De Becker case, one of the two cases which have so far been submitted to the Court, the Commission has had to give an opinion on the question of how far such imperative requirements warranted certain limitations on freedom of expression, when applied as a penal sanction to a Belgian journalist convicted of collaboration with the enemy during the war. In cases of this type the Commission and the Court thus might be called upon to contribute to the actual definition of what is meant by a democratic society. A similar question arose recently in the Iversen case, in which the Commission found that obligatory public service in certain parts of the country, imposed upon Norwegian dentists at the beginning of their careers, did not constitute forced and compulsory labor of a nature forbidden by the Convention.

Without entering into the details of the developing jurisprudence of the Commission and the Court, it can be said that the Convention, as it stands, constitutes not only a profession of faith, affirming the democratic principles of our civilization, but also a sign of health, in that the contracting states do not fear to submit to international supervision the manner in which they apply these principles.

Thus the European Convention on Human Rights, born of the conviction that the safeguarding of human rights and fundamental liberties is essential to the maintenance of true democracy, constitutes at once a safety valve as regards the operation of the existing national law of the contracting states, a bulwark against the possible weakening of democratic order in these states, a starting point for an evolution toward still greater protection for human dignity, and a noteworthy addition to the status of the individual under international law.

If, finally, we ask how the work for the promotion of human rights which is thus being carried on within the framework of the European Convention is related to the corresponding task undertaken by the United Nations on the universal level, the answer will be that there is in no case any contradiction between the two. On the contrary, since the legal implementation through the United Nations of the Universal Declaration of Human Rights still seems remote, as Mr. Blaustein has pointed out in his lecture, the experience gained with the European Convention, largely inspired, as it is, by the same basic concepts

THE UNITED NATIONS
AND ATOMIC ENERGY

Sir John Cockcroft

MASTER OF CHURCHILL COLLEGE, CAMBRIDGE UNIVERSITY

Given at Cambridge University, November 26, 1963

I have been invited by the Dag Hammarskjöld Foundation to give one of a number of memorial lectures which are being delivered in universities throughout the world. I am very glad to be able in this way to pay my personal tribute to a very great international civil servant whom I knew well through my membership on the United Nations Scientific Advisory Committee, which was founded in 1955 and was chaired by Hammarskjöld until his tragic death.

This lecture will be concerned with Dag Hammarskjöld's influence in promoting world collaboration in science and technology. His first major opportunity came after President Eisenhower's speech at the United Nations General Assembly in the autumn of 1953. President Eisenhower spoke about the tremendous dangers of nuclear war and the possibility of the destruction of civilization. He proposed the foundation of an International Atomic Energy Agency to which governments should transfer nuclear fissile materials. This agency was finally founded two years later, but in the meantime the United States suggested in April of 1954 the calling of an International Conference on the Peaceful Uses of Atomic Energy.

Up to this time the development of atomic energy even for civil purposes had largely been shrouded in secrecy, due mainly to the United States Atomic Energy (McMahon) Act and the difficulty of distinguishing between the military and civil applications of atomic energy. This proposal for an international conference was followed by the appointment of one of my friends, Professor I. I. Rabi, Higgins Professor of Physics at Columbia, to chair a United States committee to prepare the way for the conference. In August, 1954, he visited Cambridge for informal discussions of the conference agenda with me and other Cambridge scientists, including Lord Adrian. In this way, the ground was prepared for Mr. John Foster Dulles to make a formal proposal to hold the conference. He made this proposal to the United Nations General Assembly in October, 1954, and it was agreed to with enthusiasm. Mr. Hammarskjöld then arranged for the Assembly to appoint a Scientific Advisory Committee to the Secretary-General, first to supervise the arrangements for the conference. This committee was formed from representatives of the United States, Britain, Russia, Canada, France, India, and Brazil. The committee was chaired by Hammarskjöld and he attended all its meetings until the Congo operation began.

This was the first time that a Scientific Advisory Committee had operated at this level within the United Nations. It has met twice a year since its foundation and has worked very harmoniously with practically no political difficulties. This harmony was due in the first place to Hammarskjöld's great abilities as a chairman. He was very good at picking out the essential points in the discussion and in summing up to reach an agreed decision. But this harmony was also helped by the fact that most of the members were well known to each other personally and scientifically; it was a kind of club. In addition to Professor Rabi and myself, we had, as the Canadian representative, Dr. W. B. Lewis, an ex-fellow at Caius College, an ex-university lecturer of physics in Cambridge University; Dr. Homi Bhabha, distinguished theoretical physicist from India, an honorary fellow at Caius College, well known for his activities in Cambridge in the 1930s; Bertrand Goldschmidt, a French scientist who was one of the founder members of the Canadian Atomic Energy Project in the war years; D. V. Skobeltsin, a Russian experimental physicist well known to us in the chemistry department, and so on. Naturally we all got on well together.

The committee had to work fast since there were only eight months from the time of its first formal meeting to the assembly of the conference in Geneva in August of 1955. But a very effective United Nations secretariat was set up and the vast resources of the United Nations enabled preprints of over 1,300 papers to be ready by the time of the conference, when 1,400 delegates and as many observers assembled in the Palais des Nations at Geneva. By then this building had been transformed by erecting scientific exhibits in its broad corridors and all available halls while, in addition, in the grounds, a pavilion had been erected and the United States had flown in and assembled a working atomic reactor.

Mr. Hammarskjöld spoke as follows at the opening session of the conference:

We have left behind us the times when man, exploring what might have been inert matter, discovered tremendous energy coiled up at the very heart of atoms. We then entered a phase when, within the lifetime of an individual, this energy assumed destructive shape and threatened to become our nemesis. The Conference whose inauguration we are celebrating today might well mark the beginning of a phase during which man will have left his bewilderment and his fear behind and will begin to feel the elation of one of the greatest conquests made by his mind.

The conference was held in a very friendly spirit with a notable absence of the political speeches which are a regrettable feature of some international scientific conferences today. Apart from the formal conference sessions there were innumerable informal discussions, evening lectures, social functions, and exhibitions providing a great opportunity for East and West to mingle to their mutual advantage. The conference had the very important result of strengthening the hands of those scientists responsible for recommending declassification and it achieved a virtually complete removal of secrecy from civil nuclear power development.

I was very pleased to be chairman of one of the conference sessions when a Russian speaker described their first nuclear power station, which was already generating 5,000 kilowatts of energy of electricity. Sir Christopher Hinton described the plans for the Calder Hall nuclear power station, then about two-thirds built, and forecast to the conference that nuclear power could be generated in subsequent commercial stations for about 0.6*d.* per kilowatt hour provided a "reasonable allowance was made for the value of the plutonium produced." The reasonable allowance was then thought to be about 0.3*d.* per unit, resulting in a gross cost of 0.9*d.* per unit. It turned out in the course of time that this estimate of the credit for the by-product was a good deal too high.

He also forecast that electrical power output of the first four British nuclear power stations would be 400,000 to 800,000 kilowatts. The output of these stations is now expected to be about 1.4 million kilowatts. It was forecast that by 1965 eight nuclear power stations in Britain of this general type, in which heat is developed by uranium fission, would produce well over 1.0 million kilowatts. The present forecast is that by the end of 1966 we will have an installed capacity of 3.6 million kilowatts.

I had the difficult task of summarizing the proceedings of the conference in a final evening lecture. I said that the consensus at the conference was that capital costs of nuclear power stations would be 50 to 100 percent higher than the capital cost of coal-fired stations, but that fuel costs would be less than half that of coal. I went on to say that the whole history of engineering development showed how rapidly capital costs fall in the early stages of important new developments, and there was good reason to believe that in the second decade, that is to say in 1966–76, the cost of nuclear power would fall below that of power from coal and oil.

Experience gained during the eight years since the conference shows that the capital costs of the first of the commercial stations—Berkeley and Bradwell in the United Kingdom—were higher than the forecast even though the output was about twice that forecast. The original estimated capital costs of Berkeley and Bradwell were about £143 per kilowatt including some allowance for overheads but, as a result of modifications to take account of developing knowledge of the behavior of large reactors and of the general rise in prices in recent years, the cost has increased to about £175 per kilowatt for the two stations.

It was further found that the credit for plutonium originally envisaged was too high, as a result of falling costs of the competitive fissile material U–235. At present the Central Electricity Generating Board assumes no credit—a somewhat conservative assumption. A further factor increasing generating costs was that capital charges rose from

4 percent to 8 percent in the period, partly owing to a Treasury ruling that nationalized industries should earn $2\frac{1}{2}$ percent on their capital, thus effectively increasing by 40 percent the capital cost component of power. The Central Electricity Generating Board figures for the generating cost at Bradwell and Berkeley are now $1.2d$. and $1.1d$. per unit on the assumption of a 75 percent load factor and twenty-year life. However, the load factors achieved at Bradwell and Berkeley have for a period been appreciably higher than the conservative figure of 75 percent. This bears out the experience of Calder Hall and Chapel Cross, where load factors have been 90 percent over a period of a year. There are also good grounds for regarding a twenty-year life as conservative.

The forecast of progressively falling capital costs has been realized as a result of the usual process of engineering development combined with increases of output from 300,000 kilowatts to over 1.0 million kilowatts in the ninth of the series being built at Wylfa. The total generation costs for the Oldbury station coming into commission in 1966 are estimated by the Central Electricity Generating Board at $0.66d$., assuming 75 percent load factor, twenty-year life, and 8 percent interest and profit; if the station achieves an 85 percent load factor and a twenty-five-year life, and 6 percent interest is assumed, this figure would be $0.51d$. The prediction that fuel costs would be half those of coal-fired stations seems likely to be realized since Wylfa running costs are forecast as $0.22d$. per unit sent out and the contemporary 2.0-million kilowatt Thorpe Marsh coal-fired station at $0.4d$. per unit.

We are looking beyond 1968 to changing the type of nuclear power station in Britain to a more advanced design—a design which is already built in prototype at Windscale and is generating 30,000 kilowatts.

The so-called advanced gas-cooled reactor of this power station uses uranium oxide fuel elements in stainless steel sheaths and can therefore operate with fuel surface temperatures of 650° C. This enables gas outlet temperatures to be increased by more than 200° C. over earlier stations and should allow steam to be generated at 1,050° F. and 2,350 p.s.i. with steam cycle efficiencies of 43.5 percent in stations of 500,000 kilowatts output. The experimental station at Windscale has been constructed to prove the technology of the system to enable the Generating Boards to take a decision about ordering a major unit and has so far worked well.

Because of the higher temperature of operation, capital costs of a 1.0-million kilowatt station are forecast to be about £80 per kilowatt with the likelihood of further reductions to below £70. The cost per unit sent out at the first stations of the series is forecast to lie beween 0.4*d*. and 0.5*d*. per unit depending on the economic assumptions used, possibly falling to 0.35*d*. or less with more ambitious designs.

The progress of development in the United States has shown a similar trend of falling capital costs and generating costs. The first nuclear power station at Shippingport, using a pressurized-water reactor with a design output of 60,000 kilowatts, cost about $1,000 per kilowatt; its subsequent competitor at Dresden in the United States, using a boiling-water reactor with a design output of 180,000 kilowatts, cost $280 per kilowatt.

The United States Atomic Energy Commission has predicted (in its Report to the President of 1962) that 500,000-kilowatt power stations coming into commission in 1970 should be built for $140 a kilowatt exclusive of overhead, interest during construction, and site charges, so the steep decline of costs is continuing. I learned during a recent visit to Philadelphia that bids at ever lower prices are now being received by utility companies.

It would appear that, although there are substantial differences in estimated capital costs between different reactor systems, the over-all costs of generation in the early 1970s from the United Kingdom advanced gas-cooled reactor type of station, the United States boiling-water reactor and pressurized-water reactor power stations, and the Canadian competitor—the heavy-water reactor power station—should be very similar to each other. This gives very considerable confidence in predicting that nuclear power costs will fall below conventional power costs in the 1970s. The way seems to be clear therefore for a considerable expansion of nuclear power in Britain, the United States, and Canada and other advanced countries in the 1970s.

Contrary to the general impression fostered by the press, the Geneva Conference did not forecast any spectacular application of nuclear power to underdeveloped countries since it was recognized that many of them had large underdeveloped hydroelectric capacity and that this would provide energy more cheaply than nuclear power stations. It was also foreseen that, apart from mining areas such as the "Copperbelt," over-all loads and load factors would be small; under these conditions the high capital cost of nuclear power stations would make them uneconomic. These conditions still hold.

In spite of this discouragement the Geneva Conference undoubtedly encouraged undue optimism about the prospects of atomic energy in many underdeveloped countries and no less than fifty-seven atomic energy commissions have been founded and a large number of research reactors have been installed, mainly by United States companies with the help of United States Atoms for Peace Program grants.

In many cases the commissions do not have the trained staff to operate and use the reactors in a worth-while way. There have, however, been one or two exceptions to this experience. Japan and India are heavily industrialized in certain regions, and during the 1958 Geneva Conference it was forecast that India would have 500,000 kilowatts installed by 1965 and Japan 750,000 kilowatts. Since then India has placed an order for a 380,000-kilowatt power station with the United States and a 200,000-kilowatt station with Canada, and Japan has placed an order for a 160,000-kilowatt station with Britain.

The second Geneva Conference, in 1958, introduced a major new topic—the possible generation of power from the fusion of hydrogen isotopes. Until early 1958 the work in this field carried out in the United States, the United Kingdom, and the USSR was secret because it was thought that the generation of neutrons by fusion reactions might possibly enable fissile material to be produced more cheaply than from fission reactors. Aleady in 1957 this was seen to be unlikely and the United Kingdom and United States scientists recommended declassification of the whole field. At the 1958 Conference a very spectacular exhibit of experimental equipment being used in the United States, the United Kingdom, and the USSR was staged.

At that time the leader of the Harwell team, Dr. Thonemann, forecast that because of our very limited understanding of plasma physics it would take at least ten years before we could reach the break-even point when the energy generated by the fusion of hydrogen isotopes in a hot plasma would exceed the energy input and that it would take a further ten years before economic fusion power was possible.

We are now about halfway through the first decade. Good progress has been made in understanding the behavior of hot plasmas, and in particular the diagnostic techniques for measuring plasma temperatures and other parameters have been greatly improved. The original ZETA of Harwell has continued to provide invaluable information on plasma physics but is now being supplemented at Culham by other machines including Phoenix, a so-called injection mirror machine. In this machine the hydrogen plasma is contained in a "magnetic bottle" and formed and heated up by injecting neutral hydrogen atoms of high velocity which can pass easily into the magnetic bottle, converting them by interaction of the excited hydrogen atoms with the magnetic field to charged particles. The objectives of the applied plasma physics program are to reach simultaneously high temperatures of the order of 100 million degrees, densities of the order of 10^{15} ions per cubic centimeter, and containment times of the plasma of the order of a second. One of the major difficulties has been to achieve a stable plasma, but within the last year Russian workers have increased the containment time of the plasma by a factor of 30 by modifying the shape of the magnetic lines of force. High temperature plasmas have been contained for $\frac{1}{10}$ of a second but at the moment the density is only about 10^{10} particles per cubic centimeter whereas 10^{15} is required. So two out of the three requirements have been attained, which shows that good progress is being made.

The 1955 Conference discussed the industrial applications of radiation from the fission products, such as radio caesium, which are inescapable by-products of nuclear fission. It was thought then that they could be applied to the sterilization of pharmaceuticals, medical supplies, and foodstuffs and that chemical synthesis was another possible application. Since then we have found that sources of radiation of 100,000-curies intensity could be made more cheaply by irradiating cobalt in nuclear power stations such as Calder Hall. An experimental radiation processing plant giving sterilization doses of a million Rads was built at Wantage and has been very much used by industry to study the sterilization of hospital supplies and other materials. This has led to the construction of a commercial radiation sterilization plant in Australia and three such plants are under construction in Britain. The latest of these, the Gillette plant at Reading, will be used for sterilization of expendable scalpels and will ultimately use a 750,000-curie source of radiation.

The use of powerful radiation sources as catalysts in industrial chemistry has been slow in development but recently there was an announcement that Esso was building in America a plant to produce a new detergent using radiation catalysis. The new detergent, sodium alkane sulphonate, permits almost complete biodegradation of the detergent by bacteria in normal sewage treatment and should avoid the increasingly acute problem of foaming in water supplies. The Dow Chemical Company has constructed a plant for the production of ethyl bromide by the reaction of ethylene with hydrogen bromide catalyzed by gamma radiation.

Apart from this there has been a progressive increase in the use of radioisotopes in industry for process control, especially for controlling the thickness of materials from rolling mills. The number of British firms now using radioisotopes is about 1,200, with estimated annual savings of about £4.5 million. The output of the isotopes from the Radiochemical Center at Amersham is now worth about £1.5 million per annum, with a growth rate of 20 percent per annum. The greatest contribution of radioisotopes has undoubtedly been to biological research, where they are now all-pervading.

One of the most important by-products of atomic research has been in the field of radiobiology. The first Geneva Conference had some very important papers on the genetic effects of radiation which gave us for the first time a quantitative estimate of the dose of radiation required to double the mutation rate in mammals. This led to the realization that by far the greatest contribution to the genetically important radiation dose of human beings came from exposure in hospitals for diagnostic purposes; the report of a committee chaired by Lord Adrian has had a very marked effect in reducing radiation exposure to patients in Britain.

A further outcome of radiobiological work has been to show the exceptional sensitivity of embryos to radiation, and this has led to a realization of the great care needed in exposing expectant mothers to radiation.

A further important by-product was the development by the MRC unit at Harwell of techniques which made it possible to see human chromosomes for the first time. This led almost at once to the discovery that a number of serious genetic defects are due to chromosome anomalies. Mongolism is due to the triplication of one chromosome and one form of anemia is due to chromosome anomalies. Research into the chemical basis of genetics, the structure of DNA, and the mechanism of cell division has been greatly helped by the use of tritium-labeled precursors of DNA, which have helped to prove the Crick-Watson model of replication.

The International Atomic Energy Agency, a specialized agency of the United Nations, was founded at Vienna in 1956. The original objective of President Eisenhower in calling for establishment of the Agency—to serve as a kind of world bank for fissile materials withdrawn from military uses—has not so far materialized. The Agency may, however, play an important role in the future in taking over bilateral agreements between suppliers of nuclear power stations and users to ensure that plutonium produced in these nuclear power plants should not be used for military purposes. Bilateral safeguards of this kind are applied to the nuclear power stations provided by Britain to Japan and Italy and by the United States to Japan, Italy, and India. Later, if nuclear disarmament develops and fissile material from nuclear weapons is diverted to civil purposes as proposed in the draft disarmament treaties, the agency may take up again this major role proposed by President Eisenhower.

The Agency has been most active in the education and research fields by providing fellowships for students of atomic energy problems, by providing research grants, especially in the field of radiobiology, and by arranging five or six small conferences a year in specialized fields. The Agency has recently decided to found an Institute for Theoretical Physics, to be established in the first instance at Trieste for four years, to help to train theoretical physicists from the less developed countries. This was largely done at the insistence of representatives of these countries, led by Professor Abdus Salem.

The initiative of the United Nations and Dag Hammarskjöld in helping to promote the development of atomic energy has therefore borne fruit and it is becoming more and more clear how important in the long run this great new source of energy and its by-products will become for the world.

THE UNITED NATIONS FAMILY OF AGENCIES: ORIGINS AND RELATIONSHIPS

Luther H. Evans

FORMER DIRECTOR-GENERAL OF UNESCO

Given at the Nigerian Institute of International Affairs, Lagos, September 27, 1963

Though Dag Hammarskjöld will be remembered primarily for his leadership in the United Nations, he should also be remembered for his work in the wider context of that sprawling complex of associated international organizations working in a loose but meaningful harmony, which we call the United Nations family of agencies.

The activities of the specialized agencies were for only brief moments from time to time the focus of the Secretary-General's attention, but a more detailed study than I can present at this time would show, I believe, that Dag Hammarskjöld regarded the harmonious development of United Nations family policies and programs as an essential condition for the realization by the United Nations proper of its own goals. As Director-General of one of the specialized agencies during the first five years of his service as Secretary-General, I found myself heartily in accord with his point of view. It was for this reason that I strove to have the United Nations Educational, Scientific and

Cultural Organization play its role in realizing the larger purpose, with understanding and humility.

I have tried to prepare a lecture directly on the subject of Dag Hammarskjöld and the development of cooperation in the United Nations family, only to find the canvas entirely too large for any effort short of a monograph. Hence, my purpose on this occasion is limited to a description of how the family came to be what it is, with a few personal reflections on the way it worked when I was a participant in it.

I

Since the rise of the modern state as the principal power structure, the main transnational agencies prior to the League of Nations were specialized in function and powers. With the creation of the League in 1919–20 an effort was made to set up a general peace-keeping agency. Alongside the League were many independent specialized agencies which went their way with autonomy. The Treaty of Versailles, which provided for the League (Articles 1–26), also contained the basic document for another agency, the International Labor Organization (Articles 387–427). Although some provisions were made to link the two, they actually led quite separate lives. There is no mention of the ILO in the League Covenant, but the ILO articles of the Treaty of Versailles involve the League in various ways. For example:

The members should be the same as the League members (Article 387). The ILO should be established at the seat of the League "as part of the organisation of the League" (Article 392). The League Council should decide any question as to which are the members of "chief industrial importance" for representation in the Governing Body (Article 393). The secretariat (International Labor Office) "shall be entitled to the assistance of the Secretary-General of the League of Nations in any manner which it can be given" (Article 398). The expenses of ILO should be provided for by the League; the Director of ILO "shall be responsible to the Secretary-General of the League for the proper expenditure of all moneys paid to him in pursuance of this Article" (Article 399). The ILO conventions and ratifications of them were to be registered with the Secretary-General

(Article 405). The Commissions of Inquiry to be set up for dealing with complaints as to the observance of a convention were to be chosen by the League Secretary-General (from a panel drawn up by the Governing Body), and were to report back to him, after which he should send the report to the governments concerned and publish it (Articles 414–15). Amendments to the ILO part of the Treaty were to be made by two-thirds majority of votes cast by the delegates present in the ILO Conference, to take effect when ratified by the states whose representatives composed the League Council and by three quarters of the Members (Article 422).

Although this was a cumbersome arrangement, it seems to have worked rather well. But it is easy to understand why international institutional planners some twenty to twenty-five years later would desire somewhat simpler relations between the proposed United Nations on the one hand and the ILO and other specialized agencies on the other.

A footnote may be added here to the effect that, despite the links between the ILO and the League, the United States was received as a member of the former in 1934 without becoming a member of the latter.

In the League Covenant there were certain other provisions of concern to our subject. Article 23 provided as follows:

Subject to and in accordance with the provisions of international conventions existing or hereafter to be agreed upon, the Members of the League:

(a) will endeavour to secure and maintain fair and humane conditions of labor for men, women, and children, both in their own countries and in all countries to which their commercial and industrial relations extend, and for that purpose will establish and maintain the necessary international organisations;

(b) undertake to secure just treatment of the native inhabitants of territories under their control;

(c) will entrust the League with the general supervision over the execution of agreements with regard to the traffic in women and children, and the traffic in opium and other dangerous drugs;

(d) will entrust the League with the general supervision of the trade in arms and ammunition with the countries in which the control of this traffic is necessary in the common interest;

(e) will make provision to secure and maintain freedom of communications and of transit and equitable treatment for the commerce of all Members of the League. In this connection, the special necessities of the regions devastated during the war of 1914–1918 shall be borne in mind;

(f) will endeavour to take steps in matters of international concern for the prevention and control of disease.

Paragraph (a) obviously refers to the ILO; paragraphs (b), (c), (d), and (e) apparently did not envisage any specific organizations, but rather defined certain functions which the League should perform. The forecast is implicit of the United Nations interest in non-self-governing territories (par. (b)), of the abortive international trade organization, of the International Civil Aviation Organization, and of the World Health Organization. One could interpret the reference to "freedom of communication and transit" to mean that the League was interested in the work of the Universal Postal Union.

Article 24 of the Covenant carried the matter further, by providing that "there shall be placed under the direction of the League all international bureaux already established by general treaties if the parties to such treaties consent. All such international bureaux and all commissions for the regulation of matters of international interest hereafter constituted shall be placed under the direction of the League." A further provision in the same article stated: "The Council may include as part of the expenses of the Secretariat the expenses of any bureau or commission which is placed under the direction of the League."

On July 27, 1921, the Council of the League adopted a report presented to it by M. Hanotaux of France concerning "International Bureaux and the League." The report indicated that more than thirty international bureaus existed from the period prior to the League, but that none of them had indicated a desire to take advantage of Article 24. There were certain requests before the League, however, concerning new bureaus. The report said that since Article 24 did not define the degree of authority to be exercised by the League, and since the bureaus were established by conventions concluded among states, "it is to be presumed that [the authors of the Covenant] meant to allow such organisations to have a large measure of autonomy and not to be merged in the League's own organisations." The authority to be exercised by the League would, in reality, "be confined to giving the Bureau the moral support which attaches to official affiliation to the League, except in cases where abuses are revealed, such as, for instance, encroachment by an office upon the sphere of action of some other international organisation, or an unjustifiable refusal on the part of a Bureau to co-operate with other bodies, or in the event of an insufficient degree of activity."

The exercise of League authority should not "imply a right to interfere in the internal organisation of the Bureau (appointment of officials, use of funds, etc.), nor a right to insist upon amendments to the established organisation (change of headquarters, extension of sphere of action, etc.)."

The League might recommend improvements in the working of a bureau. Also it might be assumed that the bureaus would be ready "to afford the League all possible assistance and information within their special spheres."

As to organizations not established by general agreements or treaties, what are known today as international nongovernmental organizations, the report indicated that the League might use a wider discretion as to what it would require. An application would have to be made to the League by the governing body of the organization, and conditions of acceptance might be laid down, after an inquiry concerning the constitution, personnel, financial position, and aims of the bureau. Such a bureau might be asked to undertake a share of the work of the League, and also to permit the League to supervise, to some extent, the employment of its financial resources. To place a bureau under the League would imply no financial obligation on the part of the League, though the Council could at its discretion assume such an obligation.

On September 26, 1927, the League Assembly adopted a resolution calling upon the Council to have the question of "institutes or bodies set up under the authority of the League" studied by the Council and a report submitted to the Assembly the following year.

The Council adopted its report on June 27, 1928, again prepared by M. Hanotaux. On September 20, 1928, the Assembly adopted the report as its own.

This document is of such crucial importance in understanding the League's philosophy regarding specialized agencies that a few paragraphs concerning it seem justified. The report observed that though the Covenant used the strong term "direction" (Fr. *autorité*) to denote the League's relation to the international institutions,

the authors of the Covenant . . . had no intention of bringing such a variety of international institutions indirectly within the framework of the League or of encroaching upon their internal autonomy or statutory provisions in regard to their headquarters, etc. They did, however, desire to make the League a centre of co-ordination for the work of the various international institutions. Hence, the League's authority might be defined as the exercise by the League of a general mission in regard to the examination and co-ordination of the various manifestations of international life. On this hypothesis, the League should see that the organisation in question always preserves a strictly international character and that its work is carried on in an efficient manner. The necessity of avoiding overlapping must also be borne in mind.

Based on these views, the report went on to point out that in practice certain obligations should be imposed:

The Secretary-General should be entitled to receive publications and official documents exchanged between the institutions and the states represented on them; he should attend in person or by deputy all meetings of such organizations; the institutions should, on request, give the League opinons coming within their special competence; and an annual report should be sent to the League for its examination.

All of these stipulations should, it was made quite clear, be made formal in a legal act, namely, a resolution of the Council.

Under Article 24 the League accepted authority over the following international agencies:

The International Bureau for Relief to Foreigners (June 27, 1921)
The Hydrographic Bureau (October 2, 1921)
The Office for Control of Liquor Traffic in Africa (January 11, 1922)
The International Commission for Air Navigation (September 30, 1930)
The Office for Refugees (January 19, 1931)
The International Exhibitions Office (May 20, 1931)

Although no case seems to have arisen, it is to be assumed that, had the ILO wished to absorb a related international organization, it could have done so only by action of the League Council under Article 24.

The only organization to affiliate with the League by special agreement was the International Institute of Agriculture, but this arrangement did not change substantially the internal dispositions of power or the procedures of the two organizations.

Discussions took place with a view to the absorption by the League of the International Health Office (created 1907, located in Paris), but the United States objected (not being a member of the League), and the result achieved was that the office became an advisory body to the League's health organization.

The following and many other organizations went their way as autonomous agencies:

The Universal Postal Union

The International Telegraphic Union (after 1934 the International Telecommunication Union)

The International Bureau of Weights and Measures

The International Wine Office

The International Bureau of Commercial Statistics

The International Institute of Commerce

The International Institute of Refrigeration

The International Union of Railway Freight Transportation

The International Union for the Publication of Customs Tariffs

The Interparliamentary Union for the Promotion of International Arbitration

The International Penal and Penitentiary Commission

The Permanent International Association of Navigation Congresses

various scientific unions

various river commissions

It is also important to note that many new organizations were established without reference to the League. A few examples are as follows:

The International Sugar Council (1937)

The Committee of Control of the International Zone of Tangier (1923)

The International Criminal Police Commission (1923)

The International Bureau of Education (1925)

On the creative side, the League experience laid the foundations in its health organization for the World Health Organization established in 1948, while not absorbing an organization in the field since 1907, the International Health Office. In the field of communications and transit the League also created a semi-autonomous technical organization called the Organization for Communications and Transit. The secretriats of these two organizations were part of the League Secretariat. Among the functions of OCT was that of bringing about cooperation in air navigation. To this end the League absorbed the International Commission on Air Navigation.

The League established an International Committee on Intellectual Cooperation in 1921, and gave it an Organic Statute in 1925. In 1938 the Institute of Intellectual Cooperation was set up by international act, with its own director and governing body. The Act entered into force on January 31, 1940. After World War II the Institute was taken over by UNESCO.

The merits of having centralized control by the League versus allowing a spate of burgeoning and relatively uncoordinated agencies to develop were given attention in the interwar period, though one could hardly say that a well-rounded and generally accepted philosophy was developed.

Writing in 1934, Pitman B. Potter posed the question (*Geneva Special Studies,* Vol. V, No. 6): "Would one all embracing world organization be preferable to the number of only loosely integrated international organizations we now have?"

In trying to answer this question, Professor Potter pointed out:

All sorts of problems are involved, from that of pluralism versus monostatism to the relative merits of the independent bureau or commission in public administration, and even, probably, that of federalism versus the unitary state. . . . The framers of Article XXIV certainly expected more from it than has been attained, in the direction of coördination and unification . . . greater centralization is desirable. . . . The confused and uncertain relations between organizations which have grown up empirically in the past, with their duplications and uncertainties and conflicts, call for unification and systematization.

He felt that not only the International Bureaus Section of the Secretariat and the Assembly should push along this movement, but that perhaps the Member States should do likewise.

In my opinion, to be voiced more strongly later in this paper,

Professor Potter put his finger on the problem when he placed a responsibility on the Member States to bring about coordination. Since any move had to be unanimous by the states creating and sustaining an organization, the desire to cooperate had to arise in them and then express itself through two channels, one to the League and the other to the other organization concerned.

II

When the Charter of the United Nations was being developed as a proposal in the bureaucracies of foreign offices and in intergovernmental meetings formal and informal, it was always clear that a general peace-keeping agency would have to be set up after World War II, superseding the League but with jurisdiction considerably broader than that of the League. It was equally clear that an undetermined number of specialized agencies would also exist, including some which did not exist before the war. Indeed, planners saw a great need for new specialized agencies which would be set up autonomously, even if in some cases with the stimulus of the main organization, the United Nations itself. While minority views existed, they do not seem to have been taken seriously in the foreign offices of the leading allied Powers.

Thus it was that before an effort was made by certain of the allies to think through the basis of the United Nations at Dumbarton Oaks in the autumn of 1944, moves had been made by the same states and others to establish the United Nations Food and Agriculture Organization (Hot Springs, May–June, 1943), as well as the International Bank for Reconstruction and Development and the International Monetary Fund (Bretton Woods, July, 1944). Certain discussions also took place in 1942–44 concerning proposals for an educational reconstruction agency, but the United States held up definitive talks until after Dumbarton Oaks. Later (February, 1945) it went along with plans to set up an agency which later became the United Nations Educational, Scientific and Cultural Organization. This was two months before the United Nations Conference convened in San Francisco. In 1943 preparations were afoot for setting up an organization in the civil aviation field, and the formal agreement stage was reached a few weeks after the Dumbarton Oaks conversations.

The Dumbarton Oaks Proposals (drafted August 21–September

28, 1944) contain certain provisions which deserve to be noted. In the chapter on the General Assembly it is stated:

6. The General Assembly should initiate studies and make recommendations for the purpose of promoting international cooperation in political, economic and social fields and of adjusting situations likely to impair the general welfare.

7. The General Assembly should make recommendations for the coordination of the policies of international economic, social, and other specialized agencies brought into relation with the Organization in accordance with agreements between such agencies and the Organization.

In the chapter on the Security Council it was provided:

7. The action required to carry out the decisions of the Security Council for the maintenance of international peace and security should be taken by all the members of the Organization in cooperation or by some of them as the Security Council may determine. This undertaking should be carried out by the members of the Organization by their own action and through action of the appropriate specialized organizations and agencies of which they are members.

In the chapter on Arrangements for International Economic and Social Cooperation it was provided:

A2. The various specialized economic, social and other organizations and agencies would have responsibilities in their respective fields as defined in their statutes. Each such organization or agency should be brought into relationship with the Organization on terms to be determined by agreement between the Economic and Social Council and the appropriate authorities of the specialized organization or agency, subject to approval by the General Assembly.

The functions and powers of the Economic and Social Council were defined to include the making of "recommendations, on its own initiative, with respect to international economic, social and other humanitarian matters"; "to receive and consider reports from the economic, social and other organizations or agencies brought into relationship with the Organization, and to coordinate their activities through consultations with, and recommendations to, such organizations or agencies"; "to examine the administrative budgets of such specialized organizations or agencies with a view to making recommendations to the organizations or agencies concerned." Also, the Council "should make suitable arrangements for representatives of the specialized organizations or agencies to participate without vote in its deliberations and in those of the commissions established by it."

Without examining into the course of the discussions at the United Nations Conference in San Francisco (April 25–June 25, 1945), let us review briefly the results, in the form of the important provisions of the Charter as they concern the United Nations family of agencies.

The fundamental provision concerning the specialized agencies is Article 57, which reads as follows:

1. The various specialized agencies, established by intergovernmental agreement and having wide international responsibilities, as defined in their basic instruments, in economic, social, cultural, educational, health, and related fields, shall be brought into relationship with the United Nations in accordance with the provisions of Article 63.

2. Such agencies thus brought into relationship with the United Nations are hereinafter referred to as specialized agencies.

Article 63 provides that the Economic and Social Council may enter into agreements with any of these agencies, "defining the terms on which the agency concerned shall be brought into relationship with the United Nations." But such agreements require the approval of the General Assembly. By referring to Article 18, it is to be assumed that the ratification of the agreements would not fall in the class of "important questions" requiring more than a majority vote of the members present and voting.

Article 63 goes further and provides that the Economic and Social Council "may coordinate the activities of the specialized agencies through consultation with and recommendations to such agencies and through recommendations to the General Assembly and to the Members of the United Nations."

In Article 64 the measures were taken further by providing that the Economic and Social Council "may take appropriate steps to obtain regular reports from the specialized agencies." It was also empowered to make arrangements with United Nations Members and the specialized agencies "to obtain reports on the steps taken to give effect to" recommendations by the Council and the General Assembly. The Council was also authorized to "communicate its observations on all of these reports" to the Assembly.

Article 70 authorizes the Economic and Social Council to make arrangements for representatives of the specialized agencies to participate, without vote, in its deliberations and in those of the commissions established by it, and for its representatives to participate in the deliberations of the specialized agencies.

The Economic and Social Council is empowered by Article 66 to give services, with the Assembly's approval, to the specialized agencies, at their request.

The Trusteeship Council is authorized by Article 91, when appropriate, to avail itself of the assistance of the specialized agencies "in regard to matters with which they are respectively concerned."

Article 96 provides that the General Assembly may authorize specialized agencies to request advisory opinions of the International Court of Justice "on legal questions arising within the scope of their activities."

Article 65 of the Statute of the Court authorizes the Court to give an advisory opinion on any legal question at the request of whatever body may be authorized by or in accordance with the Charter of the United Nations to make such a request.

The General Assembly is given the duty to "consider and approve any financial and budgetary arrangements with specialized agencies . . . and [to] examine the administrative budgets of such specialized agencies with a view to making recommendations to the agencies concerned" (Article 17). The only "budget" and "expenses" mentioned as being under the Assembly's approval power are those of "the Organization," meaning the United Nations (Article 17).

A very interesting provision of the Charter is found in Article 48, which refers to the carrying out of the decisions of the Security Council for the maintenance of international peace and security. There it is said that "such decisions shall be carried out by the Members of the United Nations directly and through their action in the appropriate international agencies of which they are members."

Sensing that the galaxy of agencies might not be completed by the initiative of the Members of the United Nations, authors of the Charter stated in Article 59 that "the Organization shall, where appropriate, initiate negotiations among the states concerned for the creation of any new specialized agencies required for the accomplishment of the purposes set forth in Article 55." This article was quoted above.

At the San Francisco Conference there were attempts by various delegations to specify in the Charter fields in which specialized agencies should be established (raw materials, health, culture, etc.). These ideas were rejected, but a declaration was put in the report of the appropriate commission of the Conference in favor of creating agencies in the fields of health, culture, and migration.

It is relevant to note here the Charter description of certain of the functions of the United Nations since they have a bearing upon the work of the specialized agencies. Despite the reference in Article 57 to the responsibilities of the specialized agencies "in economic, social, cultural, health, and related fields," the Charter nevertheless states in Article 55 that the United Nations

shall promote:
a. higher standards of living, full employment, and conditions of economic and social progress and development;
b. solutions of international economic, social, health, and related problems; and international cultural and educational cooperation; and
c. universal respect for, and observance of, human rights and fundamental freedoms for all without distinction as to race, sex, language, or religion.

In defining the functions and powers of the General Assembly, the Charter in Article 13 clearly instructs the Assembly to "initiate studies and make recommendations for the purpose of: . . . b. promoting international cooperation in the economic, social, cultural, educational, and health fields, and assisting in the realization of human rights and fundamental freedoms for all without distinction as to race, sex, language, or religion." This does not indicate precisely to whom recommendations may be made, but one could not be wrong, I think, in saying that they could be made to Members and to specialized agencies, and, of course, to the Economic and Social Council.

Article 13 also gives the Assembly the "further responsibilities, functions and powers" referred to in Article 55, quoted above.

In describing the functions and powers of the Economic and Social Council, the Charter in Article 62 authorizes that organ to "make or initiate studies and reports with respect to international economic, social, cultural, educational, health, and related matters and

. . . make recommendations with respect to any such matters to the General Assembly, to the Members of the United Nations, and to the specialized agencies concerned." It may make recommendations on human rights and also may prepare draft conventions for submission to the Assembly and call international conferences on matters falling within its competence.

The above provisions clearly establish a wide overlapping of jurisdiction between the United Nations and the specialized agencies. The key words in the constitutions of various of the specialized agencies are duplicated in Articles 13 and 62 in defining the powers of the General Assembly and the Economic and Social Council, particularly in the case of *health, education, culture.*

It may be said, however, that the Charter was written before UNESCO and the World Health Organization were set up, and that the subsequent creation of these two agencies should be considered as weakening the actual responsibilities of the United Nations in their respective fields. The failure of the Charter to mention specifically the fields of labor (it does mention full employment), agriculture, civil aviation, banking and currency stabilization—fields of five specialized agencies (ILO, FAO, ICAO, the Bank, and the Fund) already established—lends weight to this view. Nevertheless, one cannot maintain that the power of the United Nations is rendered a nullity when such power is also granted to a specialized agency by its constitution.

The above must also be read in the light of Article 7, which authorizes the United Nations to "establish in accordance with the present Charter such subsidiary organs as may be found necessary." If UNESCO had not been established by intergovernmental agreement, this provision would seemingly authorize the establishment of an organ to perform duties of a similar kind.

III

On June 26, 1945, when the United Nations Charter was signed, the governments also signed an agreement entitled "Interim Arrangements." In this document a Preparatory Commission was created, consisting of a representative of each of the fifty signatories of the Charter. The Commission was charged with convoking the first session of the General Assembly; preparing the provisional agenda of the first sessions of the principal organs of the Organization, and preparing documents and recommendations relating to all matters on these agenda; formulating recommendations concerning the possible transfer of certain functions, activities, and assets of the League of Nations; examining the problems involved in the establishment of the relationship between specialized intergovernmental agencies and the Organization; etc.

The Commission met at San Francisco the day after the signature of the Charter, then shifted its seat to London, where it was instructed to meet as soon as possible after the Charter came into force. The Commission was to die as soon as the Secretary-General was elected.

The Executive Committee of the Commission, representing the states which were represented on the Executive Committee of the San Francisco Conference, met on August 16, and the Commission met on November 24, the Charter having come into force on October 24. The Report of the Preparatory Commission bears the date of December 23, 1945. Let us take a look at its recommendations that have an important bearing on our subject.

The Preparatory Commission recommended that the agenda of the first session of the Economic and Social Council should include an item for the establishment of a committee to report on observations on relationships with specialized agencies and any recommendations or observations to the General Assembly pertaining thereto; and arrangements for negotiating agreements with specialized agencies.

It also set forth certain considerations and recommendations concerning the commissions of the Economic and Social Council in relation to specialized agencies. One consideration was that certain agencies were already established or contemplated, whereas in others none was contemplated and hence commissions of the Economic and Social Council might be set up to help it with its work. It favored the principle that "the initial structure of the subordinate machinery of the Council has been drawn up with a view to avoiding undesirable duplication between intergovernmental agencies and the Council."

The Preparatory Commission adopted the assumption, which it admitted to be "somewhat arbitrary," that the following subjects would fall within the responsibility of specialized agencies: (a) relief and rehabilitation; (b) monetary cooperation and international investment; (c) trade policies (including commodity problems and restrictive practices of private international agreements); (d) food and agricultural policies; (e) labor standards, labor welfare, and related social questions; (f) educational and cultural cooperation; (g) health; (h) some aspects of transport; (i) some aspects of communications.

It was recommended that in these fields the Economic and Social Council should refrain for the time being from setting up commissions. If no specialized agency came into existence in any of these fields, then the Council must make suitable provision for caring for them. And there might have to be temporary arrangements in the interim.

A matter needing urgent attention, the Preparatory Commission thought, was the problem of refugees.

The Commission recommended that the Economic and Social Council should at its first session set up a human rights commission, an economic and employment commission, a temporary social commission, a statistical commission, and a commission on narcotic drugs. In addition, it was recommended that the Economic and Social Council consider the early establishment of a demographic commission, a temporary transport and communications commission, a fiscal commission, and a coordination commission to organize "the machinery for co-ordinating the activities of the various organs of the Council and of the specialized agencies."

An important suggestion which was not carried out was that a minority of "non-governmental members of commissions, with appropriate qualifications, might be chosen by the Council from among the nationals" of Members of the United Nations.

It was suggested that the Council make appropriate arrangements for specialized agencies to participate in the work of the Council's commissions and that provision for this be included in the agreements.

One of the most important subjects covered in the Report concerned the negotiation of agreements with the specialized agencies. The Commission thought that the Economic and Social Council should deal with this problem at its first session, and complete the agreements as soon as possible. At this point the Preparatory Commission observed that it would be possible for the Economic and Social Council to try to bring other kinds of intergovernmental agencies into relationship with the United Nations, besides those contemplated by Article 57, "such as those of a regional character."

The Commission then looked at the landscape of "independent bureaux and agencies functioning before the war," which are mentioned above in the section on the League of Nations, and declared: "It may be desirable for some to continue to function and to be brought into relationship with the United Nations. In a few cases, the process of merging pre-war agencies with newly established agencies is already taking place. The total number of older agencies should be reduced and brought into a more rational and unified organizational structure." There were three alternatives: liquidation, with some or all functions going to a specialized agency; liquidation, with functions going to some United Nations unit; and a merger with another intergovernmental agency. Certainly, organization men predominated in the Preparatory Commission.

The Commission saw clearly that the battery of specialized agencies in existence or under active consideration at the end of 1945 did not cover all fields which it was desirable to cover. The alternatives which appealed to it were: new specialized agencies might be set up under United Nations initiative; the Economic and Social Council might set up subordinate commissions or committees; some other type of subordinate organ of the United Nations might be created; or the Economic and Social Council might recommend that a specialized agency or other intergovernmental agency undertake additional functions.

To cover the interval before agreements were negotiated, it was suggested that the Economic and Social Council might wish to make recommendations to the Members of the United Nations concerning the agreements and other matters pertaining to the relations to be established between the United Nations and the specialized agencies.

As to the agreements, the Preparatory Commission listed ten subjects which it deemed appropriate to cover in the agreements, covered by the Charter, as follows: reciprocal representation; exchange of information and documents; coordination commission of the Economic and Social Council; recommendations to the specialized agencies; reports; decisions of the Security Council; assistance to the Trusteeship Council; requests for advisory opinions; requests for information by the Court; budgetary and financial relationships. It also listed ten not so covered but which were "considered important in the general plan of relationships with the specialized agencies," namely: liaison; proposal of agenda items; rules of procedure; common fiscal services; personnel arrangements; privileges and immunities; administrative tribunal; technical services; central statistical service; location of headquarters.

The Commission thought all twenty items appropriate for inclusion in agreements with an "extensive" range of functions in economic, social, or related matters, but some might drop out in case of agencies with "less extensive" functions. It went on to spell out its thinking concerning the content of the agreements on these various subjects, but only a few points require consideration here. As to reciprocal representation, it thought the extent might differ from one agency to another, and that specialized agency participation in the General Assembly (not mentioned in the Charter) might be included. One idea was voiced that has been proved not very realistic, namely, that most agencies would have their headquarters near the United Nations headquarters. When this was not so, it was recommended that permanent liaison officers be stationed at United Nations Headquarters. It was also suggested that the Economic and Social Council might find it useful to have liaison officers at specialized agency headquarters.

As to coordination machinery, the Commission recommended that the Economic and Social Council provide for a coordination commission, including the chief executives of the specialized agencies, or their deputies, with the United Nations Secretary-General or his deputy as chairman. One of the functions of the coordination commission would be to help in the scheduling of the meeting of the various principal organs and subsidiary bodies and of conferences called by the various agencies. It was hoped that any form of procedure adopted by the United Nations for international meetings would be adopted as far as applicable by the specialized agencies.

It was recommended that each specialized agency undertake in the agreement to assist the Security Council upon its request in the application of measures envisaged in Article 41 of the Charter (measures short of the use of armed forces, such as interruption of economic relations, of communications, and of diplomatic relations).

As to advisory opinions by the International Court of Justice, the Commission thought that the General Assembly might want to have a general authorization included in the agreements, perhaps of limited duration, and with or without approval in each case by the Economic and Social Council. In any case it was recommended that any specialized agency request for an advisory opinion should be called to the attention of the Economic and Social Council. Also, specialized agencies should be asked to agree to supply the Court with any information it might request under Article 34 of the Statute.

Concerning the subject of budgetary and financial relationships, the bureaucratic impulse again showed itself in a bad light. The United Nations Charter says in Article 17 that the General Assembly "shall consider and approve any financial and budgetary arrangements with specialized agencies referred to in Article 57 and shall examine the administrative budgets of such specialized agencies with a view to making recommendations to the agencies concerned." Now, what did the Commission think these simple words meant? It said: "The primary object . . . is to encourage and develop a large measure of fiscal and administrative co-ordination in the interest of greater efficiency and economy in operation for the entire structure" of the United Nations and the agencies. This was weakened somewhat by the prior observation that it was "not considered that there was any intention to confer on the General Assembly a financial power that could be used by it to control the policies of the specialized agencies." It may be asked what "financial power" the Charter provisions did confer.

The Preparatory Commission went on to say that the provision of Article 17 concerning budgetary and financial arrangements quoted above "envisages varying degrees of relationship, from complete financial integration downwards." It "assumed" that under this provision "agreements might be concluded with some of the specialized agencies which would confer on the General Assembly the responsibility for voting their budgets." This statement was made despite the observation just quoted that no control over policies of the agencies was intended. The Commission thought that budgets prepared by the agencies could go to the Advisory Committee for Administrative and Budgetary Questions, and then to the General Assembly as parts of a consolidated budget. This would *simplify* the complicated budget process, and it would enable the United Nations Members to note all United Nations family expenses at one time and in one place. The system used by the League in reference to the ILO, which was "similar," had worked satisfactorily. That the constitutions of most of the specialized agencies would have to be amended was not a serious obstacle. The member states of the agencies which were not also United Nations Members could be allowed to vote on their respective budgets in the Assembly prior to the Assembly's final vote.

The Commission realized that specialized agencies could not be compelled to agree to any such arrangement, but it was hopeful that they would consent. As to any new agencies, the Commission hoped that Members of the United Nations would frame the new constitutions in such a way as to provide for the new idea. As to other types of "financial arrangements," the Commission mentioned the possibility that the General Assembly might in its judgment vote "special grants or subventions" to a specialized agency to carry out "a new program of international co-operation" for the United Nations.

In considering the provision concerning Assembly review of specialized agency "administrative budgets," the Commission had trouble with the adjective, but it was able to conclude that it should not be given "a restrictive interpretation." The Commission was determined to get a lot of blood from a small turnip! The provision of common fiscal services was deemed to be an even less objectionable idea than a consolidated budget. Thus it was recommended that the United Nations collect contributions from members of all agencies. It was suggested that the United Nations might administer balances and special funds, perform auditing services, etc. There might be common financial regulations. Common standards on personnel, set forth in common staff regulations, were recommended, as well as arrangements for interchange of staff. While it yearned for "the eventual development of a single unified international civil service," the Commission did not want to try for anything of the sort at the present stage. One administrative tribunal for all agencies was voted for. The United Nations passport might well cover specialized agency personnel.

In the case of agencies seated at United Nations Headquarters it would be possible to have unified technical secretarial services. A central statistical service at the United Nations for all agencies was recommended. While recognizing that certain circumstances made a uniform rule unwise, the Preparatory Commission recommended that the Economic and Social Council should make the location of specialized agency headquarters at the seat of the United Nations "a point of major importance" in negotiating the agency agreements.

The Commission concluded its report on the subject of agreements with specialized agencies by making the very wise observation that the task of coordination "can be performed only if Members individually will assist in making co-ordination possible."

The draft rules of procedure recommended by the Preparatory Commission for adoption by the general Assembly, the Security Council, the Economic and Social Council, and the Trusteeship Council reflected many but not all of the principal recommendations referred to above.

The Economic and Social Council held a general discussion on the agreements in January and February, 1946. A report later submitted by the Secretary-General of the United Nations to the Economic and Social Council describes, in words I could not improve on, "two main tendencies among members" revealed in that discussion: some envisaged a thoroughgoing centralization, including identity of headquarters and of membership, designed to mold the whole complex of agencies, and of commissions of the Council, into a closely integrated mechanism operating under the direct policy guidance of the Council. Others urged caution in the matter of centralization, both as regards site of headquarters and as regards activities, it being clearly out of the question for the Council to undertake the detailed management of a vast variety of activities, most of them of a highly specialized character, entrusted to qualified technicians. The Chairman of the Economic and Social Council, in winding up this discussion, pointed out that only the question of location of headquarters was relevant to the negotiations with the agencies. He further declared himself opposed to the doctrine of identical membership as between the United Nations and the agencies, as he felt that the Charter recognized the fact of differing memberships. The second effort to thwart the intent of the authors of the Charter was thus turned back.

The Economic and Social Council then discussed the points to be covered in the negotiations with the agencies, adopted a resolution on the subject, and named a committee of eleven, headed by the Chairman of the Economic and Social Council, to negotiate with FAO, ILO, the Bank, the Fund, ICAO, and UNESCO. This work began on May 21, 1946, and during 1946, 1947, and 1948 agreements were concluded with these agencies, with the final approval of the General Assembly, and also with the Universal Postal Union, the World Health Organization, the International Telecommunications Union, the International Refugee Organization, and the Intergovernmental Maritime Consultative Organization. At later dates agreements were concluded also with the World Meteorological Organization and the International Atomic Energy Agency. The analysis which follows ignores the two latter agreements, for convenience of presentation.

The agreements recognized each specialized agency as "responsible for taking such action as may be appropriate" for the accomplishment of its purposes as set forth in its basic instrument. The Bank and Fund agreements make specific the point that each of these institutions is "an independent international organization" and that some of their information is confidential, even in dealing with the United Nations.

As to membership in the specialized agency concerned, the UNESCO agreement gives the Economic and Social Council a veto over the admission of states not members of the United Nations, which it must exercise within six months, and the ICAO agreement gives the General Assembly a one-year period within which to veto members additional to those referred to in its basic instrument as being eligible. In the case of UNESCO, it is also provided that a state suspended or expelled from the United Nations also loses its membership in UNESCO.

Reciprocal representation is provided for in all agreements, with the terms showing a good deal of variation. Provision for participation by the agencies in United Nations meetings includes not only the Economic and Social Council and its subordinate organs and the Trusteeship Council, but the General Assembly as well when relevant subjects are discussed.

The right is also granted by each party to the other to place items on agendas of appropriate organs (limited to giving "due consideration" in the case of the Bank and the Fund).

As to "recommendations" the arrangement is one-sided, that is, the agencies agree to submit to the appropriate organ any recommendations made by the United Nations. Prior consultation before the making of recommendations by either party is required by the Bank and Fund agreements. Accepting recommendations is in no case compulsory. The United Nations recognized that it should refrain from making recommendations to the Bank "with respect to particular loans or with respect to terms or conditions of financing by the bank." Agreements generally (not the Bank and Fund, however) provide for consultation between the United Nations and the agency concerning recommendations and the reporting of action taken. The agencies agree to cooperate with any bodies established by the Economic and Social Council for carrying on the work of coordination.

All agreements provide for the exchange of documents and other nonconfidential information. The agencies agree to make regular reports to the United Nations and to provide special reports on request. Certain special provisions appear in certain agreements (UNESCO and WHO, for instance) regarding special agency roles in public information activities.

All the agreements commit agencies to cooperate with the Trusteeship Council and the Security Council, with variations in the texts. Some agencies also agree to cooperate with the United Nations regarding non-self-governing territories (not ITU, UPU, Bank, and Fund).

Each agency is given a general permission to request the International Court for advisory opinions (a move forward from the strict provision of the Charter). The agencies agree to supply information to the Court under Article 34 of its Statute.

As regards headquarters location, no provision is contained in some agreements; in others the only requirement is to consider the desirability of locating at United Nations Headquarters and to consult with the United Nations before making a decision. In fact, no specialized agency has located its headquarters in New York, but several are at the European Headquarters of the United Nations in Geneva. Regional offices of agencies are required by most agreements to be "closely associated" with such offices of the United Nations, "so far as practicable."

The agreements generally recognize the desirability of "a single unified international service"; this means the development of "common personnel standards, methods and arrangements designed to avoid serious discrepancies . . . in terms and conditions of employment, to avoid competition in recruitment of personnel and to facilitate interchange of personnel." The establishment of an International Civil Service Commission is foreseen in some agreements. Some agreements, such as those with the Bank, Fund, and UPU, are more general in character than the others.

Cooperation and the elimination of unnecessary duplication in statistical work are provided for. The United Nations is recognized as "the central agency" in this field, serving all agencies, but each agency is recognized as possessing authority in "its special sphere." The agreements generally provide for consultation to avoid competitive and overlapping facilities and services, and to establish common services, as far as practicable.

As to budgetary and financial arrangements, the most that any of the agencies would agree to was to consult concerning a consolidated budget. Naturally, provisions are made for the General Assembly to receive agency budgets and to make recommendations thereon, which the agencies then consider. The agencies may request the United Nations to collect the contributions from Member States, the details to be provided in supplementary agreements. The Bank and the Fund are almost entirely exempted from the budget examination procedure of the United Nations. The agreements provide for consultation concerning arrangements as to which agency pays for activities which the United Nations may request another agency to undertake (the Bank and Fund agreements allow these agencies to request the United Nations to undertake activities for them).

Formal agreements between specialized agencies or between one of them and any other intergovernmental organization shall be reported to the Economic and Social Council. In some cases this requirement is applied to agreements with nongovernmental organizations. The executive heads of the United Nations and each agency may make supplementary arrangements to carry out the agreements. The agreements are themselves subject to revision from time to time. The agencies have the right to use the United Nations *laissez-passer*.

IV

A few conclusions drawn from this summary of relationships among the specialized agencies of the United Nations may now be given.

The main pieces of machinery for coordination which have resulted from the constitutional and legal documents and fifteen years or more of history are:

(1) The Economic and Social Council. The Council receives written reports from the agencies, and at each summer session it hears oral presentations from and discusses matters with the executive heads of the agencies (in rare cases, with their deputies). The result is quite satisfactory at a certain informational level, and for probing into a few problems, but it is far from satisfactory in regard to the ideal role the Economic and Social Council is authorized to play in regard to helping coordinate the programs of all members of the United Nations family. The emphasis is too much on minor administrative frictions and deficiencies, and far from enough on how to solve the world's great problems by imaginative and creative action by the United Nations family. The Economic and Social Council is overburdened and has no real possibility of rising to the challenge. Too many of its debates are affected by national political policies, and the agency heads find the atmosphere bureaucratic and oppressive compared to the specialized program atmosphere of their own legislative organs.

(2) The Administrative Committee on Coordination. The ACC was established in 1946, pursuant to a resolution of the Economic and Social Council. It consists of the Secretary-General of the United Nations as chairman and the executive heads of the specialized agencies. It usually meets in the autumn in New York and in the spring in

Geneva. The grist which comes to its mill, and that of its preparatory committee, is largely administrative, but there is also a significant element of important policy and program business. Much of the business is transacted in secret and in informal group conversations. But many formal decisions are reached, usually by unanimous consensus, and reported to the Economic and Social Council. The family of agencies works much better because of the ACC's existence. Dag Hammarskjöld found the ACC very useful, and he quite clearly enjoyed his work with a group of colleagues with whom he could talk freely about world-shaking issues. But he also found his experience somewhat frustrating. On the one hand he saw the need for more coordination and concerted action than generally existed, and he yearned to be a more dynamic force among his colleagues on ACC than he dared try to be. The embarrassment came from the fact that he was legally only *primus inter pares,* not prime minister, when more of the latter quality was needed. It became my self-assumed role during my five years of association with him to push, on occasion, for the kind of concert of action under his leadership which he wanted but could not press for.

(3) The General Assembly's Advisory Committee for Administrative and Budgetary Questions. This is the organ which considers in detail the budgets of the agencies and makes recommendations thereon for the Assembly's consideration. While the Advisory Committee is helpful on minor matters, its general effect on important program matters has not been great. It has contributed little to making the United Nations family more dynamic or creative, and had more attention been paid to its advice the results would have been generally depressing.

(4) The Technical Assistance Board. The TAB was established to help the Economic and Social Council administer the expanded Program of Technical Assistance set up under the stimulus of President Truman's Point 4 program. It consists of the representatives of the executive heads of the specialized agencies, with a representative of the United Nations Secretary-General as executive chairman. On the whole TAB has functioned well, but there has been some evidence of particularistic agency points of view going against an over-all United Nations family conception of how the system should work. It was

primarily for this reason that Dag Hammarskjöld and I strongly supported a different system for the administration of the Special Fund of the United Nations, established under a General Assembly resolution of 1958. In this case the specialized agencies do not participate in the governing mechanism, though they help develop projects and in many cases are charged with their administration.

(5) Various minor boards and committees have been established to assist with personnel matters, pensions, public information, libraries, etc.

If a few conclusions were to be drawn as to how the family of agencies should be regarded, I would venture the opinion first of all that the areas in which the specialized agencies work are markedly better off than they would have been if the agencies handling them had been placed fully under the management of the United Nations. I believe the work in health, agriculture, education, and so on has developed further and faster under more dynamic leadership because of the opportunity of officers of agencies to appeal to the specialized areas corresponding to their own in governments and to take initiatives which would have been vetoed at the United Nations.

In the second place, I would say that, while coordination and cooperation have not been perfect, they have easily been satisfactory on the whole. To make them better would require: one, an increase in the consistency of points of view in Member State governments; secondly, an increase in the leadership ability of the Economic and Social Council.

Beyond cooperation and coordination in the usual sense, it remains to consider how the agencies have aided the United Nations by following its lead in dealing with world problems, including crises. Here the record is very good. When the Korean and Congo crises came, the response of the relevant agencies to the call for help from the United Nations ranged from good to excellent. In the technical assistance program, the record is genuinely good. The same may be said for the Special Fund programs, though there has been some complaining at the United Nations about slowness of administrative action by the agencies in some cases. The deficiency is one of capacity probably more than of good spirit. In their responses to the General Assembly and Economic and Social Council requests, which have been very numerous and sometimes not very well conceived, I would say that the record of the agencies has been quite good.

In administrative and personnel fields, the agencies have gone along very well on principles and systems which did not involve giving up autonomy and control of operations. They have resisted strongly, however, the idea of a consolidated budget, and they haven't been fully cooperative on ideas for common services and facilities. I would not give them a bad mark on these points, however, because I think the process of bureaucratization would quickly be overdone if the agencies were not resistant, and that economies or clarifications would not be worth the efforts most of them would require.

It is a fad among publicists, when they see something as complex as the United States government or the United Nations family, to say right off, and without study, that there is no doubt a great deal of overlapping, duplication, rivalry, and confusion. After years of living in the system, I have no hesitation in saying that a serious criticism of the United Nations family on these grounds has no basis. There are some ill-defined areas, but in nearly every one of them practical solutions have been found by the secretariats of the agencies concerned. Duplication of effort is at a minimum, and there is very little rivalry or confusion. There have been cases when the United Nations acted and UNESCO stepped aside or where UNESCO acted and the International Atomic Energy Agency might have—but understanding, agreement, and cooperation have prevailed.

As a final word, I would say that the United Nations family is a good family, it is resilient, it is capable of adding new members, and its accomplishments are a credit to the authors of the Charter and of the constitutions of the specialized agencies. The long participation of Dag Hammarskjöld as the nearest thing to a father in the family is one reason why the record has been even better than the documents of the founders gave promise that it would be.

BIOGRAPHICAL SKETCHES

Jacob Blaustein has long been a leader in the international human rights movement. He was a consultant to the United States delegation at the United Nations Conference in San Francisco in 1945, a member of the United States delegation to the tenth session of the United Nations General Assembly in 1955, and National Chairman for the observance of the 10th Anniversary of the Universal Declaration of Human Rights in 1958. He is a member of the Board of Trustees of the Dag Hammarskjöld Foundation and of the United States Committee of the Dag Hammarskjöld Foundation. He is a former president and now honorary president of the American Jewish Committee. He has served on various United States governmental assignments. With his father, he was co-founder of the American Oil Company and is a director of a number of major business corporations, including Standard Oil (Indiana), and of educational and philanthropic organizations.

Ralph J. Bunche joined the United Nations Secretariat in 1946 and has been an Under-Secretary since 1955, working directly under the Secretary-General on such special political assignments as the United Nations Emergency Force (UNEF) in the Middle East, the United Nations Congo operations, the United Nations Truce Supervision Organization in Palestine, the United Nations Force in Cyprus, and other missions. After the assassination of Count Folke Bernadotte, the United Nations Mediator in Palestine, in September, 1948, Mr. Bunche was appointed Acting Mediator by the Security Council and directed the negotiation in 1949 of the four armistice agreements between Israel and the Arab States which have continued in effect ever since. For this he was awarded the Nobel Peace Prize in 1950. He is a member of the Board of Trustees of the United States Committee of the Dag Hammarskjöld Foundation and the Secretary-General's representative on the Foundation.

Sir John Cockcroft, the British physicist, was awarded the Nobel Prize in Physics in 1951 and the Atoms for Peace Award in 1961. He was Director of the Atomic Energy Research Establishment of the Ministry of Supply from 1946 to 1958 and became a member of the British Atomic Energy Authority in 1954. He has served on the Scientific Advisory Committee of the United Nations Secretary-General and was a Vice-President of the 1955 and 1958 International Conferences on the Peaceful Uses of Atomic Energy organized by the United Nations. He is Master of Churchill College, Cambridge University.

Douglas Ensminger became representative of the Ford Foundation in India and Pakistan in 1951 and since 1953 has served as the Foundation's Representative in India and Nepal. In this post he has organized and directed the very successful Ford Foundation programs of technical assistance and community development on the subcontinent. He has also been a consultant to the Agency of International Development and the United States Department of State and a Visiting Professor at Columbia University. In earlier years he was with the United States Department of Agriculture.

Luther H. Evans was Director-General of the United Nations Educational, Scientific, and Cultural Organization (UNESCO) from 1953 to 1958. He served on UNESCO's Executive Board as United States member from 1949 to 1953. He was Chief Assistant Librarian of Congress from 1940 to 1945 and Librarian of Congress from 1945 to 1953 after earlier service as Director of the WPA Historical Records Survey and of the Legislative Reference Service. He became Director of International and Legal Collections at Columbia University in 1962.

Ernest A. Gross was Deputy United States Representative to the United Nations from 1949 to 1953 and a member of several United States delegations to the General Assembly. Among his earlier government posts were those of Legal Advisor of the Department of

State and Assistant Secretary of State. He was President of Freedom House in 1953 and in 1954 became a member of the New York law firm of Curtis, Mallet-Prevost, Colt, and Mosle. He is a member of the State Department's Advisory Committee on International Organizations and is the author of *The United Nations: Structure for Peace* and numerous articles. He is a member of the Board of Trustees of the Dag Hammarskjöld Foundation and of the United States Committee of the Dag Hammarskjöld Foundation.

Paul G. Hoffman has been Managing Director of the United Nations Special Fund since its establishment in 1959. He was reappointed for a second four-year term in 1963. Mr. Hoffman is a former President and Chairman of the Board of the Studebaker Corporation. He helped organize the Committee for Economic Development and served as Chairman of its Board of Trustees from 1942 to 1948. He was appointed in 1948 by President Truman as the first Administrator of the Economic Cooperation Administration (the Marshall Plan). He served in this post until 1950. From 1951 to 1953 he was President of the Ford Foundation. He was a member of the United States delegation to the eleventh session of the General Assembly in 1956. He is a member of the Board of Trustees of the United States Committee of the Dag Hammarskjöld Foundation.

Philip C. Jessup has been a judge of the International Court of Justice since 1961. He was appointed Deputy United States Representative to the United Nations Security Council in 1948 and served as United States Ambassador-at-Large from 1949 to 1953. In 1949 he negotiated at the United Nations the agreement which ended the Berlin blockade. He was Assistant Secretary-General at the founding conferences of the International Bank and Monetary Fund at Bretton Woods in 1944 and served with the United States delegation at the United Nations Conference in San Francisco in 1945. He was Hamilton Fish Professor of International Law at Columbia University from 1946 to 1961. He is the author of numerous works on international law and international organization.

Muhammad Zafrulla Khan of Pakistan was President of the seventeenth session of the United Nations General Assembly in 1962–63.

He has served Pakistan as Minister of Foreign Affairs and was leader of its delegations to the General Assembly and to the Security Council for consideration of the India-Pakistan dispute, from 1947 to 1954. Sir Zafrulla was a judge of the International Court of Justice from 1954 to 1961 and then became Permanent Delegate of Pakistan to the United Nations. He was reelected a judge of the International Court in 1963. In earlier years he had been a delegate to the Indian Round Table Conferences, President of the All-India Muslim League, and Judge of the Federal Court of India.

Mrs. Alva Myrdal has been chairman of the Swedish delegation at the United Nations disarmament negotiations in Geneva since 1962. She is a former Principal Director of the Department of Social Affairs in the United Nations and of UNESCO's Department of Social Sciences. She served from 1955 to 1961 in India, Ceylon, Burma, and Nepal as Swedish Ambassador. Mrs. Myrdal has served as first President of the Dag Hammarskjöld Foundation. She is the wife of Karl Gunnar Myrdal, the economist and author, who was executive secretary of the United Nations Economic Commission for Europe from 1947 to 1957.

Julius K. Nyerere was elected President of Tanganyika in 1962 and is now President of the United Republic of Tanganyika and Zanzibar. He was his country's first Prime Minister when it became an independent sovereign state and a Member of the United Nations in December, 1961. Formerly he had served as Chief Minister. A teacher at St. Mary's Roman Catholic School and St. Francis' Roman Catholic College who studied at Makerere College in Uganda and at Edinburgh University, he became the founder and President of the Tanganyika African National Union in 1954 and a member of the Tanganyika Legislative Council.

Mrs. Vijaya Lakshmi Pandit was President of the United Nations General Assembly in 1953 and chairman of the Indian delegation to the Assembly from 1946 to 1950 and again in 1963. She was India's first Ambassador to the USSR from 1947 to 1949, Ambassador to the United States and Mexico from 1949 to 1952, High Commissioner of India in London from 1954 to 1961, and since 1962 has served as Governor of Maharashtra State. In earlier years Mrs. Pandit was an active participant in the national movement for Indian independence and became the first woman in India to hold ministerial rank. She is a member of the Board of Trustees of the Dag Hammarskjöld Foundation. She is a sister of the late Jawaharlal Nehru, Prime Minister of India from 1947 to 1964.

Lester B. Pearson became Prime Minister of Canada in 1963. He was Secretary of State for External Affairs from 1948 to 1957 and was leader of the Liberal Party and the Opposition from 1958 to 1963. He was a member of the Canadian delegations to the Food and Agriculture Conference at Hot Springs in 1943, the United Nations Conference at San Francisco in 1945, and subsequent sessions of the United Nations General Assembly. He was chairman of the Canadian delegation to all sessions of the General Assembly from 1948 to 1957 and served as President of the fifth session in 1950. He has also headed Canadian delegations to NATO meetings and was chairman of the North Atlantic Council in 1951–52. Mr. Pearson is a member of the Board of Trustees of the Dag Hammarskjöld Foundation.

Sture Petrén is President of the Svea Court of Appeal in Sweden. He was head of the Legal Department of the Swedish Ministry of Foreign Affairs from 1949 to 1963 and legal adviser to the Swedish delegation to the United Nations General Assembly from 1948 to 1960. He has been a member of the European Commission of Human Rights since 1954 and its President since 1962. He has been a member of the Permanent Court of Arbitration since 1955 and of the United Nations Administrative Tribunal since 1952. He is also a member of the Board of Trustees of the Dag Hammarskjöld Foundation.

Galo Plaza (Lasso) was President of the Republic of Ecuador from 1948 to 1952. Previously he had served as Minister of National Defense and as Ambassador to the United States. He was chairman of the United Nations Observation Group in Lebanon in 1958 and served the United Nations also on a special mission to the Congo in 1960 and as a member of the Latin American Common Market

Committee of the United Nations Economic Commission for Latin America in 1958–59. In 1964 he served as Special Representative of Secretary-General U Thant in Cyprus and then as Mediator.

Mrs. Agda Rössel served as Permanent Representative of Sweden to the United Nations from 1958 to 1964, when she became Ambassador to Yugoslavia. She was a member of Swedish delegations to the United Nations from 1952 to 1958. She is a former Vice-President of the International Federation of Business and Professional Women who early in her career served as Secretary of the Union of Women Employees of the National Telephone Company of Sweden and later held various advisory posts. Mrs. Rössel, as Swedish permanent representative to the United Nations, has been an *ex officio* member of the Board of Trustees of the Dag Hammarskjöld Foundation.

Dean Rusk became Secretary of State of the United States in January, 1961. A former Rhodes scholar and educator, he served during the war in two campaigns in the Burma theater, where he became Deputy Chief of Staff. Mr. Rusk was Special Assistant to the Secretary of War in 1946–47 and Director of the Offices of Special Political Affairs and United Nations Affairs in the Department of State from 1947 to 1949, when he was appointed the first Assistant Secretary of State for United Nations Affairs. From 1950 to 1952 he was Assistant Secretary of State for Far Eastern Affairs and then became President of the Rockefeller Foundation in New York.

Philippe de Seynes has been Under-Secretary for Economic and Social Affairs of the United Nations since 1955. In this capacity he has represented the Secretary-General in the Economic and Social Council and other organs concerned with United Nations economic policies and programs. Previously he had served in the French Ministry of Finance, as Deputy Secretary-General of the Allied Reparations Agency in Brussels, and, from 1949 to 1954, as a member of the French mission to the United Nations. For several years he was its permanent representative for economic and social questions. In June, 1954, he was appointed an adviser to the former Premier Pierre Mendès-France.

Mongi Slim, Secretary of State for Foreign Affairs of Tunisia, was President of the sixteenth session of the United Nations General Assembly in 1961. He served as Permanent Representative of Tunisia to the United Nations and Ambassador to the United States and Canada from 1956 to 1961. Before and during World War II he was a leading member of the Tunisian nationalist movement, was a political prisoner of the French from 1938 to 1942, and was elected Director of the Neo-Destour Party in 1945. As Minister of State he conducted negotiations for Tunisian self-government in 1951 and was Minister of the Interior from 1955 to 1956. Mr. Slim is a member of the Board of Trustees and of the Executive Committee of the Dag Hammarskjöld Foundation.

Adlai E. Stevenson became United States Representative to the United Nations and a member of the Cabinet in January, 1961. This appointment renewed an association with the United Nations dating from the days before he was elected Governor of Illinois in 1948 and twice nominated for the Presidency—in 1952 and 1956—by the Democratic Party. In 1945 Mr. Stevenson served with the United States delegation at the San Francisco Conference and was chief of the United States delegation to the Preparatory Commission in London. Subsequently he was a member of the United States delegations to the first and second sessions of the United Nations General Assembly in 1946 and 1947. Mr. Stevenson is a member of the Board of Trustees of the United States Committee of the Dag Hammarskjöld Foundation.

Ingvar Svenilson is Vice-President and Professor of Economics at Stockhom University. Since World War II he has been a leading figure in Swedish national planning. He was a colleague of Dag Hammarskjöld in the days of the Marshall Plan and chairman of the productivity committee of the Organization for European Economic Cooperation (OEEC). He is the author of major studies on economic growth and international trade and is a member of the Board of Trustees of the Dag Hammarskjöld Foundation.

U Thant of Burma has served as Secretary-General of the United Nations since November, 1961. He was Permanent Representative of Burma to the United Nations and chairman of its delegations to the General Assembly from 1957 to 1961. He was a Vice-President of the General Assembly in 1959 and chairman of the Committee on the United Nations Development Fund and of the United Nations Congo Conciliation Commission in 1961. He is a former educator who served the government of Burma as Press Director, Director of Broadcasting, and Secretary of the Ministry of Information before coming to the United Nations. He is the author of *History of Post-War Burma, League of Nations,* and other works. U Thant is an *ex officio* member of the Board of Trustees of the Dag Hammarskjöld Foundation.

Willard L. Thorp was Assistant Secretary of State for Economic Affairs in the United States Department of State from 1946 to 1952. Before that he had served in various government and academic posts. Since 1952 he has been Professor of Economics at Amherst College, where he also served as Acting President in 1957. He was the United States Representative on the United Nations Economic and Social Council from 1947 to 1950, and chairman of the United States delegations for the General Agreement on Tariffs and Trade (GATT) from 1950 to 1952. In 1963–64 he served as chairman of the Development Assistance Committee of the Organization for Economic Co-operation and Development (OECD). Mr. Thorp is a member of the Board of Trustees of the United States Committee of the Dag Hammarskjöld Foundation.

Barbara Ward (Lady Jackson) is an internationally distinguished political economist, author, and lecturer. She is a former Foreign Affairs Editor of *The Economist,* with which she maintains her connection, and the author of such books as *The Rich Nations and the Poor Nations, Faith and Freedom, A Policy for the West,* and *India and the West.* She was invited by the government of India to study its five-year plans and has spent a great deal of time in Africa. Miss Ward has also served as Governor of the British Broadcasting Corporation and the Sadler's Wells and Old Vic Theatres.

DATE DUE